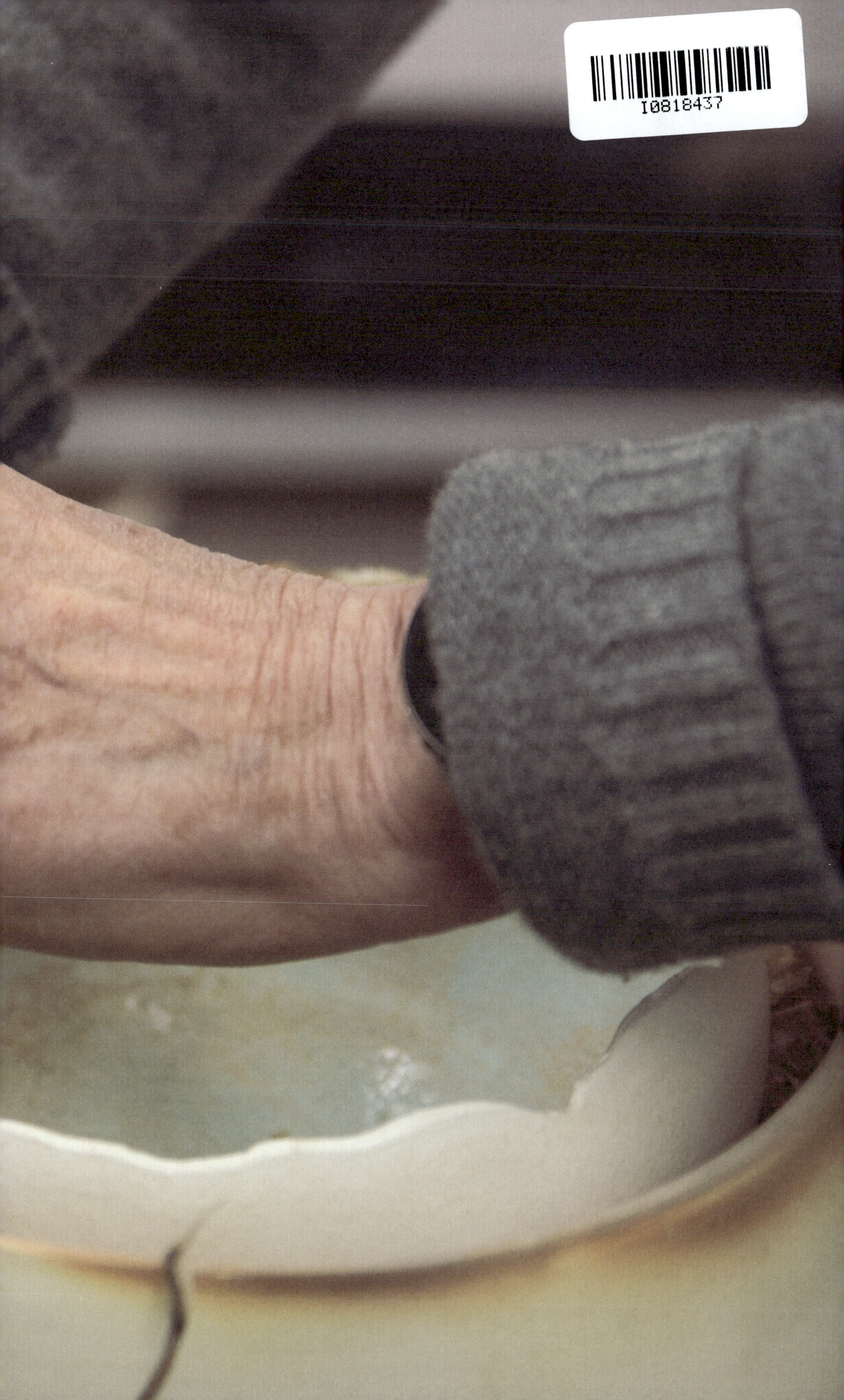
I0818437

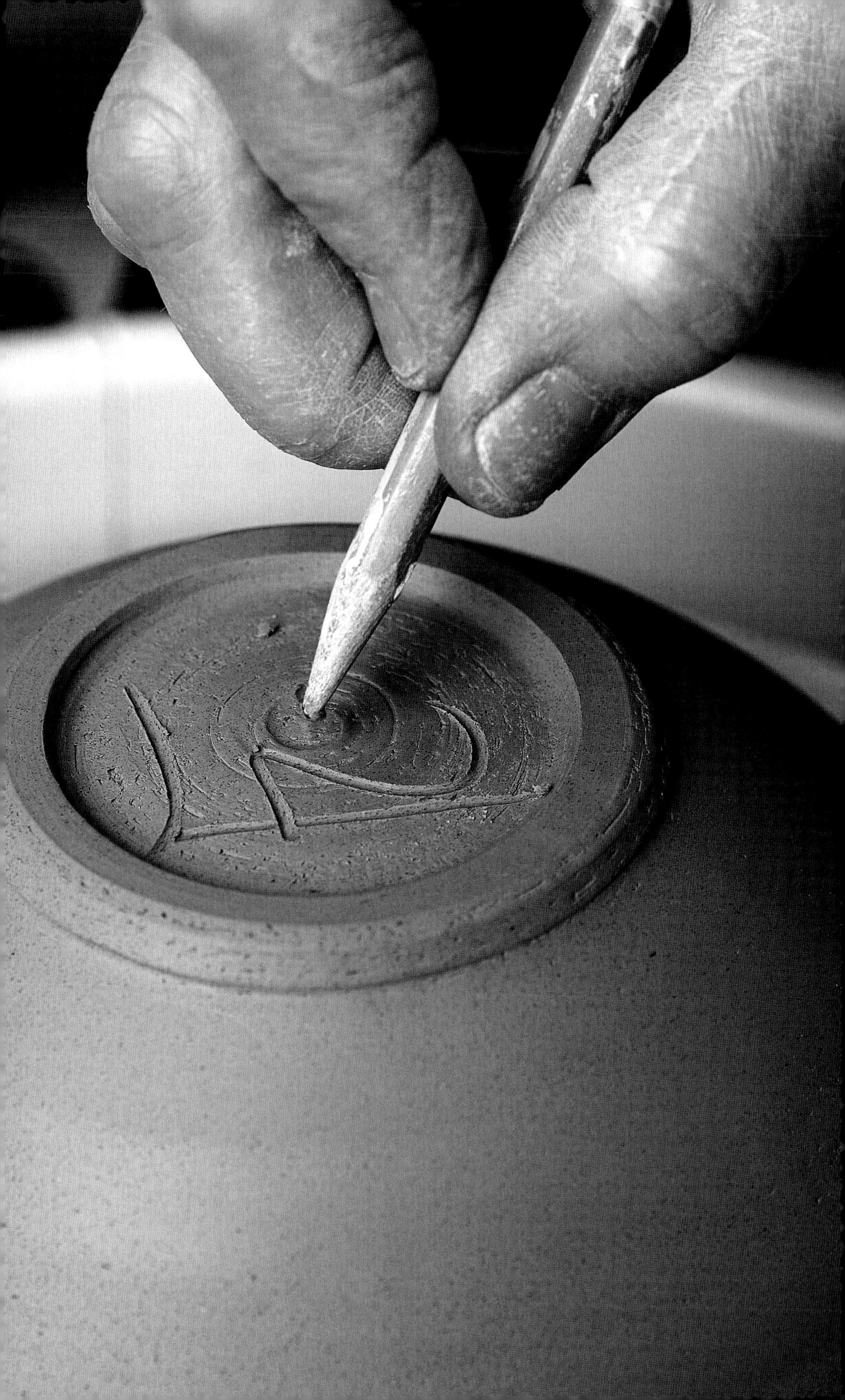

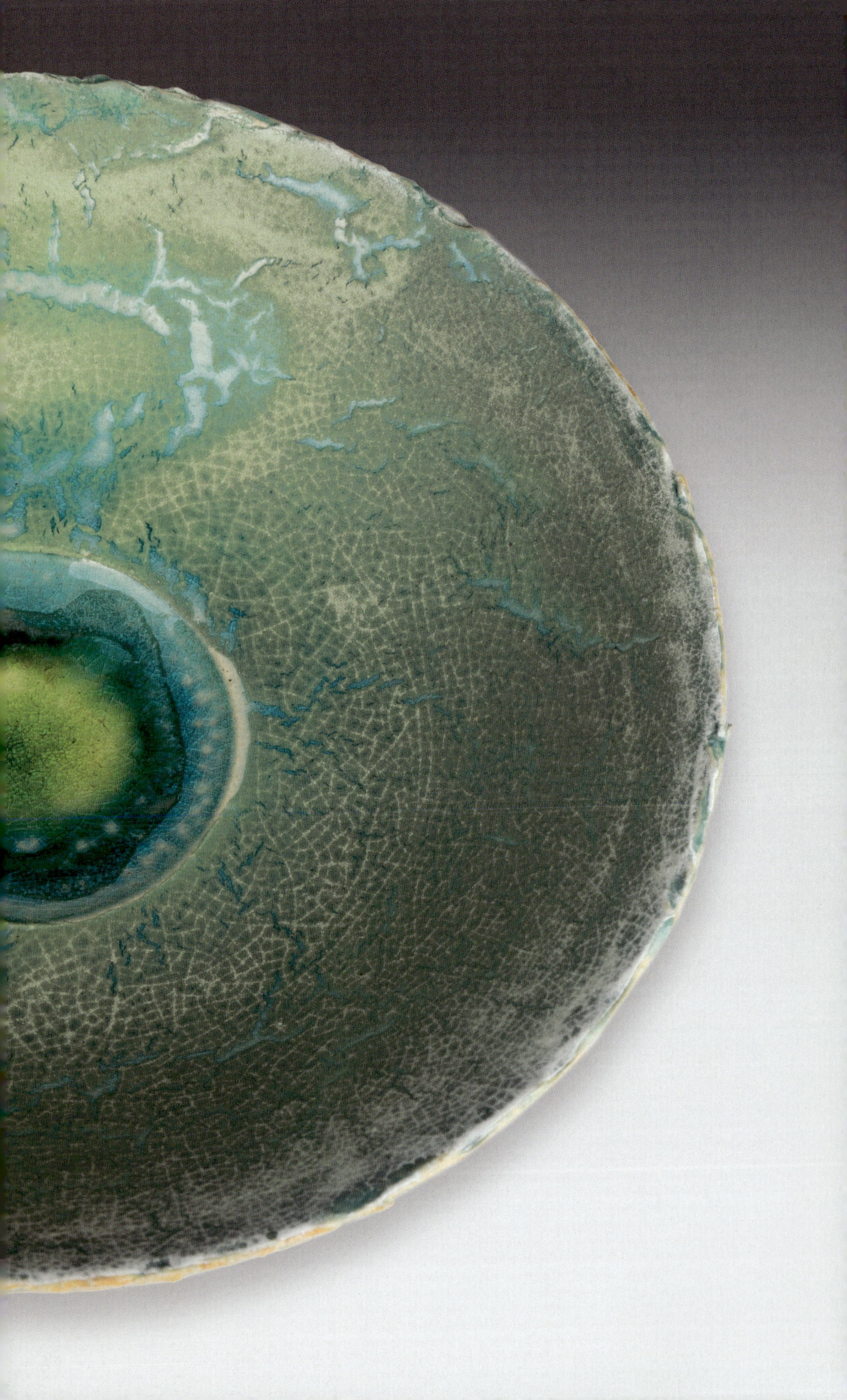

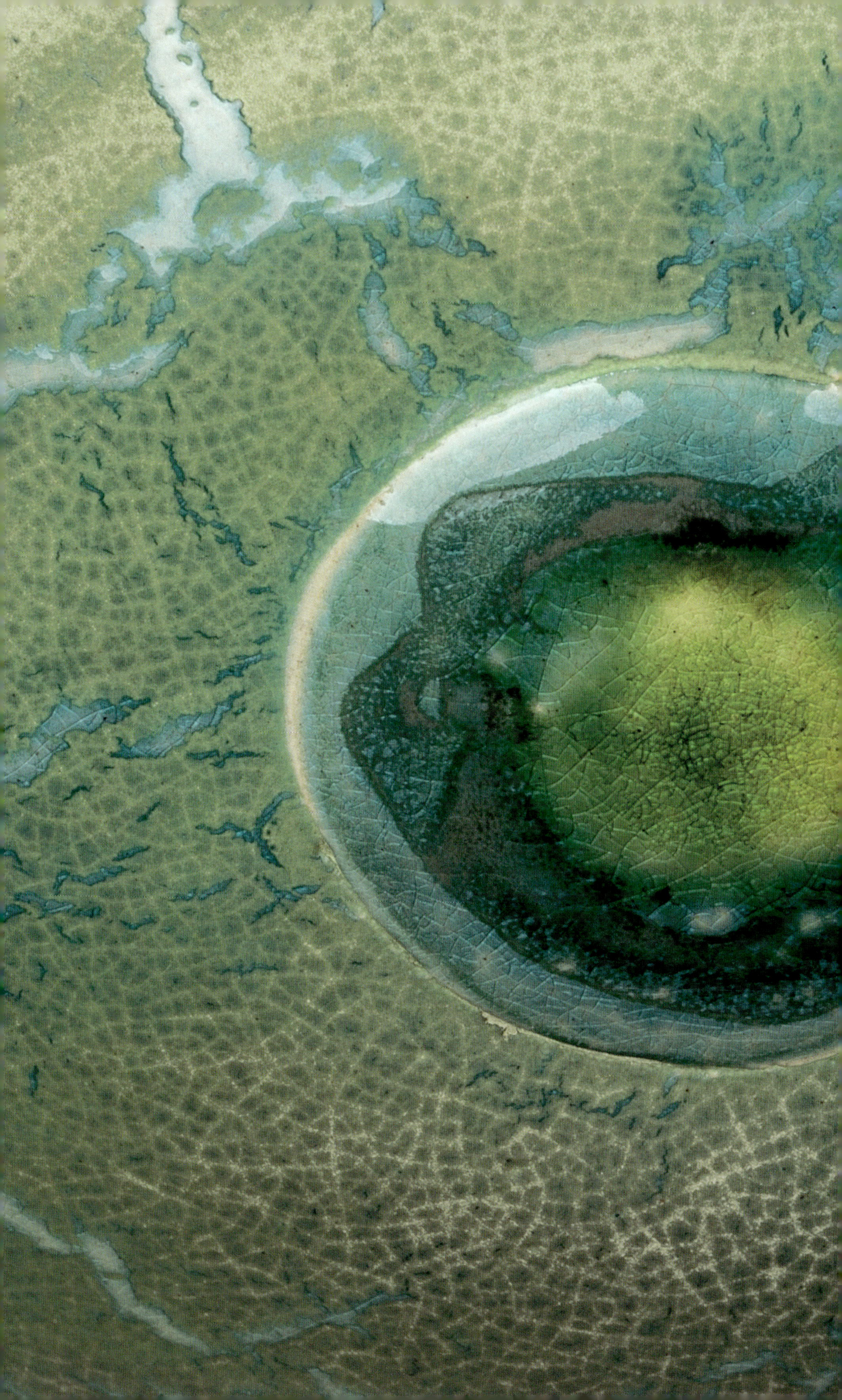

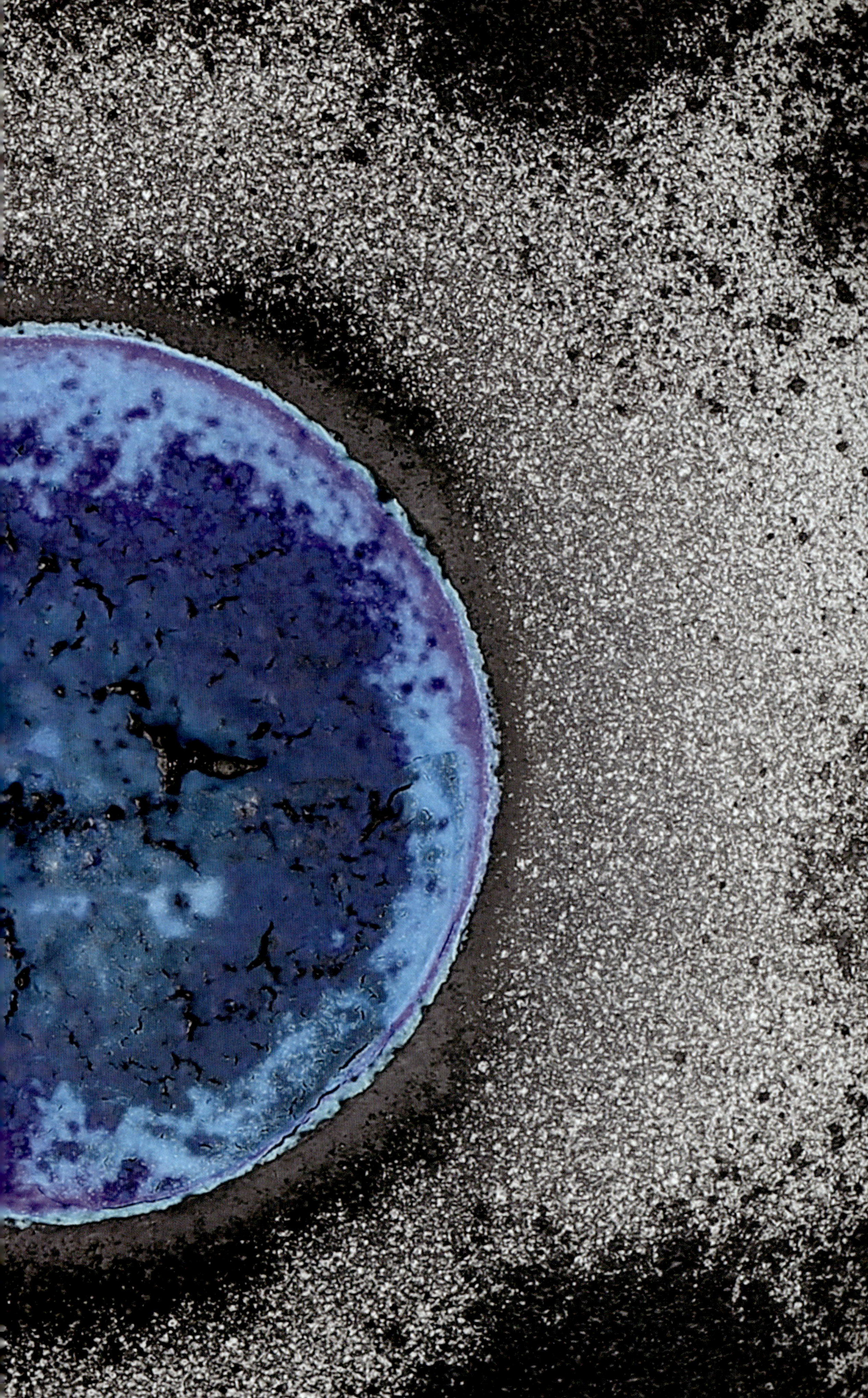

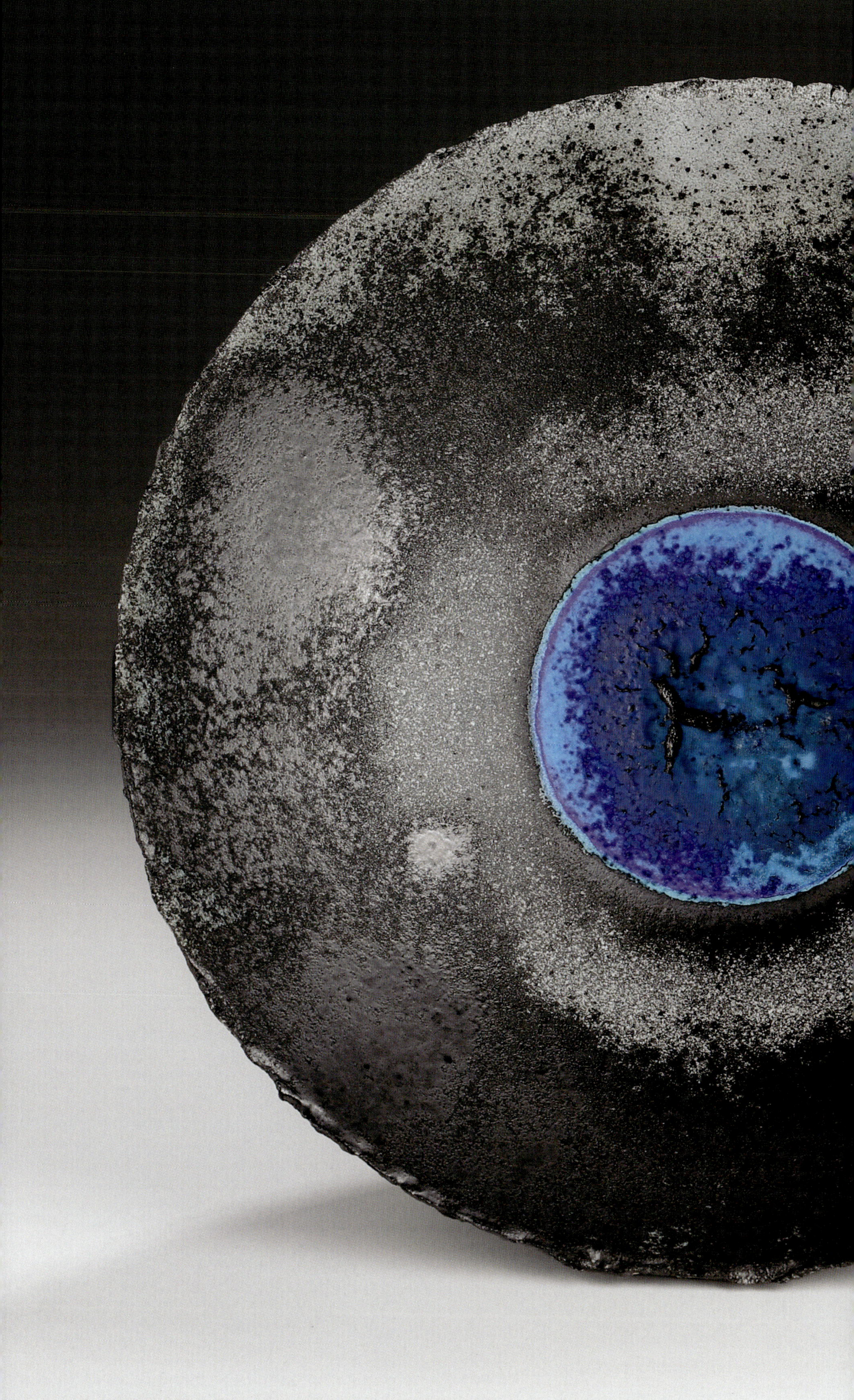

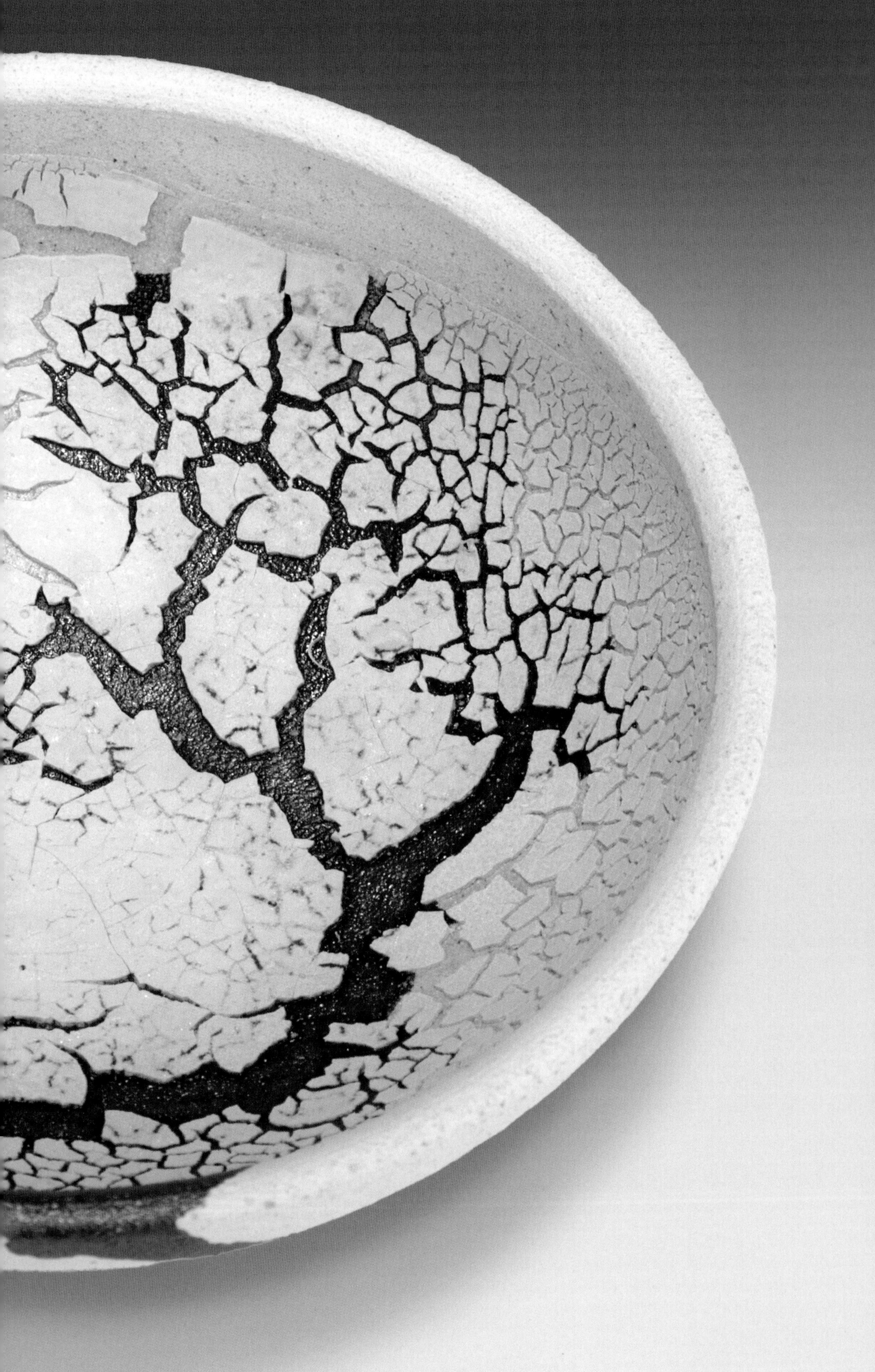

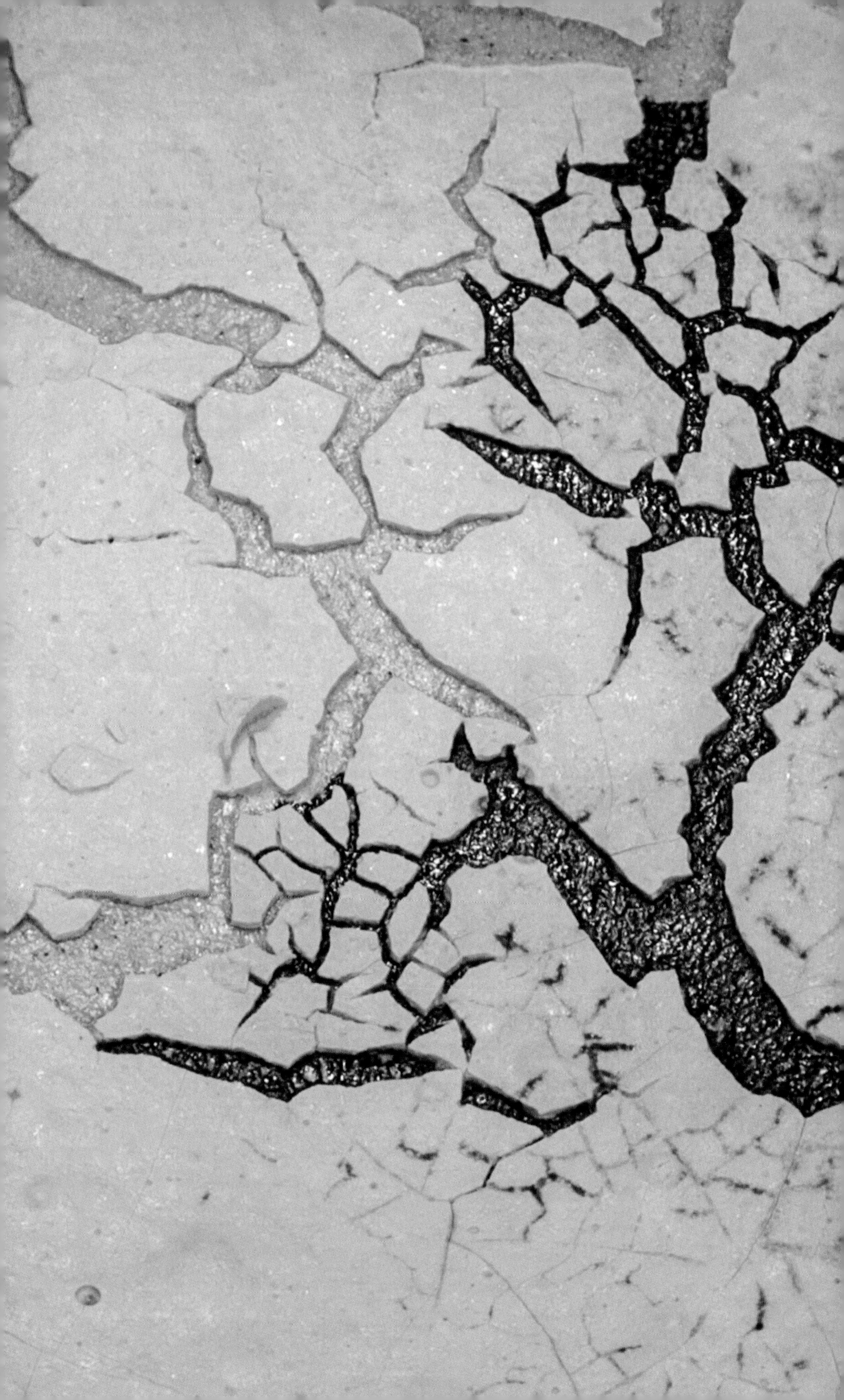

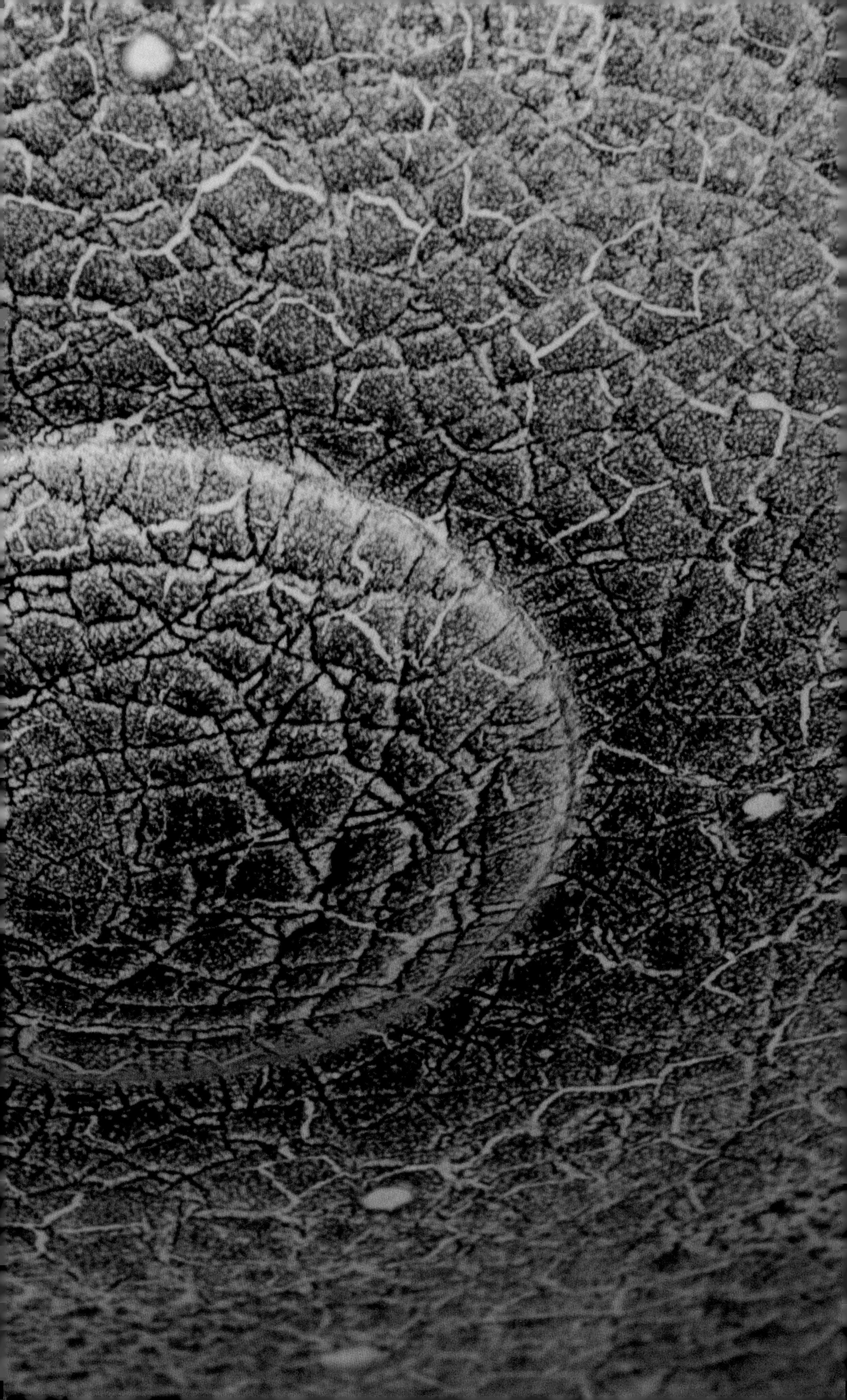

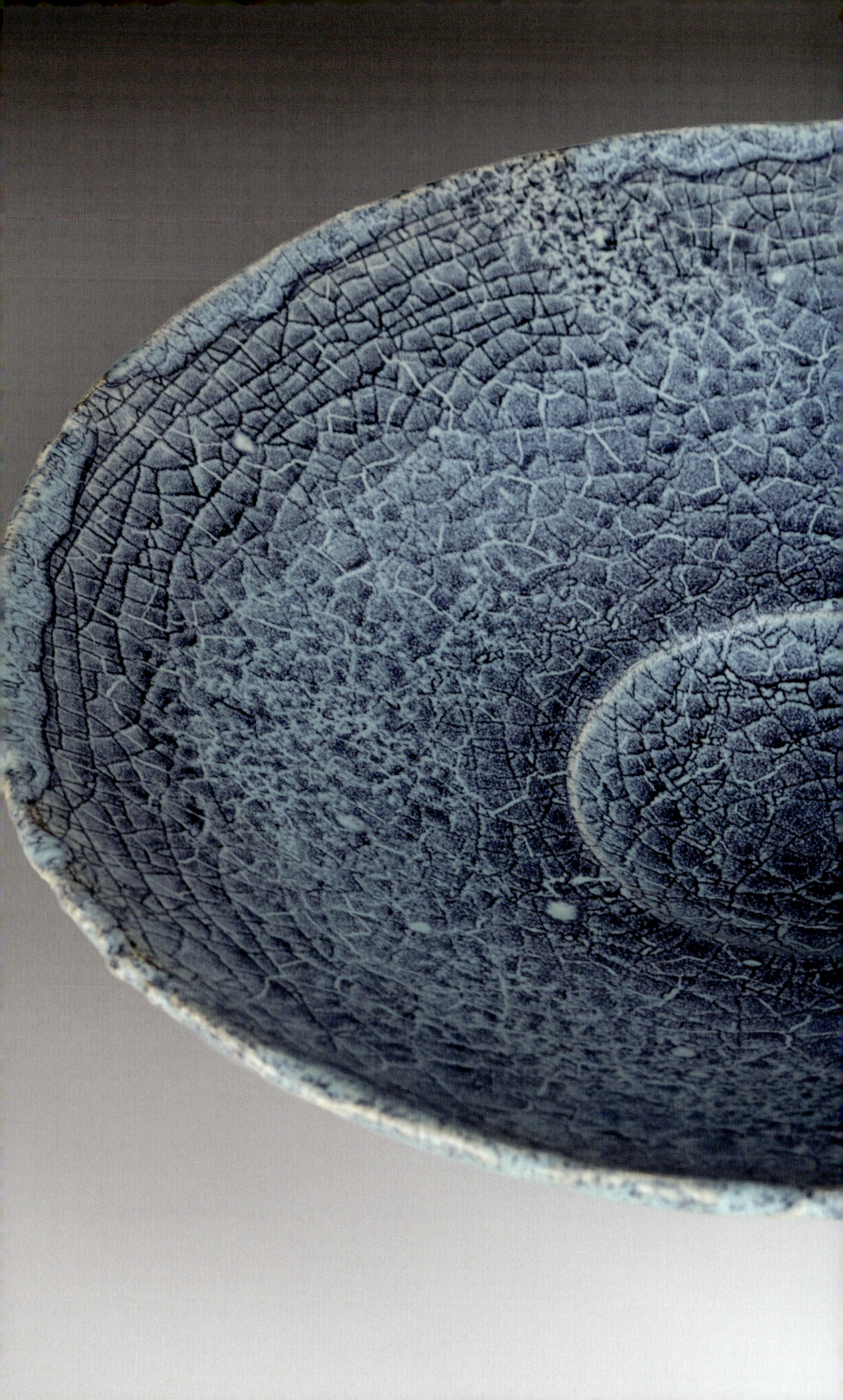

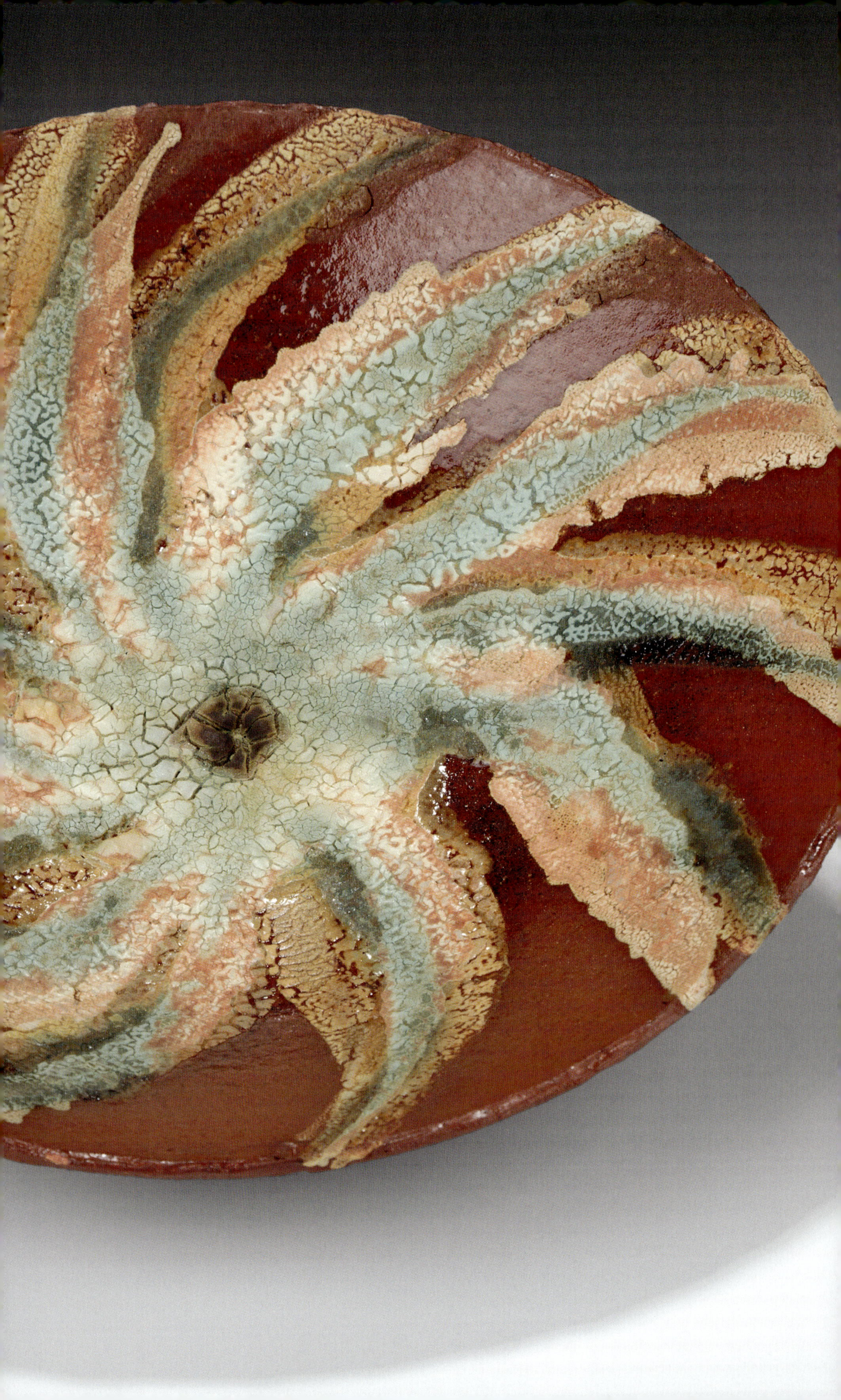

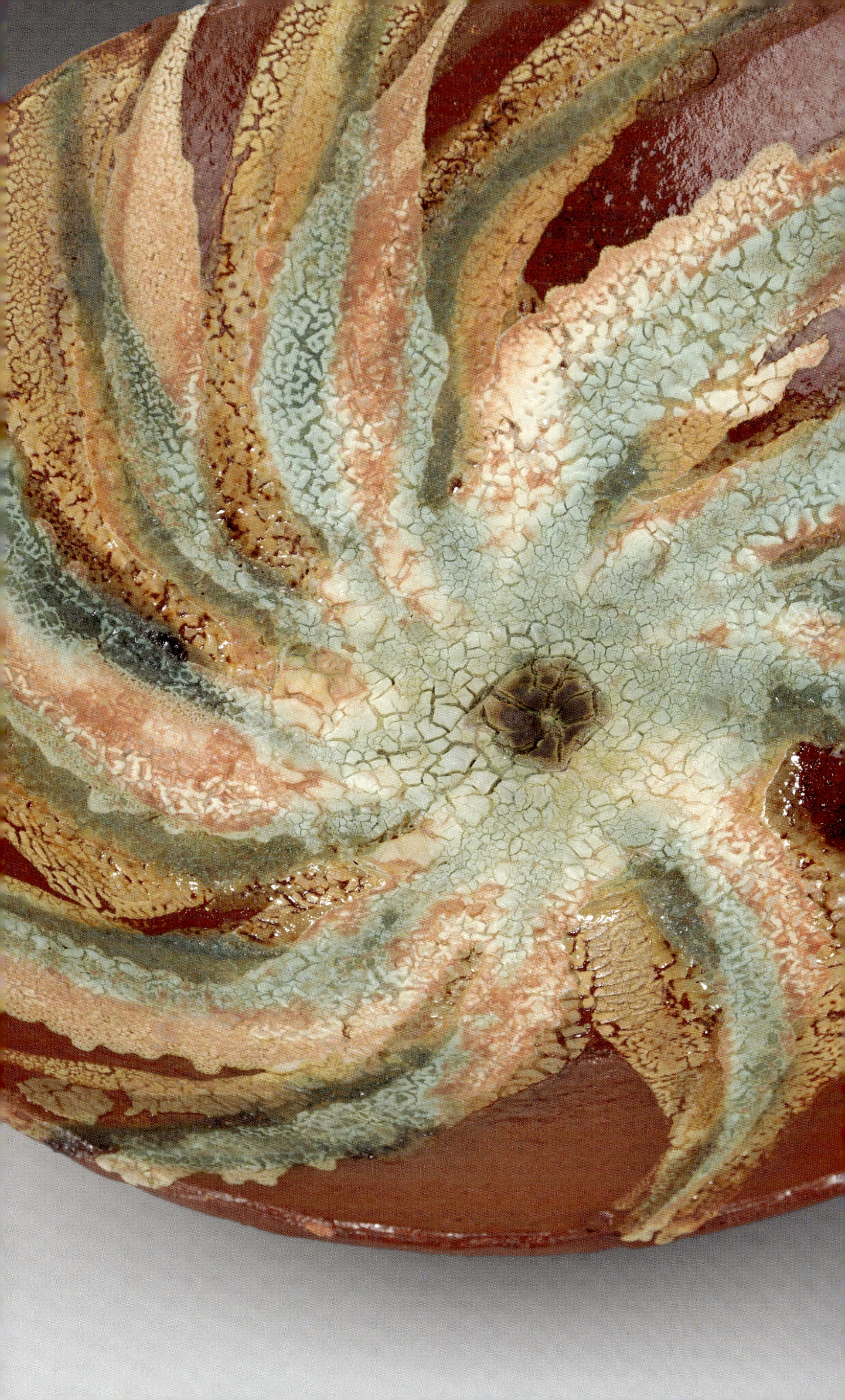

MARY FOX

DEVELOPING GLAZES

LOW-FIRE REDUCTION AND OXIDATION

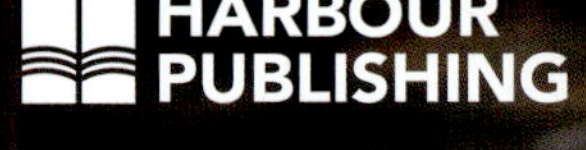

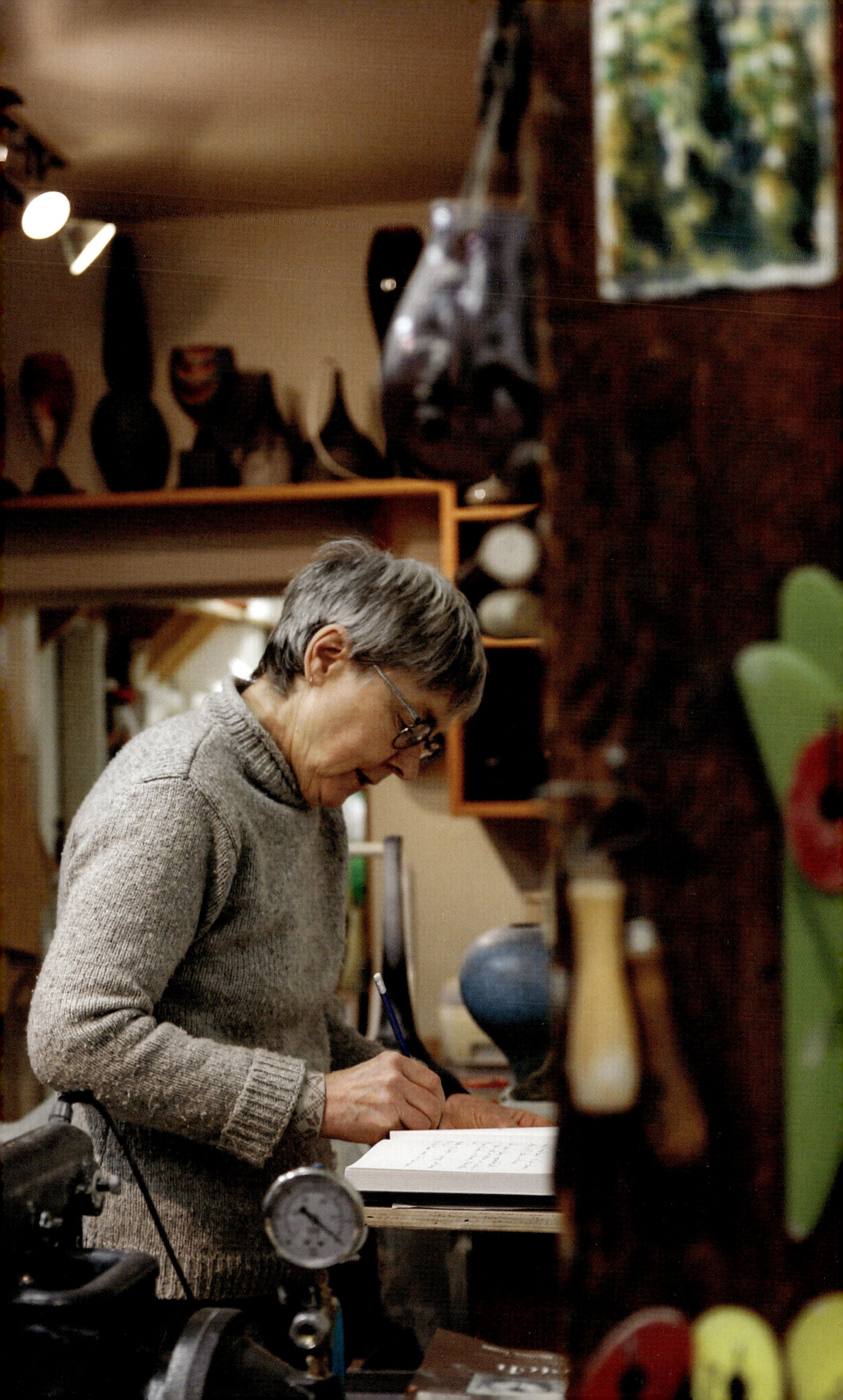

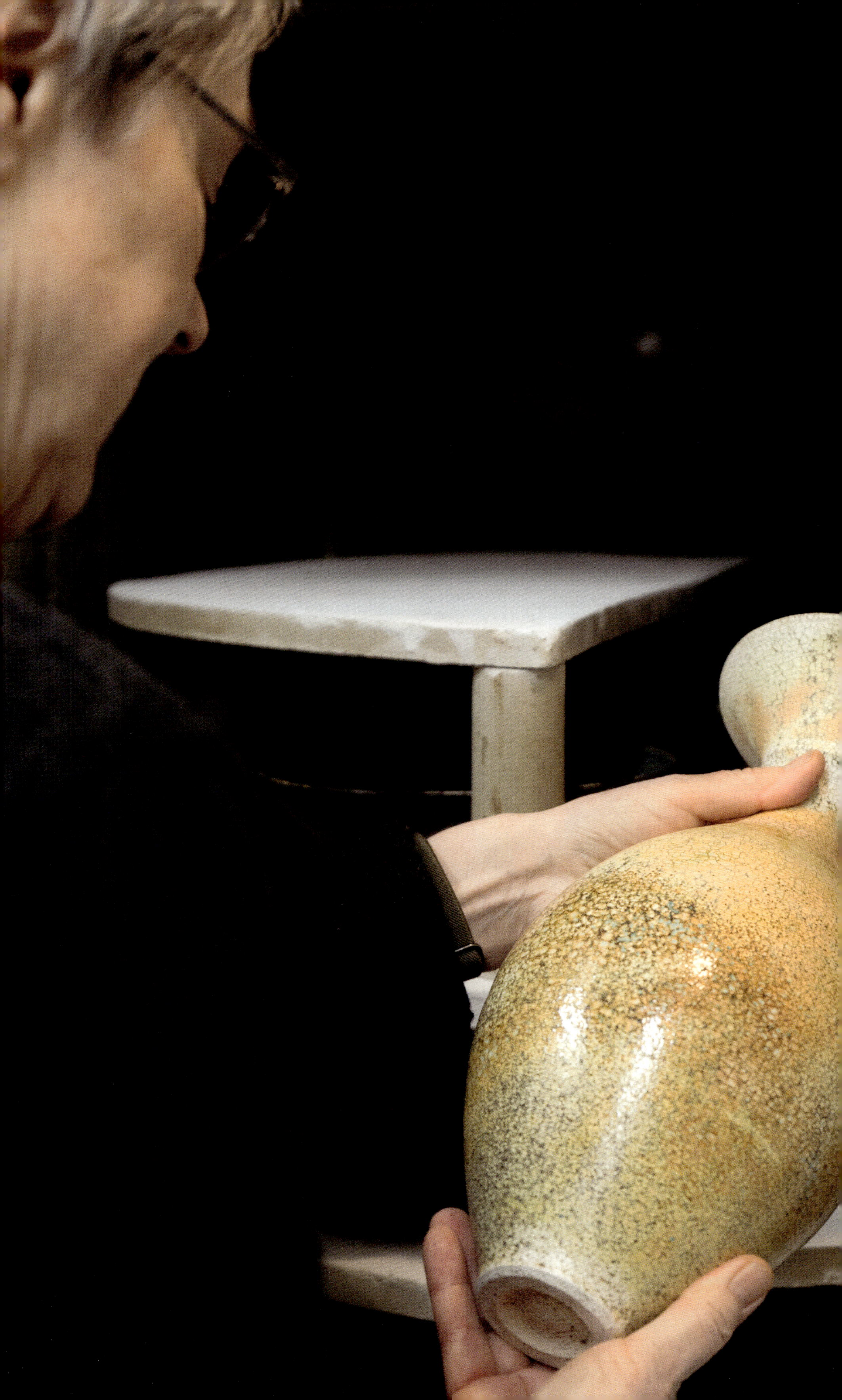

Dedicated to all potters who are nervous about glazing and want to find ways to bring fun and joy into the process.

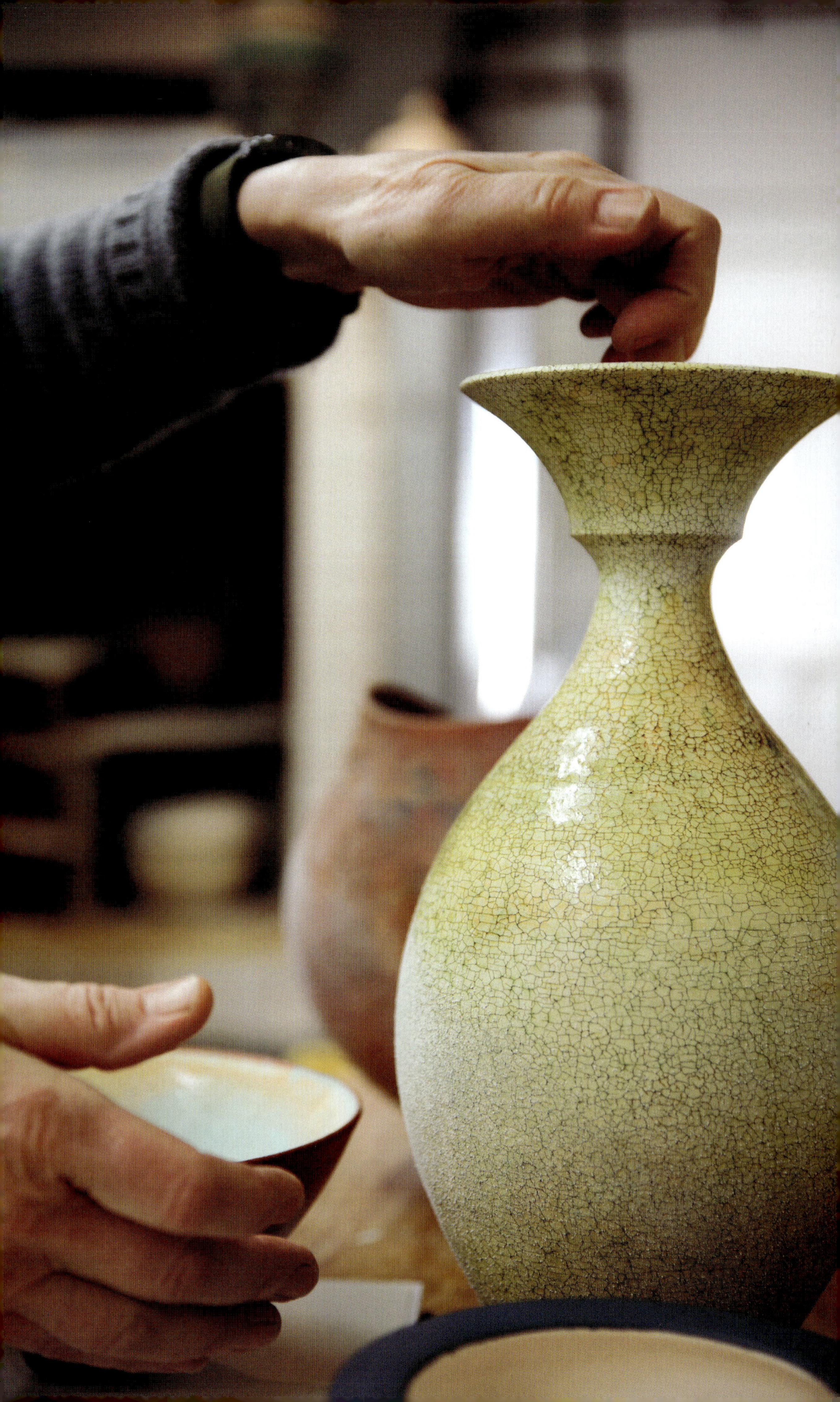

CONTENTS

INTRODUCTION

Glazes, glazes, glazes—so beautiful and yet so frustrating at times! Over the years, I have frequently been asked how I come up with such unique and beautiful glaze effects. Potters from all over the world visit my studio and are curious to know more about my techniques. As a result, I have come to realize that it would be enormously helpful if I shared, step by step, how I get the unusual glazes people discover when they visit Mary Fox Pottery.

I used to think that I really wasn't that great at glazing, that I just played around and got lucky. But now, on reflection, I know that my results were never just flukes. In my quest for different ways to dress my vessels, I have consistently followed what I refer to as my "rabbit-trail" approach and have developed into a serial glaze experimenter.

When you first start to pot, it can be quite intimidating when you get to the glazing stage. You've struggled along learning to throw on the wheel and, gosh, that was hard enough, but now you're going to take your hard-won pots and risk ruining them with unsatisfactory glaze results. Yikes! Fear and trepidation often take over, so when you eventually get some results you are happy with, you stick with them. Why risk more glaze grief if you don't need to? I remember this stage well, having carried out loads of glaze tests, only to discard most of them as "not-good glazes." It would be years before I began to truly understand how dramatically glaze results are affected by the way a glaze is applied and how the piece is fired. Fortunately, the development of computerized kilns has helped immensely with controlling and duplicating firing methods, and these days there are many books, videos and online resources devoted to glazes.

So, why write a book on glazes when the topic is already so well covered? Well, for starters, many of the glazing techniques I describe here are experimental and not discussed in existing resources. And further, I explore glaze results achieved through firing at lower temperatures, particularly in a reduction atmosphere, an area that few potters are delving into. While most glazes do best in oxidation, there are some that are great in either oxidation or reduction, and, in this book, I want to introduce you to the fascinating world of reduction firing. Wherever I can, I show you how a glaze looks fired in both oxidation and reduction, focusing on the lower firing ranges, cone 06 to cone 04.

LOW-TEMPERATURE FIRING

Low-temperature kiln firing is under-researched, and there is very little written about low-fire reduction other than works focused specifically on lustreware, raku, saggar or pit firing. But the more I work with this firing method, the more I am convinced that it offers a vast world of hidden secrets and avenues to explore. For example, since being a young potter, I've wondered, *why don't potters try a process similar to raku using their gas kilns? Why not try firing the work fast and reducing during the firing, then cooling the kiln as quickly as possible? What kind of effects would this create?* It was decades before I acquired the tool I needed to finally explore this and other questions that have percolated in my mind—a Blaauw gas kiln, ideal for experimenting with reduction firing.

In this book, I share some of my exciting discoveries, though I've explored only a fraction of the possibilities. All the decorative reduction work that I am showing you here has been fired fast—taking 3 hours to reach a top temperature of 1870°F–1940°F. You don't need to fire this fast, but I wanted to emulate the speed of my previous raku firings with an old electric kiln that took 3 hours to get to 1900°F.

As reduction firing requires a gas kiln, some of you may be wondering if this book is for you if you don't have a gas kiln. The answer is yes, as I also offer a variety of ideas about glazing and experimenting with low-temperature oxidation firing, as well as introduce the fascinating world of reduction.

Another reason for focusing on low-temperature firing is the benefit to the environment. In recent years, I have been asking myself, *why, during this time of climate change, are young potters flocking to wood and soda firing?* Wood firing is laborious, the results can be disappointing unless you really know what you are doing and a good percentage of the work is unexciting. Then there is the enormous amount of wood consumed in a single firing—often enough to heat one or two houses for a year. Recently, I have encountered articles that address this issue and am pleased to see that potters are starting to build more efficient wood-burning kilns and to explore lower temperatures for soda/salt firing. These efforts are good and timely, but when it comes to lowering your carbon footprint, you can't beat the Blaauw for fuel efficiency. I am discovering that you can get similar results firing at low temperatures in the Blaauw as you can with energy-intensive, high-firing methods.

I think firing low is the way of the future. Not only does it use a lot less energy, but also it saves a considerable amount of money. With climate change and its effects all around us, reducing our carbon footprint by firing at lower temperatures can only be a good thing.

EXPERIMENTING WITH GLAZES

As I thought about how to write a book that would inspire potters to create their own glazes, I reflected on how I started out as a beginner by testing loads of glazes. It's hard to get across to young potters that this is not necessarily the most helpful strategy and, in many ways, may actually make things harder. Then I came up with the idea of giving myself a challenge as a way of approaching this book. *What if I started working with glazes and methods I hadn't yet explored?* Since I have decades of experience, it wouldn't be the same as starting as a novice, but it would be a fun way to show you how I develop ideas and techniques. At the outset, I had no idea how much this exercise would end up affecting my own work, not only in the glazes I was developing, but also even the forms I was creating.

I started by picking some glaze recipes from online sources. As some ingredients are becoming too expensive or challenging to source, I chose glazes with ingredients that are readily available and aren't overly expensive. Where some of the ingredients were expensive, such as lithium, I limited myself to recipes that used a small percentage. I also gave myself free rein to use minerals by themselves, along with terra sigillata and a couple of common raku glazes. Though focusing primarily on glazes meant for non-functional artwork, I also explored low-fired tableware, both in oxidation and reduction. In these pages, I share how I went about experimenting with these glaze materials—taking risks, but with method in my madness.

A book such as this would have been game-changing for me when I was starting out. I hope it will open many creative doors for you and show you just how much fun glazing can be. If you are creating work that isn't designed with function in mind, the handcuffs are off, so to speak. You really can try anything. Think of your decorative finishes as you might think about cooking. In the kitchen, we are constantly playing around with recipes or improvising from scratch. What if you started to approach glazing with that kind of freedom? Doesn't that sound like way more fun?

Join me as I explore new ways of glazing and firing my work. Buckle up—it's going to be an exciting ride!

CHAPTER 1

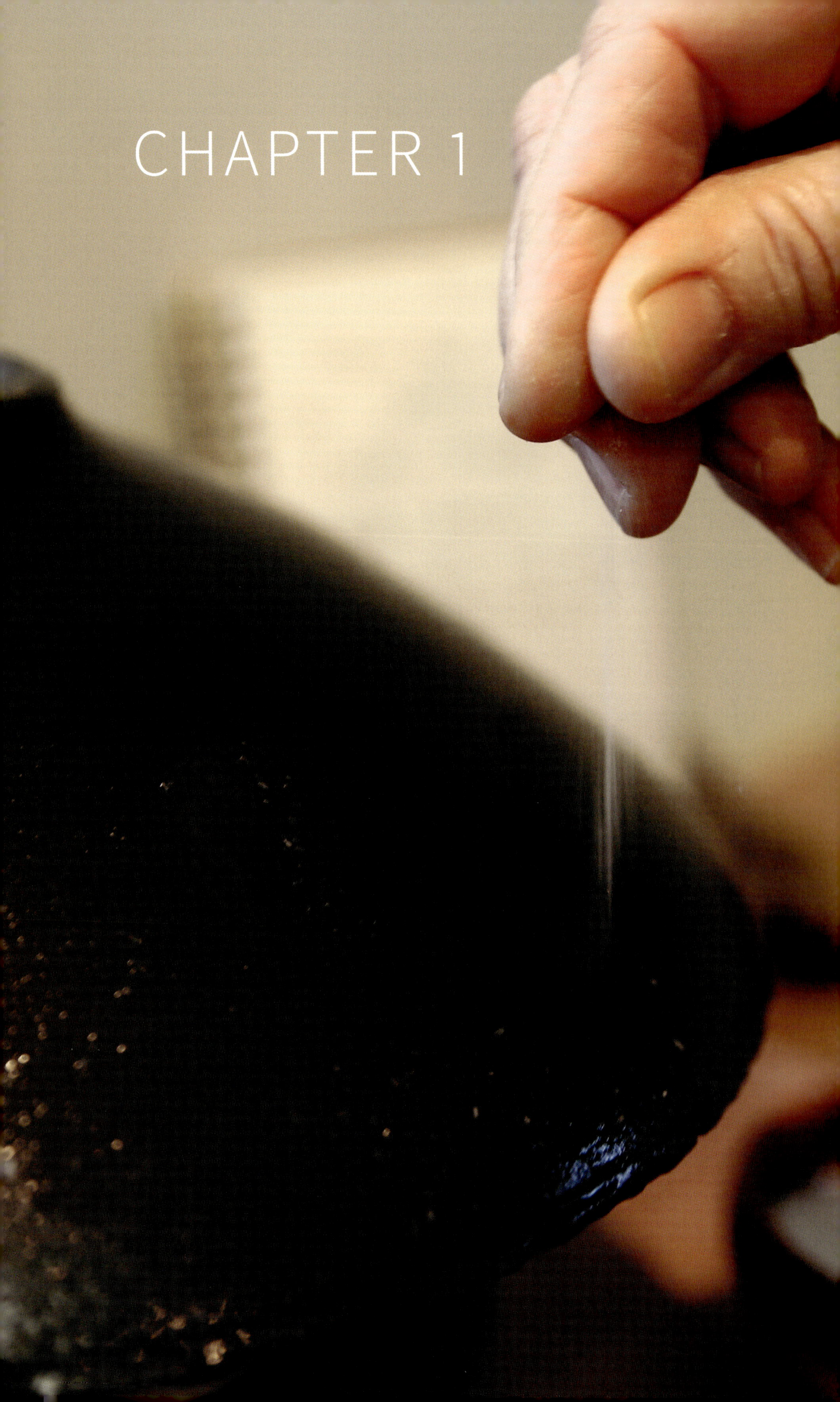

WHO KNEW YOU COULD DO SO MUCH WITH BORAX?

In my first book, *My Life as a Potter*, I shared with you how I started down the lithium trail by putting small amounts of dry minerals on test tiles and firing them to see what would happen. I have wanted to go further with testing dry minerals, and this book was the perfect excuse to dive in. Let's start our explorations with a simple ingredient that many of us are familiar with, borax. Yes, the same stuff that is widely used as a household cleaner and a booster for laundry detergent. I am constantly amazed by this one simple glaze ingredient and the multiple effects it can create. I think you will be, too, so let's get going by starting with how it began and how it led to the discovery of multiple new glaze effects.

I had been experimenting with solubles to encourage more haloing with my crawl glazes. This led me to pay more attention to borax, as I figured out it was the key to the halo effect. I was intrigued by this discovery and started to play. My first experiments began with lowering the bisque temperature to cone 06, then pouring the crawl glaze only on the inside of the vessel to see how much would seep through and make patterns on the outside surface. *Seaworm's Bloom* is an example of what haloing can look like.

My next experiments were inspired by Kate Marotz. One evening, as I was researching borax online, I came across an article by Kate that described how she was using borax washes in her work. The article sparked a lot of the ideas and led me to develop the techniques I will be sharing with you here.

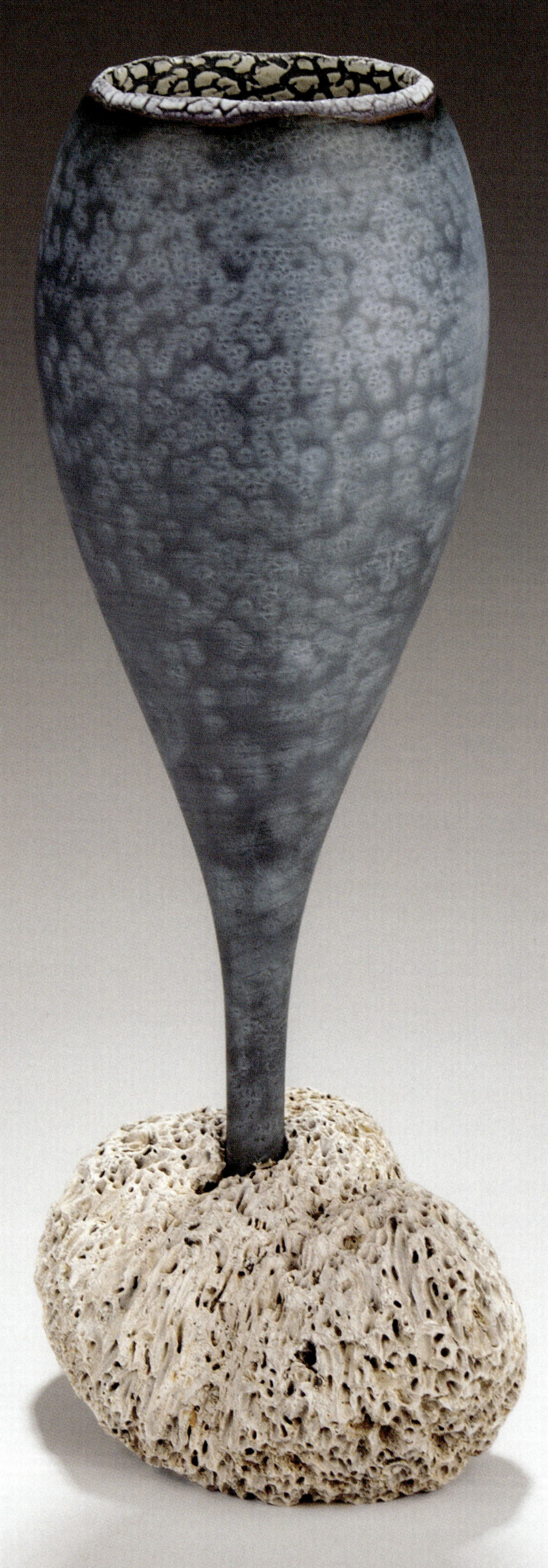

Seaworm's Bloom

A couple of years ago, a woman came into my gallery carrying a beautiful, uninhabited worm colony rock. She was clearly very attached to it and told me all about finding it on the beach while on holiday. It had been her treasure for decades, and now she wondered if I would like it. Like it, indeed! I immediately began imagining it as the base for a chalice.

As I turned it over in my hands, I saw that it had a recessed area that might work for drilling a small hole. Drilling into my base rocks takes extreme care, as they can easily crack if everything doesn't go right. Fortunately for me, my stone sculptors are skilled and gentle, and I don't lose many bases. When they sent the worm colony back to me, I could see that it was going to need a piece with a delicate glaze to match its texture.

How did I achieve the softly marked glaze surface on the chalice you see here? The pattern on the outside is brought about by solubles in the interior crawl glaze that have seeped through to the outside surface and left these wonderful patterns on the sigillata. A low bisque of 06 or lower helps encourage this to happen. I rather think this woman is no longer with us, but I think of her each time I look at her treasure from the beach.

OPPOSITE
Seaworm's Bloom, terra sigillata, crawl glaze mounted in seaworm casting, 14 cm W × 34 cm T.

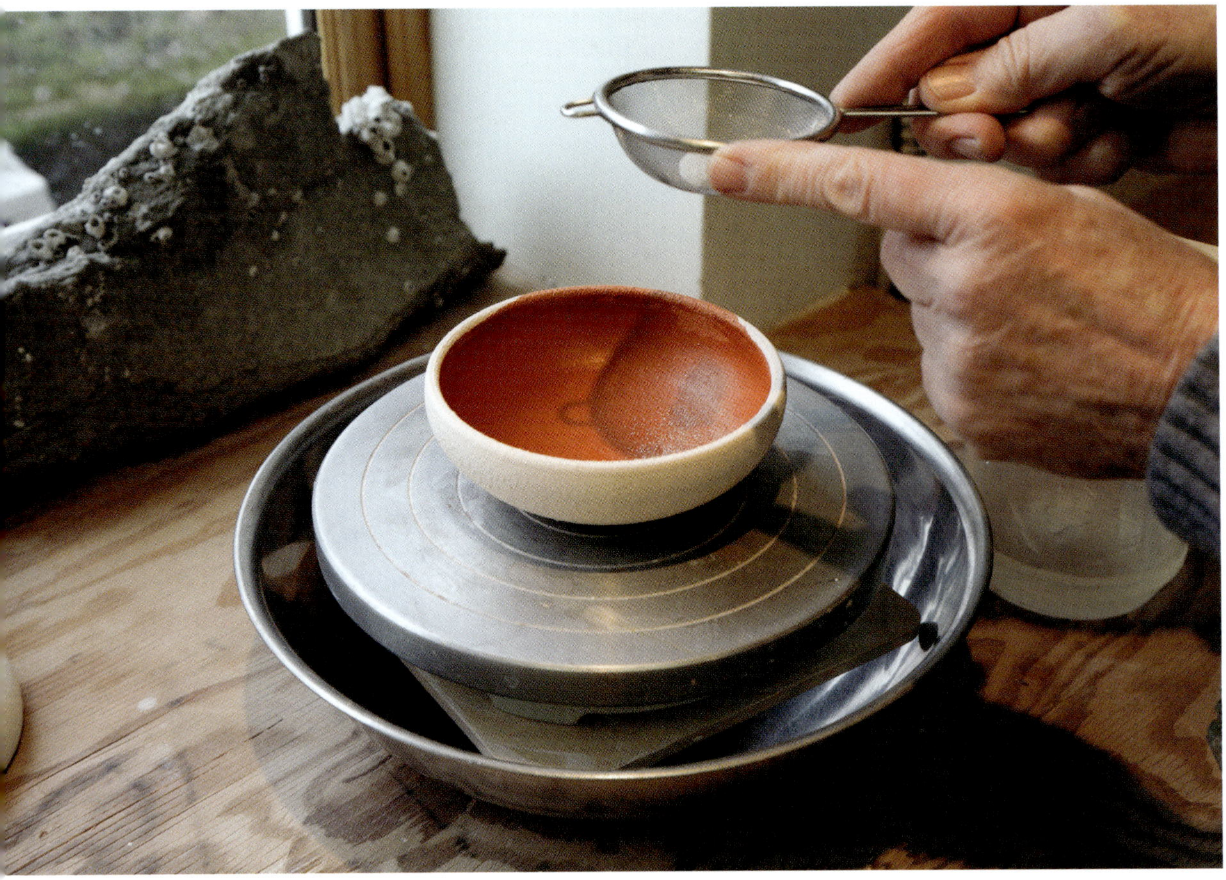

Applying borax to a test bowl.

After seeing what borax did on a test bowl, I decided to try it out on a small bisque vessel that had white terra sigillata on the body and orange sigillata applied to the top collar. I got my supplies ready—a large kitchen sieve, borax and gum to hold the borax on the pot. I started by brushing on the gum, but as I hadn't used gum in this way before, I soon got into trouble. I got gum on all right, but it was a very uneven layer and there were drips of it everywhere, including on my hands. It was the beginning of a royal mess.

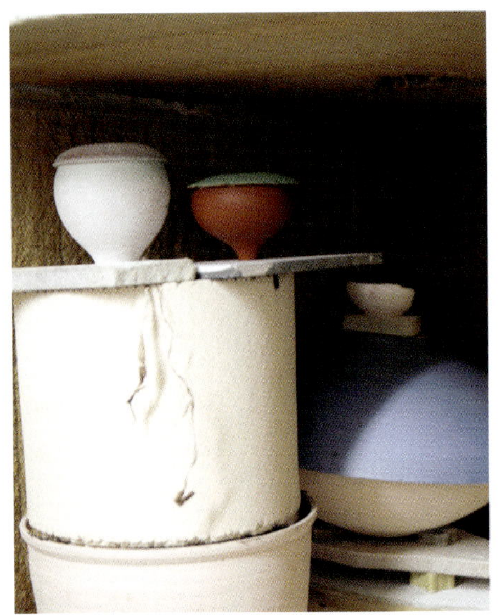

This little pot (far left, perched on top of a saggar) was about to inspire a whole new avenue of exploration for me.

I now had a very gummy pot, but suddenly realized I hadn't thought through how to get the borax on the sides of the pot. The top would be easy, but the rest of it, not so much. I was going to have to hold it sideways, turning it as I sprinkled—not easy to do by yourself. Now I was getting really flustered, my hands were sticky and there was borax everywhere.

During this process, my apprentice Sarah Wilson had been keeping her head down at the wheel nearby, gamely trying to stay focused on the pot she was making and block out the circus going on a few feet away. But I think she sensed that she was going to be called into service, and of course I soon did just that. She grasped what the problem was, as she had hardly been able to ignore my fussing, but understanding what I wanted her to do was another matter. When I am flustered, I do not give very clear instructions.

I asked her to hold the pot sideways and to turn it while I sprinkled the borax. She looked at this gummy pot and said, "Where do I hold it?" In my mind it was obvious, but when I looked at the pot, I realized that it wasn't going to be that easy. In exasperation, I replied, "Wherever you can!" And then I grabbed the sieve, which was rapidly spilling borax everywhere, and started to sprinkle. A delicate controlled affair it was not! At some point while I was barking orders, Sarah's hands hit the side of the pot, scraping off some of the borax. Once the sprinkling was done, I examined the streak her hand had left and thought, *Hmm, what to do?* I decided to leave well enough alone. I had a reduction firing loaded and ready to go, so I popped the pot on top of a saggar and started the kiln.

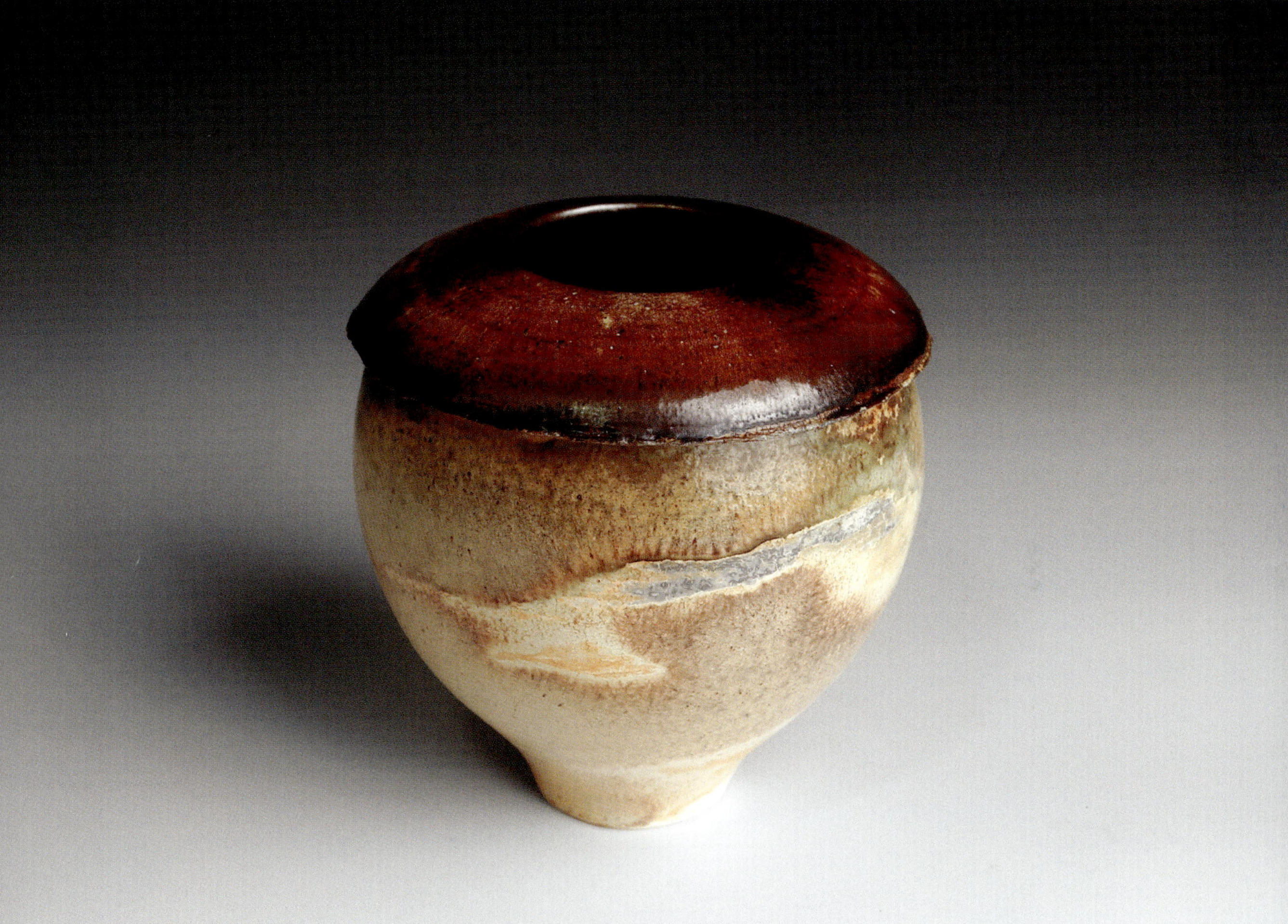

I can't tell you how much I learned from this one little pot. It was my first discovery of some of the hidden possibilities of borax and excited me to no end. The area on the right, where Sarah's hand had brushed off most of the borax, had turned grey in the reduction. Because of this accident, I got a hint of what could happen if I intentionally applied borax in varying thicknesses. And the collar of the pot gave me clues about how orange terra sigillata would behave in reduction.

My prize, the first hint of what was to come.

Vessel, white terra sigillata, orange terra sigillata, borax, cone 06, reduction, 12.5 cm W × 13 cm T.

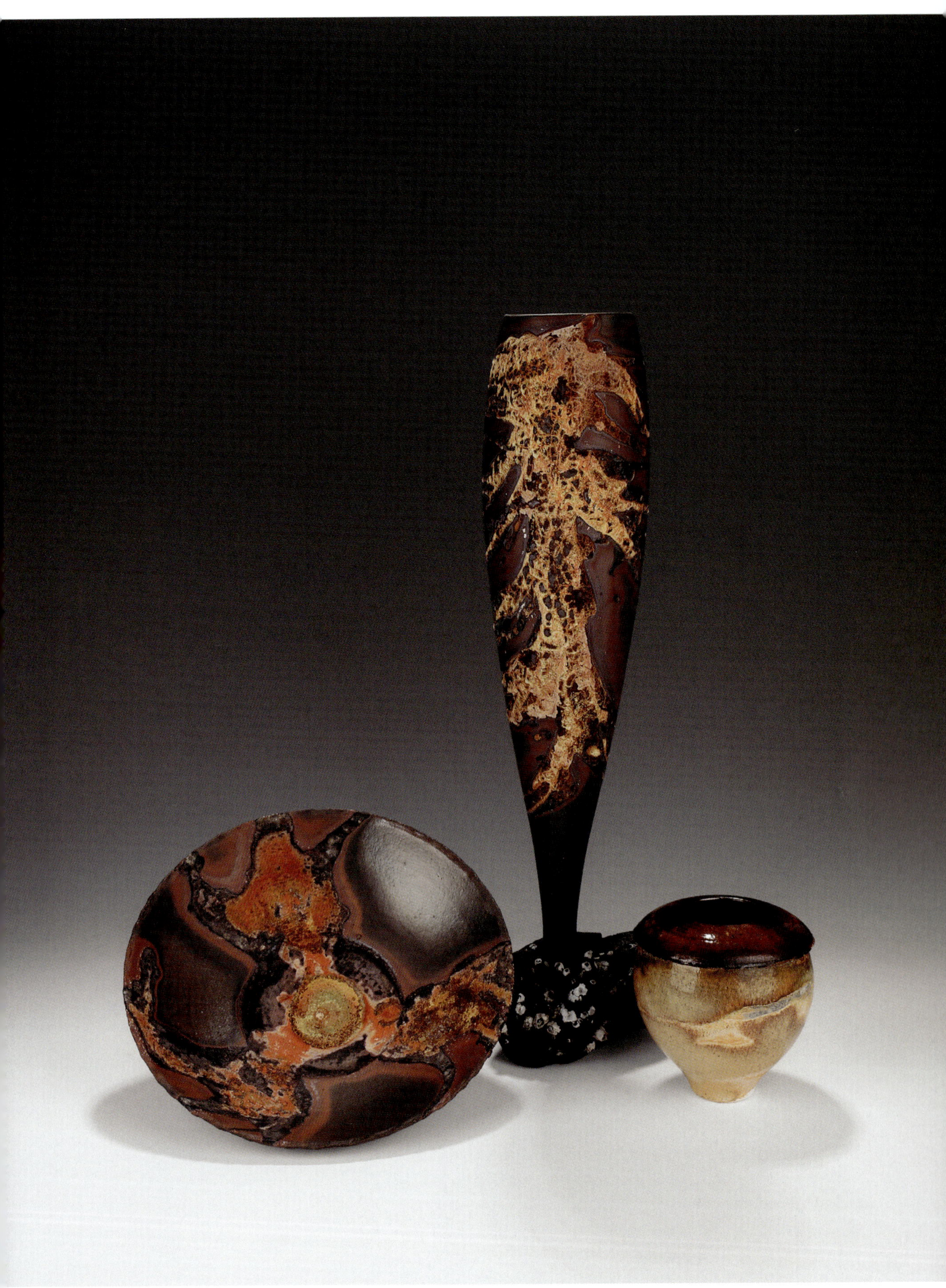

The two other pieces in this photo were also in the firing and have a base layer of orange terra sigillata with Lana Wilson's chartreuse applied. This was the LR1 firing with the reduction starting at 1102°F, or 594°C. I like to play around with the level of reduction, as the effects can be lovely, especially with the orange terra sigillata. If the reduction is lower, the terra sigillata produces lighter streaks of colour rather than turning completely shiny black, as it does in heavier reduction. The bowl on the left was in an area of the kiln that got more reduction, and you can see there is very little variation in the sigillata, but look at the gorgeous haloing, the beautiful shadow around the glaze edges! The chalice also has some of that variation in the upper part of the form, going darker toward the stem.

My first borax experiment after the little pot was this flower bowl, fired in oxidation. Years ago, I started calling this style of bowl a "flower bowl" because of its resemblance to a flower opening from the central core. I refer to them this way throughout the book. For this piece, I sprinkled borax starting from the outer edges, applying it heavily at the edge and lighter toward the centre. I had brushed Alkaline Blue 04 glaze onto the centre, but not being used to brushing glazes, I had forgotten how the glaze doesn't necessarily flow

OPPOSITE, FROM LEFT

Bowl, orange terra sigillata, Lana Wilson's chartreuse glaze, cone 05, reduction, LR1, 30 cm W × 8 cm T.

Chalice, orange terra sigillata, Lana Wilson's chartreuse glaze, mounted in rock, cone 05, reduction, LR1, 16 cm W × 54 cm T.

Vessel, white terra sigillata, orange terra sigillata, borax, cone 06, reduction, 12.5 cm W × 13 cm T.

BELOW

Orange terra sigillata, white terra sigillata, borax, Alkaline Blue 04 glaze, oxidation, 29 cm W × 8 cm T.

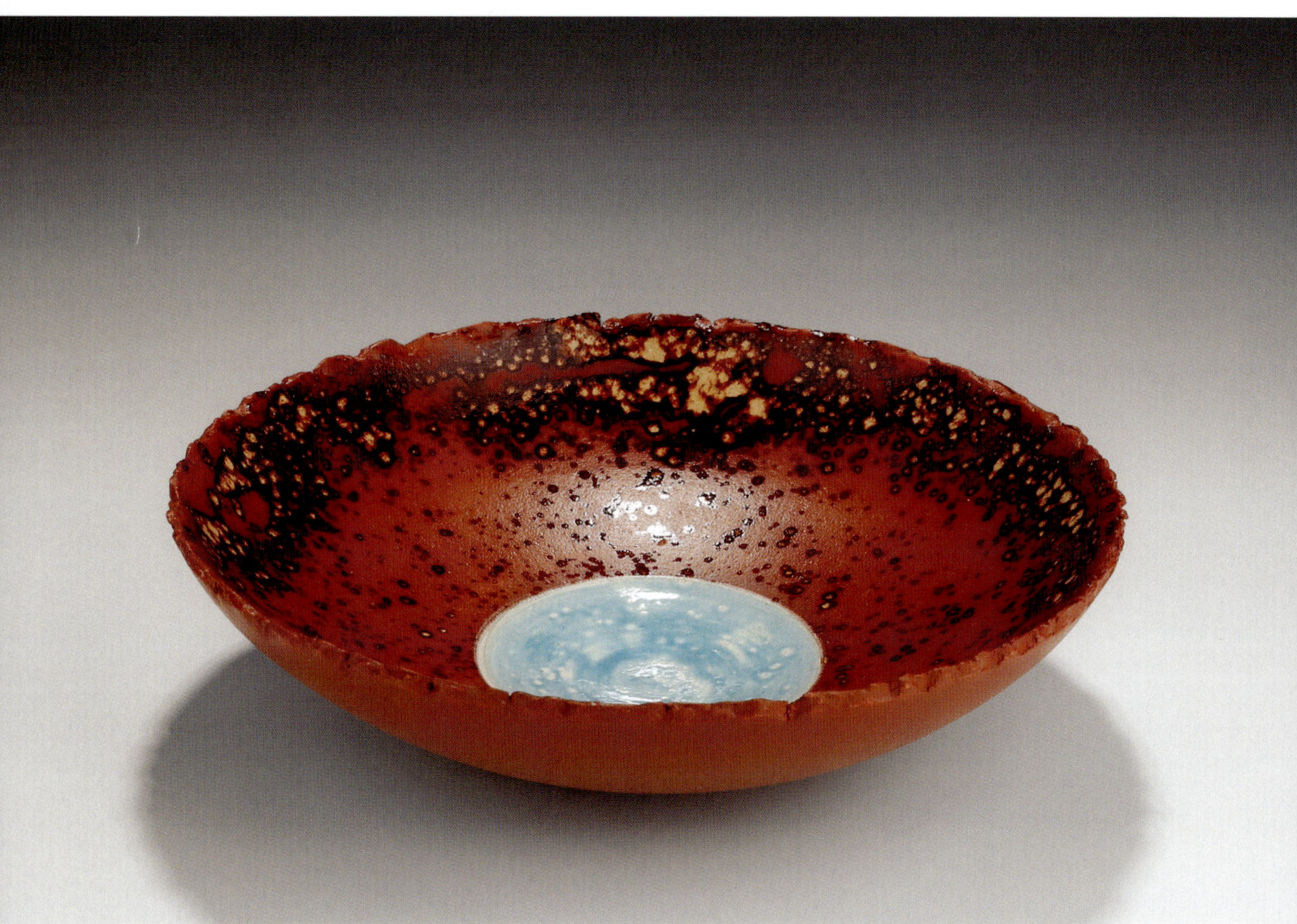

Glaze solubles

In ceramics, certain compounds used in glazes can dissolve into water. The compounds stay mixed into the water and will not settle out. These solubles are usually flux materials such as borax, soda ash and nepheline syenite.

When you apply a glaze, the clay body soaks up the water, along with anything dissolved in it. The solubles may migrate through the clay to the other side of the clay wall. As the glaze dries, the solubles are left in the clay, sometimes showing up as marks on the surface. You may see this if you pour a glaze on the inside of a vessel and then wait until later to glaze the exterior. When you come back to glaze the exterior, the solubles will show on the outside surface of the piece.

smoothly off the brush, hence the uneven glaze layer. Adding gum to the glaze will help with this problem. The creamy coloured spots are where the borax is thickest, while the darker areas are where it's thinner.

Now that you've had a taste of experimenting with borax applied to a terra sigillata base, we can start to go a bit deeper into the world of terra sigillata.

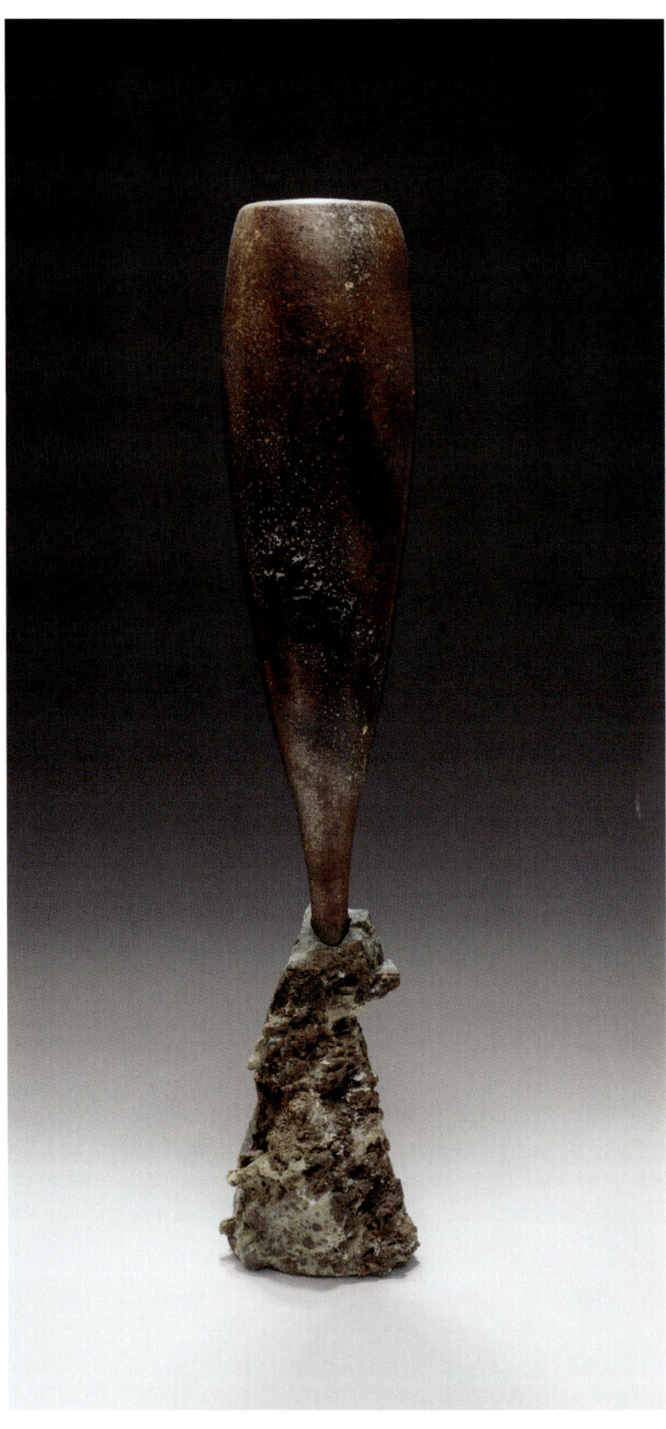

Chalice, terra sigillata, borax, reduction fired, mounted in rock, cone 04, 2024, 14 cm W × 68 cm T.

Halo effect

The halo effect refers to the beautiful line of colour that sometimes appears on the outer edges of a glaze. It is usually brought about by solubles in the glaze that have been soaked up into the clay. As the water evaporates, it leaves behind whatever is dissolved. When the piece is fired, these solubles burn and create the halo effect.

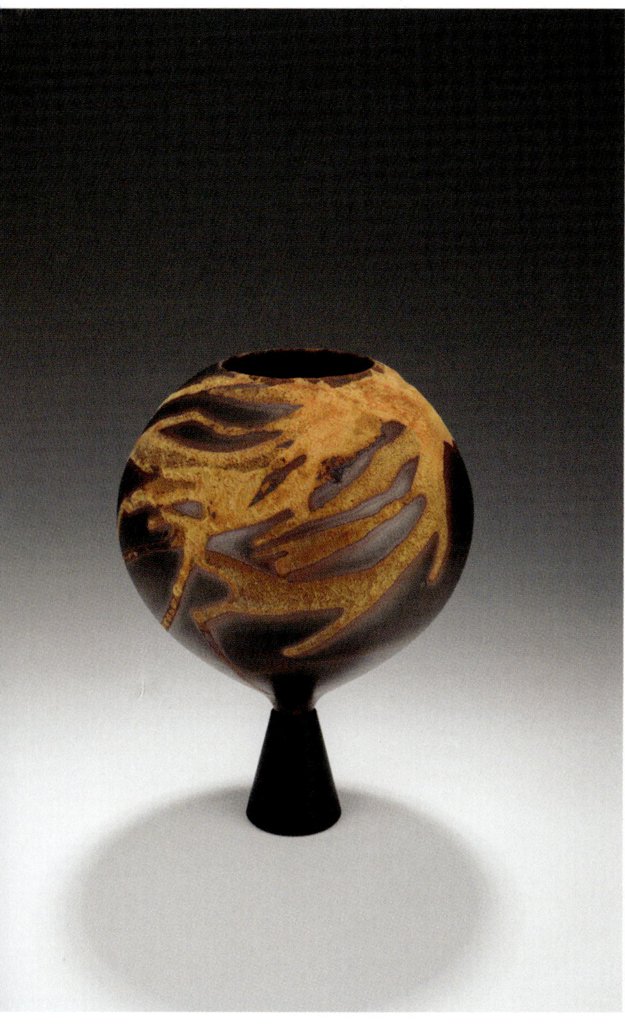

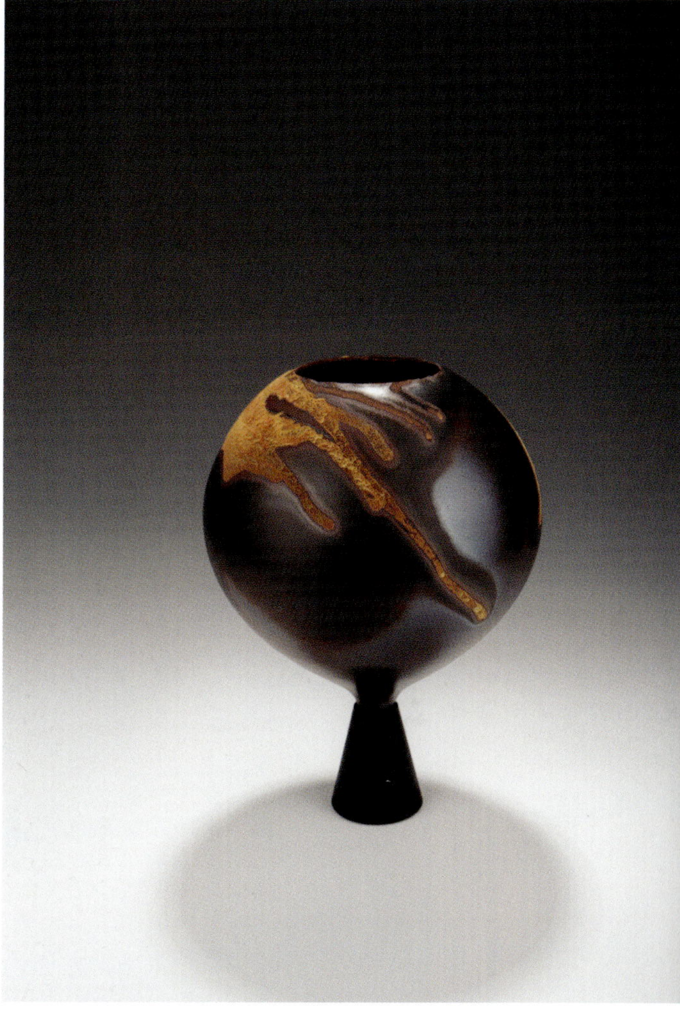

Chalice, terra sigillata, Lana Wilson's chartreuse, reduction fired, mounted in metal, cone 05, 2021, 20 cm W × 19 cm T.

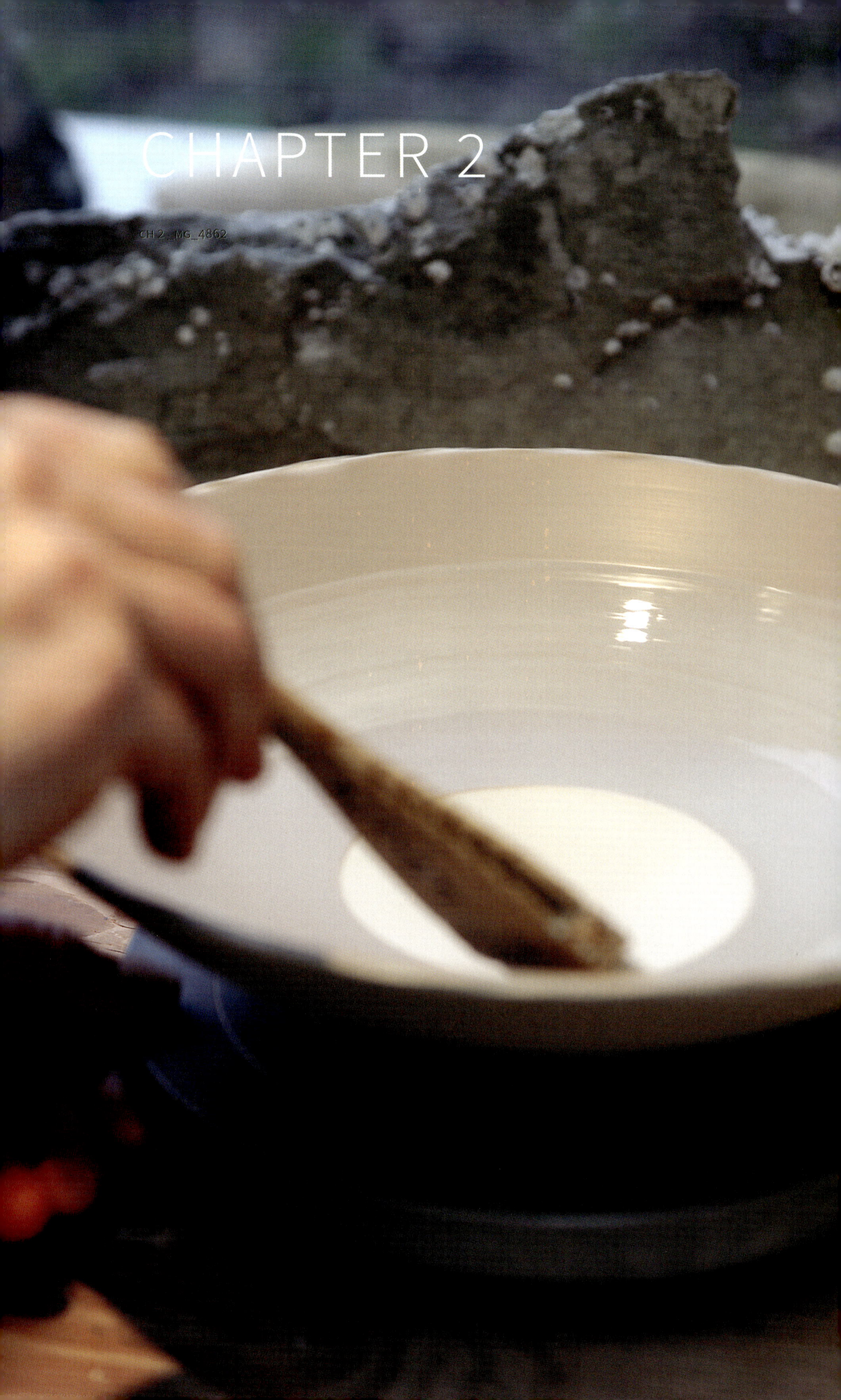

CHAPTER 2

CH 2_MG_4862

THE TRANSFORMATIVE MAGIC OF TERRA SIGILLATA

My experiments with terra sigillata started decades ago with my crawl glaze work. I think of terra sigillata as providing a base layer to build on, much like the undercoat that painters apply to start a painting.

There is definitely a steep learning curve when it comes to making and applying terra sigillata, but it's well worth the effort. In this chapter, I give you a taste of what terra sigillata can bring to your work. Not all the techniques I use are explained here, but don't worry; there is much more to come in the next chapters.

MAKING TERRA SIGILLATA

Terra sigillata is made by mixing clay with water and a deflocculant, then leaving it to sit for at least 24 hours, so that the heavier particles settle. You then siphon off the finer particles above, discarding the heavier sludge below.

If you are lucky, you will be able to see three distinct layers once the mixture has settled—watery liquid on top, sigillata in the middle and particulate sludge on the bottom. If so, you can siphon off the top watery layer and discard it, then move on to siphon the sigillata layer, leaving the sludge at the bottom.

When I used Calgon decades ago as a deflocculant, the three layers showed up nicely. But since the Calgon recipe was changed, I switched to other deflocculants, and they don't produce the same clearly distinct layers after settling. So, now I siphon off the top two layers and throw out the bottom

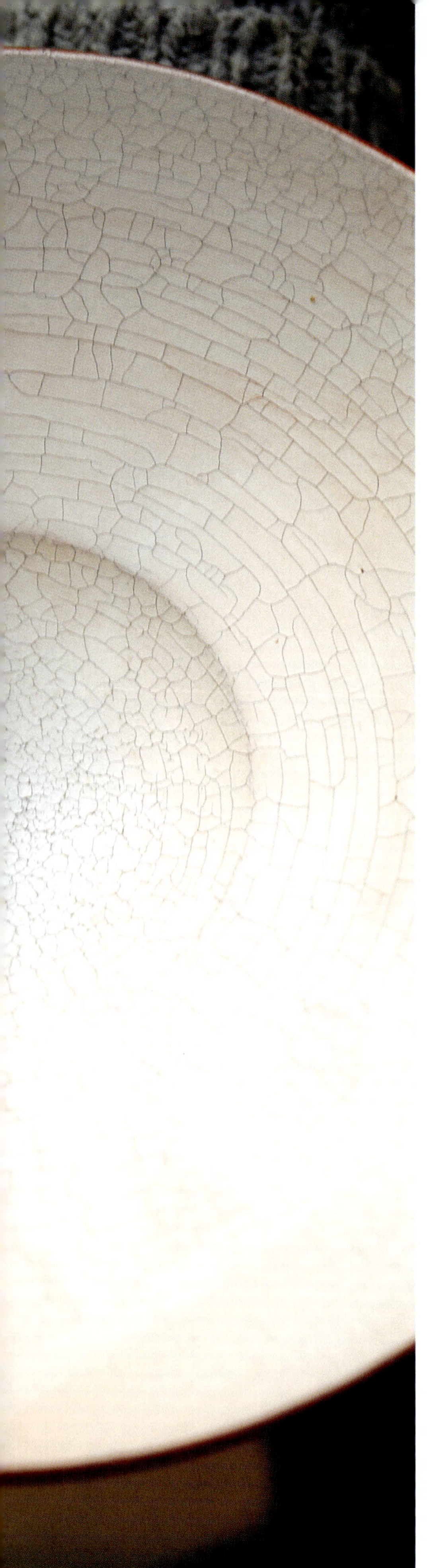

layer of sludge. Then I leave the terra sigillata to settle for a few weeks before I remove the top layer of water to reveal the terra sigillata underneath.

There are many articles online about how to make terra sigillata, but I include a basic recipe for you here.

WHITE TERRA SIGILLATA

Test batch: 1 L (.26 gal) water, 400 g ball clay, 2 g sodium silicate, 2 g soda ash. If using Darvan 7 in place of sodium silicate, omit the soda ash and use 11 g of Darvan 7.

5-gallon batch: 19 L (5 gal) water, 7,600 g ball clay, 38 g sodium silicate, 38 g soda ash. If using Darvan 7, mix the following: 19 L (5 gal) water, 7,600 g ball clay, 209 g Darvan 7.

ORANGE TERRA SIGILLATA

Orange terra sigillata is made the same way, substituting Cedar Heights Redart clay for the ball clay.

When your terra sigillata is made, you can take things a step further by adding minerals or stains to it.

DARK BLUE TERRA SIGILLATA

For the dark blue terra sigillata you see in this book, use:

2 cups white terra sigillata and 12 g copper oxide, 20 g cobalt oxide, 10 g manganese dioxide.

If you want your terra sigillata to be a darker blue-black, use 1 cup of white terra sigillata instead of 2 cups.

You can also add minerals to the terra sigillata to influence whatever you apply over it. To 1 cup of terra sigillata, add 1 tsp of any of the following: tin oxide, spodumene, petalite, soda ash, borax.

I did quite a few tests with each of these combinations and was pleasantly surprised by the results. But more about that later.

APPLYING TERRA SIGILLATA

For the most part, I brush the terra sigillata onto my pieces when they are bone dry, though you can apply it to bisque

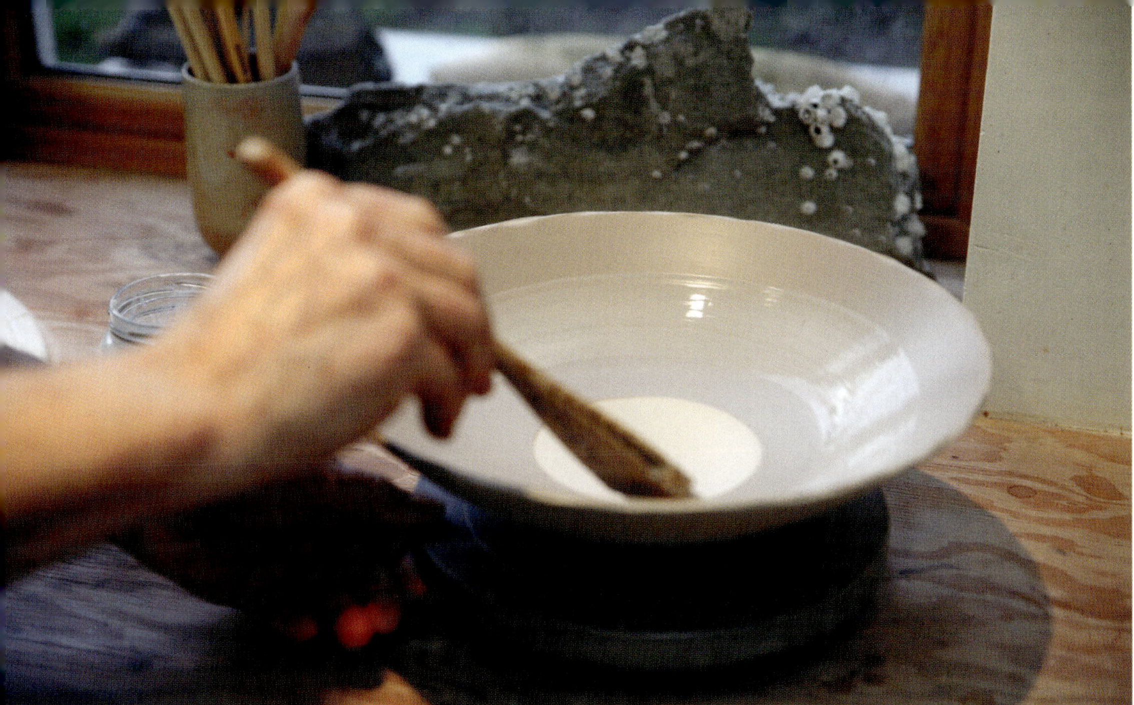

ware as well. Be very careful when brushing it on. If you have drips or loose brush hairs, these will show, as will fingerprints if you handle the piece before it is fully dry. The terra sigillata needs to be a thin slip, with a specific gravity between 1.10 and 1.20, around the consistency of skim milk. Usually, three to four coats will suffice, as you can run into problems with crazing or flaking if it is applied too thickly. It can be polished after the last coat. However, for most of my work, the polishing isn't necessary, as I am using the terra sigillata primarily as an undercoat for what will be applied on top of it.

Brushing white terra sigillata onto a bone-dry bowl.

As I like to play around, I often apply the white terra sigillata fairly thickly to encourage crazing. Over the years, I have sought to create a feeling of unearthed antiquities in my work, and a crazed surface achieves that nicely.

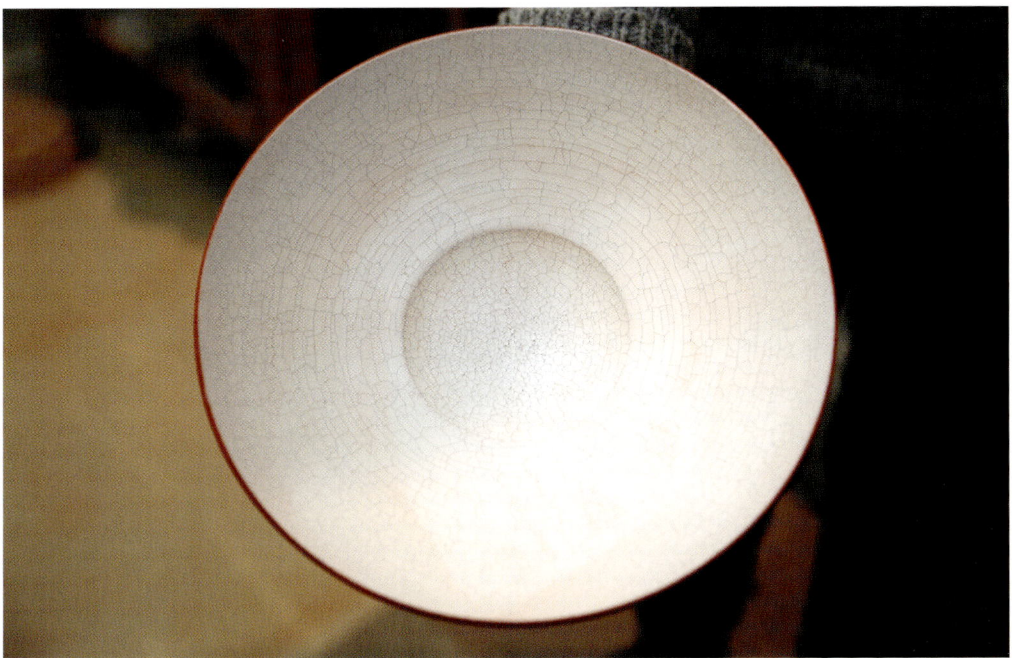

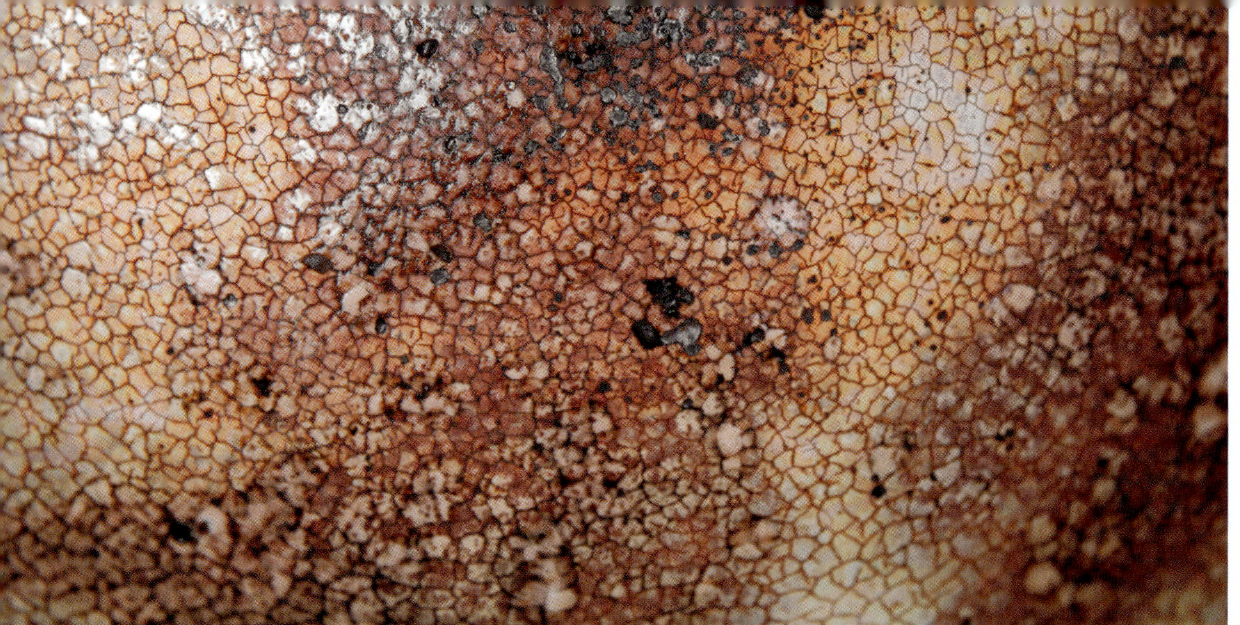

Terra sigillata, borax, copper wash, cone 05, reduction.

This is how the crazed terra sigillata surface looks after the bisque firing. I have applied a wash and wiped it off to show the craze lines more clearly. Now, I move on to the layering up stage, where I apply individual layers, firing between each layer, to slowly build up the surface.

You can also spray on the terra sigillata. I prefer to brush on the base layer, as I think the surface looks better, and then spray on added layers, if desired. In these examples, I've done a little of both.

EXPERIMENTING WITH MULTIPLE FIRINGS

To begin illustrating the differences between oxidation and reduction, I've made twin bowls to show you how results change, depending on which atmosphere they are fired in.

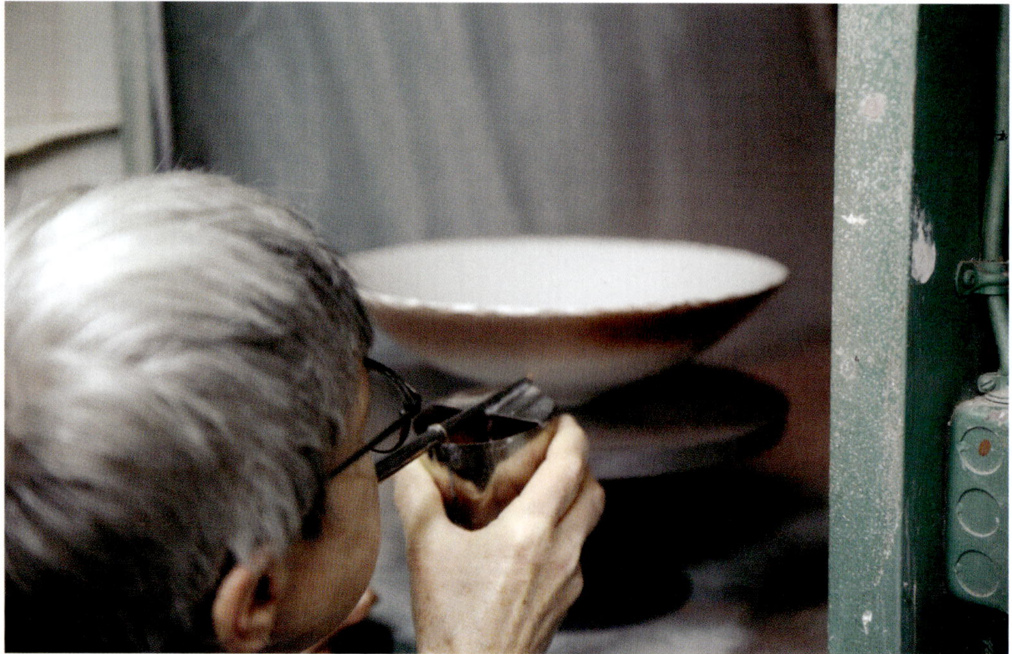

Using an atomizer to spray orange terra sigillata over a first layer of white terra sigillata with tin added to it.

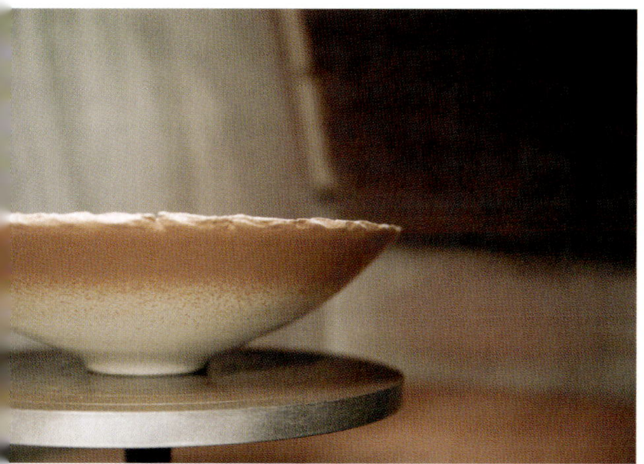

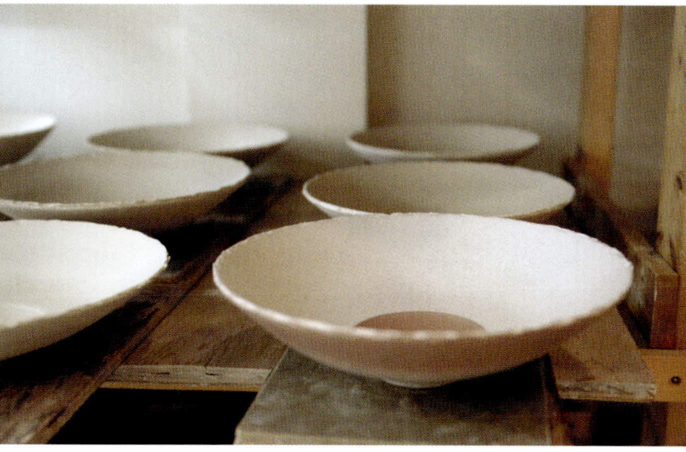

On each bowl, I have applied a first base layer of white terra sigillata containing tin oxide to the outside and inside, except for the centre of the interiors, to which I've applied a layer of orange terra sigillata. Finally, I have used an atomizer to apply a dusting of orange terra sigillata to the outside and inside walls of the bowls.

After being coated with layers of terra sigillata, these bowls are lined up and ready to pop into the next bisque firing.

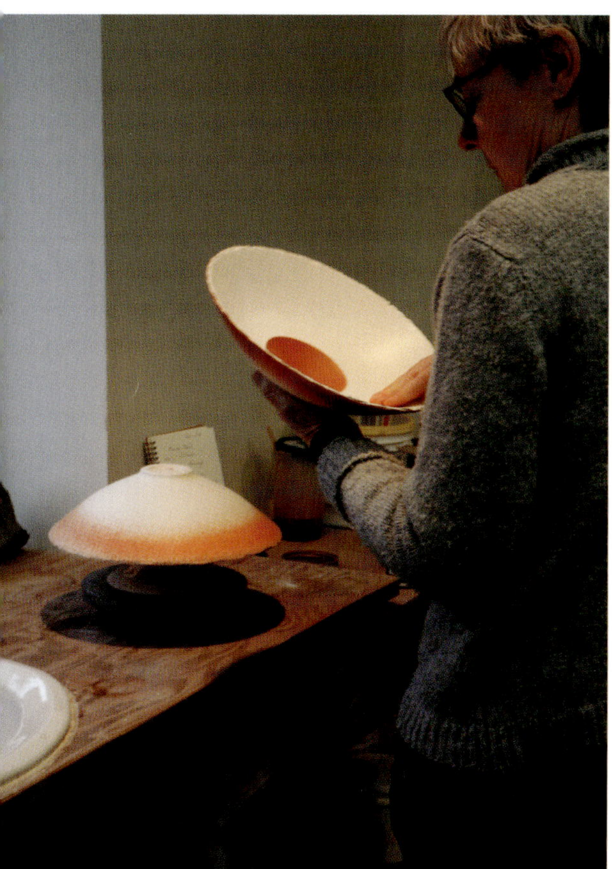

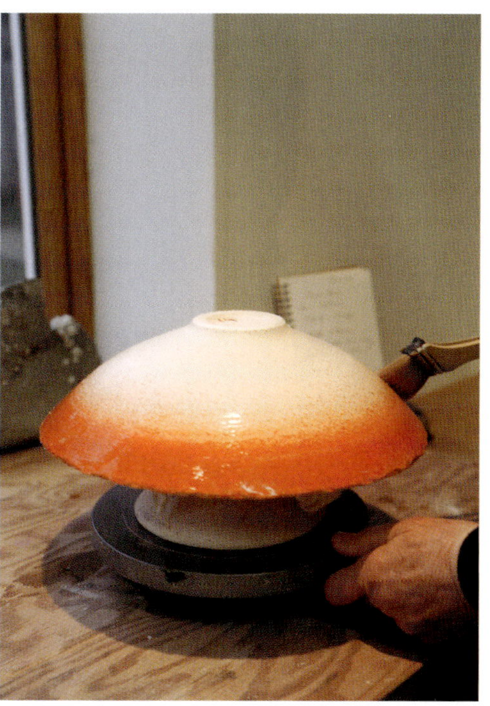

I brush on a coat of gum for the borax to stick to, before firing one bowl in oxidation and the other in reduction.

Examining the bisque-fired bowls and contemplating my next move, I decide to apply borax to some areas on the bowls.

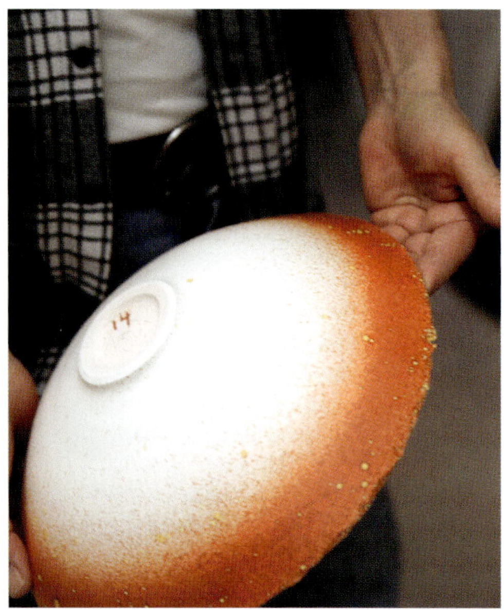

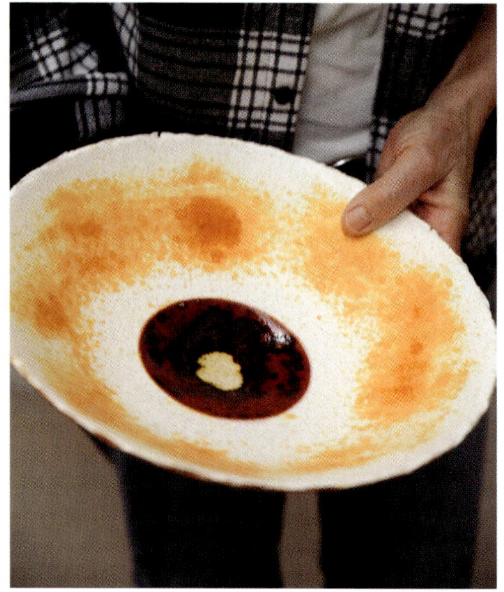

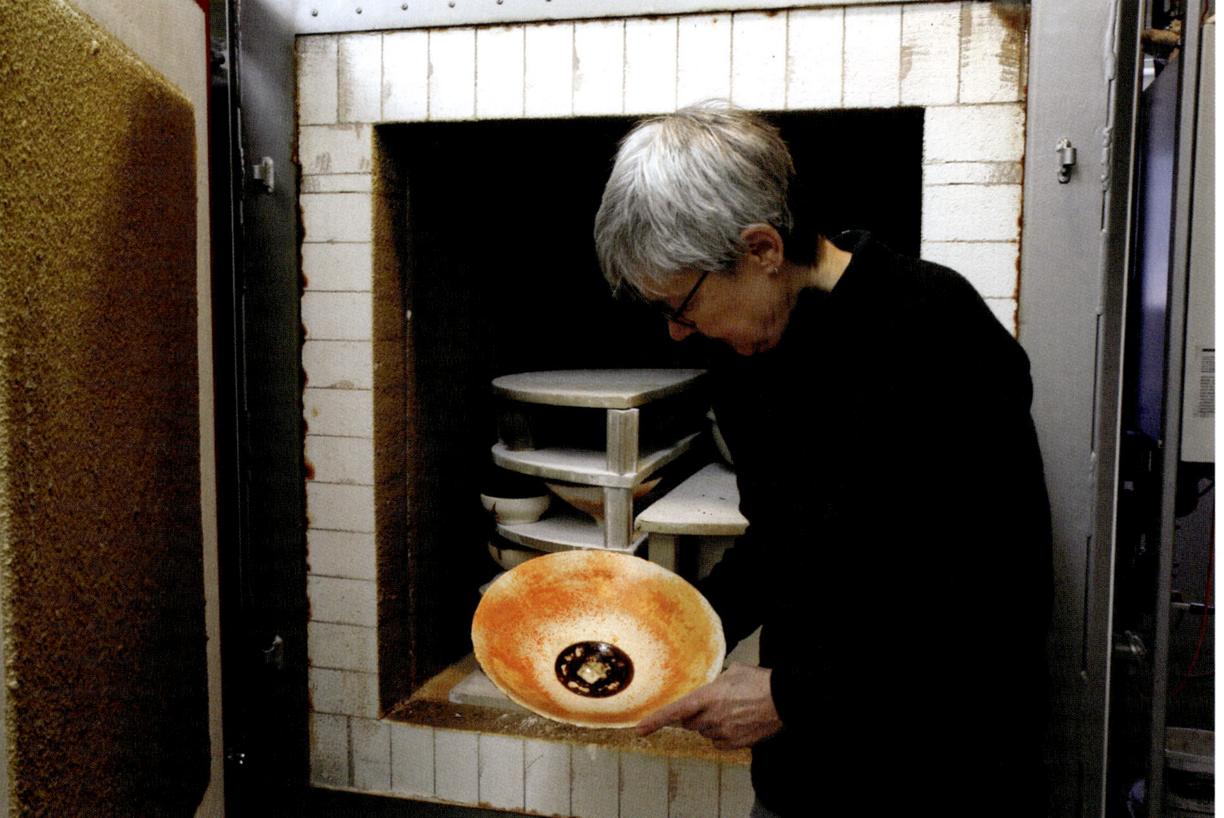

TOP
Bowls fired in oxidation.

BOTTOM
Unloading the kiln, seeing the subtle differences brought about by the reduction firing.

So far, all I've added to these bowls is borax. When you sprinkle borax over white terra sigillata with tin in it, you get a marvellous orange colour. Over the orange terra sigillata in the centre of the bowls, I've sprinkled the borax a bit thicker and placed a wee clump of borax in the middle. I was a bit disappointed by the fact that there wasn't a big change in colour on the LR1 bowl, and neither bowl looked finished to me, so I contemplated my next step.

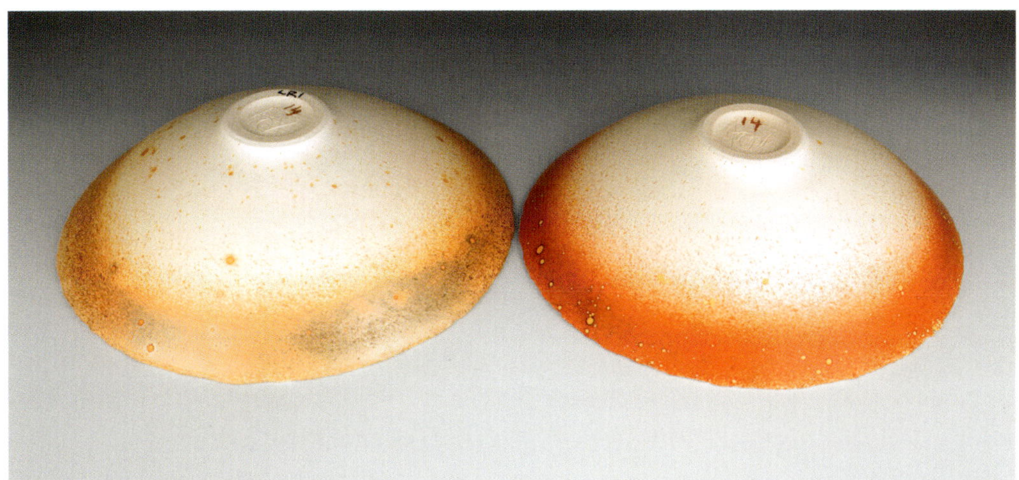

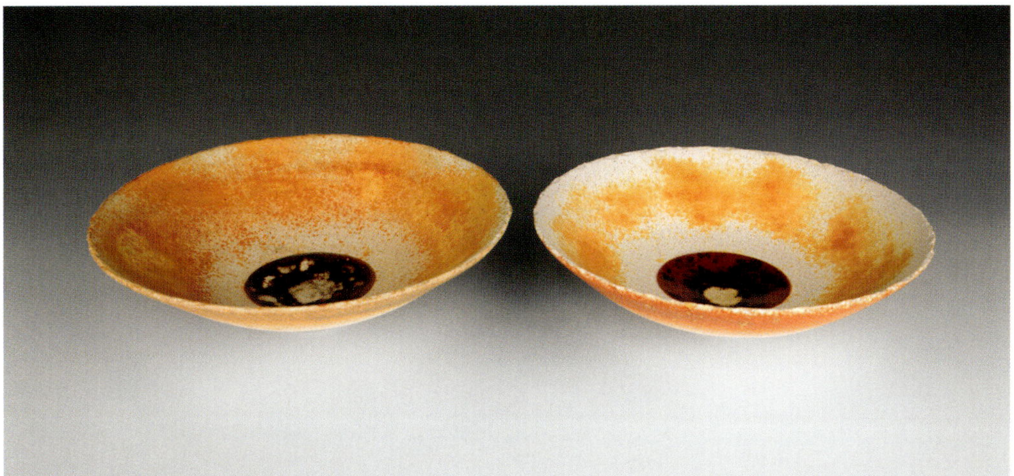

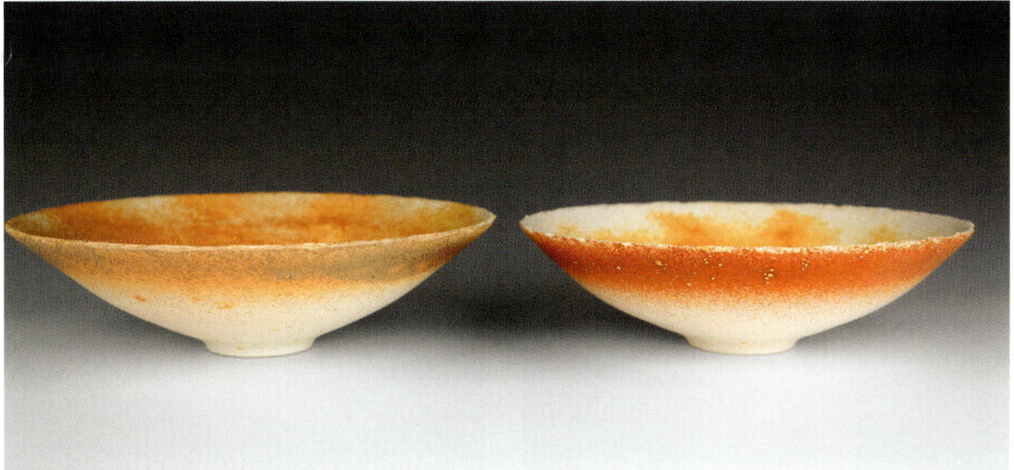

I decided to apply a new glaze I've been playing with, Crusty Mudflat, over the orange terra sigillata/borax layer on the LR1 bowl and leave the centre of the other bowl alone. I then used the atomizer to spray a light dusting of orange terra sigillata over the borax area and popped them both in an oxidation firing.

In each photo, the bowl on the left has been fired in reduction (LR1), and the one on the right in oxidation. Notice how the orange terra sigillata has become browner in reduction.

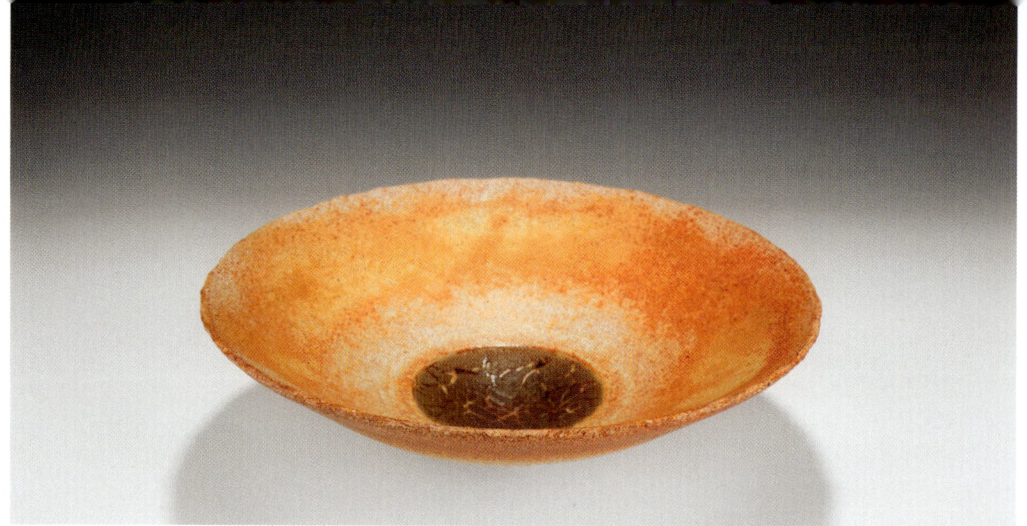

Previously reduction-fired bowl with Crusty Mudflat and a bit more terra sigillata applied, fired in oxidation.

When they came out of the firing, I felt that the light dusting wasn't enough, so I set aside this reduction bowl for the time being and went back to the oxidation only bowl. I sprayed on more terra sigillata, but this time I held the atomizer much closer to the bowl, so that the force of the spray was greater near the lip and lighter as I went closer to the centre.

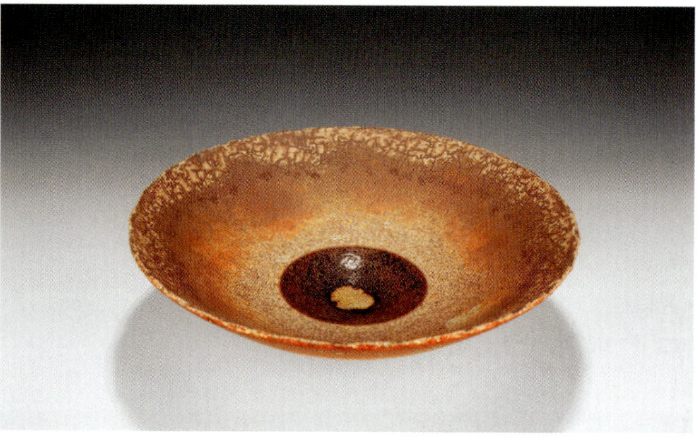

In this photo, you can see how different the terra sigillata looks when applied to a previously fired, semi-glazed surface. I suspected the terra sigillata would run when I applied it, as the bowl hadn't been preheated to help the terra sigillata stick. And run it did, but in the most beautiful way! When I stopped spraying to look at it, I knew I had nailed it.

Bowl, terra sigillata, borax, cone 05, multifired in oxidation, 30 cm W × 9 cm T.

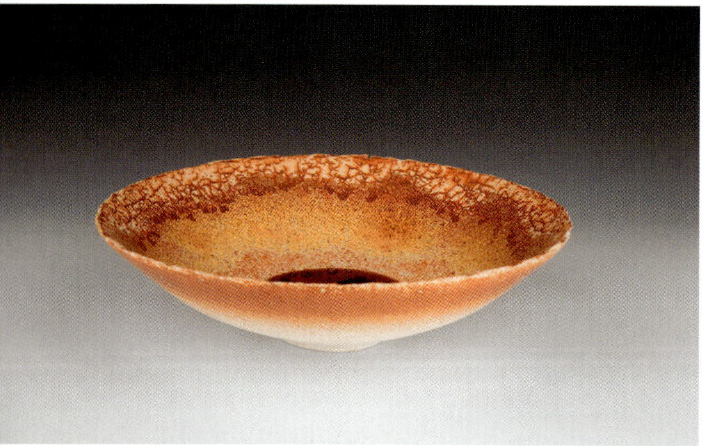

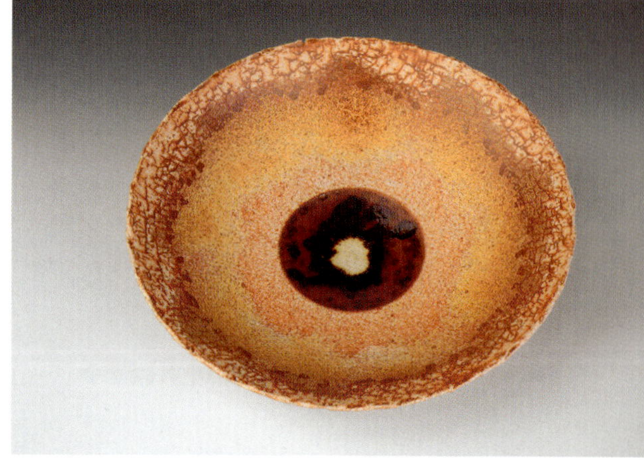

I have to say this is one of my favourite bowls, and it's all done with terra sigillata and borax. Oh, and that beautiful pattern at the top? That's brought about by the terra sigillata seeping into those craze lines that I was talking about earlier.

What happened to the other bowl you may wonder? Well, I sprayed on another layer of orange terra sigillata, slightly thicker than on the previous bowl, added more Crusty Mudflat glaze to the centre and fired it again in reduction. Only this time, I set the first reduction ramp at 80 per cent and then raised it to 85 per cent once I hit 1562°F, resulting in a much more heavily reduced surface.

Bowl, terra sigillata, borax, glaze, multifired, cone 05, reduction, 30 cm W × 9 cm T.

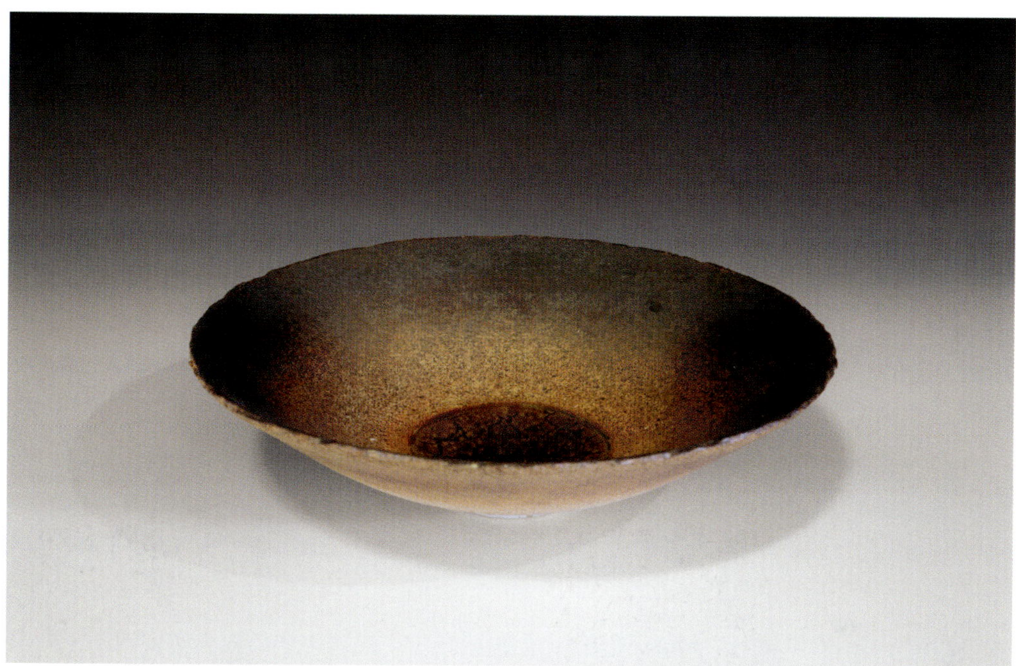

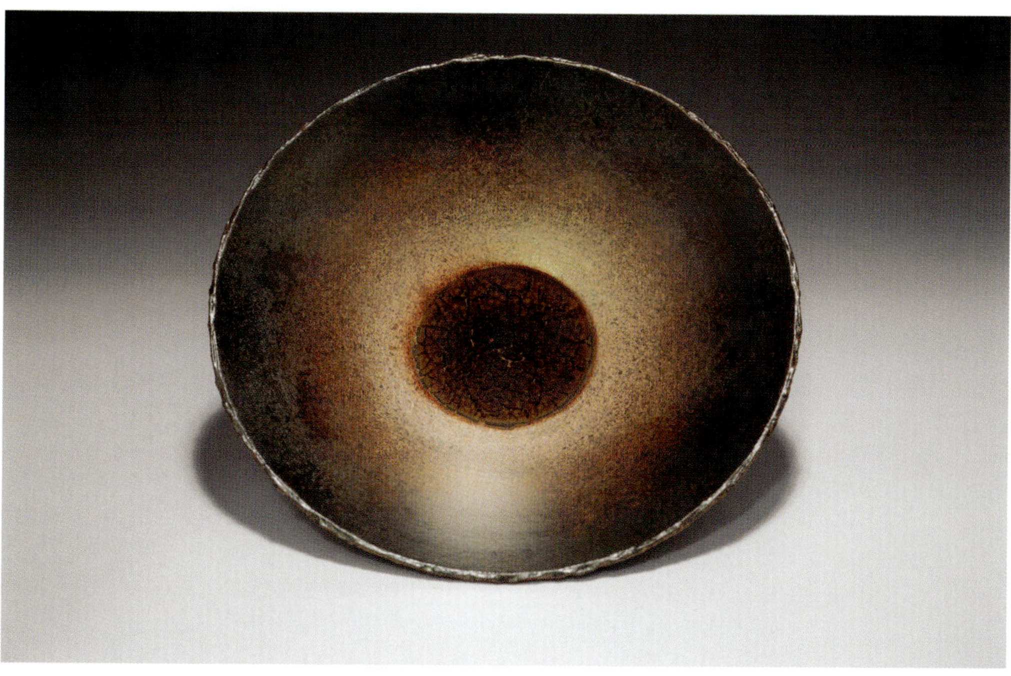

Those first two bowls whetted my appetite for more experiments with the terra sigillata and borax combination, leading to these next bowls, which showed vastly different results with just the smallest variations in finishing processes. Though I followed almost exactly the same procedures for each, the main difference was that for the second bowl I brushed a layer of gum over the base layers of sigillata and then sprinkled borax on pre bisque to see what would happen. Both were fired in oxidation.

RIGHT
Bowl 1 after bisque firing.

BELOW
Bowl 1, final firing, cone 05, oxidation, 28 cm W × 7.5 cm T.

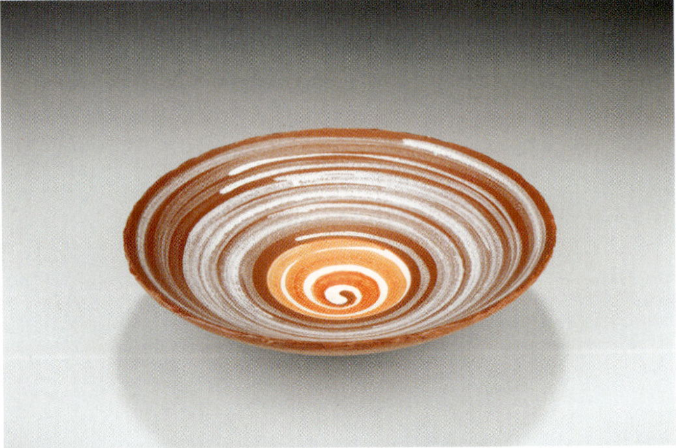

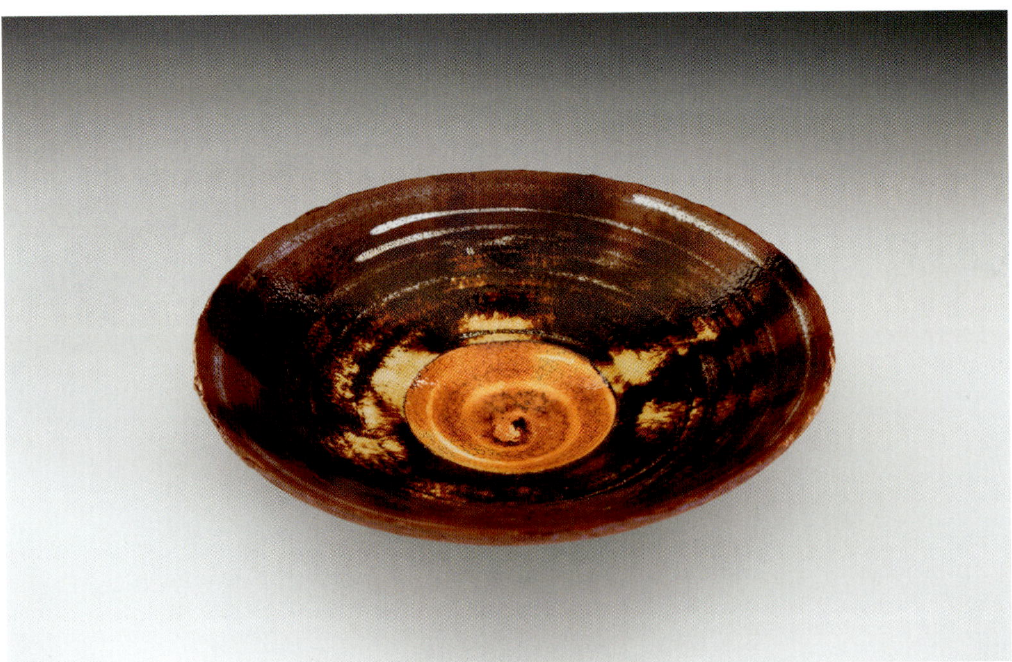

The steps involved for *Bowl 1* were:

1. Orange terra sigillata on body with white terra sigillata spirals overtop, white terra sigillata and tin on the flower, followed by a swirl of orange terra sigillata, bisqued.

2. Gum, borax sprinkled overall, fired.

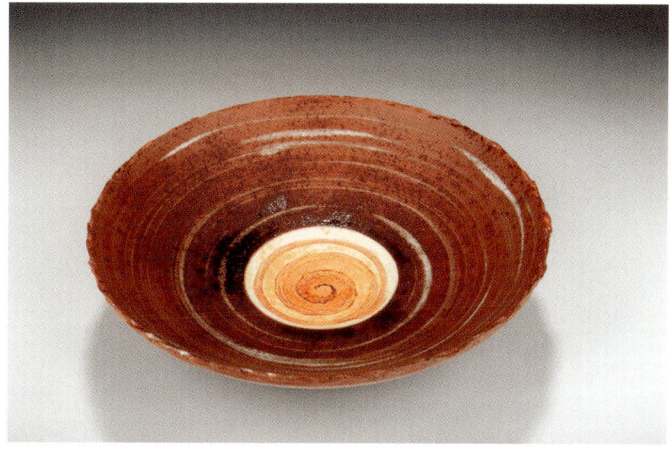

LEFT

Bowl 2 after bisque firing. Note the difference created by sprinkling the borax straight onto the terra sigillata before the bisque.

BELOW

Bowl 2, final firing, cone 05, oxidation, 28 cm W × 7.5 cm T.

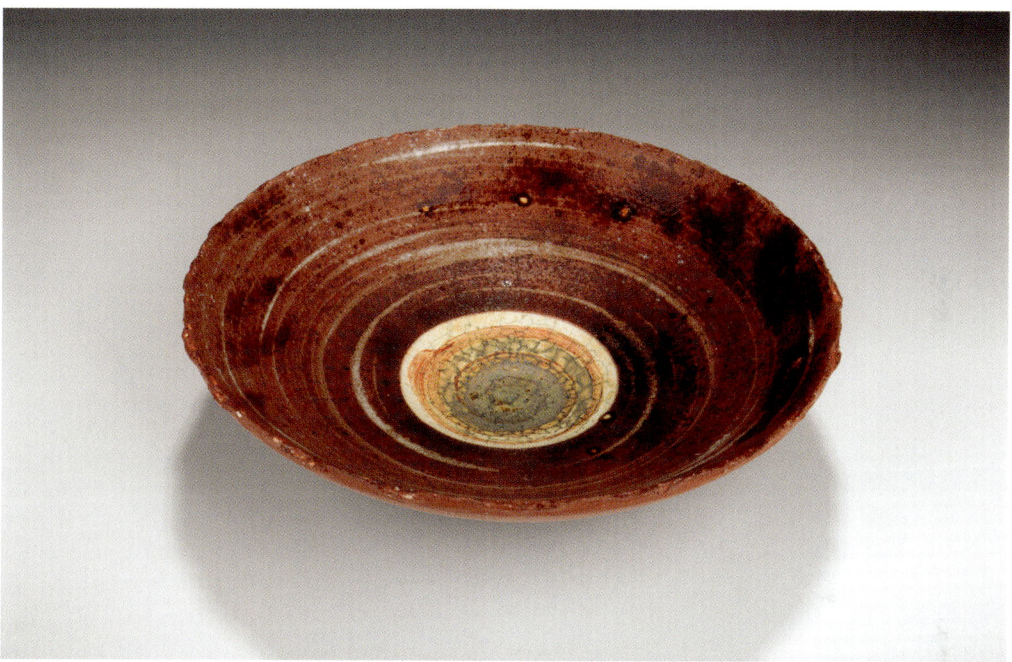

After the second bowl had been bisqued, I brushed more white terra sigillata spirals onto the orange and applied a copper wash to the flower, adding a final sprinkling of borax before firing again.

I found the results from these bowls very exciting. So much variety from only four ingredients, and we're just getting started!

My next experiments involved adding other minerals to white terra sigillata and then sprinkling borax on top to see how it would react with the minerals. I found that there wasn't much of a difference when the borax was sprinkled over spodumene, petalite or soda ash blends, but there was a big difference with the tin blend. I tested the blends in oxidation and reduction, but didn't notice much variation in results between the two atmospheres.

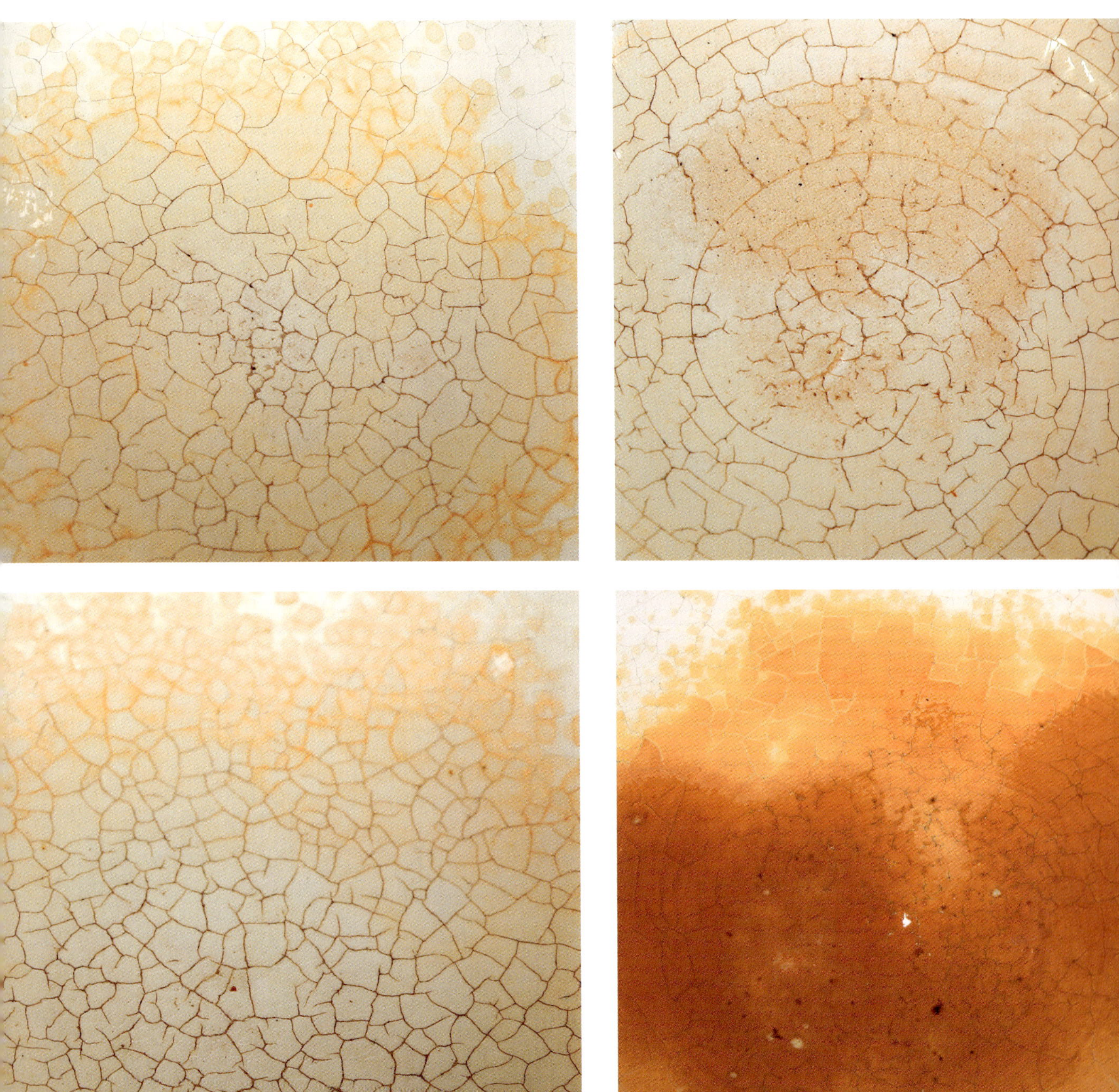

TOP LEFT
White terra sigillata with soda ash.

TOP RIGHT
White terra sigillata with spodumene.

BOTTOM LEFT
White terra sigillata with petalite.

BOTTOM RIGHT
White terra sigillata with tin.

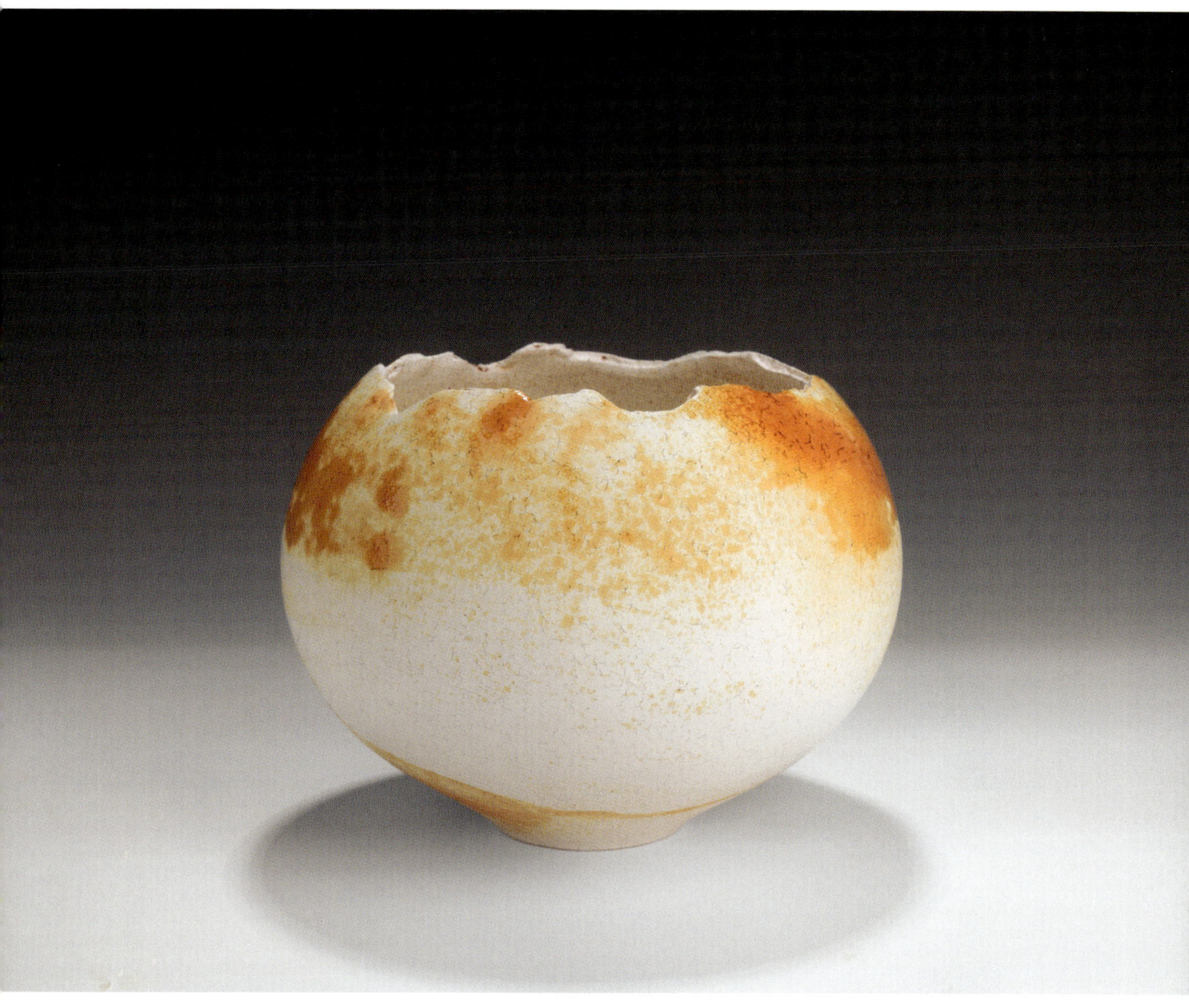

Egg-white terra sigillata with tin, borax sprinkles, cone 05, oxidation, 20 cm W × 15 cm T.

All the mineral test blends were made to the ratio of 1 cup terra sigillata to 1 tsp mineral. Here are the steps I used:

1. Applied the terra sigillata blends and fired the test bowls to cone 05 in oxidation.

2. Sprinkled on borax and fired again to cone 05 in oxidation.

The white areas on this piece have very little to no borax. The bold yellowy-orange is where more borax was sprinkled.

Now, let's move on to explore what you can do with coloured terra sigillatas.

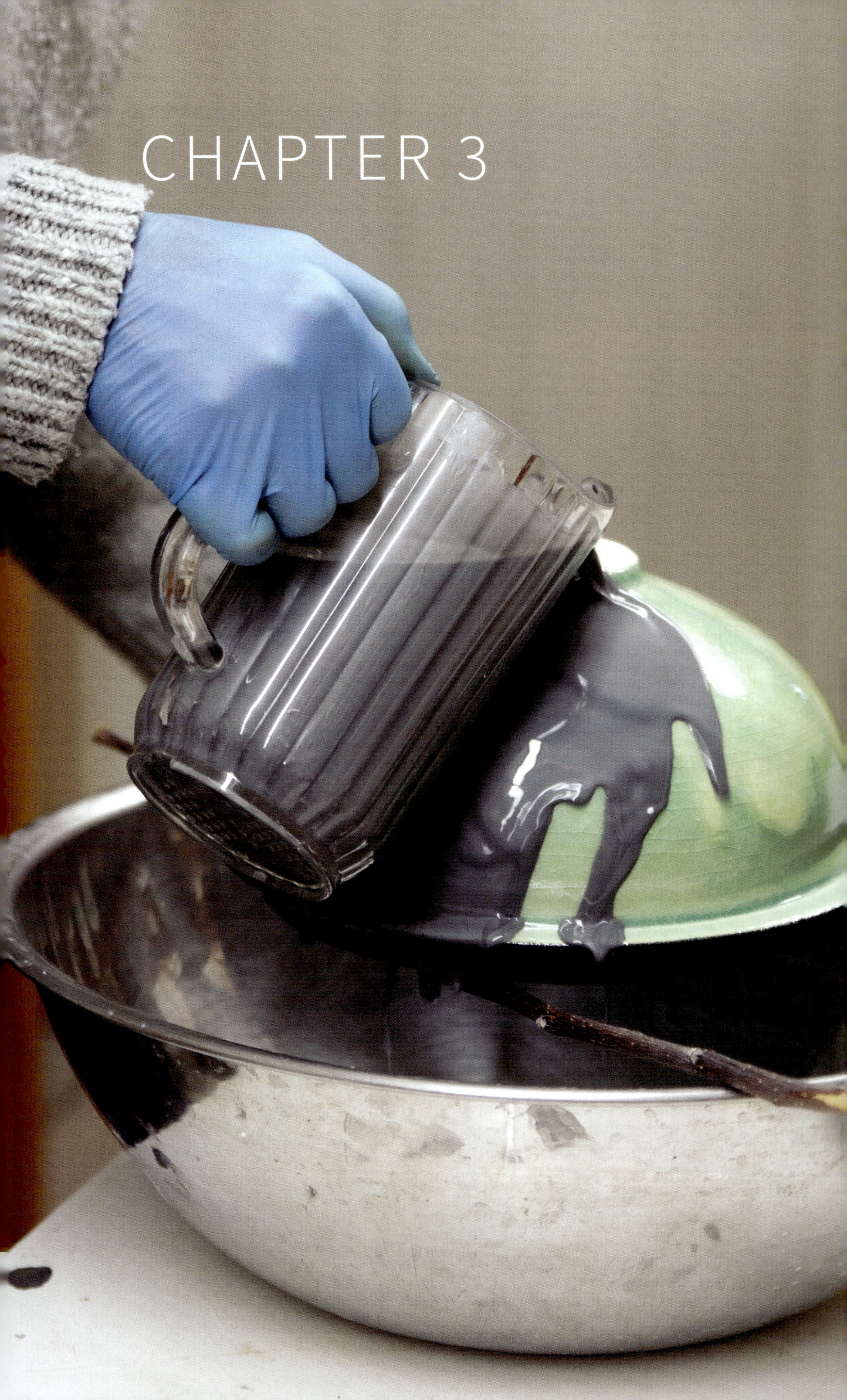

CHAPTER 3

ENLARGING YOUR PALETTE WITH COLOURED SIGILLATAS

After seeing what adding minerals to the terra sigillata could do, I was flooded with inspiring ideas. It was time to try the next step: sprinkling borax on coloured terra sigillatas.

Let's begin with a bowl that I had bisqued with a blue terra sigillata.

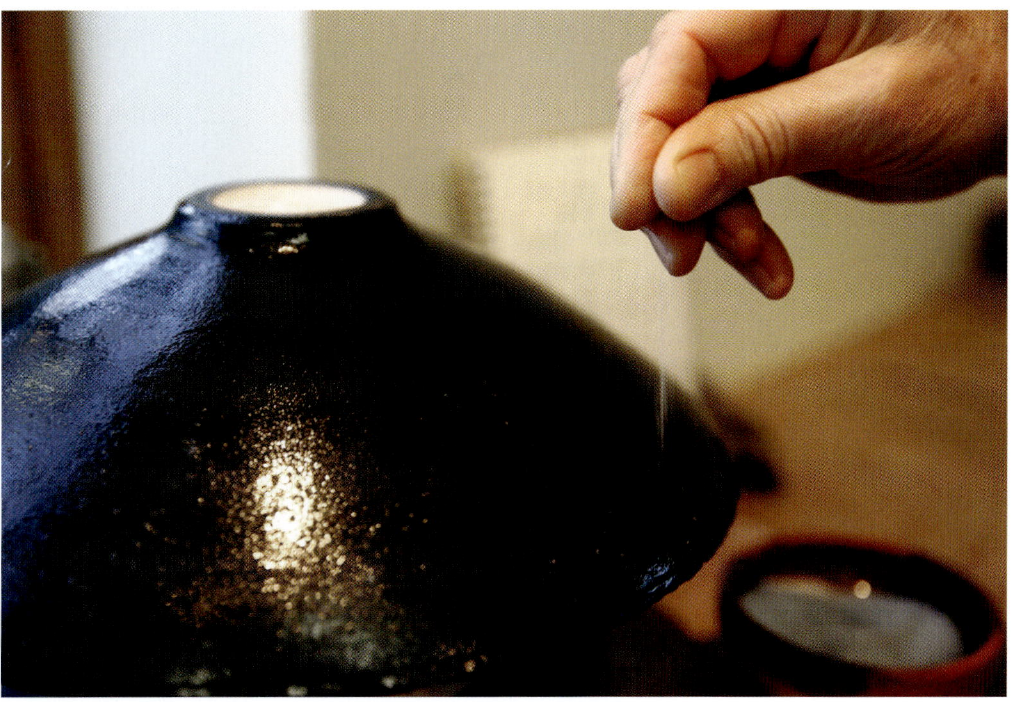

With a layer of gum covering the dark blue terra sigillata, I sprinkled borax on the exterior. For the interior of the bowl, I used a small kitchen sieve to apply the borax, lightly at the edges and then more heavily as I moved toward the centre.

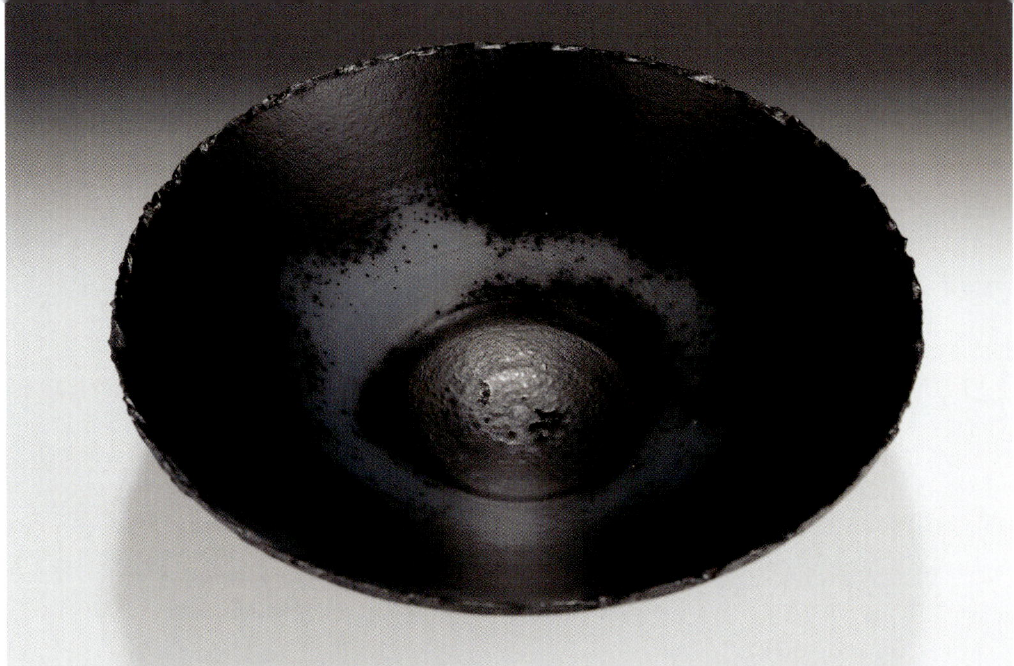

After the first glaze firing in oxidation.

When I lifted the bowl out of the kiln, I marvelled at how the colour evoked the darkness of deep space. I loved it! However, I also wanted to explore what other colour effects could happen, so I poured some Barium Matte Blue glaze that I had recently tested into the centre. With borax being a strong flux, I suspected that the barium glaze would respond nicely, possibly losing its matte finish. I had applied the borax quite thinly on the rest of the interior, so I decided to apply more to thicken it in certain areas and then fired the piece again.

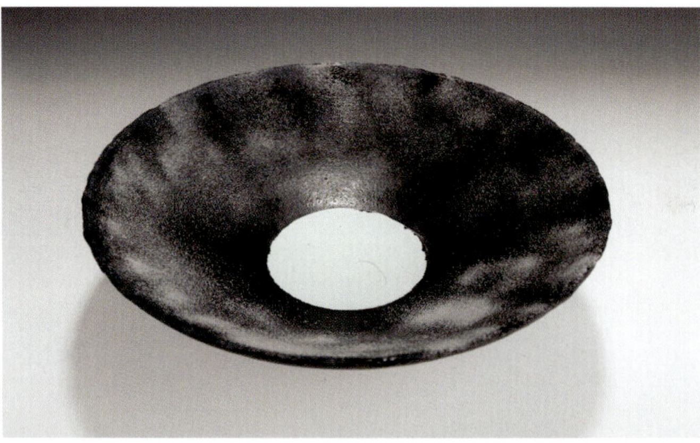

Before it went into the kiln again.

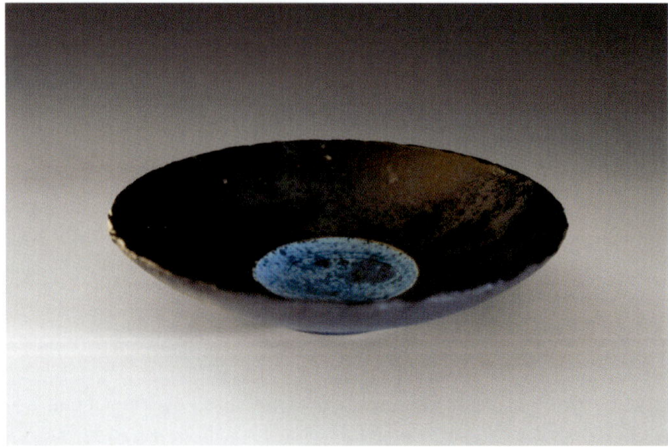

After refiring, cone 05, oxidation.

Now, I could have left well enough alone, but I had one more idea. *What would happen if I applied a dusting of white terra sigillata over some of the borax?* From the start, I had approached this bowl as a learning piece, so I forged on to firing number three.

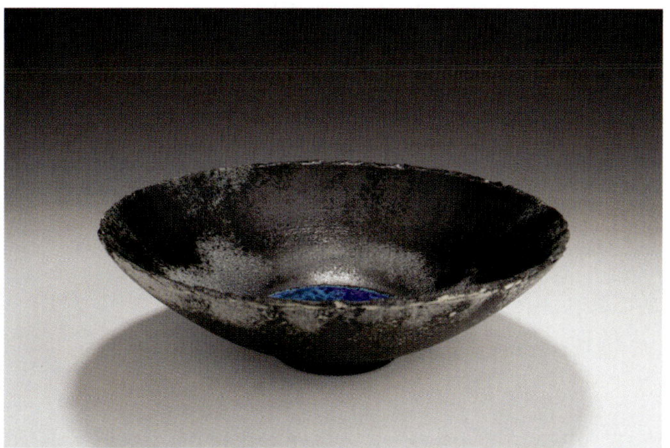

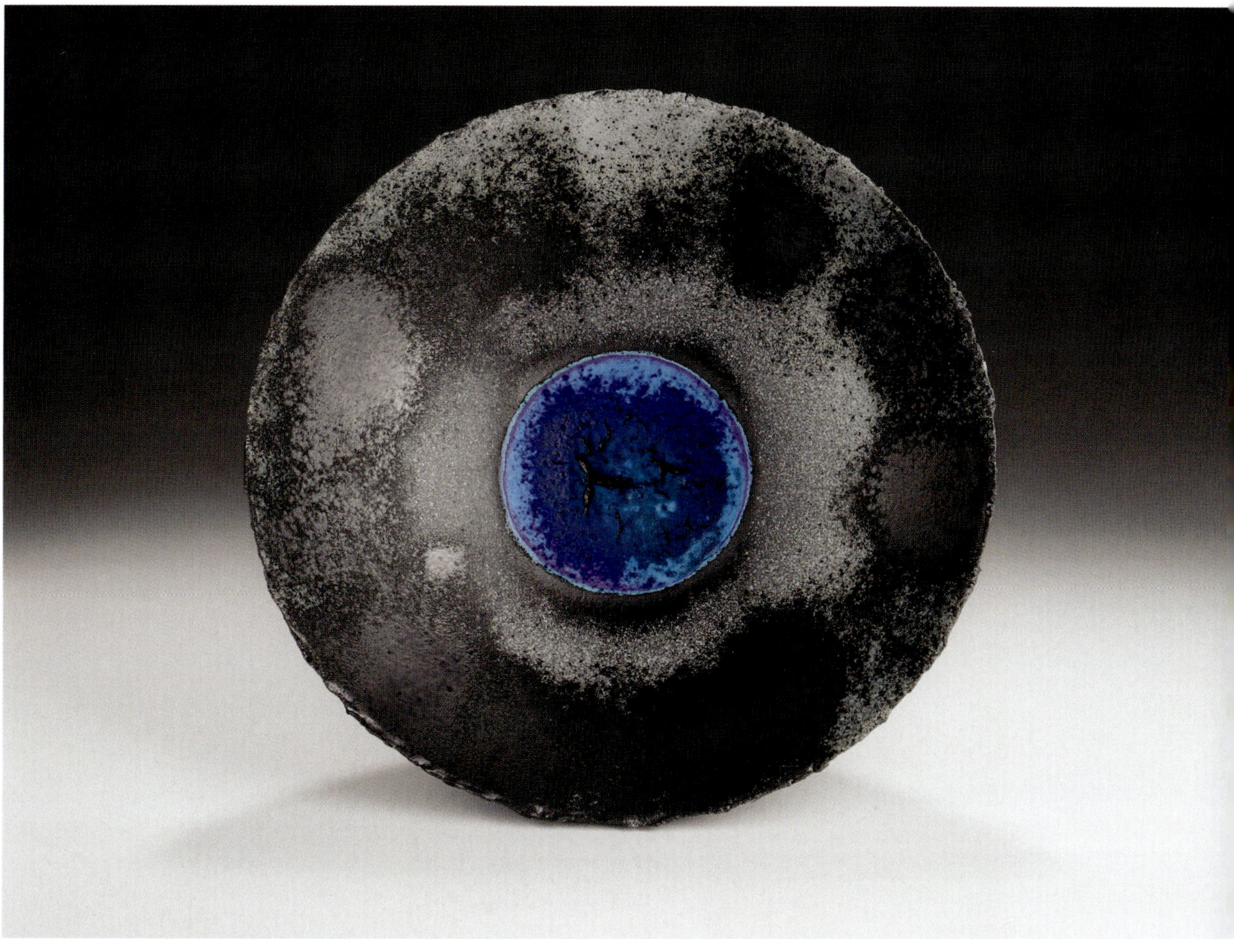

Magic! I love how the thick layer of the barium glaze has crawled in parts, letting the dark borax layer underneath shine through.

Blue terra sigillata, borax, Barium Matte Blue, white terra sigillata, cone 05, multifired in oxidation, 34 cm W × 11 cm T.

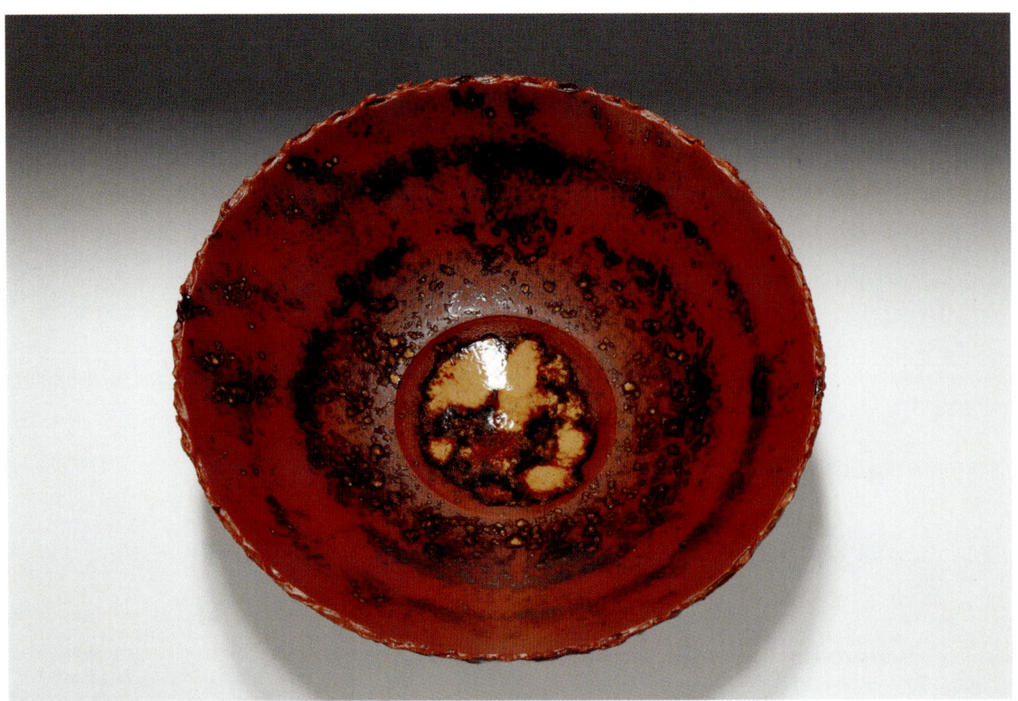

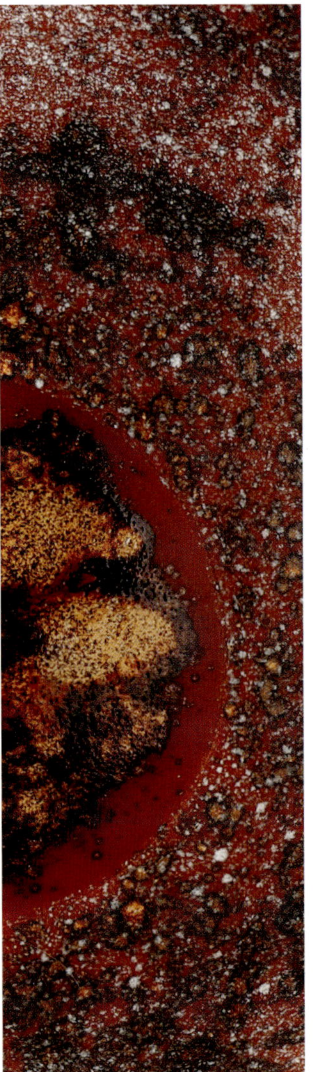

This first experiment inspired more ideas, and I immediately went on to try something similar on a bowl coated with orange terra sigillata.

See those dark areas? That's where the gum was thinner and had already started to dry, so less borax adhered to it. Where the borax was thickest, it turned the lighter orange colour you see here.

Looking good, but I wanted to play more.

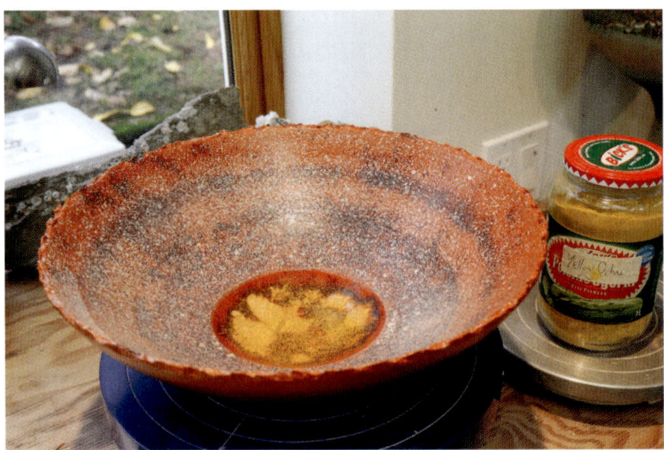

LEFT

Close-up view of centre.

ABOVE

My final step was to dust some white terra sigillata on the interior and sprinkle some yellow ochre in the centre.

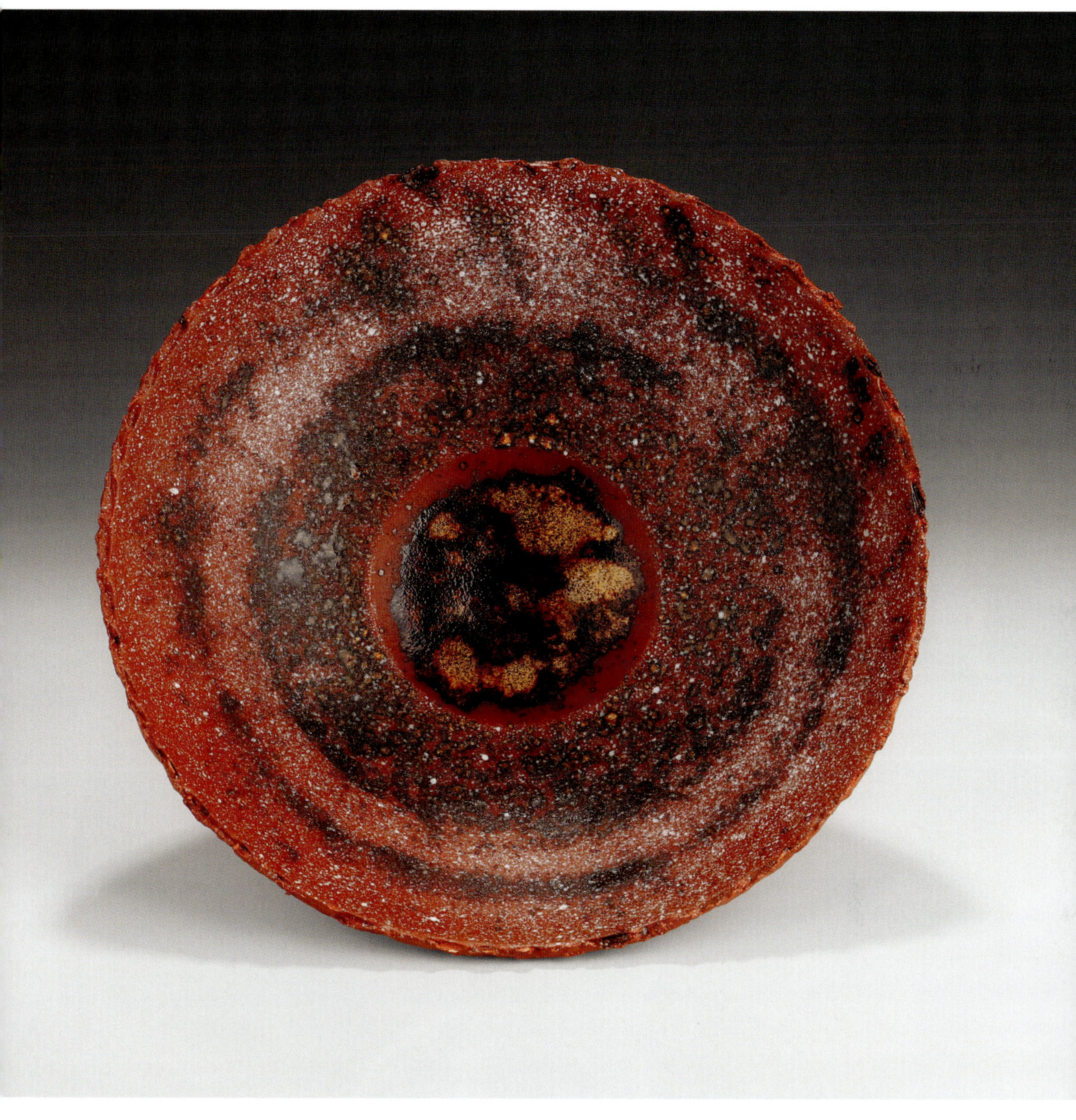

Now that you've seen what coloured terra sigillatas can do, let's look at adding mineral washes.

Orange terra sigillata, borax, white terra sigillata, yellow ochre, cone 05, multifired in oxidation, 34 cm W × 10 cm T.

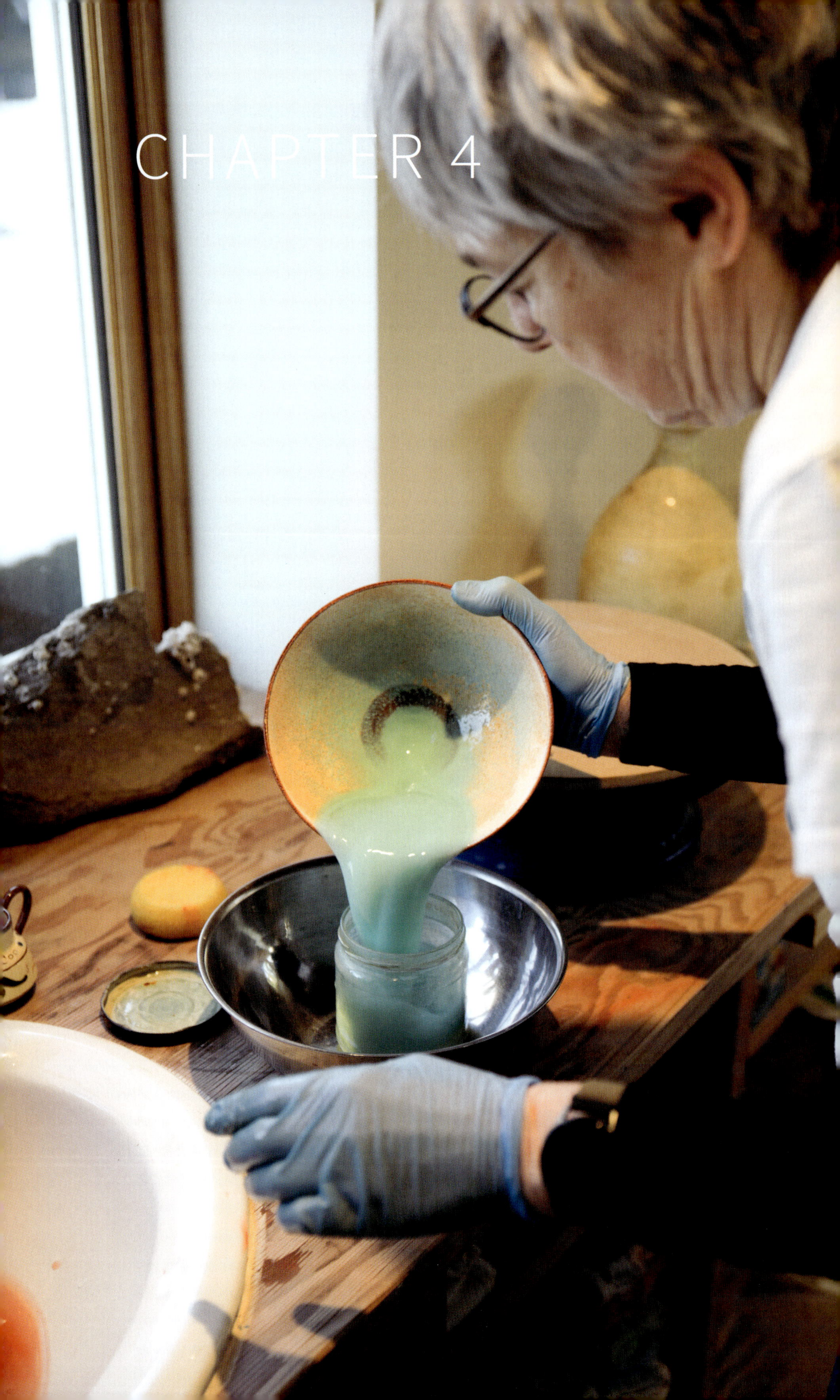

CHAPTER 4

THE WORLD OF WASHES

The last time I remember using washes was back in high school, where I brushed red or black iron oxide onto my creations, then washed it off, so it was left primarily in the textured areas. I didn't find it very exciting.

However, in my recent explorations—though I haven't yet done many pieces using this technique—I'm definitely not finding it boring! I really wish I had tried this out years ago, as I am getting such cool effects. I envision lots of playing around with washes in the future. However, like all the finishes and techniques I have explored, this one has its own idiosyncrasies. After applying a wash, I have found it helpful to take a photo to accompany my notes. The visual reminder can be invaluable, especially if a lot of time has passed between tests.

A **wash** is a mixture of water and a mineral, or minerals, that can be applied to a bisque or glazed piece. You can leave the wash on or wash it off, so that it leaves traces on the surface.

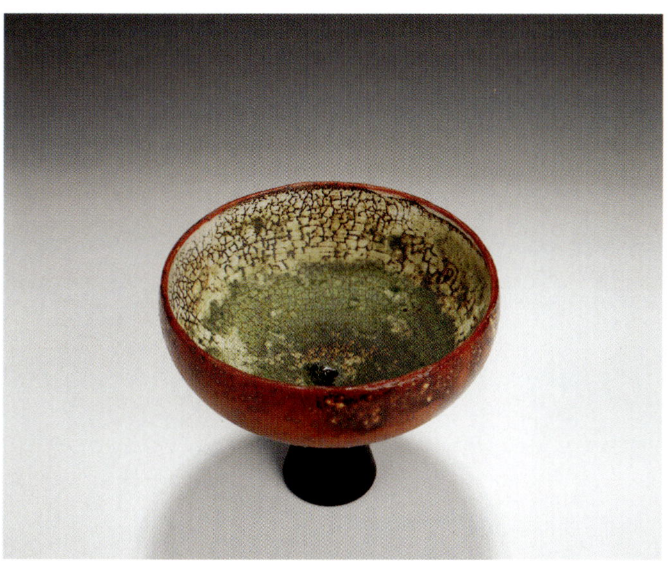

Chalice, white and orange terra sigillata, borax, copper wash, cone 05, oxidation, mounted in metal base, 17 cm W × 15 cm T.

The main wash I've been playing with is a mixture of water and copper carbonate. I'd like to say that I have carefully measured the amount of copper carbonate I added to water, but I haven't. About ½ tsp of copper carbonate to 1 cup of water would be my best guess. The copper sinks quickly to the bottom of the jar, and you need to keep stirring it, so it is hard to be precise. The nicest finishes I've attained have been where the copper isn't very thick. Where it is thick it can turn blackish, so I suggest you play around.

Here are the steps to follow when applying the wash:

1. Apply a layer of white terra sigillata, then bisque fire.

2. After the bisque firing, you will need to apply a flux that will work with the copper wash. I use a light sprinkling of borax for this and then fire the piece again.

3. Now you are ready to apply the wash. I use a small jar to pour in the wash, as you need to keep stirring or shaking up the mixture as it settles. A thin application is best, but it's easy to end up with areas where the wash is too thick. So how do you know what is just right and what is too thick? This is where learning and practice come in. Observe carefully and make notes. After a few goes, your glaze instincts will start to kick in, and you will know when you've got it right.

4. Now you are ready to fire your experiment, and cone 06 to cone 04 will suffice. You could probably go cooler or hotter if you want, but I haven't tested that out.

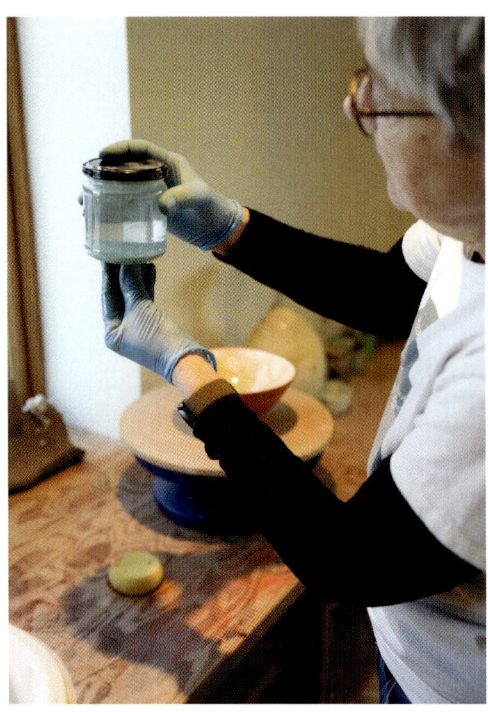

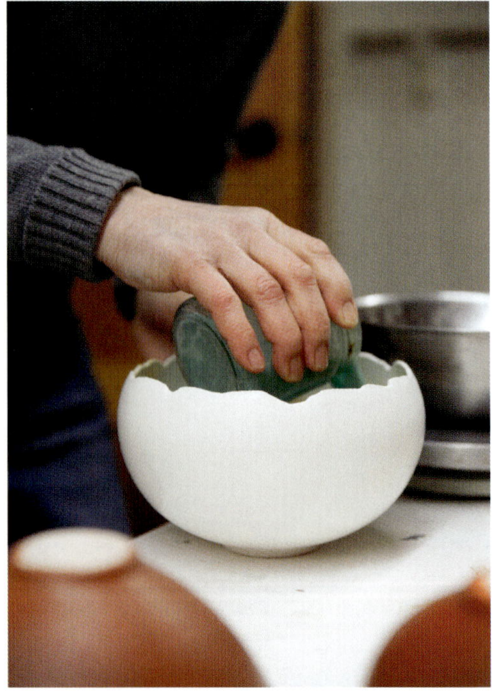

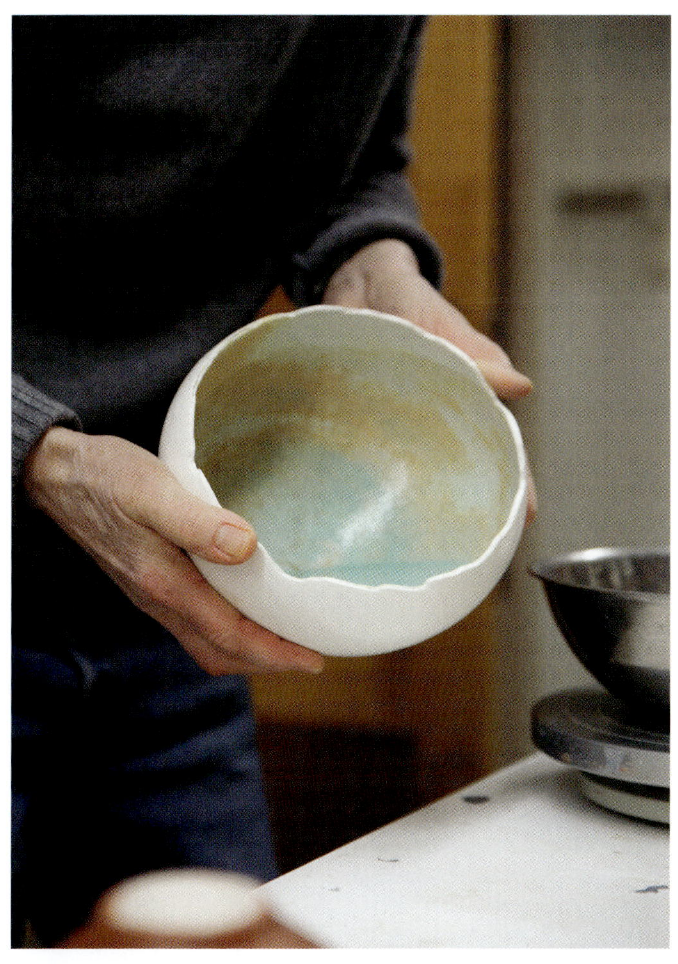

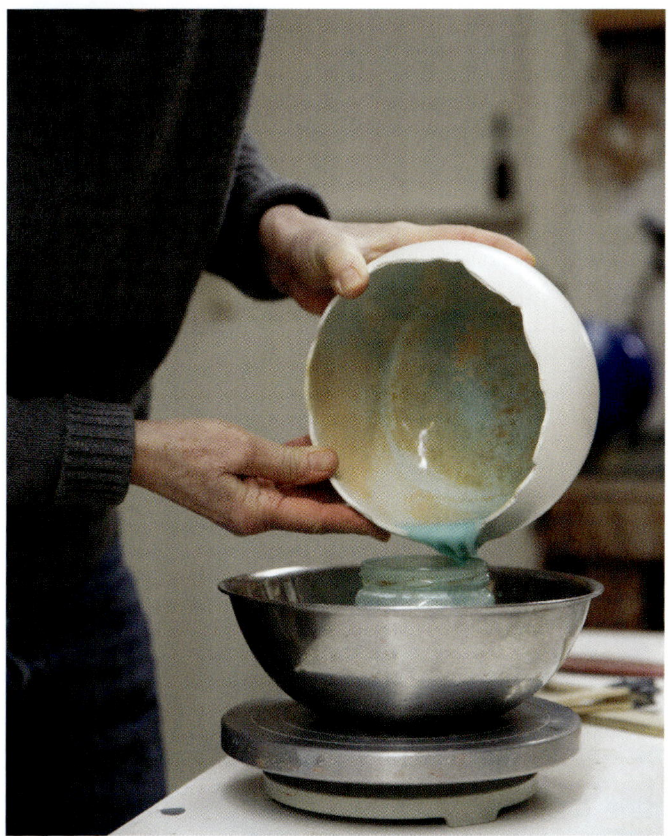

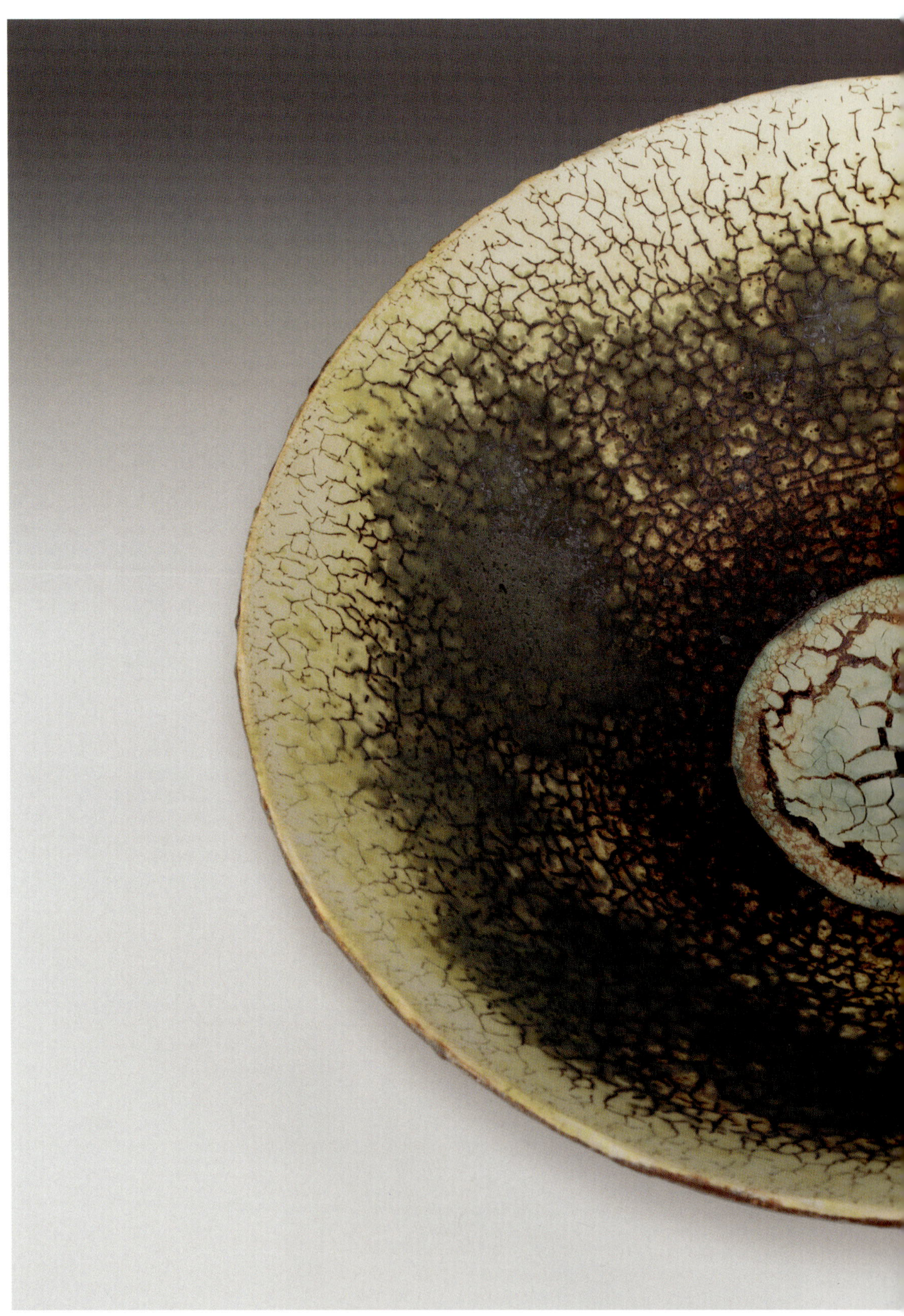

The dark areas on this bowl are a good example of what a copper wash can look like if applied too thickly.

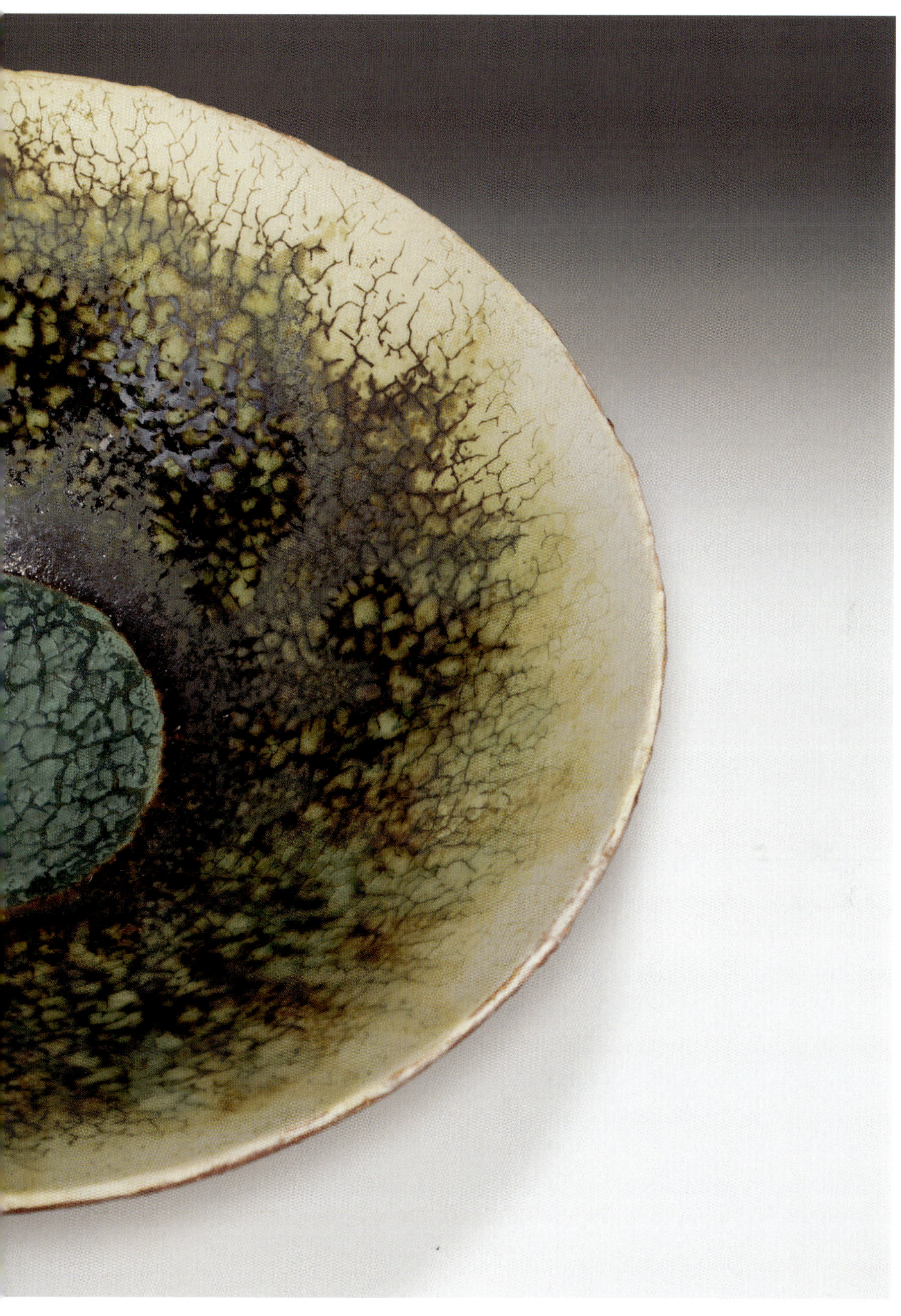

To correct the dark areas, I applied a light dusting of borax, put a little glaze in the flower and fired again.

White terra sigillata with added tin on interior, orange terra sigillata on exterior, fired; borax sprinkles applied to interior, fired again.

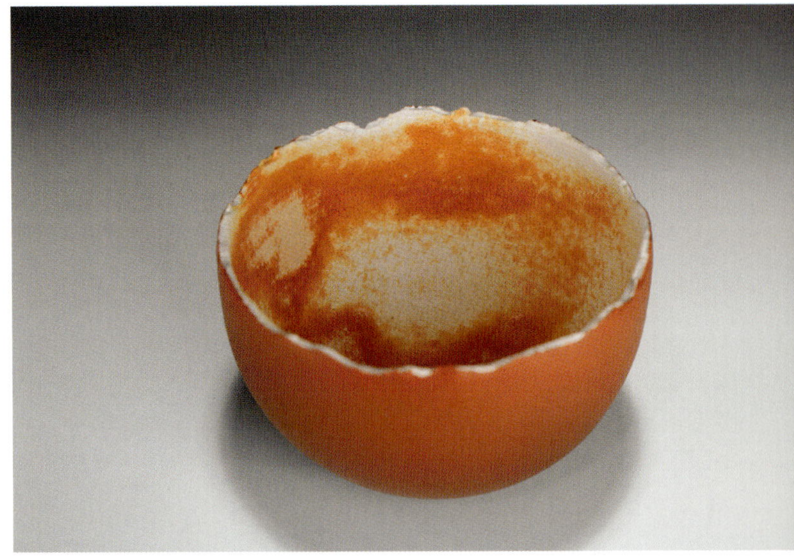

RIGHT

The vessel after an application of copper wash. You can see the copper hasn't covered the interior in a uniform way. This is what you want, as it will give the finish more variety and interest.

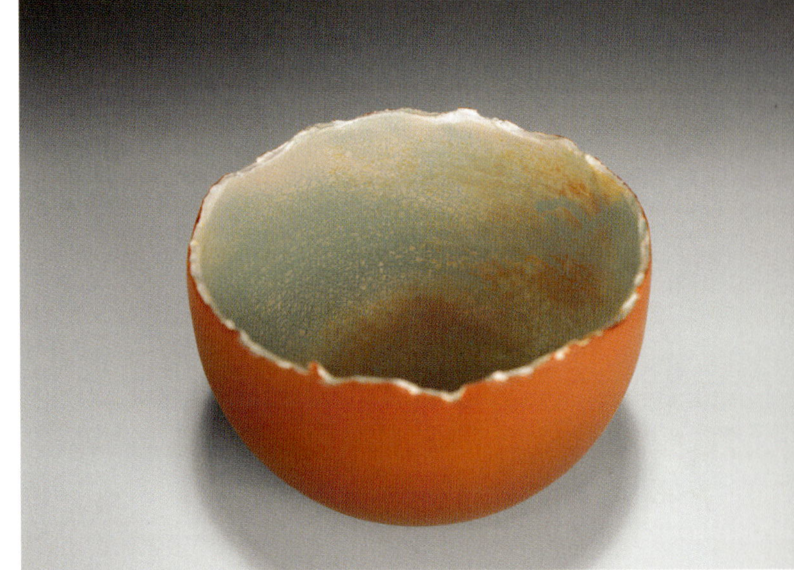

BELOW

Detail: notice how the wash follows the craze lines.

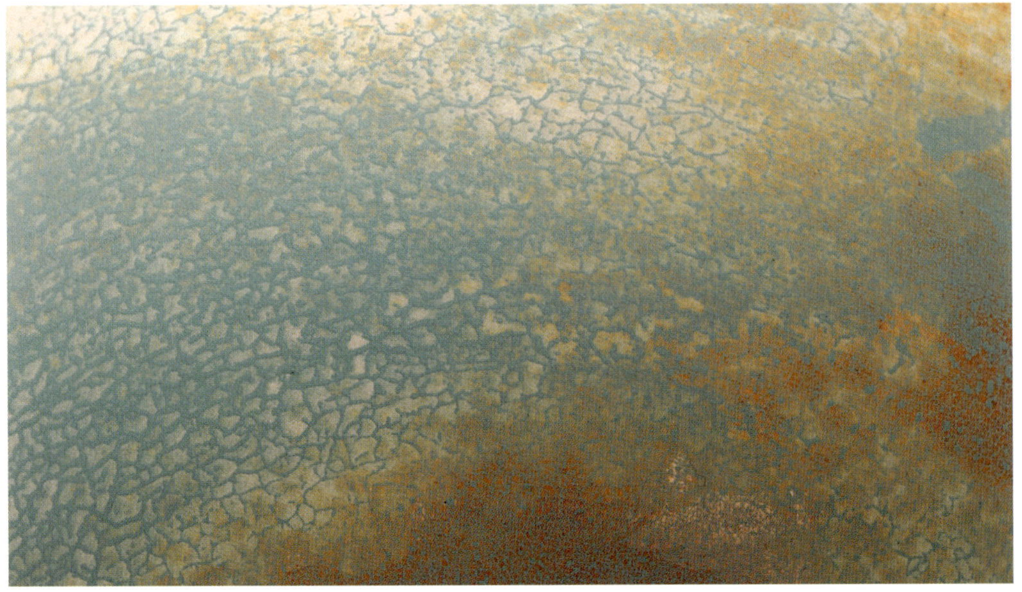

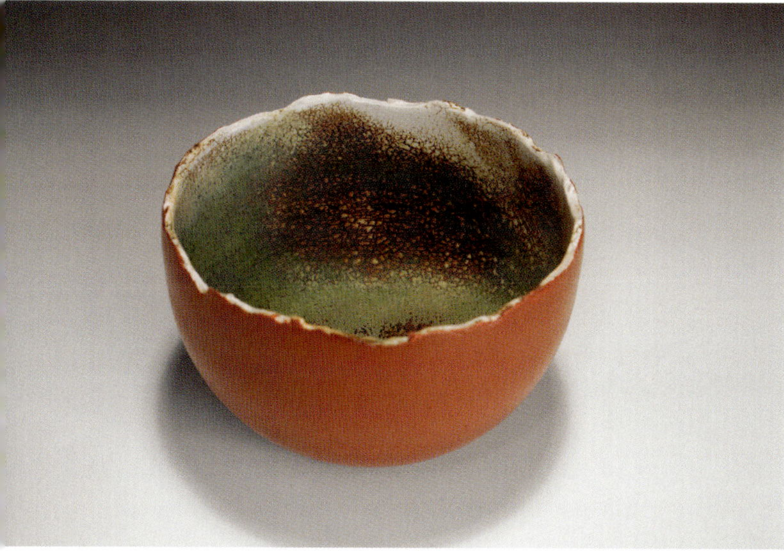

Detail after firing to cone 05 in oxidation.

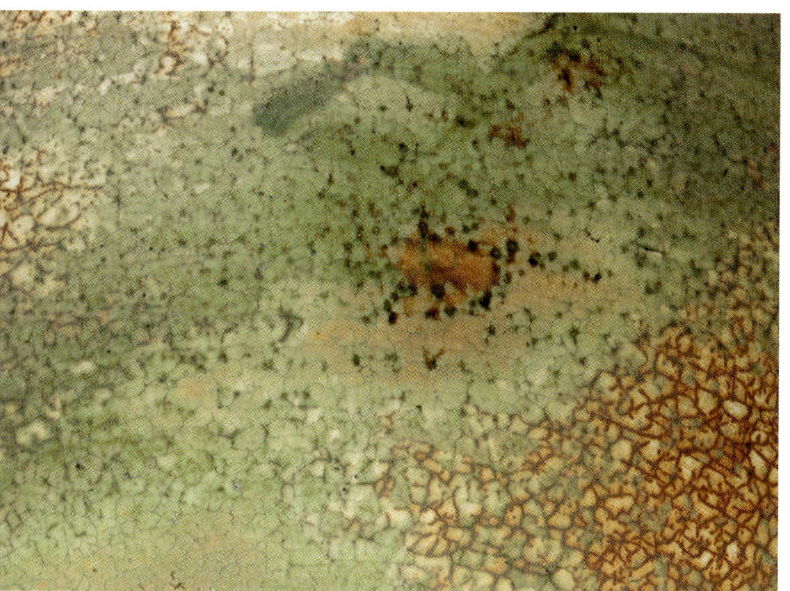

LEFT
Detail after firing that shows the copper wash following craze lines.

BELOW
The same vessel reduction fired. Terra sigillatas, borax, copper carbonate wash, cone 05, reduction, 20 cm W × 13 cm T.

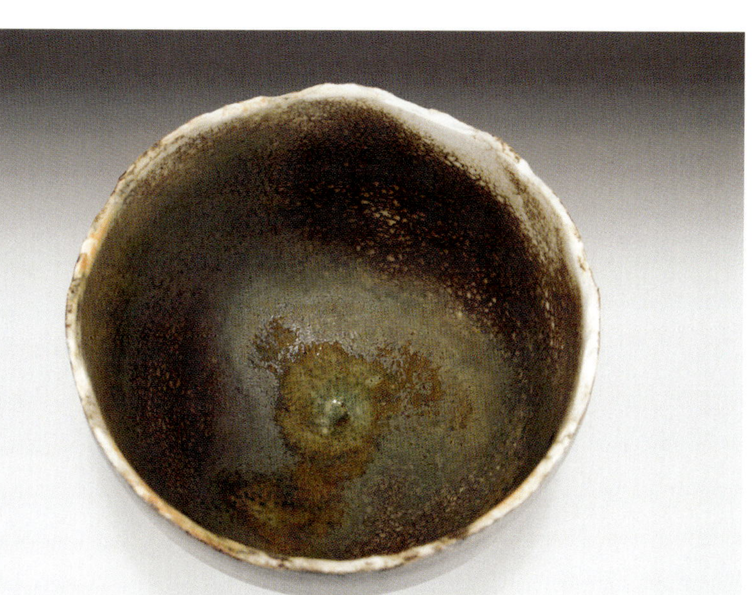

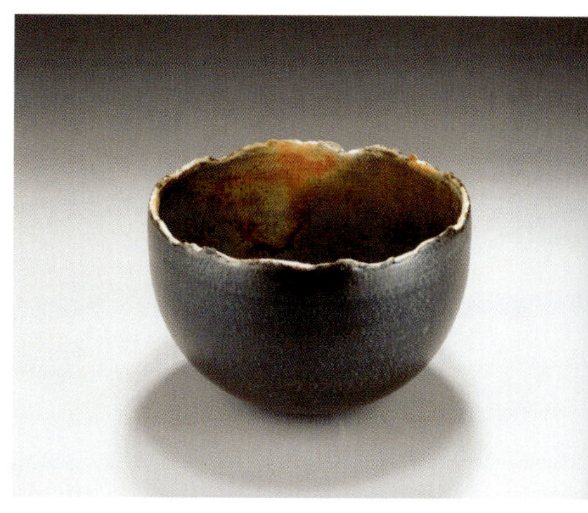

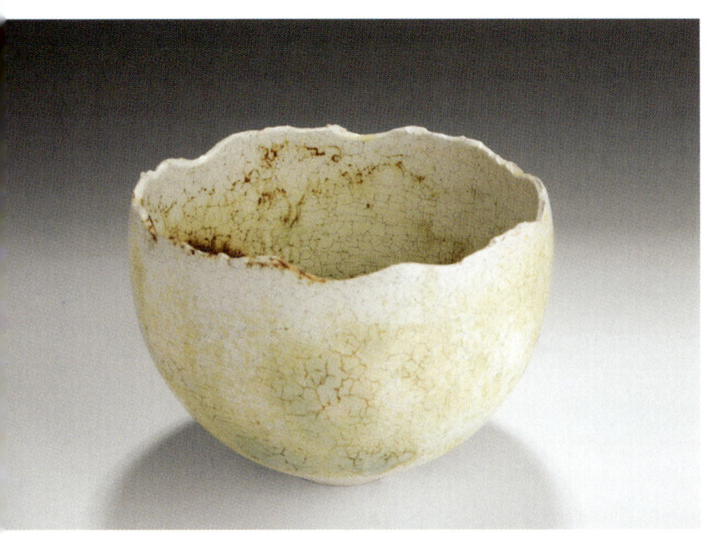

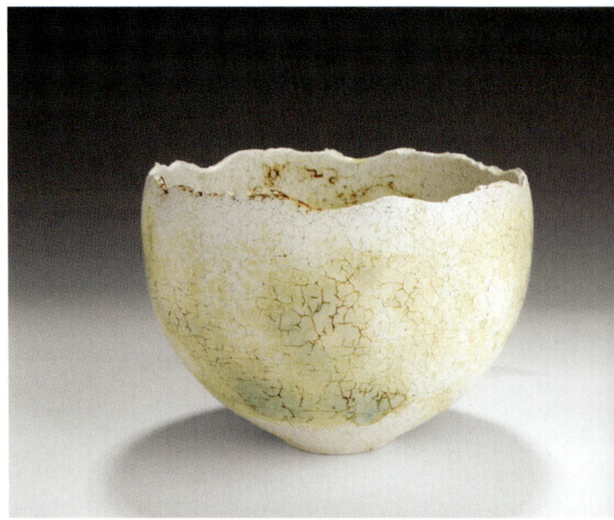

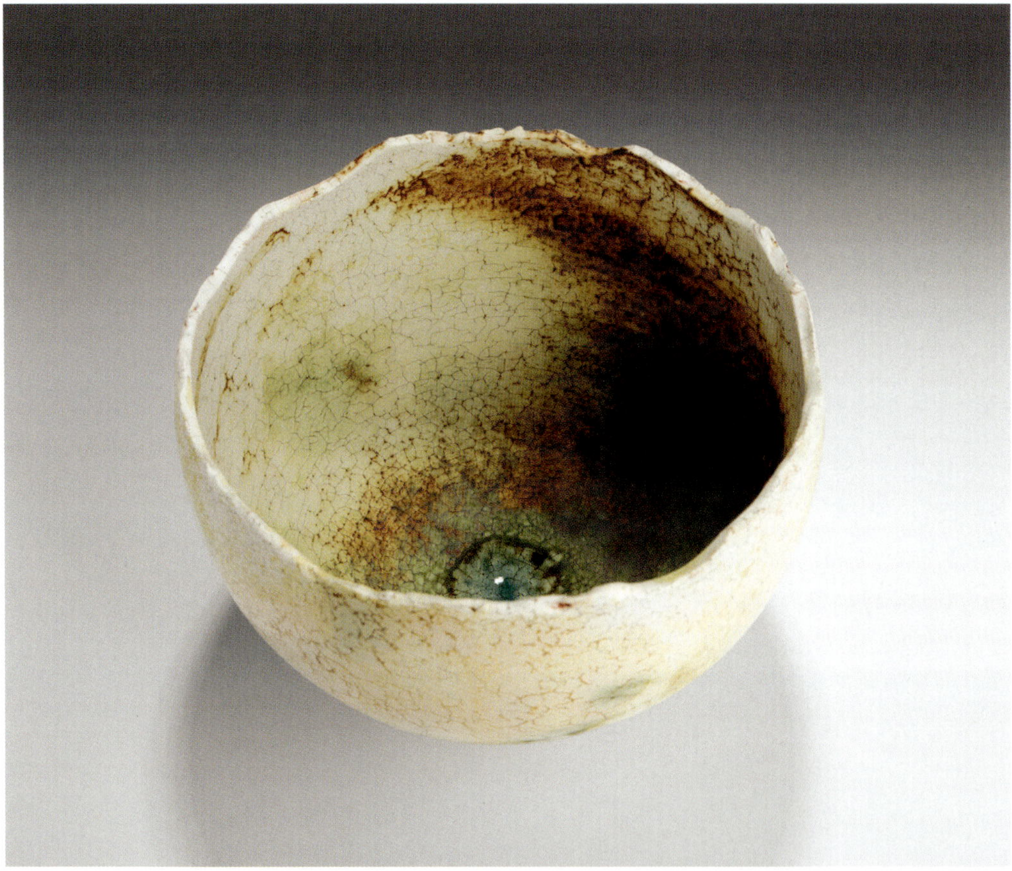

Vessel with Sculpted Rim, white terra sigillata, borax, copper carbonate wash, glaze crystal, cone 05, oxidation, 19 cm W × 14 cm T.

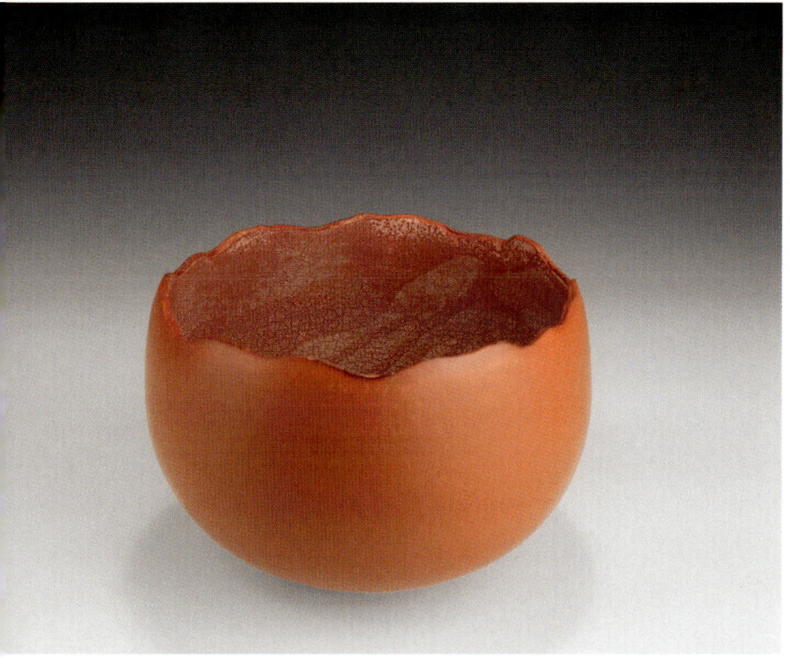

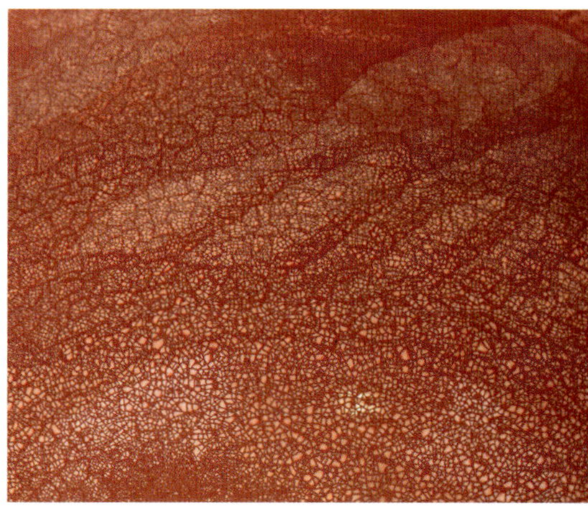

Orange terra sigillata on exterior, white terra sigillata on interior, borax, fired in oxidation; red iron oxide wash applied and vessel fired again.

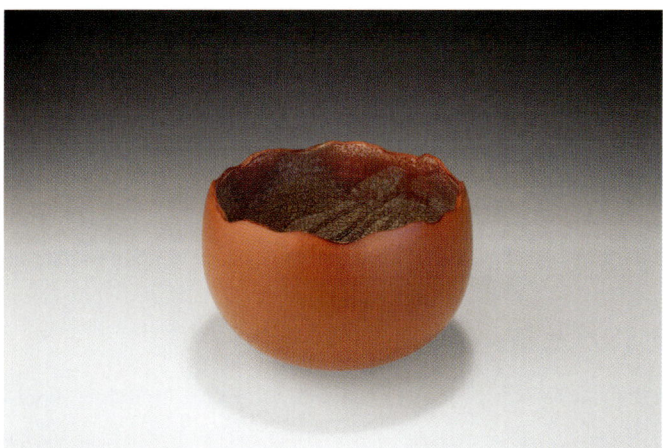

Iron-washed bowl fired to cone 05 in oxidation.

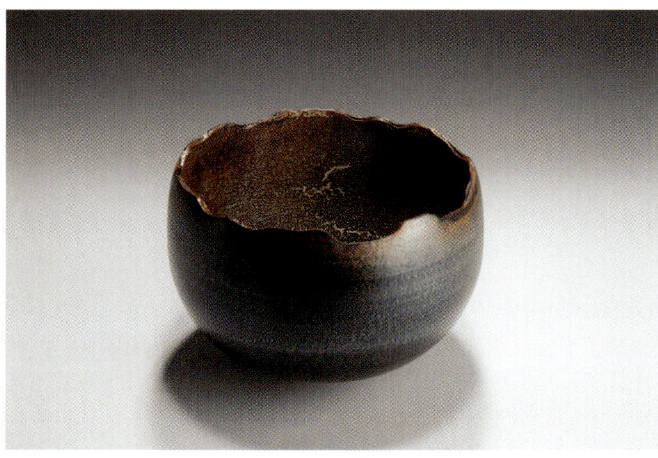

The same bowl refired in reduction, 21 cm W × 16 cm T.

CHAPTER 5

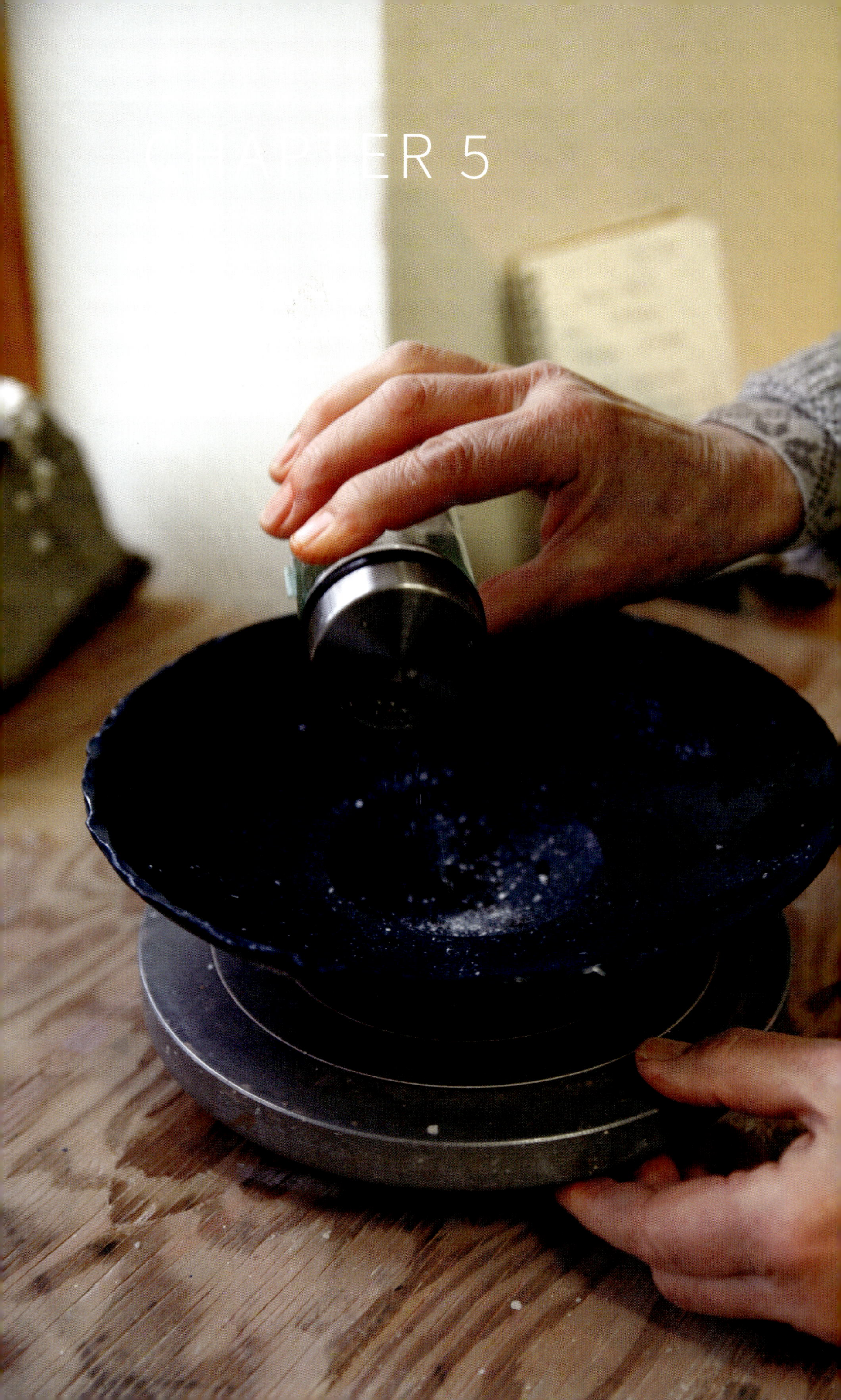

SPRINKLE, SPRINKLE!

One day when I was out walking the girls (my dogs, Amy and Sasha) musing about this book, a radical idea came to me.

What would happen if you mixed the ingredients of a glaze together, but used the mixture dry instead of adding water? Whoa—that got me going! It would be way outside the box, a completely unknown area of experimenting for me. As this book is focused primarily on decorative glazes and finishes without the concerns of functionality and durability that come with tableware, I figured, *Why not try it?*

Now that I was used to working with gum, I knew how I could get the dry glaze to adhere to a pot, so that wouldn't be an issue. However, other obstacles immediately sprang to mind, the main one being that the ingredients wouldn't blend together the way they do in liquid form. Glazes need a balance of three main ingredients: silica, alumina and flux. Each ingredient influences the other. Silica is your glass former, alumina bonds the glaze and flux lowers the melting point.

The experiments I'd done with borax had been eye-opening, and from what I had learned, I guessed that borax might work quite nicely as an underlayer to help fuse the dry glaze. I would have to pick shiny glazes that already had a low melting point. Alkaline Blue 04 fit the bill, as it's loaded up with frit and soda ash—a lot of flux!

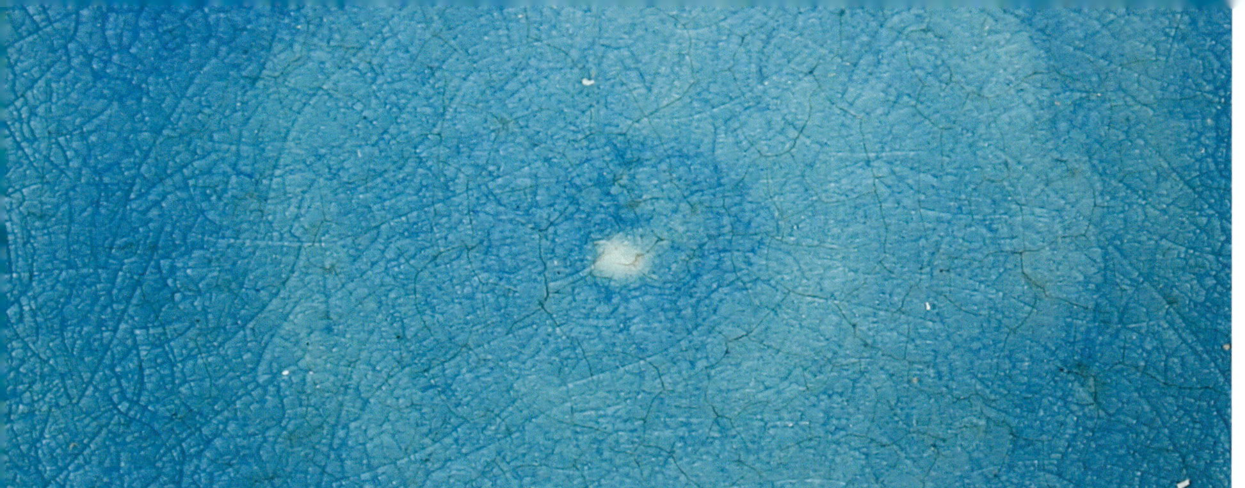

Alkaline Blue 04 glaze test.

My first glaze test showed a nicely crazed light blue. After a few further tests, I made a small batch without water, mixed it well and put it in a salt shaker with fairly big holes for sprinkling. I tried applying it quickly to a piece but was too tentative and used a very light touch—too light to really see much of a result. My next attempts were much better.

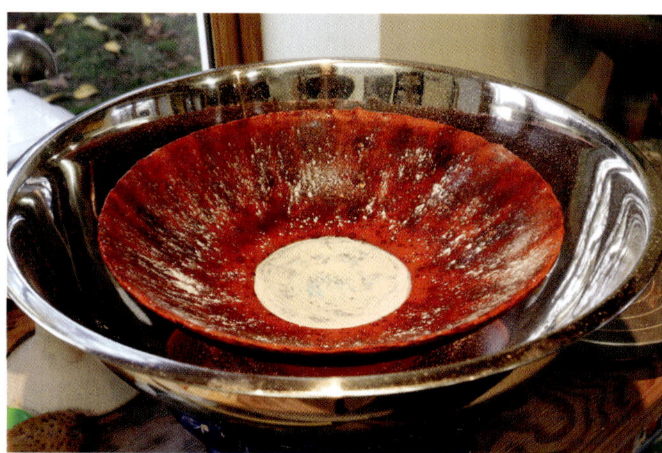

RIGHT
With the first layer of borax already fired on, I added glaze to the centre and a sprinkling of dry glaze to the rest of the bowl.

BELOW
This bowl had already been fired a few times, but needed a bit more work, so I sprinkled on more dry glaze and fired again.

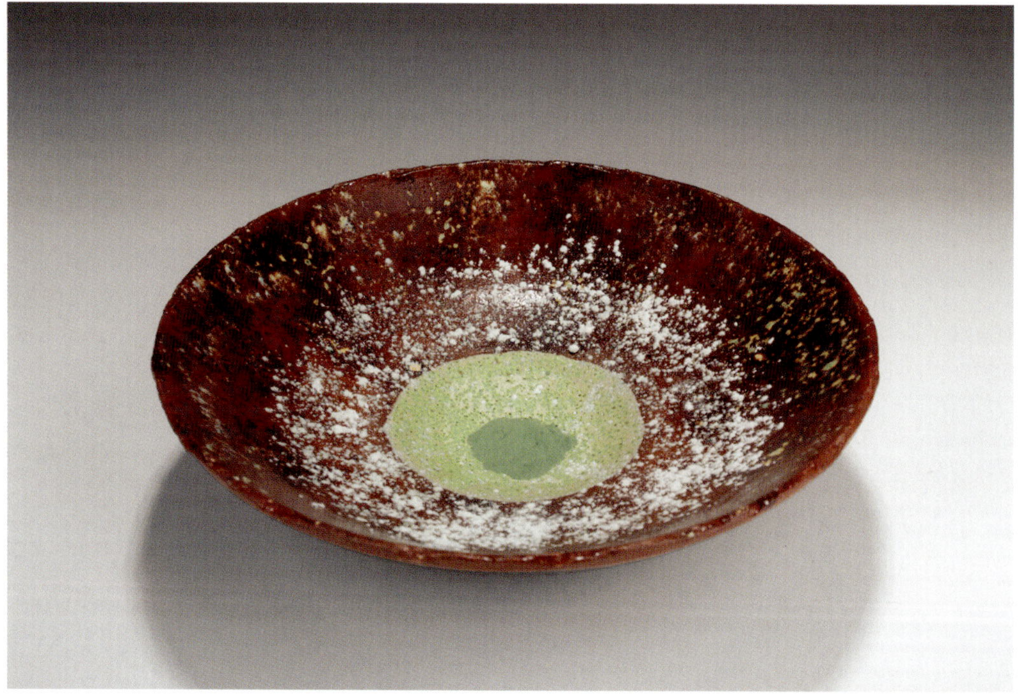

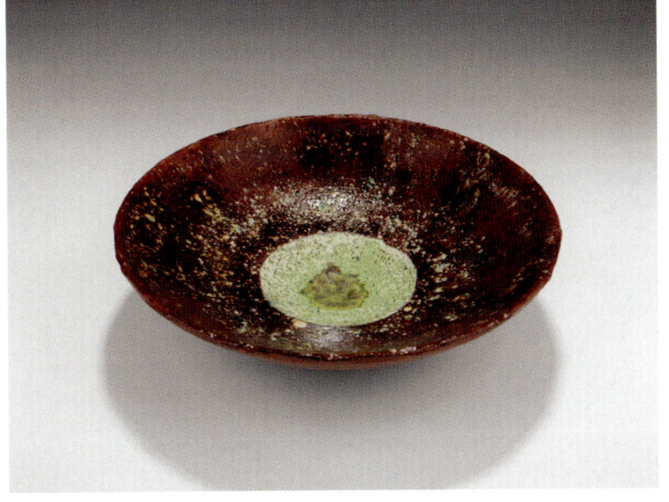

Bowl: orange and white terra sigillata, borax, dry Alkaline Blue 04 and Moonelis. Flower: borax, wet Moonelis, Moonelis crystal placed in centre, cone 04, oxidation, 27.5 cm W × 7.5 cm T.

This bowl inspired another idea. I'm sure many of you have experienced going to mix up a glaze that has been sitting around for a while, only to find there are crystallized chunks in it. I had never thought of firing one of these crystals before, but I popped one in the centre of a bowl. The results were very cool, with an almost gem-like effect. The crystal had also influenced the tone of the underlying glaze, which excited me even more, as that opened up many possibilities for colour variations. Needless to say, I am now thrilled when I find crystals in my glazes.

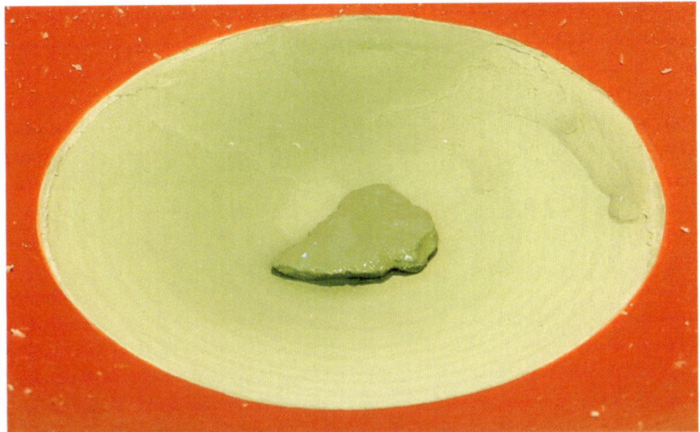

A crystal placement before firing.

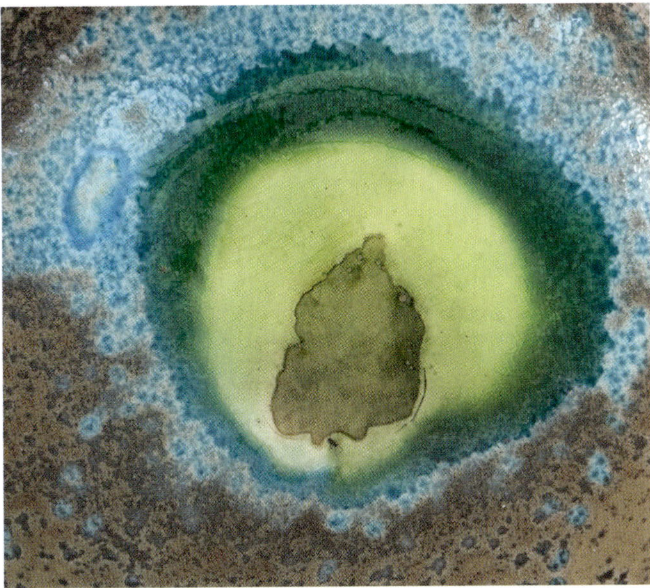

A crystal from an adapted version of Moonelis placed over Soda Blue, after firing.

Shivering occurs when a glaze compresses (shrinks) more during firing than the clay body it covers. This leads to the glaze cracking and peeling away from the clay body.

Crazing occurs when a glaze contracts more than the clay body during cooling. It appears as a network of fine hairline cracks in the glazed surface of fired ware, but generally does not result in the glaze peeling off, as with shivering. When you are using just terra sigillata and borax, you can end up with a bit of both happening.

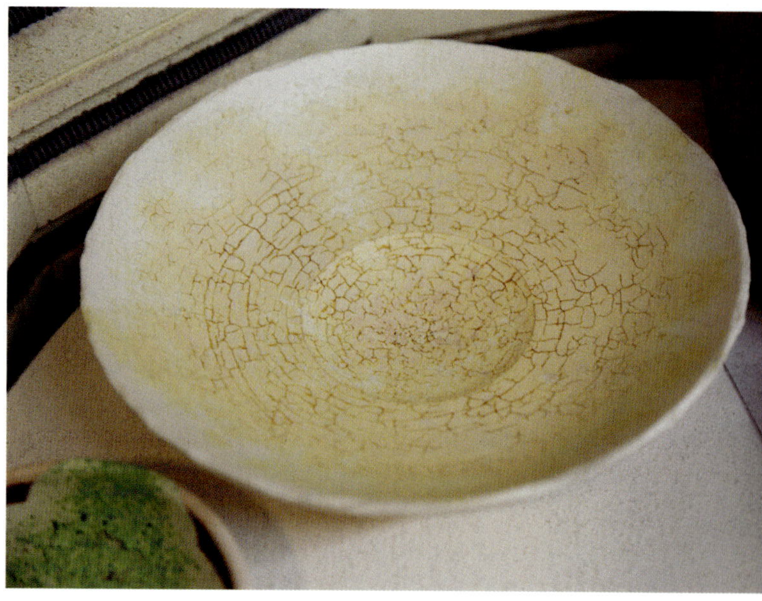

In my experience, beauty often starts with a mistake! This next piece, *Summer Meadow*, was developed as the result of a flaw; in this case, shivering. I had applied borax a tad too thickly over white terra sigillata, and when the piece came out of the kiln, I knew shivering was going to be an issue down the line.

I applied an iron wash over the borax and then sponged it off, so it remained just in the craze lines. Then I fired it again, hoping that the shivering would resolve itself, but it didn't.

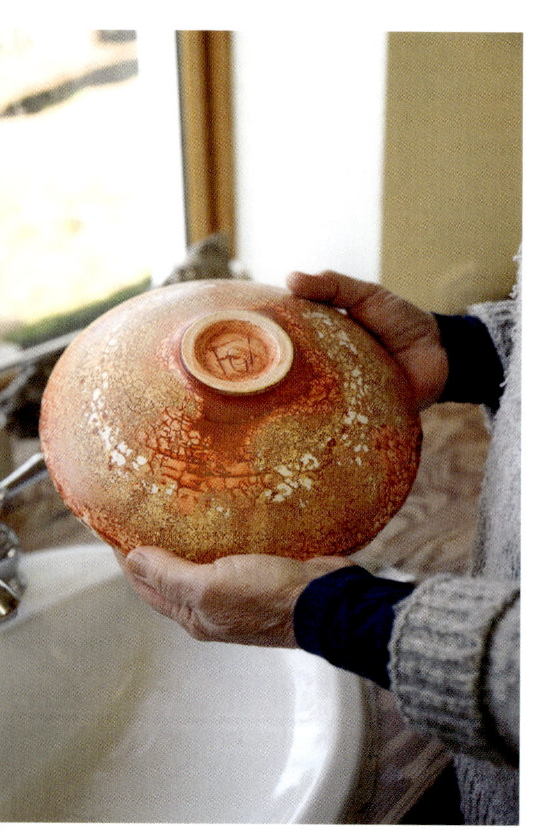

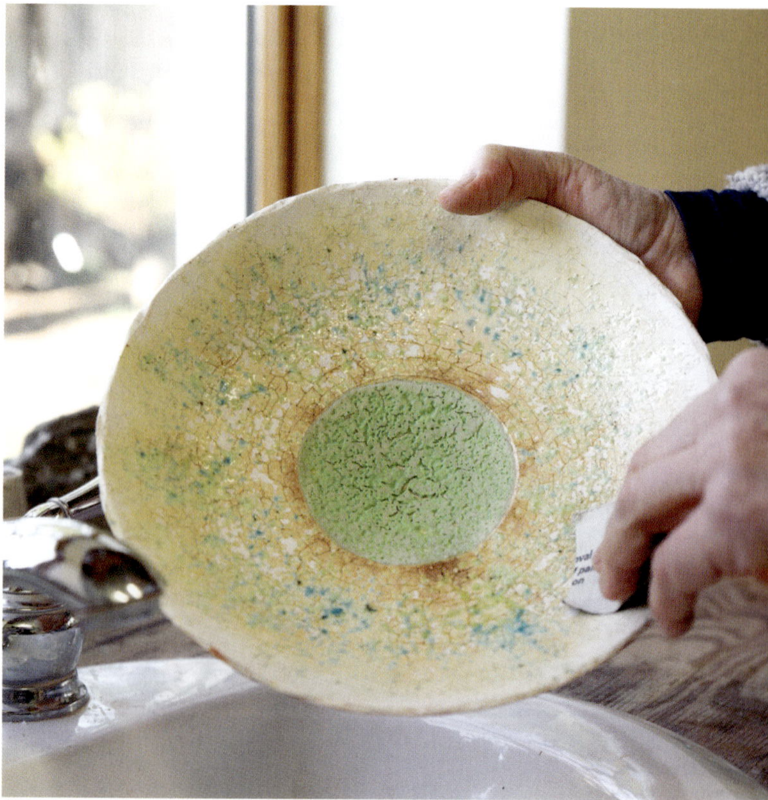

The shivering was proving to be quite persistent, so I went over the whole piece with sandpaper, taking off any suspected problem areas. I then sprayed more orange terra sigillata on the outside, sprinkled dry Moonelis and Alkaline Blue 04 on the inside and added wet Moonelis in the centre. This seemed to do the trick and produced a cool result. I thought I was going to stop there, but there was more to come!

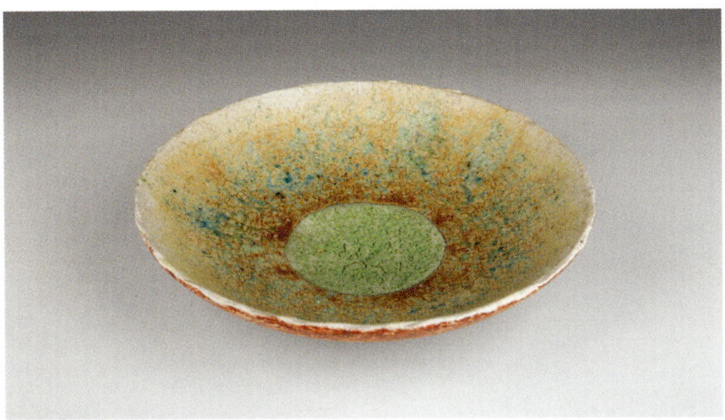

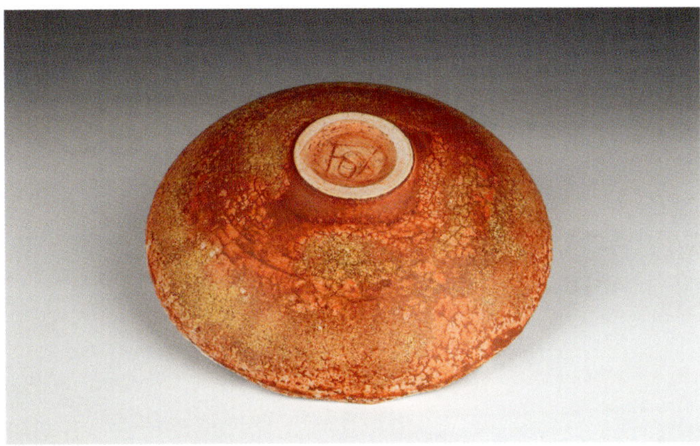

The more I lived with the piece, the more I thought it would be enhanced by a darker underside.

I had not sprayed my black crawl glaze over a surface like this before, but was pretty sure a thin coat would do the trick, and it did.

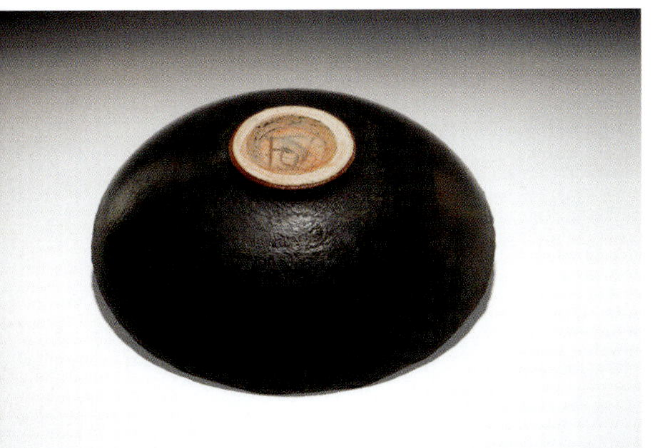

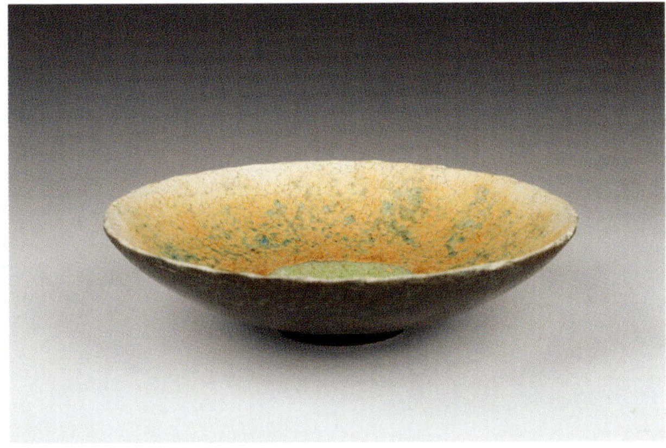

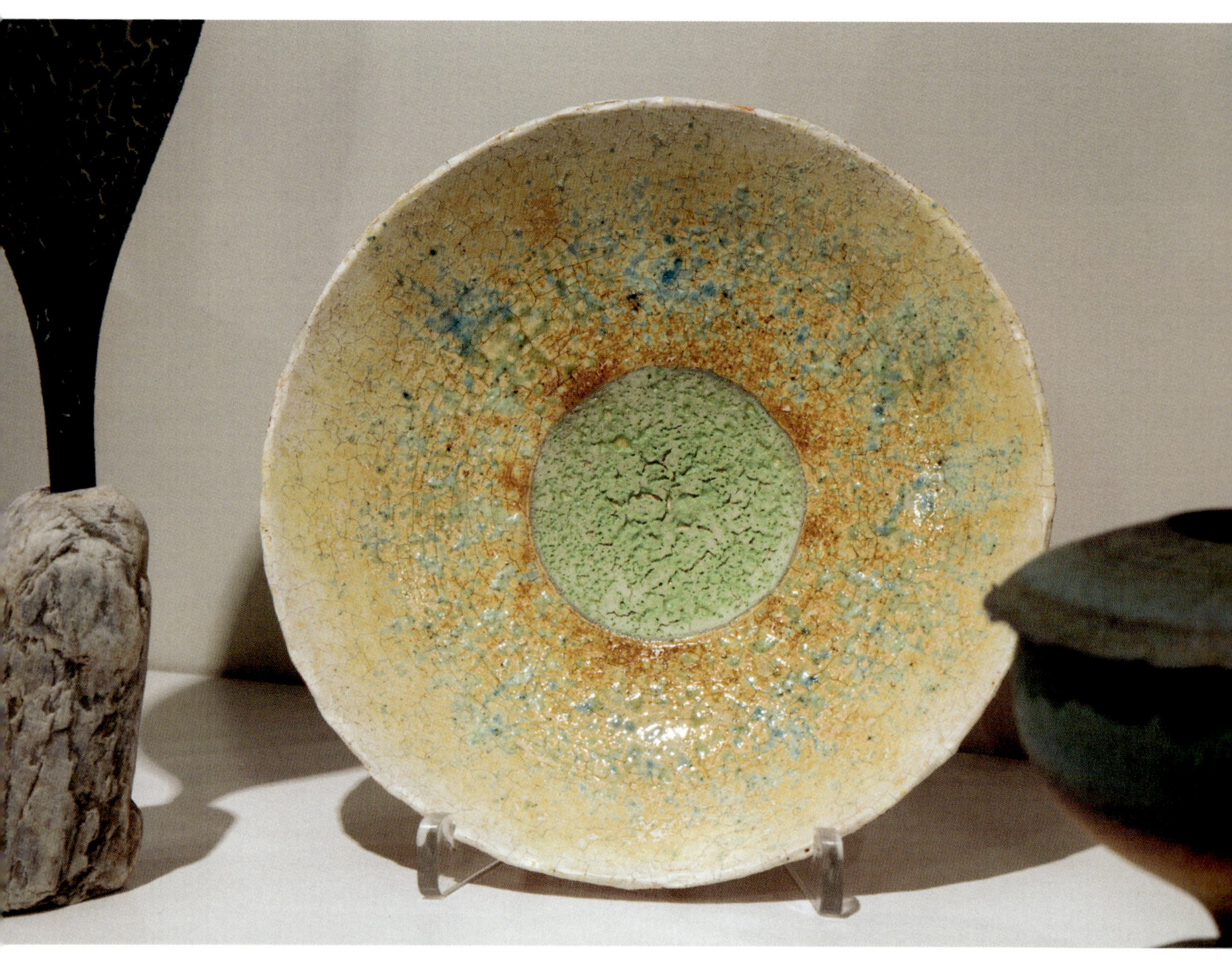

Summer Meadow, multiple
glazes and terra sigillata,
cone 04, oxidation,
25 cm w × 6.5 cm×T.

I went on to see if I could duplicate the results I got with *Summer Meadow* and was quite pleased by how close I came. Here are the steps I followed:

1. Applied orange terra sigillata on the exterior and the flower centre, white terra sigillata on the rest of the interior. Bisque fired, cone 04.

2. Sprinkled borax on the interior, going lighter on the central flower. I may have added a wee bit of dry Alkaline Blue 04 in the flower as well. Fired to cone 05.

3. Brushed a wash of red iron oxide on the interior, then sponged it off.

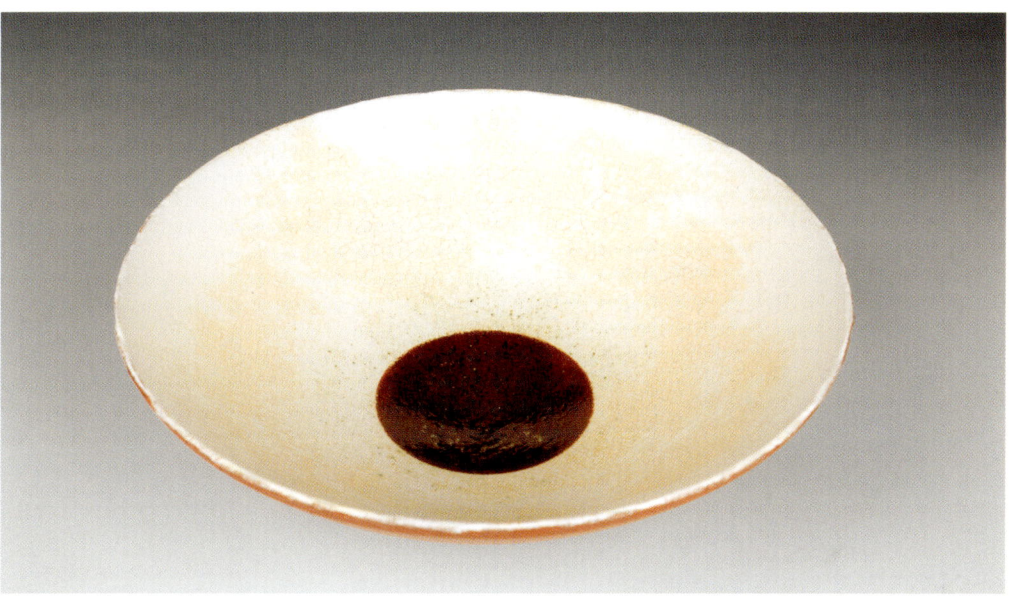

4. Sprinkled dry Moonelis and Alkaline Blue 04 in the main interior, applied a thin layer of wet Moonelis in the flower and, as a last-minute thought, popped a borax crystal in the middle. Fired again.

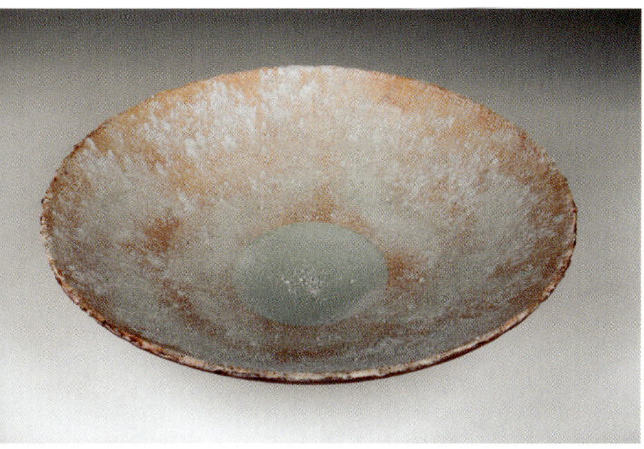

Before refiring

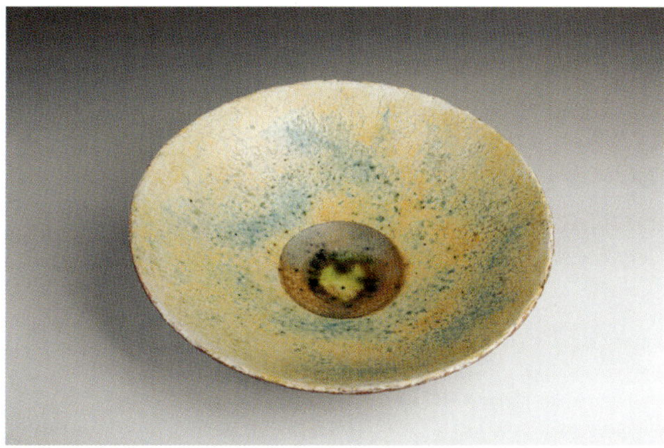

After refiring

"Yuck" is all I have to say about how the centre flower turned out. However, the effect of the borax crystal was interesting.

5. My next move was to turn to one of my favourite cover glazes, Parched Earth, and apply it to the flower centre. I then applied a light dusting of orange terra sigillata to the interior rim area. Fired to cone 04.

Before refiring

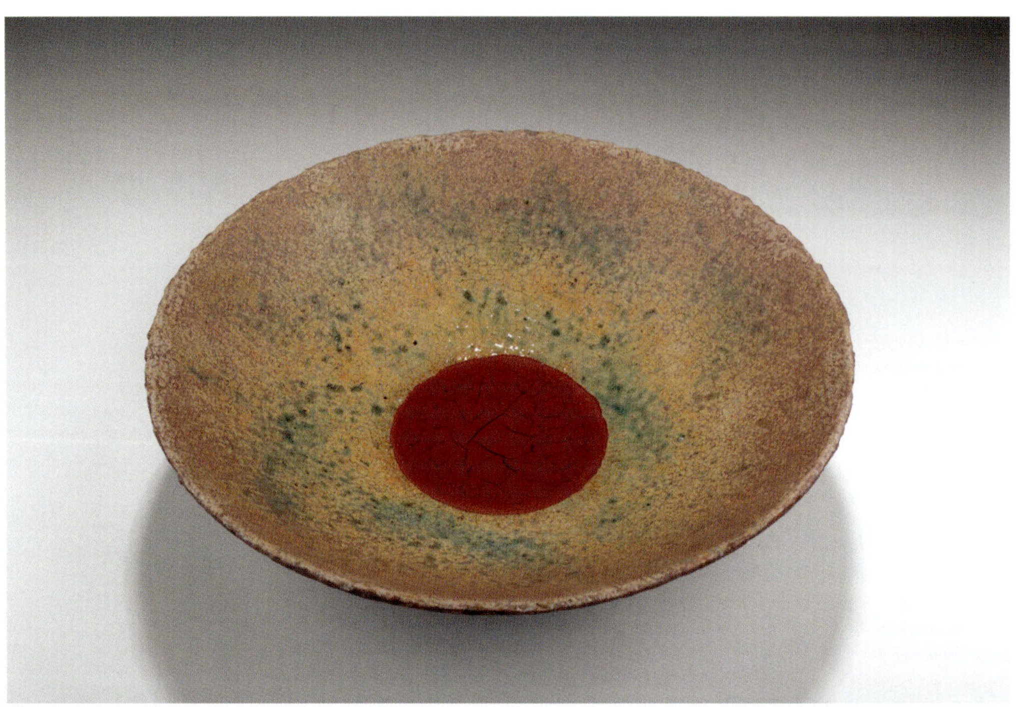

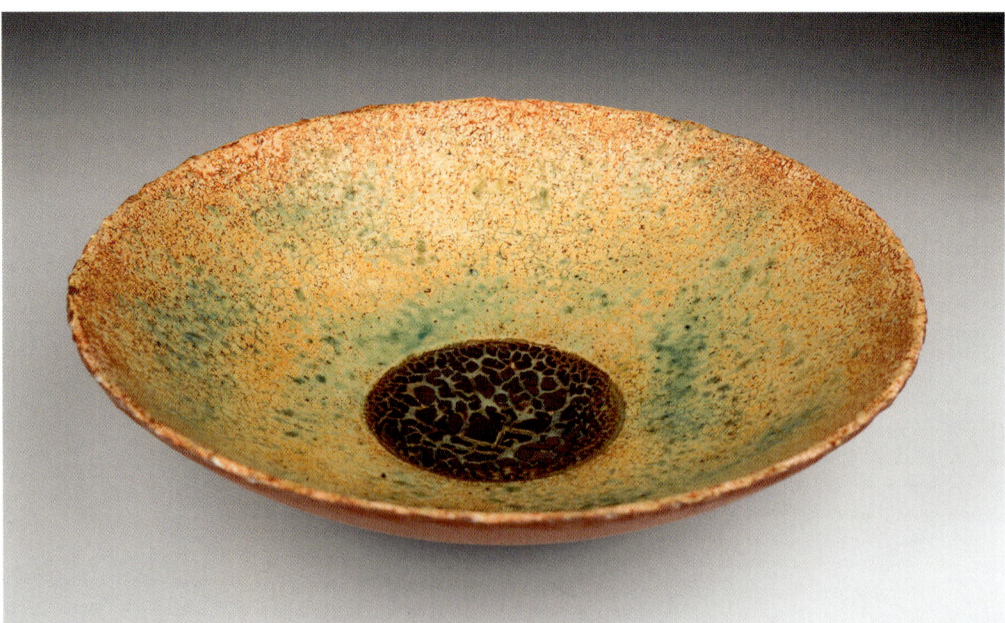

Desert Flower, multiple firings, white and orange terra sigillata, glaze, cone 05, oxidation, 29 cm W × 9 cm T.

If you look closely at the interior surface, you can see hints of the red iron in the craze lines among the specks of orange terra sigillata. The greenish areas are the dry glaze.

While I was working on *Desert Flower*, I had a duplicate on the go, so that I could show you what it would look like reduced. All the steps were the same with the exception of the borax crystal. I poured the Moonelis thickly this time, so thick that the glaze crawled as it was drying, leaving fair-sized gaps around the crawling. I looked at this as a bonus because I knew that after the bowl was fired again and ready for its final touches, whatever glaze I used would fill these gaps and accentuate the pattern that was developing.

I applied Parched Earth, and when it crawled, the platelets were smaller and settled into the gaps as well as on top of the Moonelis.

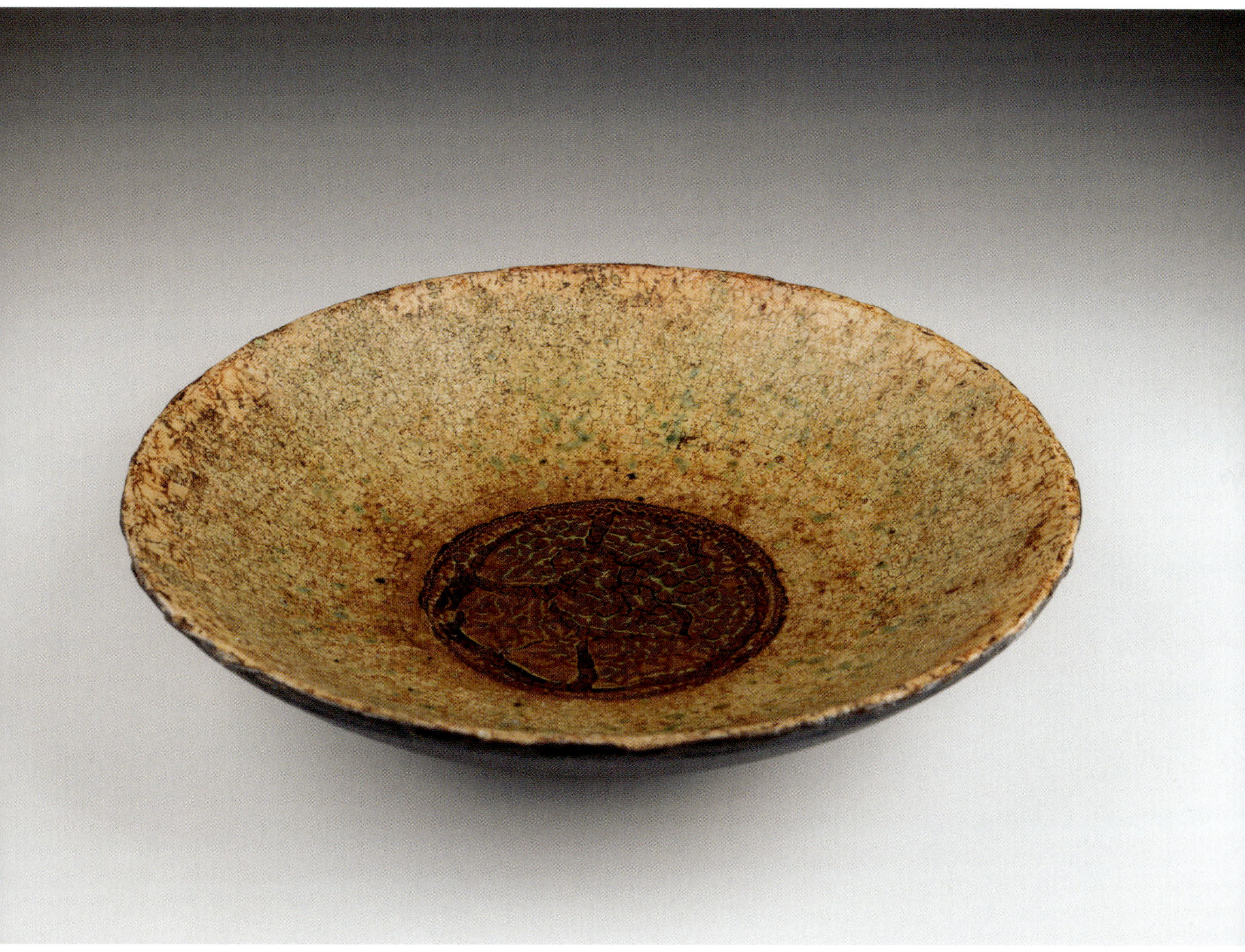

Parched Earth, multiple firings in oxidation, terra sigillata, glazes, final firing reduction, cone 04, 28 cm W × 7 cm T.

CHAPTER 6

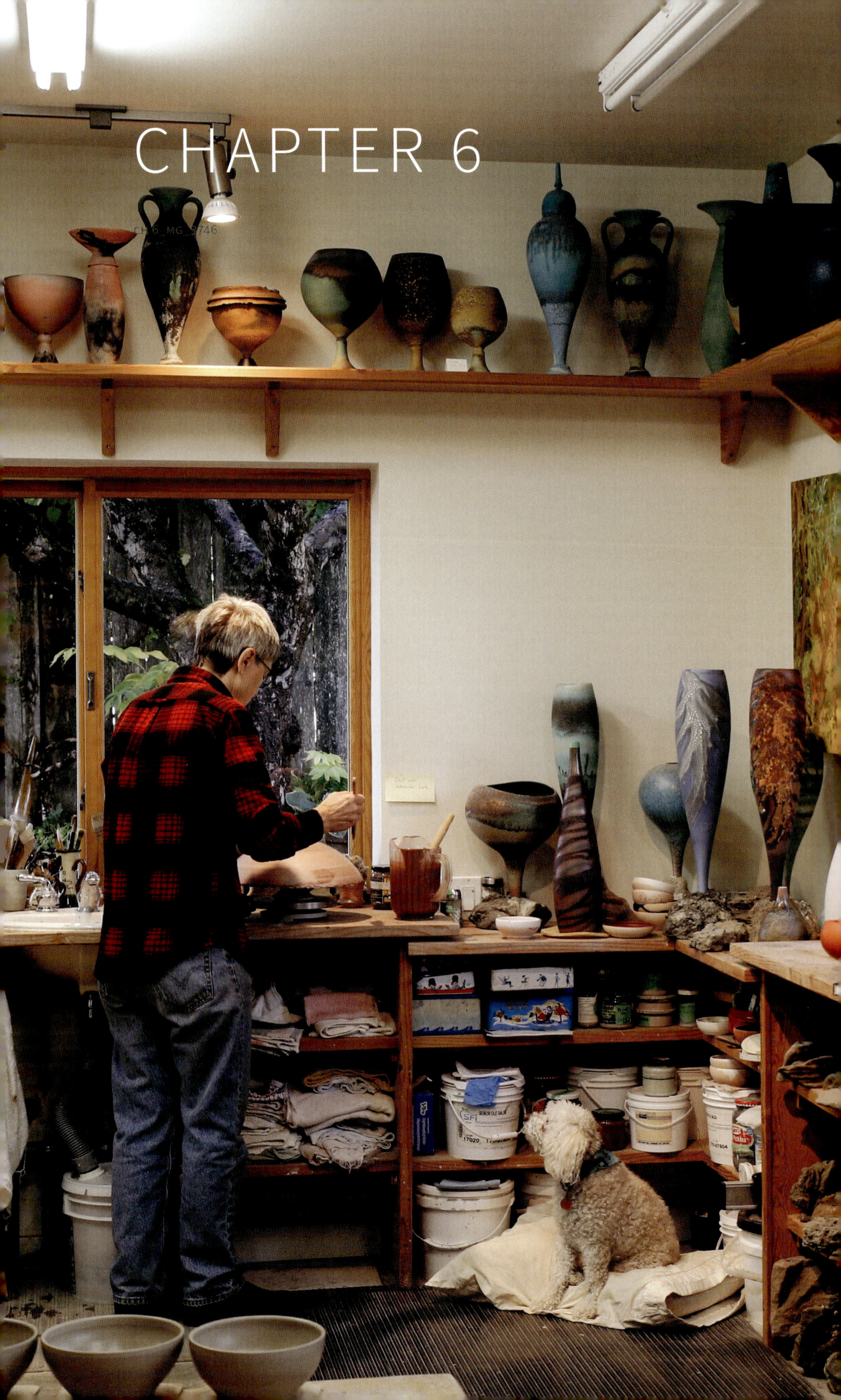

TERRA SIGILLATA AND GLAZES AS OVERLAYS

For the most part, terra sigillata is used as an undercoat, but its magical qualities don't stop there! When I went online to pick glazes I hadn't used before, one of the first I chose was Lana Wilson's Chun. I've been playing around with and learning from her chartreuse glaze for years and knew she would be a good source.

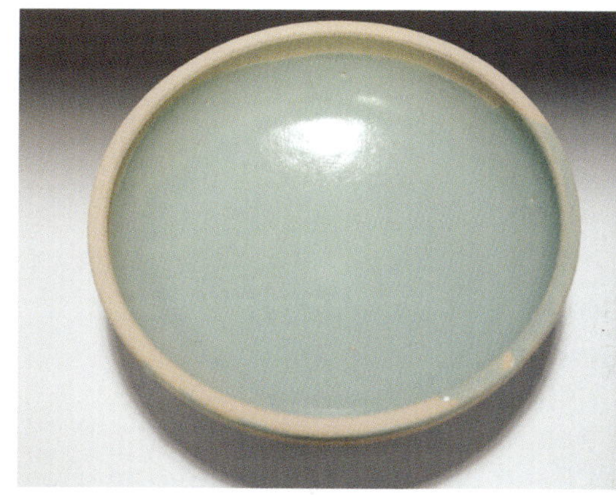

The test bowl with Lana Wilson's Chun, glazed on the thick side.

The first thing I noticed on my tests, aside from the fact that it was a beautiful glaze, was that, if applied on the thick side, it crazed. I don't see crazing as a negative, so I started to play. The test on the right is the first one I made using this glaze. As it happens, by some small miracle, I had set it aside and as I was writing this chapter, I remembered I had kept it and raced down to my studio to find it. It would be perfect for illustrating how you can use the crazing qualities of a glaze to your advantage.

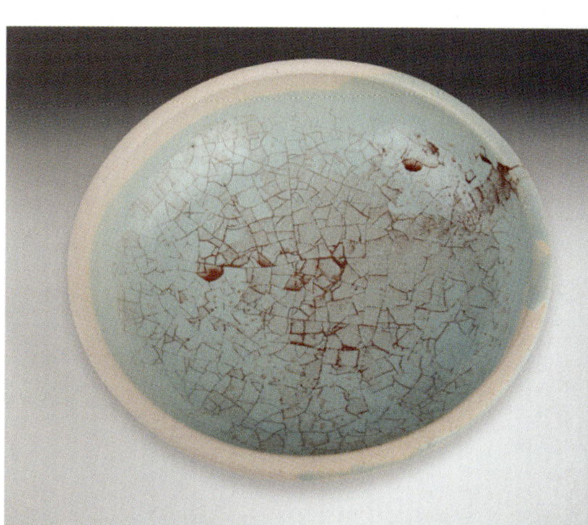

How it looked after a quick pour of red iron terra sigillata.

I had some red iron terra sigillata on my workbench, so I watered down a small amount, poured it into my test bowl, swirled it around and then dumped it out. The result highlights the craze lines, showing how they have fairly large spaces between them. If the glaze is thicker, there is more crazing with less space between the lines. When you add the terra sigillata, everything affects everything else—the thickness of the terra sigillata pour, the thickness of the piece itself and how good your first pour is.

The first pour is critical. If you don't get it just the way you want, you won't be able to do another pour right after, as the craze lines will be full and won't react the same way. Wait at least 24 hours for everything to dry and then try again. As it happens, I have two bowls to show you that illustrate this

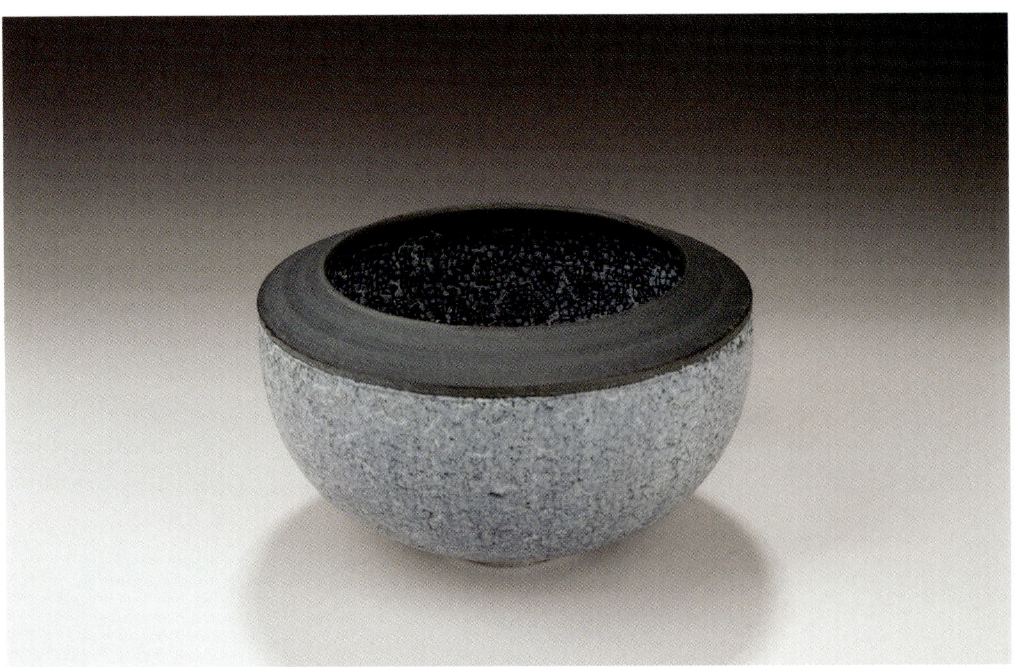

ABOVE
Bowl, Lana Wilson's Chun glaze, terra sigillata, cone 04, oxidation, 20 cm W × 13 cm T.

BELOW
Bowl in unglazed leather hard stage.

nicely. I wanted a contrast between the inside and outside of the first bowl and had thinned the blue slip a bit to achieve this, but when I went to pour it, my hand shook and it wasn't a good pour. I removed the slip from the outside with a sponge and poured again with the same thickness of slip I had used for the interior. The contrast between the interior and exterior couldn't have been better. On the second bowl, I nailed the pours on the first go, and, as you can see, there is quite a difference.

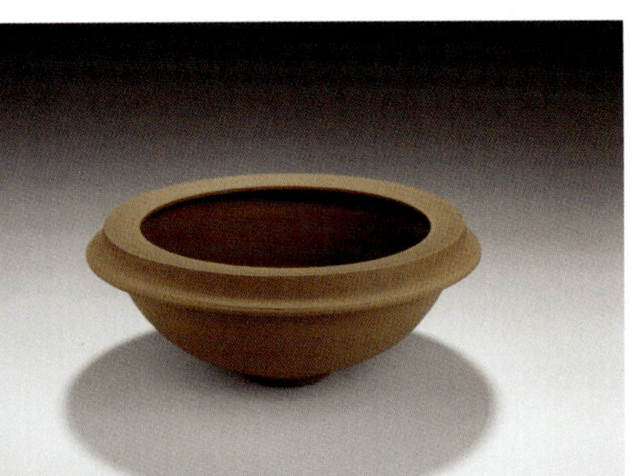

RIGHT
Bowl, Lana Wilson's Chun glaze, terra sigillata, cone 04, oxidation, 27 cm W × 11 cm T.

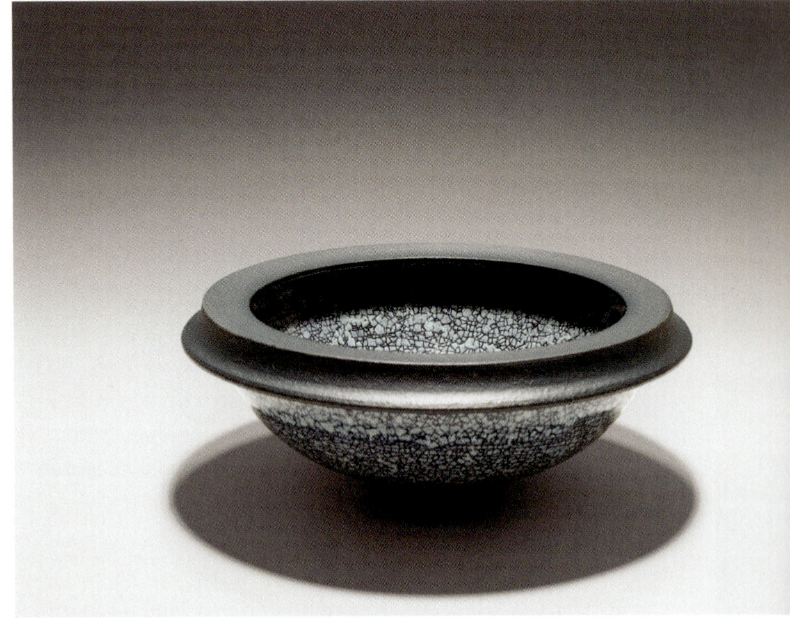

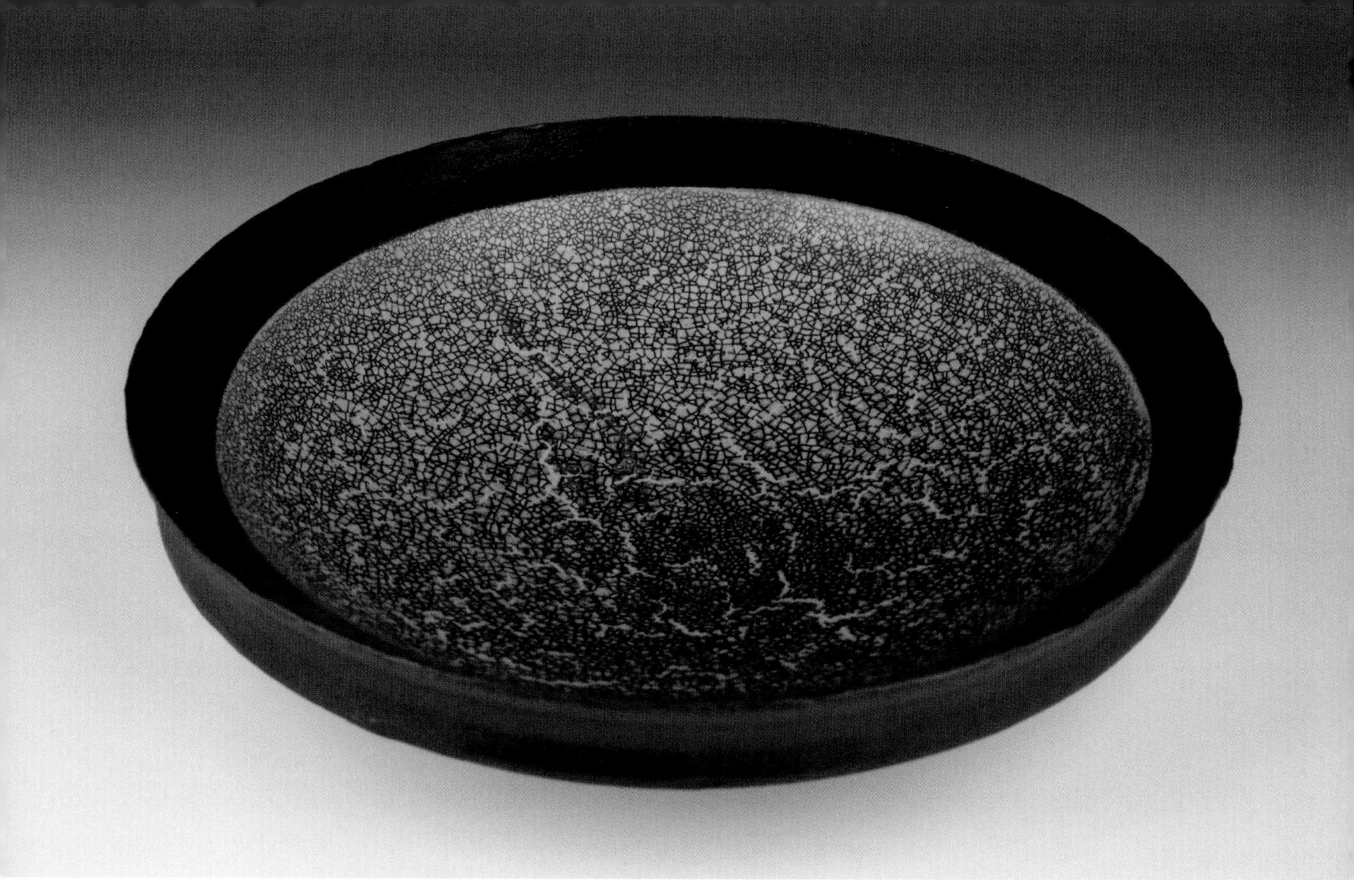

This collared bowl is a great example of finer craze lines. After it's been poured out, the remaining sigillata is still wet and naturally runs toward the middle of the piece, giving you different thicknesses, which add to the overall effect.

Collared Bowl, Lana Wilson's Chun, dark blue terra sigillata, borax (rim), multifired, cone 04, oxidation, 34 cm W × 8 cm T.

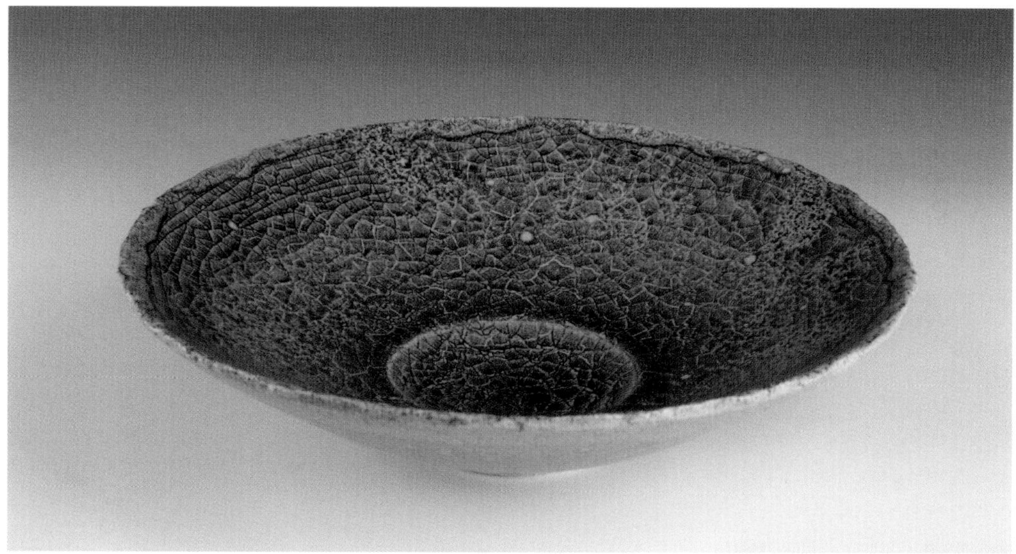

For the exterior of this bowl, I decided to see what a thin layer of sprayed terra sigillata would look like. I applied it heaviest near the outer edges and thinner as I worked my way down to the bottom. Results will differ depending on whether you spray onto a pot that is at room temperature or onto a pot that has been warmed up first. If warming it, I put it in the oven and set the temperature anywhere between 170°F and 220°F, wait a bit, then take it down to the kiln room to spray.

Flower Bowl, Lana Wilson's Chun, dark blue terra sigillata, multifired, cone 04, oxidation, 28 cm W × 7.5 cm T.

RIGHT
Dark blue terra sigillata sprayed on exterior.

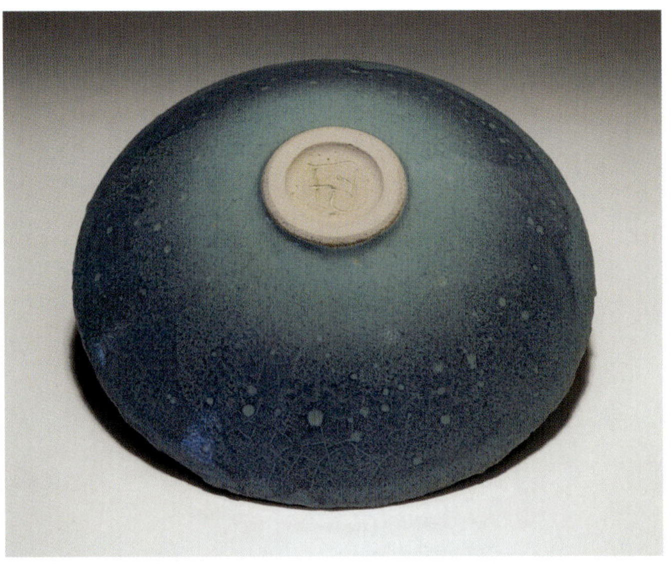

BELOW
Rimmed Bowl, Lana Wilson's Chun, dark blue terra sigillata, borax, multifired, cone 04, oxidation, 24 cm W × 10 cm T.

For the next bowl, I wanted to see what the Chun glaze would look like over the dark blue terra sigillata, so I applied that to the rim. The glaze was poured into the interior and on the exterior. The rim was sprinkled with borax.

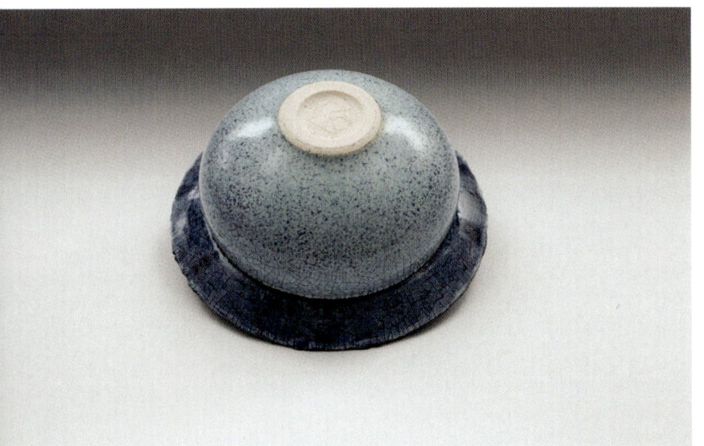

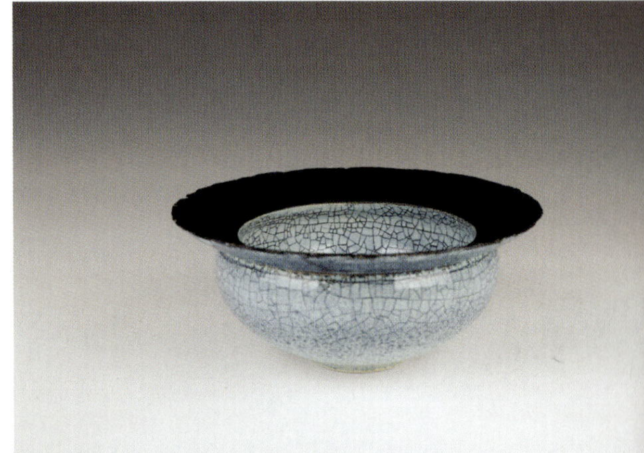

And, finally, here is an example of the terra sigillata applied thicker. The darker areas on the rim have borax sprinkles.

Bowl, Lana Wilson's Chun, terra sigillata, borax, multifired, cone 04, oxidation, 29.5 cm W × 7 cm T.

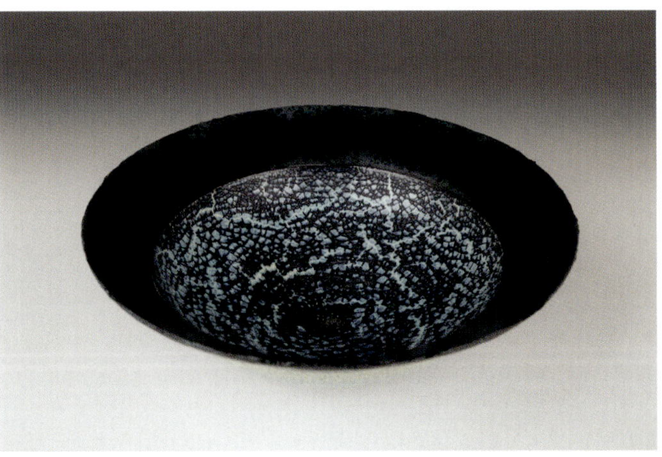

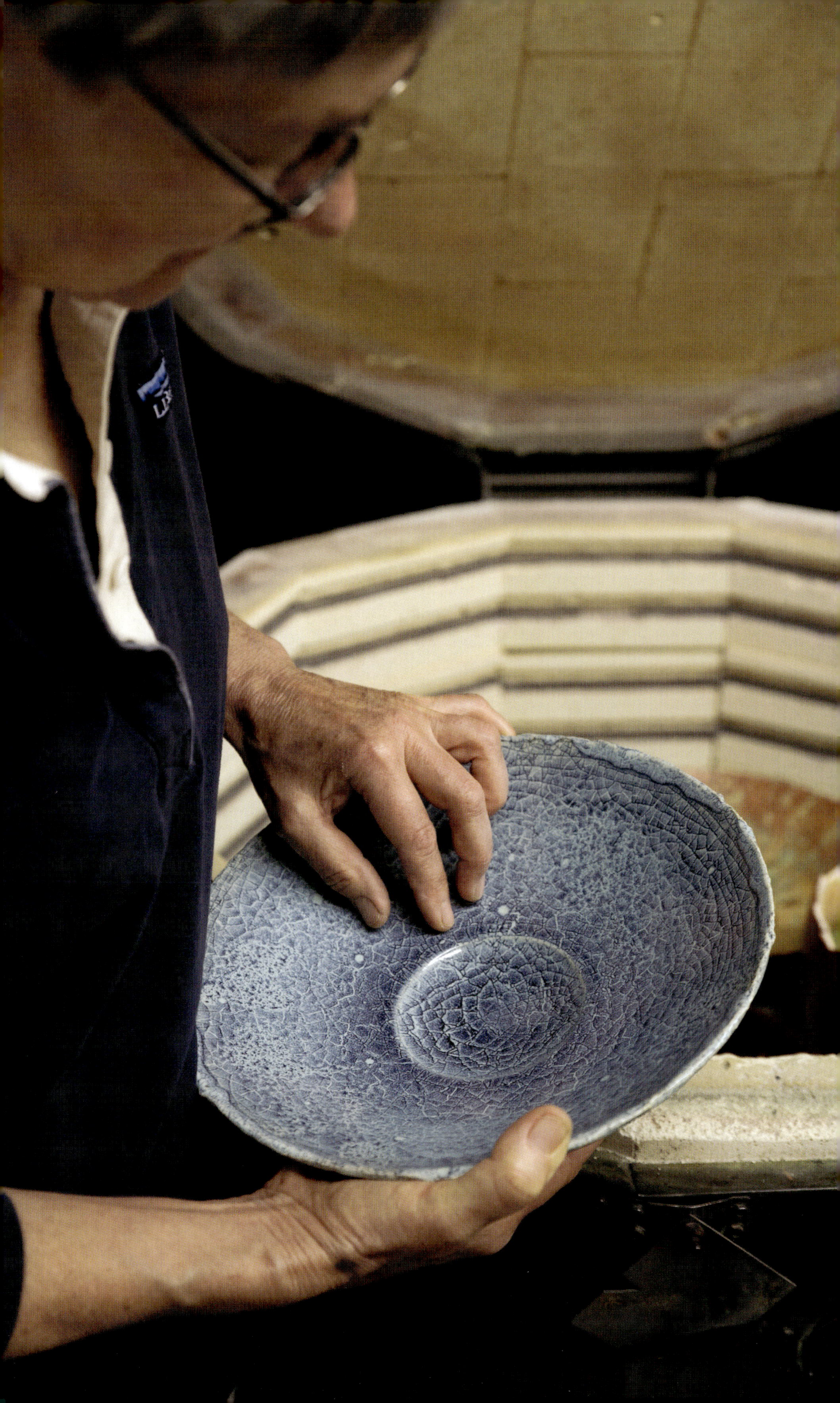

To illustrate another approach, here is an example inspired by a test bowl I had fired with Soda Blue, then had applied a thin overlay of Chartreuse Moonelis to see what would happen. I quite liked the results, which of course prompted me to play more with these glazes. I had been pondering my beautiful test bowl for months when I decided one day it was time to see if I could get close to reproducing the effect I had achieved on it.

The inspiring test bowl. Soda Blue with overlay of Chartreuse Moonelis.

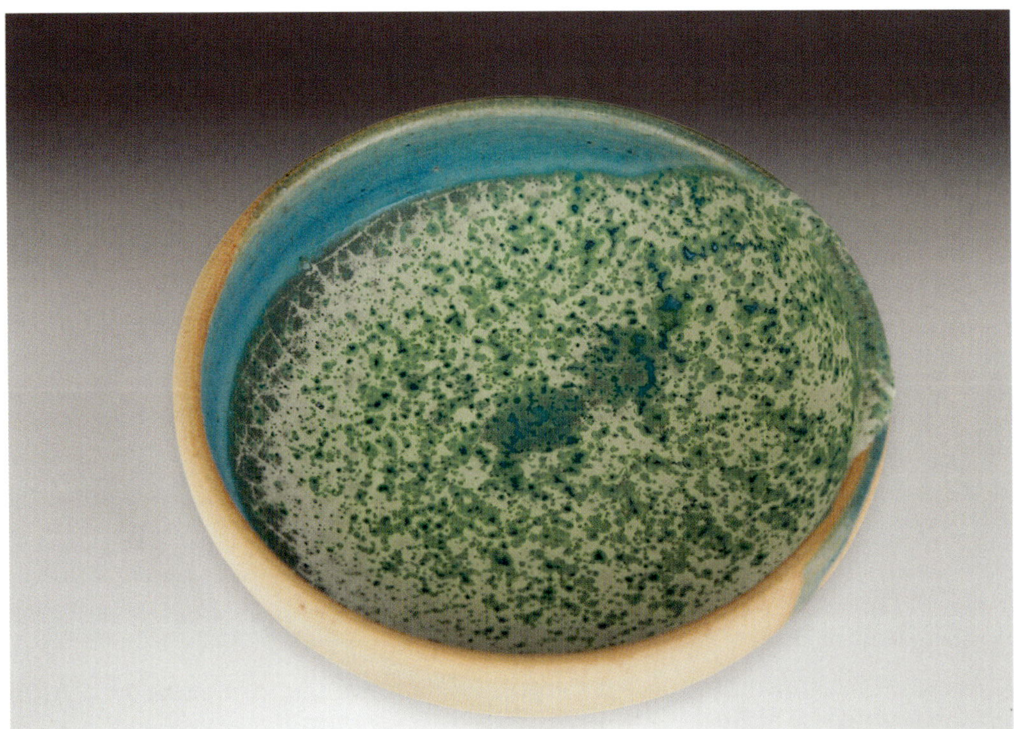

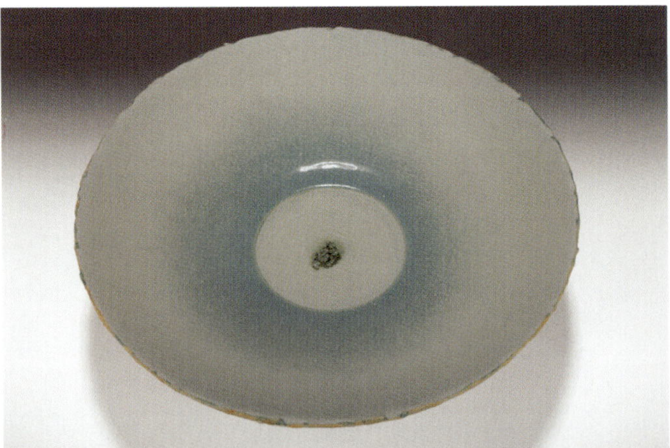

I began with the base layer of Soda Blue on this flower bowl. However, when it came out of the kiln, I could see the base layer was a bit too thin and needed some help. I warmed the bowl in the oven and then sprayed a bit more Soda Blue overtop, poured some more in the centre flower and topped the centre off with a little heap of Chartreuse Moonelis crystals.

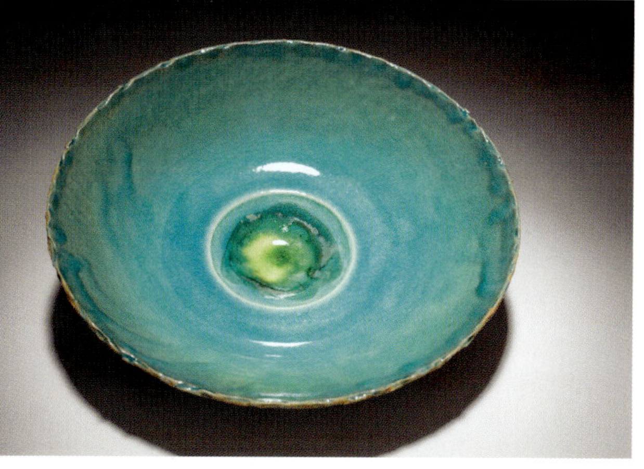

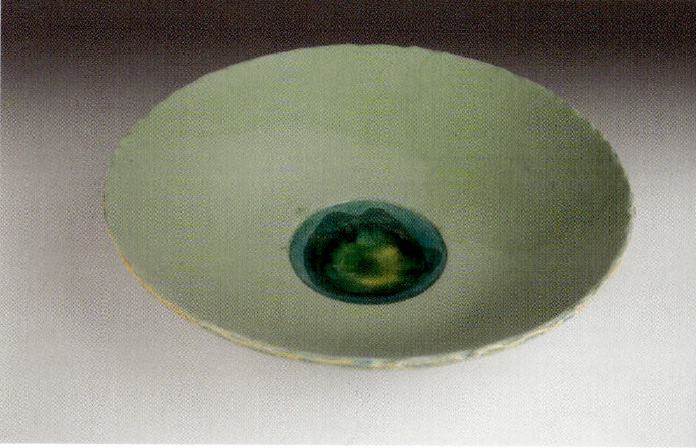

Liking it more once the Soda Blue was thicker, I was eager to see how the Moonelis would react over it and whether it would turn out like my test bowl.

ABOVE RIGHT
Bowl with Chartreuse Moonelis applied, before refiring.

I poured the Chartreuse Moonelis in and hoped for the best.

Though it didn't turn out the same as the test bowl, I wasn't disappointed. That's part of the beauty of working like this—you are bound to discover many appealing variations, even though you are using all the same ingredients. It all comes down to application, firing temperature and the kiln gods.

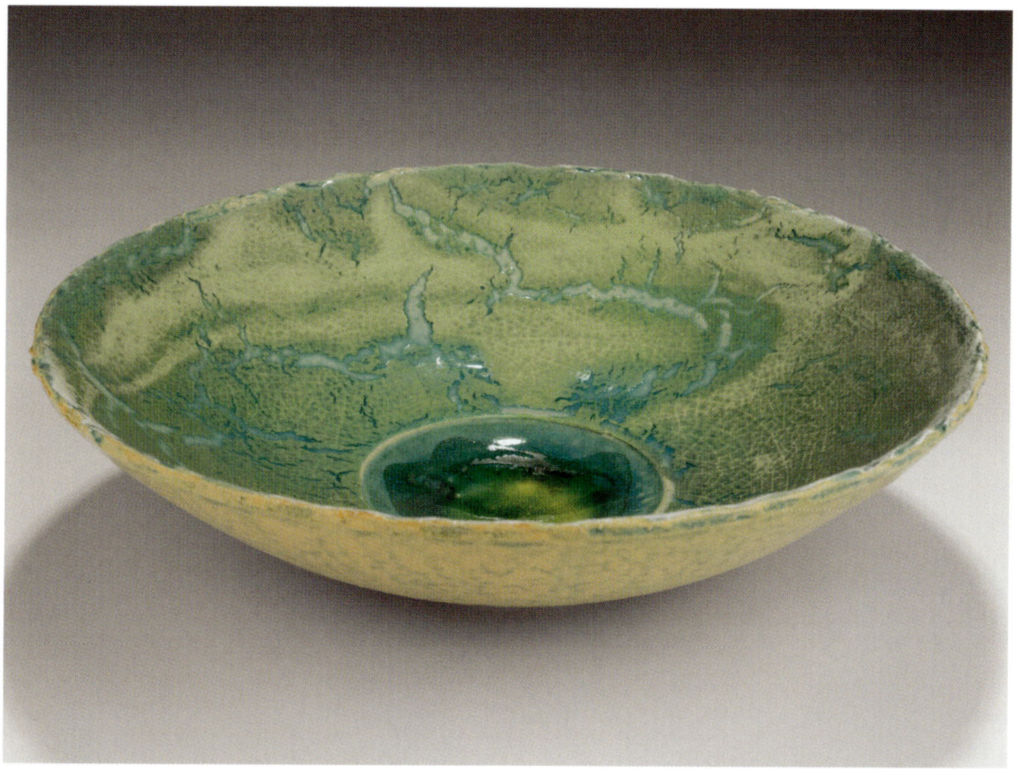

Bowl, Soda Blue, Chartreuse Moonelis, multifired, cone 04, oxidation, 30 cm W × 8 cm T.

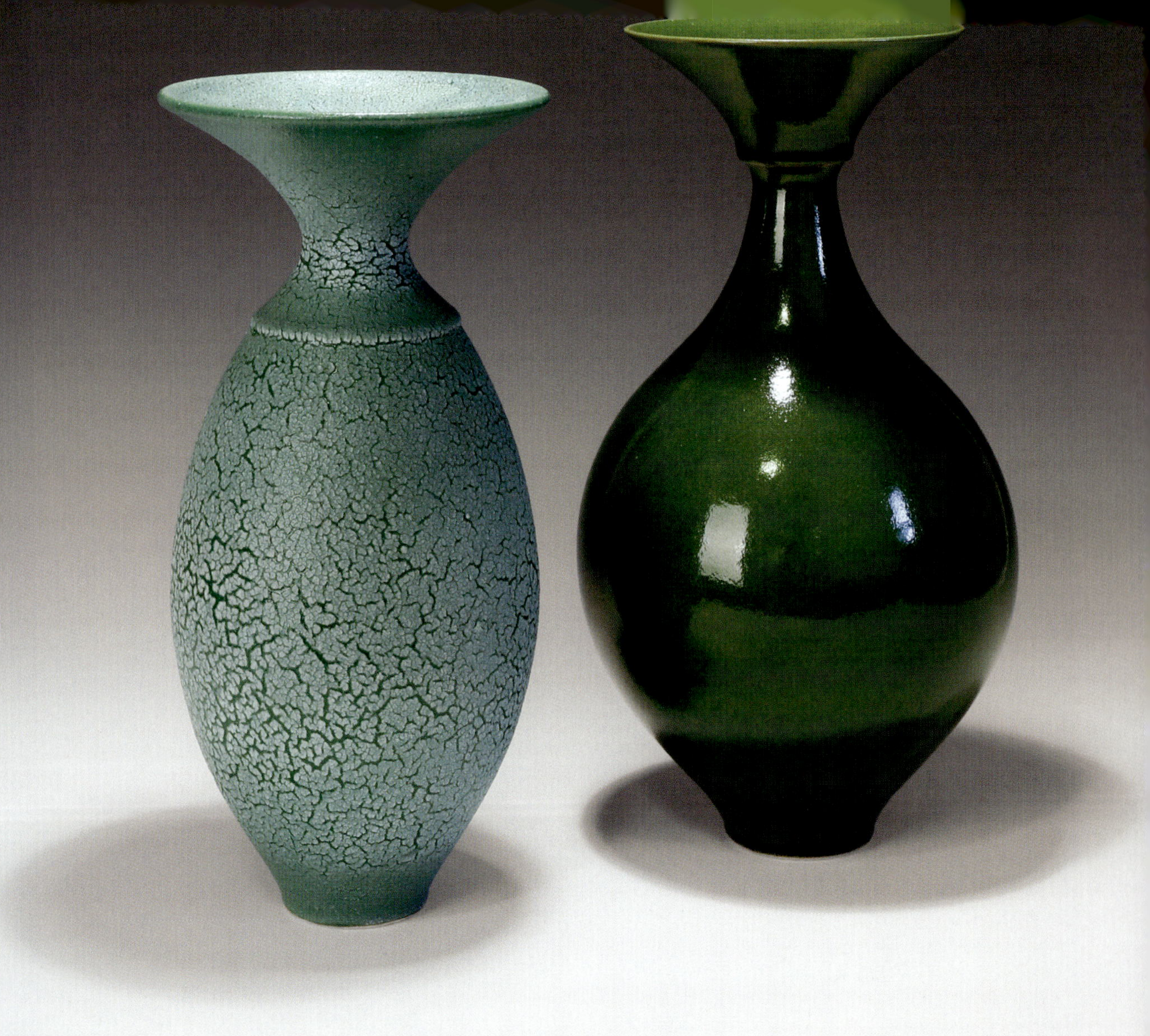

OPPOSITE, LEFT

Emerald Green underglaze, white crawl, 05, multifired in oxidation, 13 cm W × 38 cm T.

OPPOSITE, RIGHT

Emerald Green 05, fired in oxidation, 15 cm W × 38 cm T.

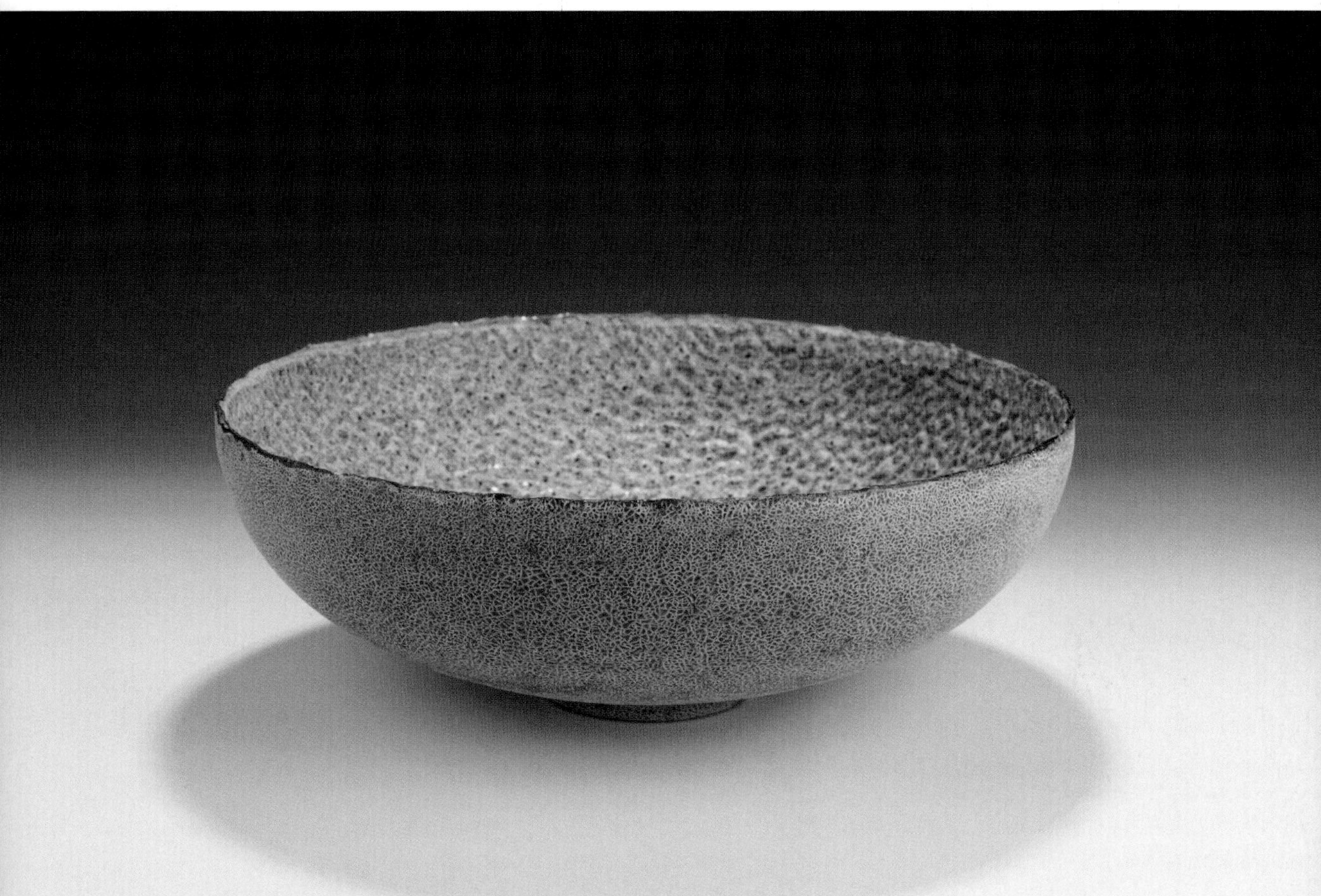

Snowy Day, dark blue terra sigillata, green crawl glaze, baking soda blue, 05, multifired in oxidation, 31 cm W × 11.5 T.

CHAPTER 7

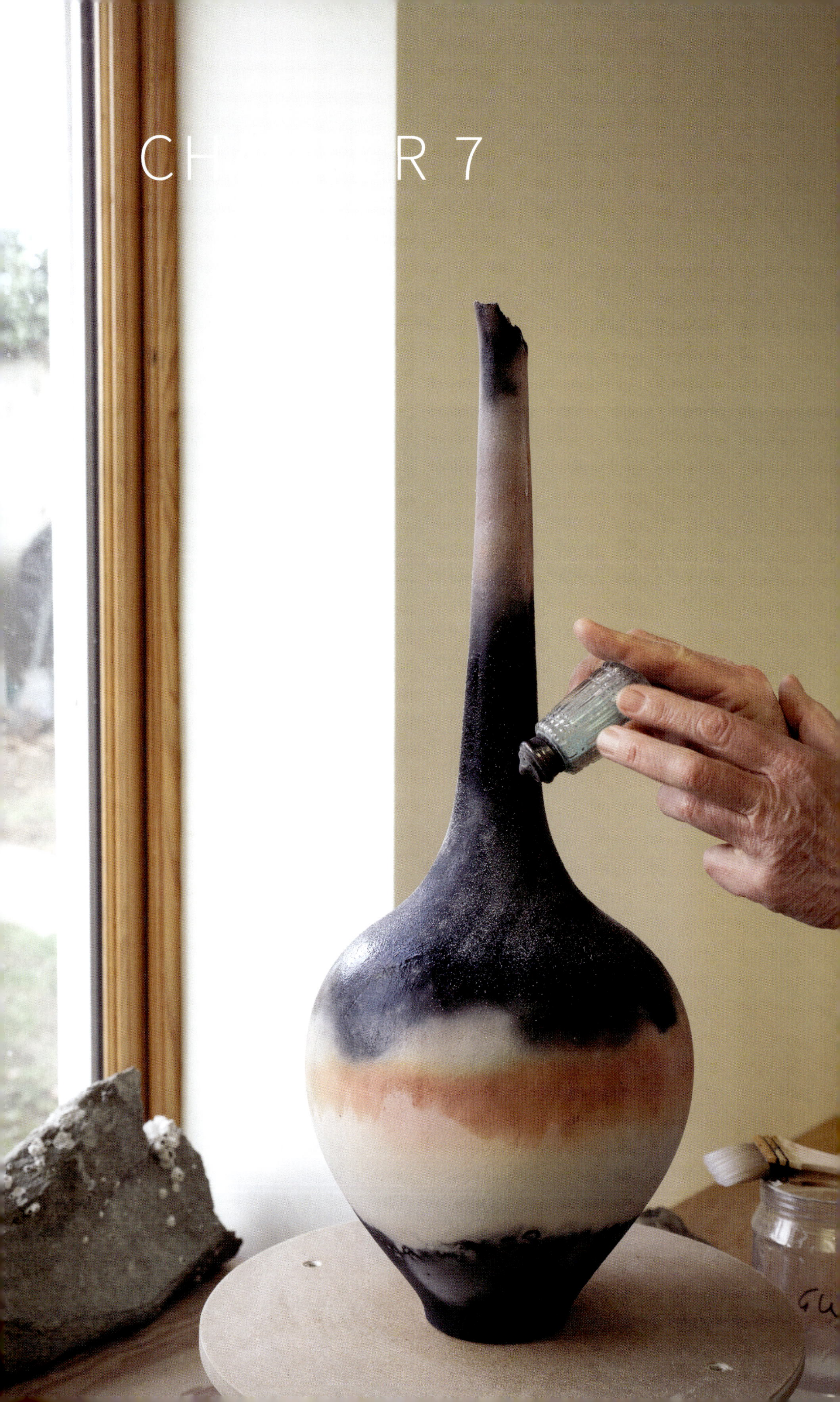

NEVER SAY DIE

I'm going to finish off my discussion of terra sigillatas and unconventional glaze techniques with one of my greatest saves ever, a fantastic example of making a silk purse out of a sow's ear. Unfortunately, it was one of my early experiments, and I didn't document all the steps, but I did take a few photos with my iPad.

This bowl started its journey coated with a layer of black terra sigillata. My original plan was to decorate it with crawl glazes, but then I realized I was curious about what the black terra sigillata would look like fired with borax applied, so the plan changed.

I started with a sprinkling of borax on both sides, applying it heavier on the interior, and adding Alkaline Blue 04 in the centre. My meagre notes say it was then fired in oxidation. When it came out of the first firing, the borax areas didn't look too bad—clear where I had put chunks of borax, and rusty brown where the borax was thin. The centre where I had applied the Alkaline Blue 04 was a very ugly brown. *What to do?* I decided to put a layer of Parched Earth overtop of the Alkaline Blue 04, fire it in reduction and hope for the best. Alas, my hopes would soon be dashed.

When I took it out of the kiln the next day, I was taken aback by the large creamy areas which had looked okay in oxidation, but now looked quite hideous. The Parched Earth layer hadn't been thick enough and had melted into the underlayer of glaze and still looked yucky. I was tempted at this point to throw in the towel. The bowl had gone through both oxidation and reduction firings and was supremely ugly.

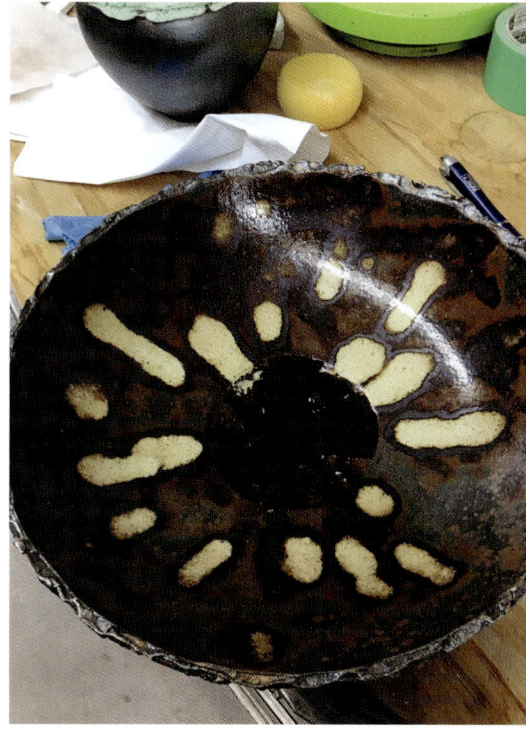

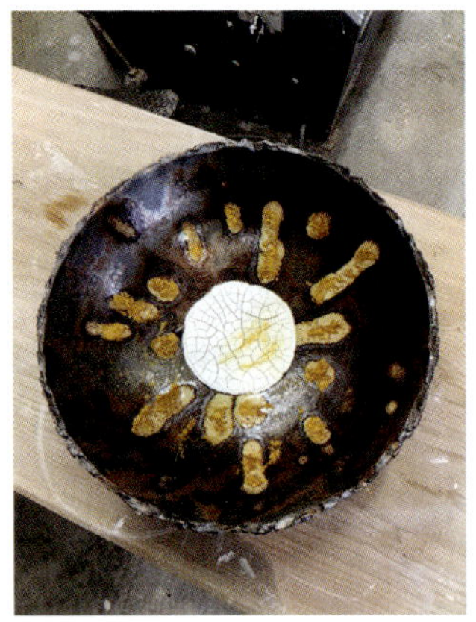

Yellow ochre applied to creamy spots, white crawl glaze added to centre, waiting for refiring.

Why continue? I put it aside, as I really didn't have any idea of what else I could do.

After a few days of pondering, I decided to try putting some yellow ochre in the creamy spots. The ochre had been sitting around in the studio for at least two decades. It may even have travelled from my Vancouver studio to Ladysmith in 1991. My guess is that I had bought it to experiment with, had not gotten great results and had just put it aside and forgotten about it. As this bowl was truly dreadful, I figured I had nothing to lose. It was a good opportunity to try anything and see what happened.

In the centre of the bowl, I applied my white crawl glaze and set aside the piece to wait for the next firing. As the reduction firings only seemed to be resulting in a darker, uglier bowl each time, I opted to go back to oxidation.

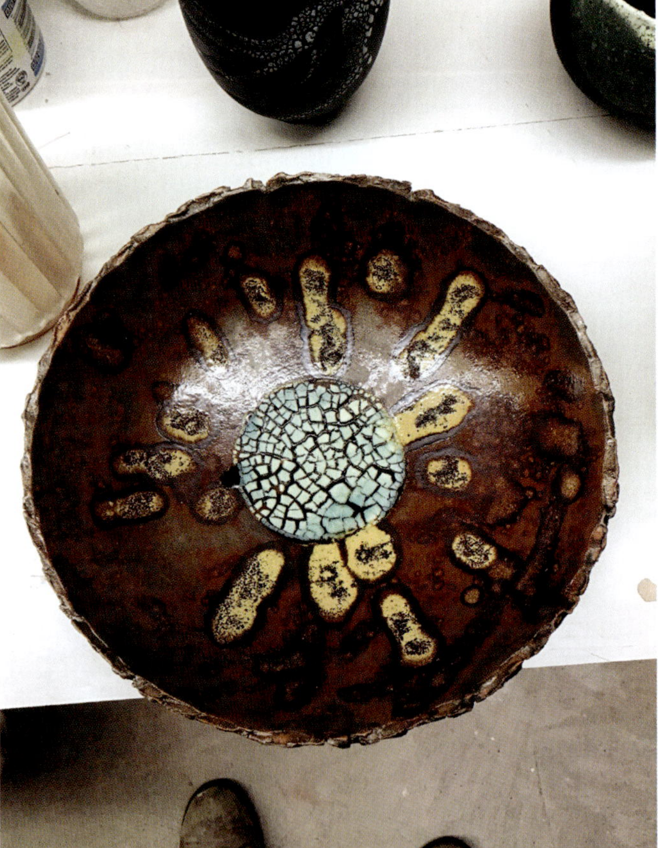

Bowl after refiring in oxidation.

This somewhat careless photo with the tips of my boots showing cracks me up. I imagine that I wasn't thinking particularly complimentary thoughts at the time. However, I was intrigued by how the ochre had become gritty, like fine sand. It had turned quite dark overall, but had little shiny flecks in spots, and the oxidation firing had lightened the background up a bit. After much thought, I decided to try covering everything except the core with a layer of orange terra sigillata and then added a thick layer of Parched Earth over the crawl glaze in the centre.

As I placed it in the kiln, I had no idea what would happen, but my expectations were low. I almost fell over when I lifted it out of the kiln the next day. Like a caterpillar emerging as a butterfly, it had absolutely transformed.

I named it *Arid Planet* and after admiring it in my living space for a few days, took it down to display in the gallery. I was a bit reluctant to sell it right away, but as I had posted it online, the cat was out of the bag, and it was snapped up the next day.

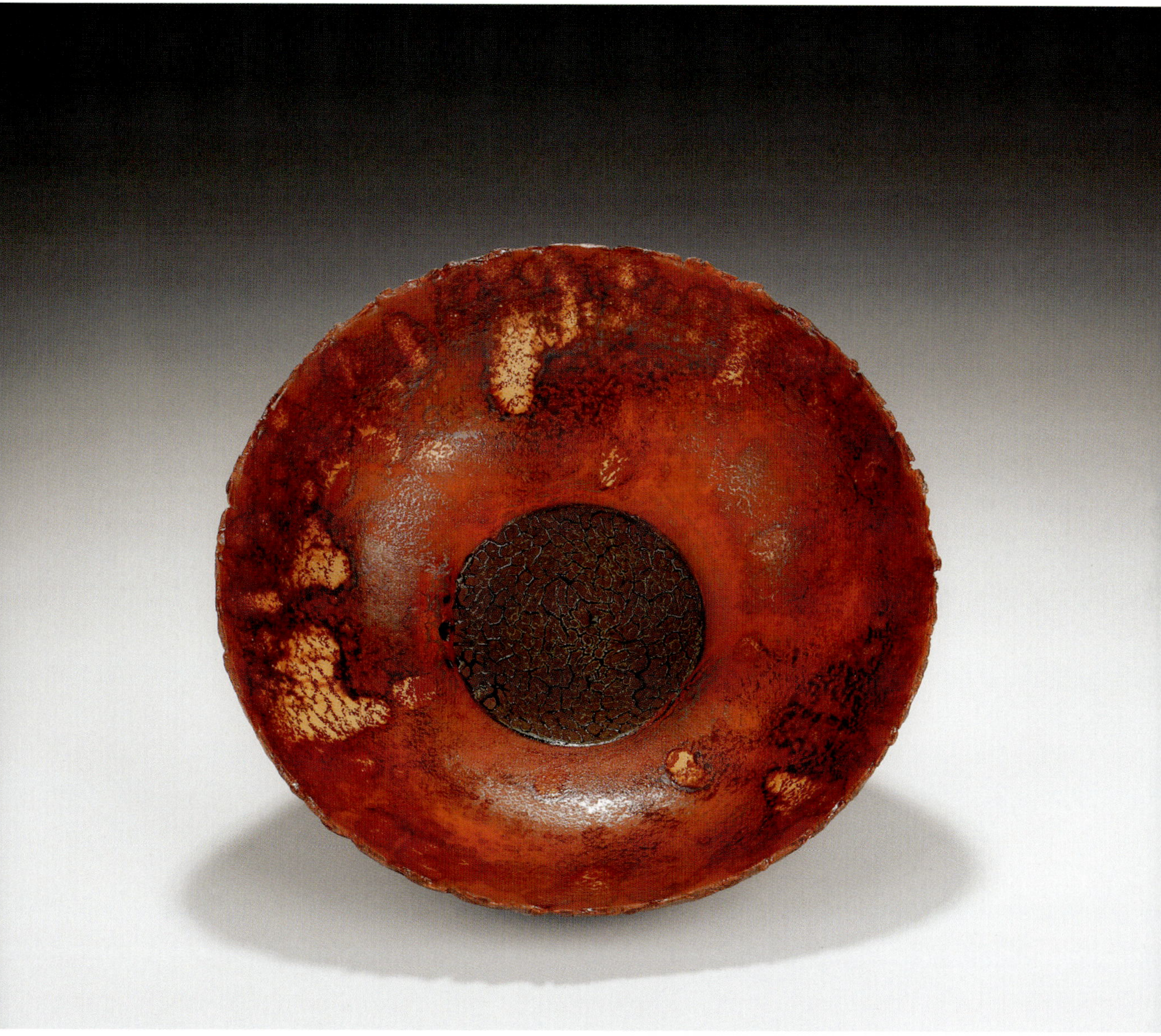

Arid Planet, layered finishes, multifired in reduction and oxidation, 33 cm W × 11 cm T.

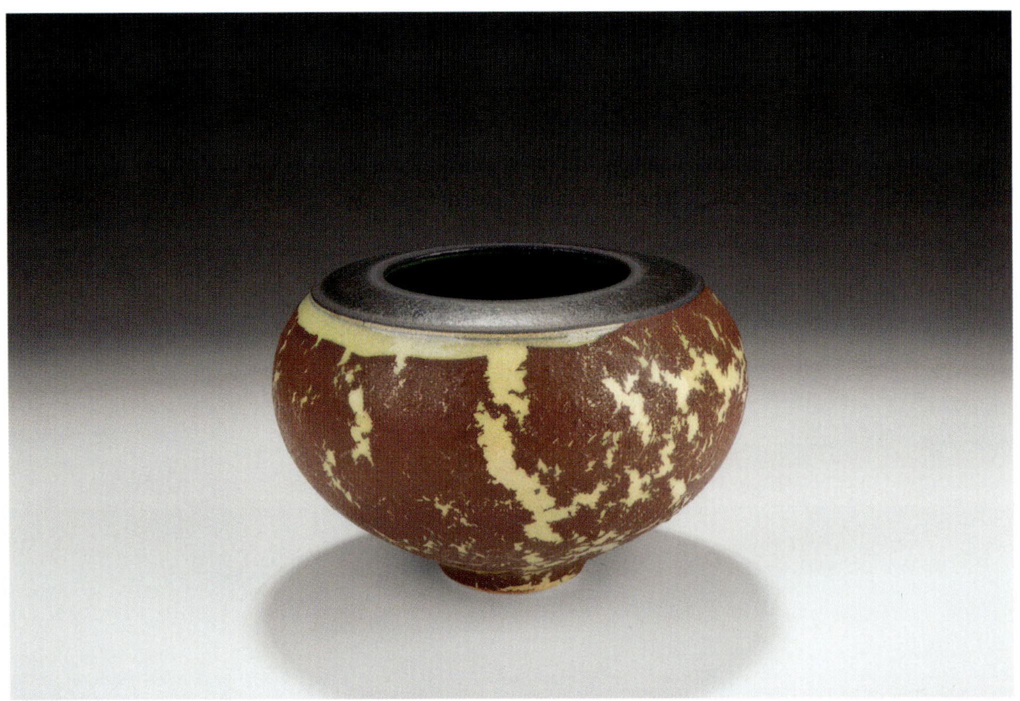

Another example of the first glaze firing not turning out as planned is this vessel. The black sigillata on the rim looked good, and the interior, glazed with Emerald Green, fired perfectly and so was left alone. The Lime Green on the outside was too pale to make much of a statement. *What to do?* I decided to put a coat of red iron oxide terra sigillata over the lime green knowing that it would shrink up in the firing and leave gaps to showing the glaze underneath. I didn't dislike how it turned out, but I thought I could do better.

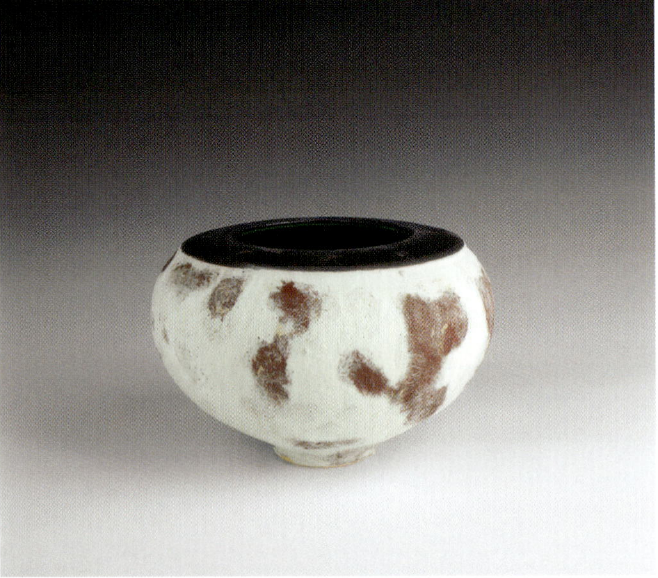

I applied Emerald Green over the Lime Green in the gaps, sponged off some so the red slip would contrast and kept some areas of the red slip as it was.

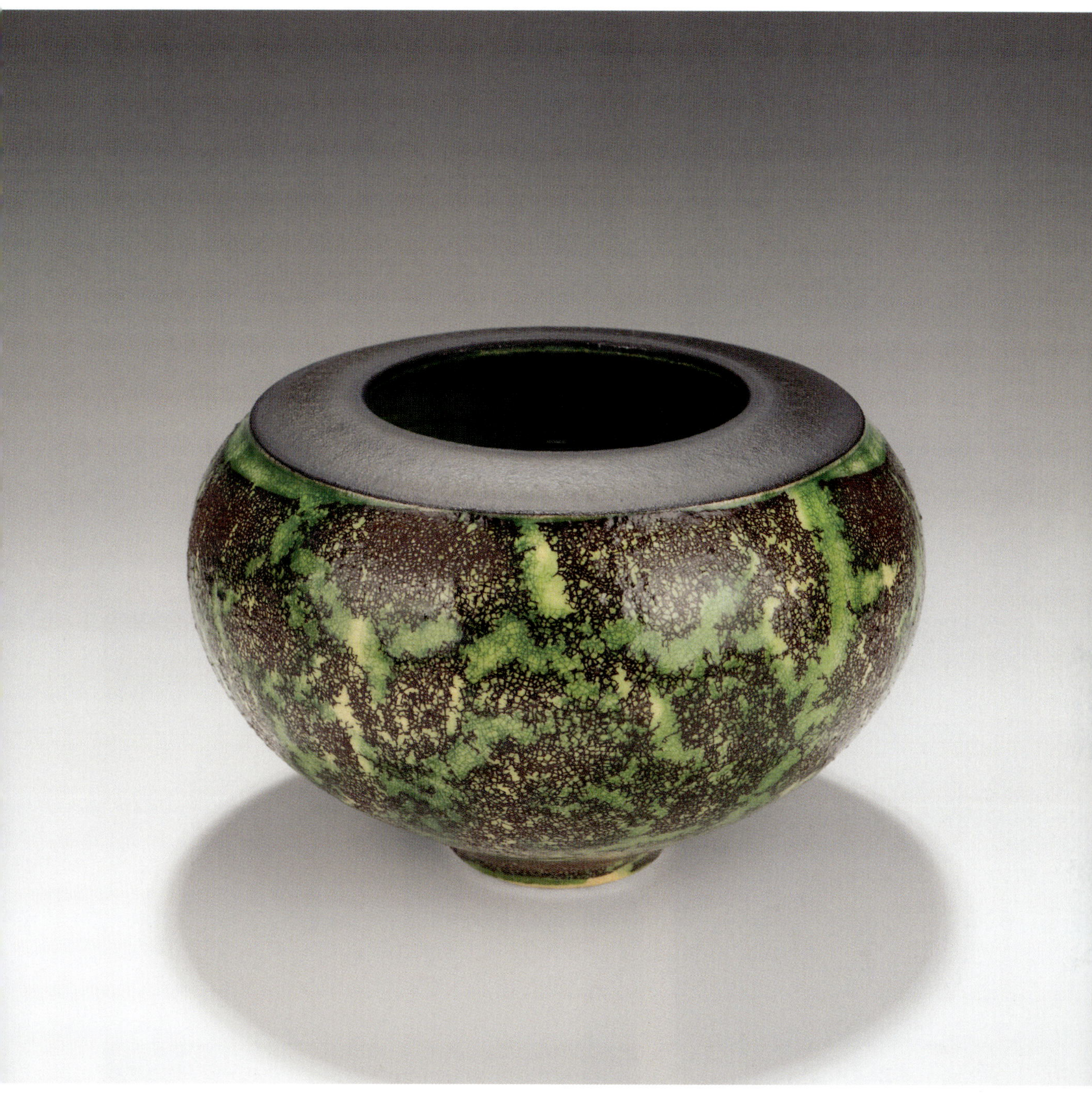

ABOVE

Collared Vessel, multiple glazes, terra sigillata, oxidation, 30 cm W × 8 cm T.

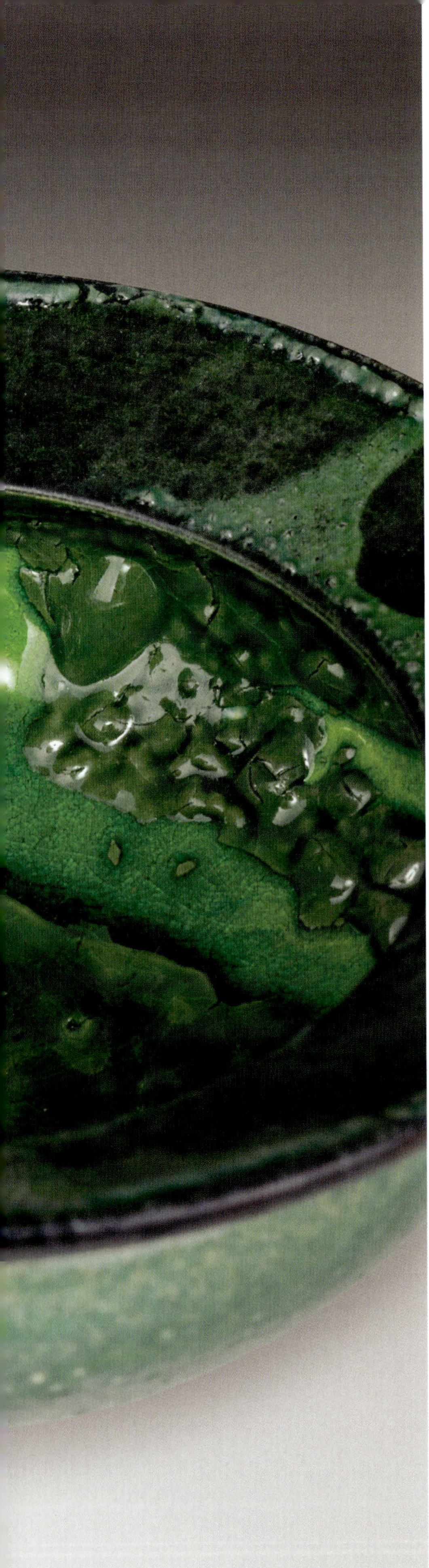

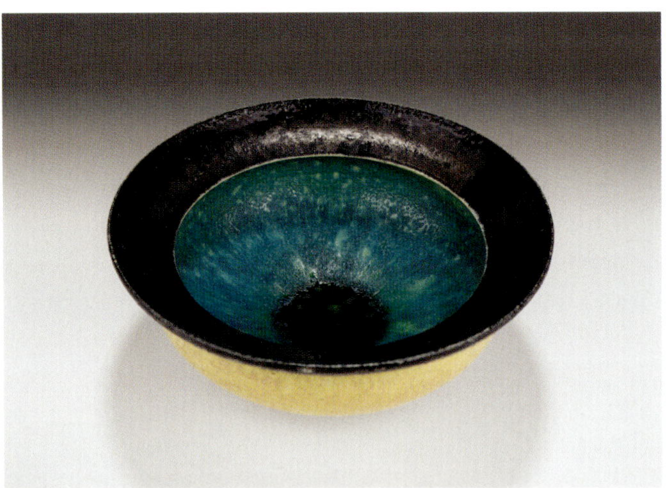

Finally, for this bowl, the first firing had dark blue terra sigillata on the collar, mystery glaze on the outside and inside, and dark blue terra sigillata on the rim, along with some borax. Turned out kind of ugly. Still unhappy I brushed Moonelis over selected areas and fired again.

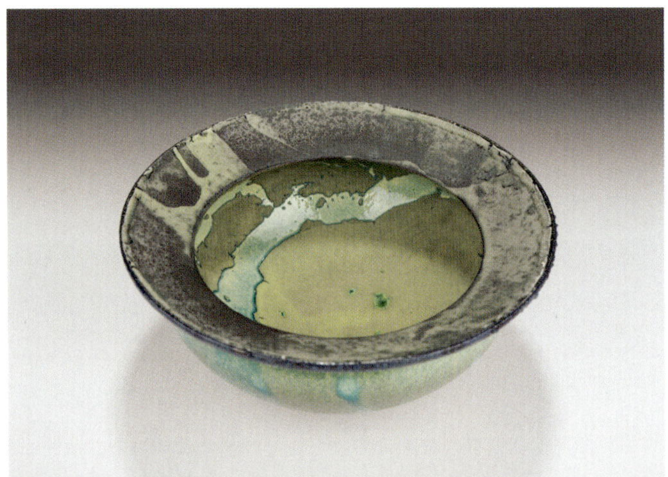

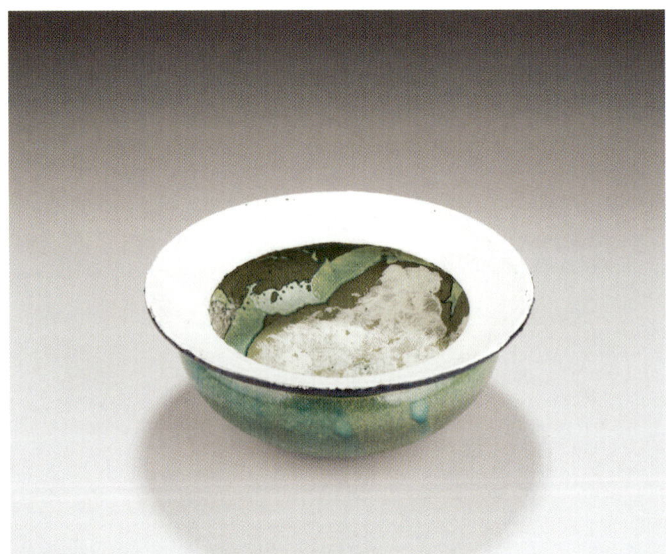

It still looked pretty yucky, and by this point I was not in the least bit hopeful. The Moonelis had bubbled where it was thick in the interior, but interestingly, these bubbles were very strong. I pushed on them with my fingers and couldn't break them, so decided to try brushing Emerald Green on the rim and over the bubbles, followed by a light spray of Emerald Green on the exterior.

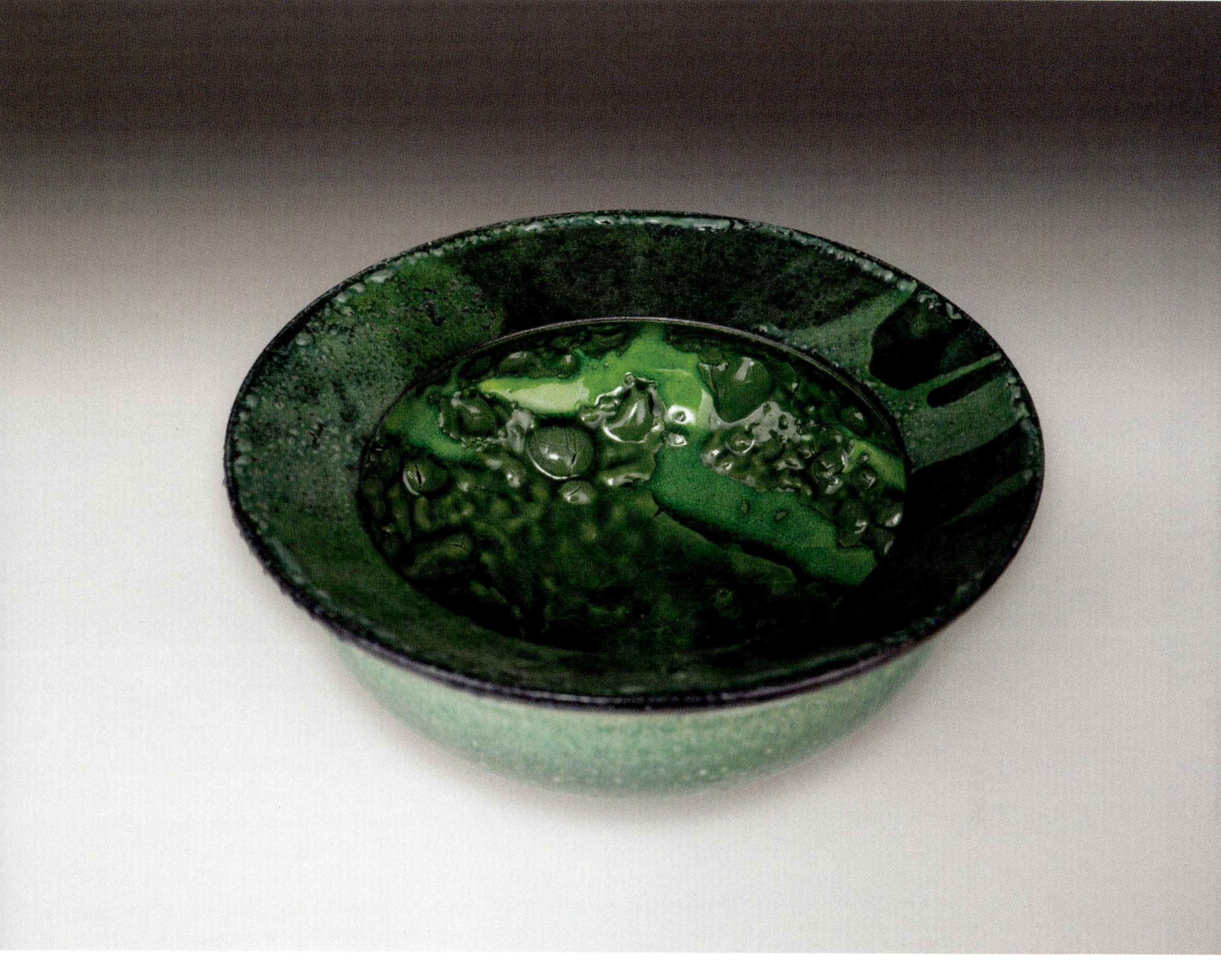

Swamp Bowl, multiple glazes, terra sigillata, multifired in oxidation, 20.5 cm W × 8.5 cm T.

Now, not everyone is going to like this piece, but I do. As luck would have it, I have a sculptural piece that I will be making soon. I want an area of it to look swampy, but had no idea how I was going to achieve that look. Now, I do.

Your brain is probably exploding with things you want to try out after reading these first chapters. You might want to take a short tea break before we dive into the next section, where we go deeper into exploring reduction.

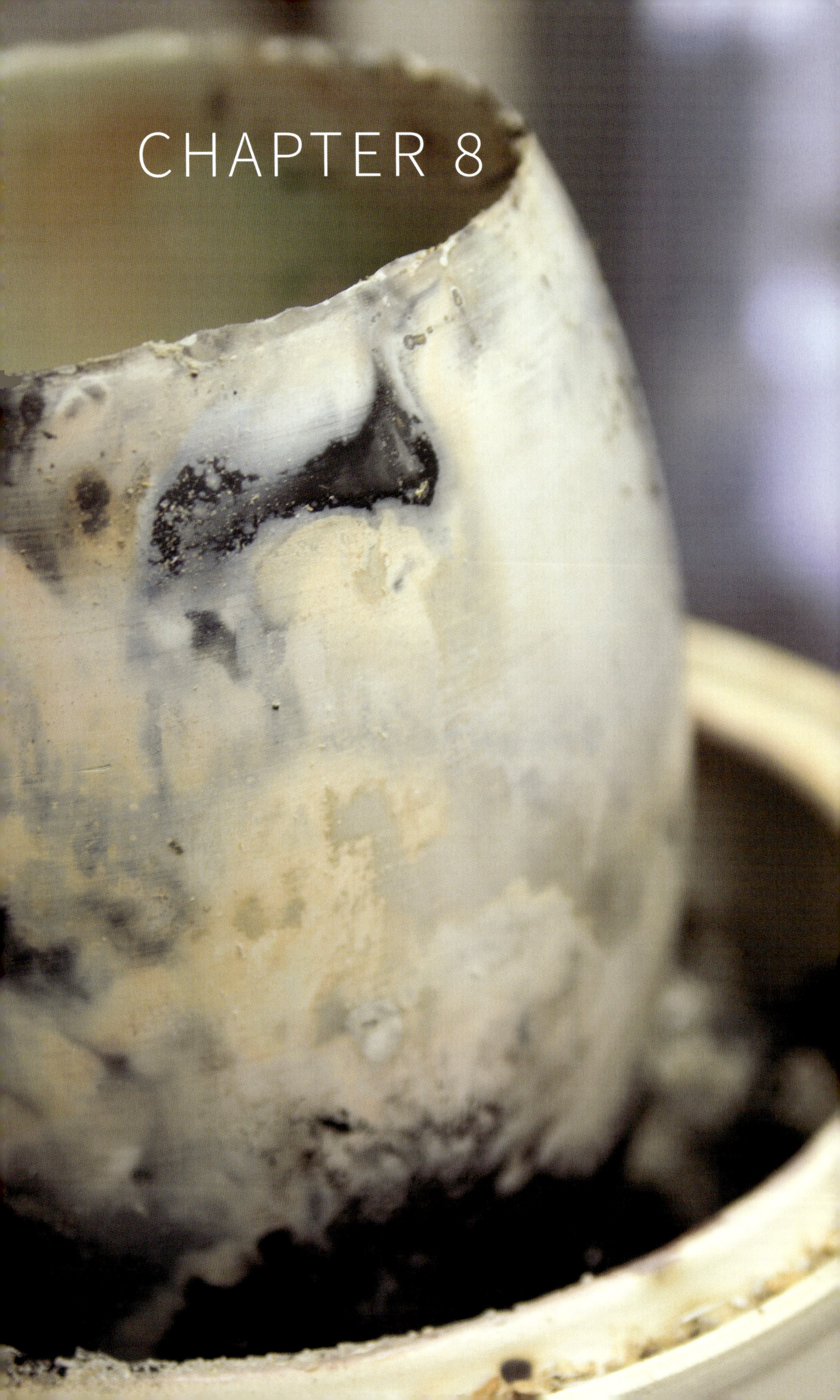

CHAPTER 8

SAGGAR IN THE LINE OF FIRE

In the next four chapters, I focus on reduction firing, which I've always wanted to explore more deeply. Back in the '70s, when I first started to work with clay and glazes in school, everything was low fired, cone 06, in oxidation, and we used small jars of premade glazes. It wasn't until I was in Grade 11 and at a new school that I got the opportunity to fire to cone 6 oxidation and to start making my own glazes. When I eventually found a few cone 6 oxidation glazes that worked reasonably well on my tableware, I stuck with them and didn't experiment further.

But as a young potter, I would often visit full-time potters' studios to learn from what they were producing. And, as I recall, they all were firing in reduction. From these visits I began to believe the popular potters' myth of the time that reduction was where it was at, and that oxidation was its poor country cousin. The word was that getting a nice glaze in reduction was easy, but with oxidation, not so much. And, for sure, most of the work I was drawn to was reduction fired.

Now, decades later, I realize that the problems potters were having back then with oxidation glazes stemmed largely from the kilns that were available. They didn't accurately reproduce firings, and the temperature throughout the kiln would often vary considerably, creating inconsistent results. Then, along came computerized kilns, and that changed everything. Now we could program the kiln to fire as we wanted and easily add soaks at any point in the firing.

I suppose it is no surprise that as a young potter curious about reduction firing, I turned my attention to the eye-catching world of raku—it was easy, fast and exciting with its unpredictable and often-dramatic results. After a few years of exploring raku, I dipped my toe into saggar firing, but only just enough to get a taste of what might be possible. So, my knowledge of reduction firing was very limited.

However, since acquiring my Blaauw gas kiln, I have been able to go to town investigating new glazing and firing techniques for reduction work. I spent the first few years with the Blaauw focusing primarily on tableware, learning to create the glazes that I had loved as a youngster. I did a little bit of low-fire reduction, but only enough to let me know that this was going to be a steep learning curve full of exciting discoveries. But now, with some experimentation under my belt, I can share some of my discoveries with you.

I start here with an example that shows how I work and how my exploration process unfolds. It begins with a saggar-fired piece that was a complete surprise to me and which led to many subsequent experiments on sacrificial pots.

I wandered down this particular rabbit hole when I placed a saggar, which had a slightly open crack, into the bottom right area of the kiln, right near the burner flame. I had packed the saggar in the usual way with sawdust, seaweed, bits of beach coal, pinecones and the like, all crammed around the outside of the vessel and against the saggar wall. I tossed a little copper carbonate in and then went on to fill the inside of the vessel with a similar mixture. During the firing, as the burner flame found its way in through the crack, it licked around the vessel, burning up any combustibles in its path.

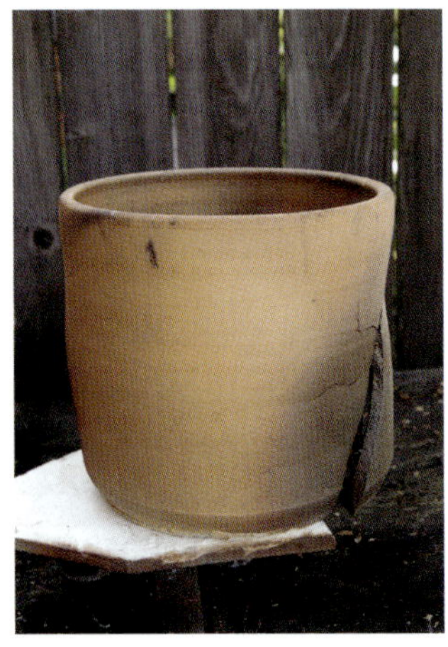

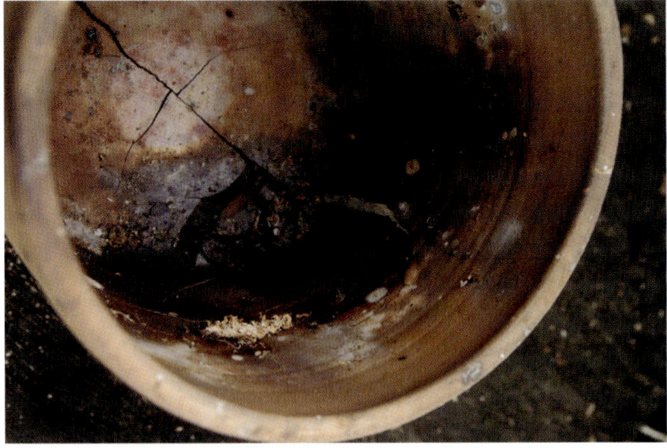

I didn't know that a happy accident was about to occur, so I didn't take a picture of the saggar in the kiln, but here it is after giving up its prize.

The next day, as I lifted the pot out of the saggar, I could see there was very little ash remaining around the exterior of the vessel. It had been well and truly incinerated. I was struck by how it reminded me of wood-fired work, while the interior of the pot had the pink and black tones of my other saggar-fired work.

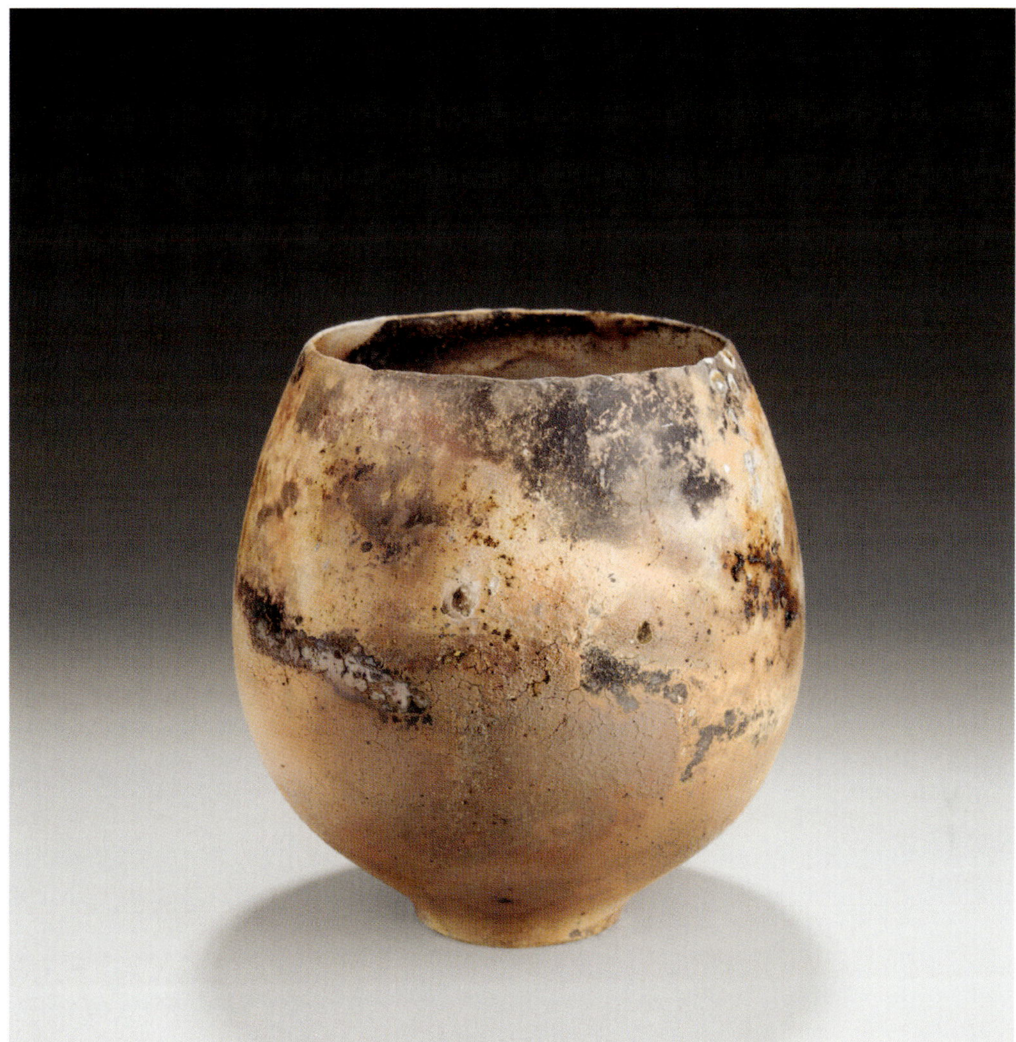

Happy accidents are often the impetus for new explorations, and this one sparked a lot of ideas. I decided to try and re-create what had happened and reinforced the saggar by wrapping wire around it to hold it together. When it came time for the next firing, I placed the packed saggar in the same spot and hoped for the best.

The piece that came out of the cracked saggar this time had a completely different feeling; beautiful in its simplicity, it emitted a soft, peaceful vibration.

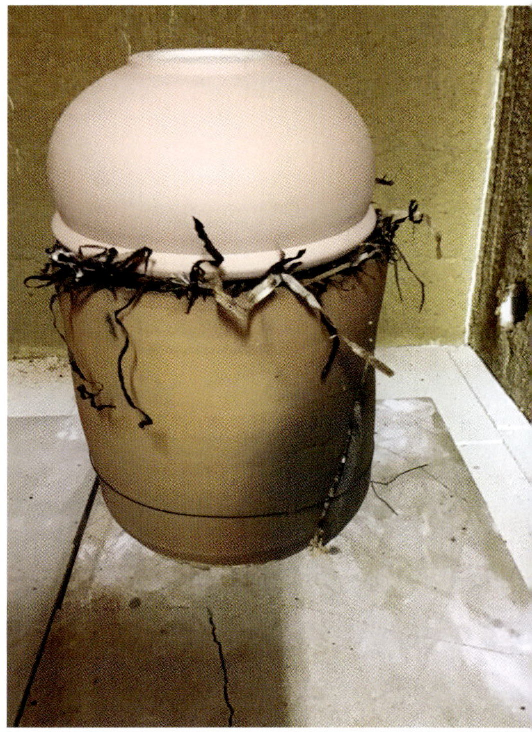

TOP
Vessel, saggar fired, 18 cm W × 21 cm T.

RIGHT
The saggar in relation to the burner. After taking the photo, I turned the saggar around, so the crack was in the line of fire.

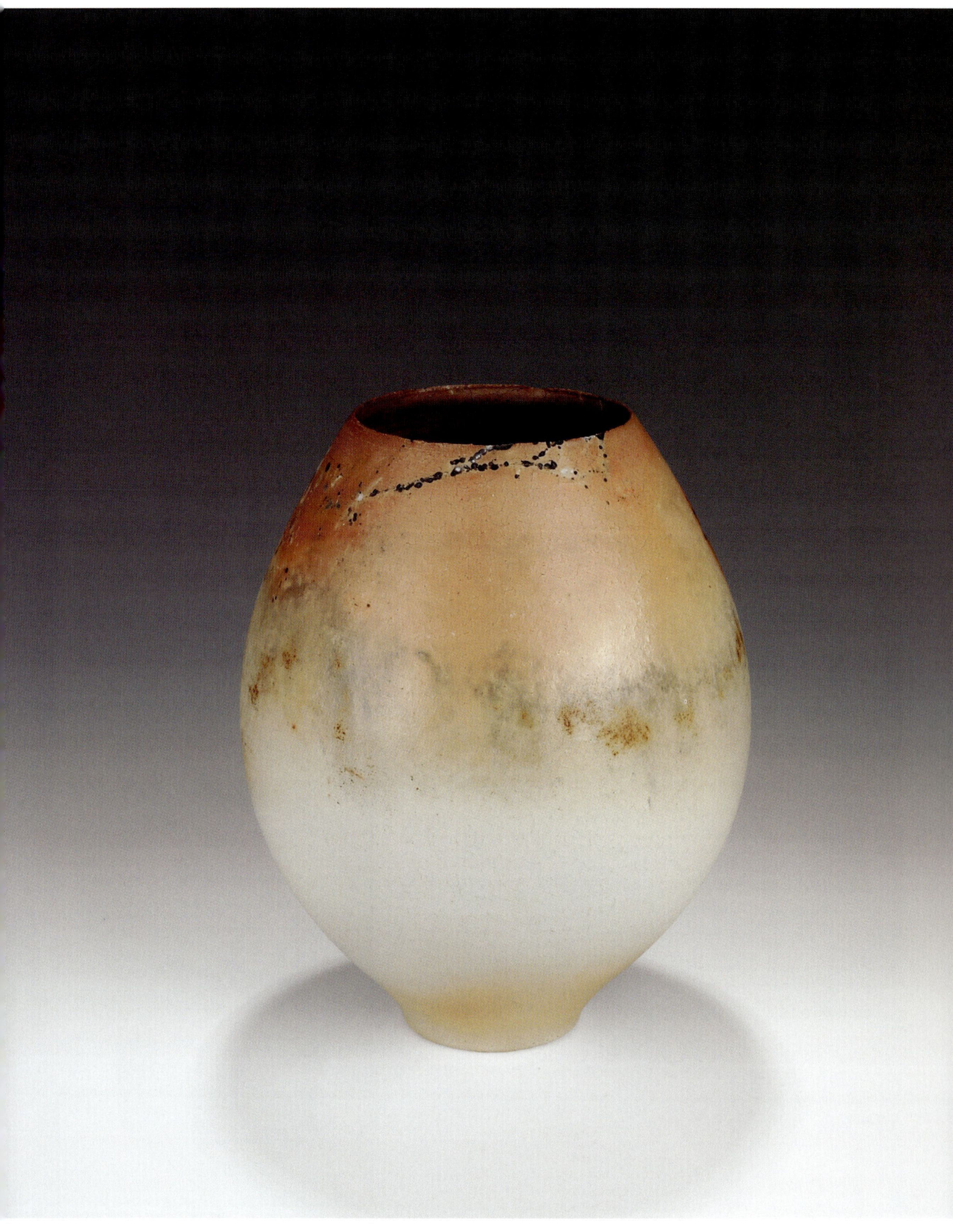

Serene Vessel, saggar fired,
15 cm W × 24 cm T.

Now, being a curious fox, I couldn't stop there. I wanted to try more with my now quite-fragile saggar. The next idea would require a sacrificial pot, and I chose an altered vessel I'd made a few years back. It was one of those pieces that I had fired multiple times but had never been completely happy with. So, even though to many eyes the vessel was quite fine the way it was, I considered it expendable for the purpose of experimentation. However, when I tried to put the vessel in the saggar, it was too large to fit, so I had to adapt my plan. I recalled that, kicking about somewhere (as I rarely throw out anything), I had an old saggar that had cracked in half. I hoped I could reinforce it with some wire and position it so the burner flame would lick through the crack and work its magic.

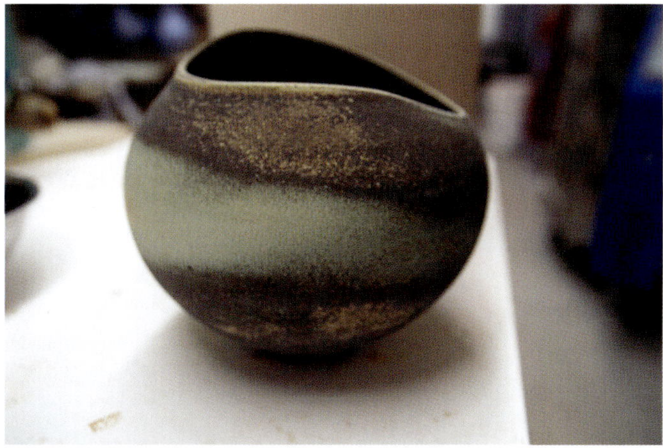

LEFT
Sacrificial altered vessel, lithium compound.

BOTTOM
Sacrificial altered vessel, several firings later. Glazes unknown; ready for experimentation.

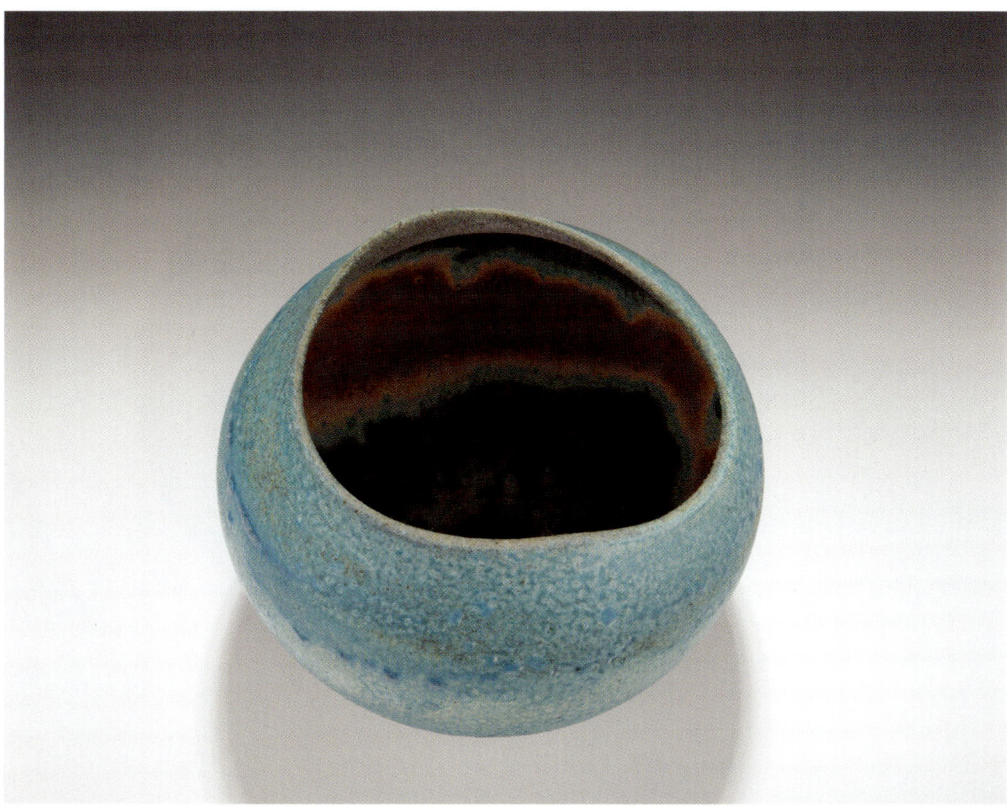

Packed and ready to put in the kiln.

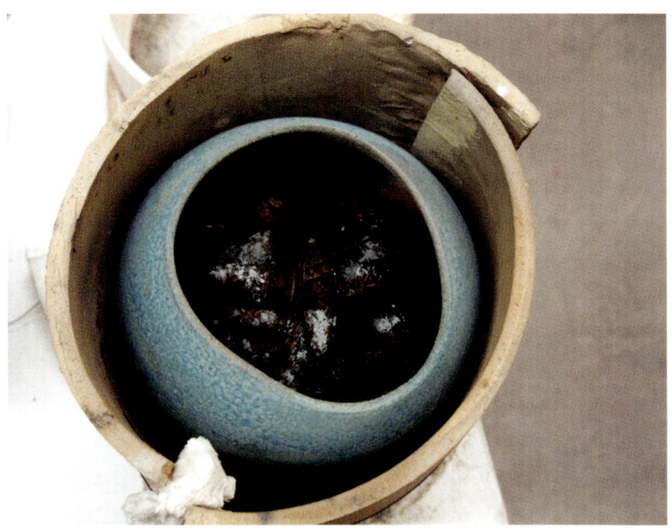

The saggar I cobbled together to place near the burner. I wrapped an old element around it to hold it together and filled the cracks with kiln fibre.

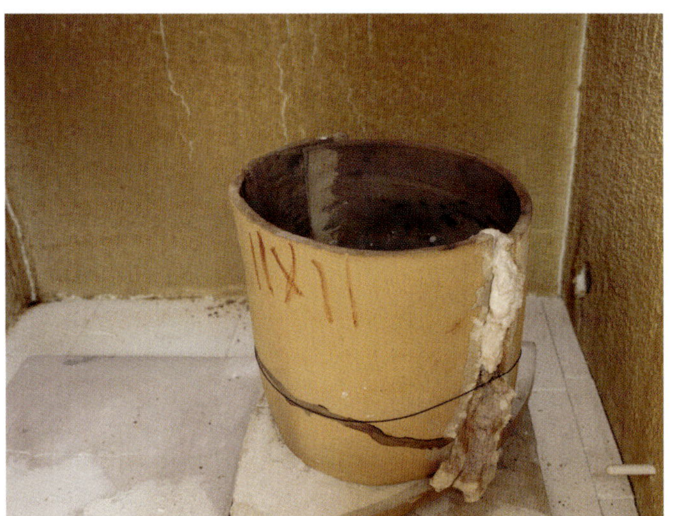

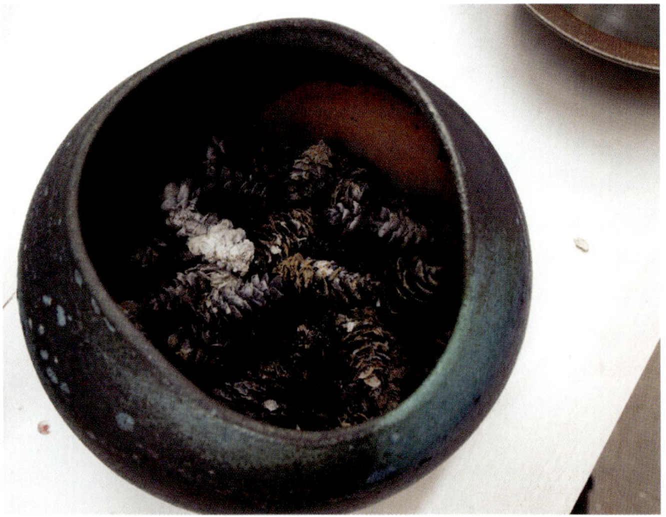

Because the piece was glazed, I opted to put combustibles and a bit of copper carbonate in the interior only. This way, the reduction would be a bit lighter, and I would see more clearly the results of the flame.

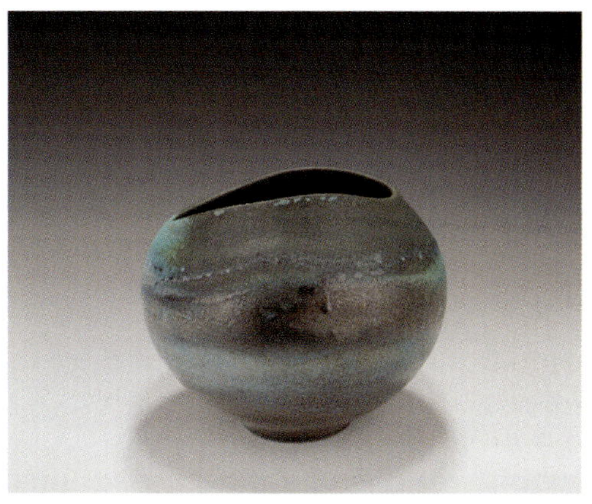

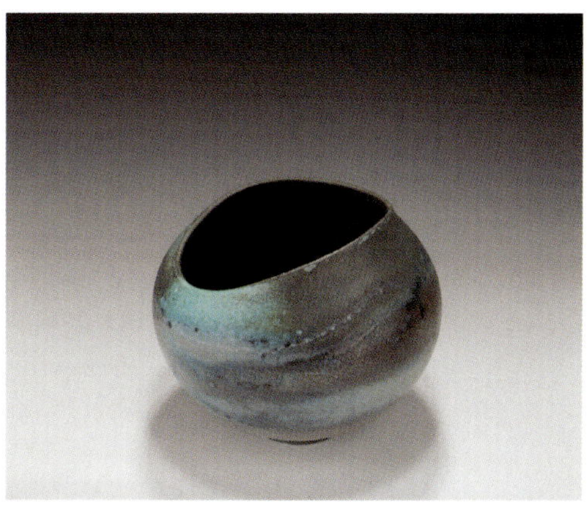

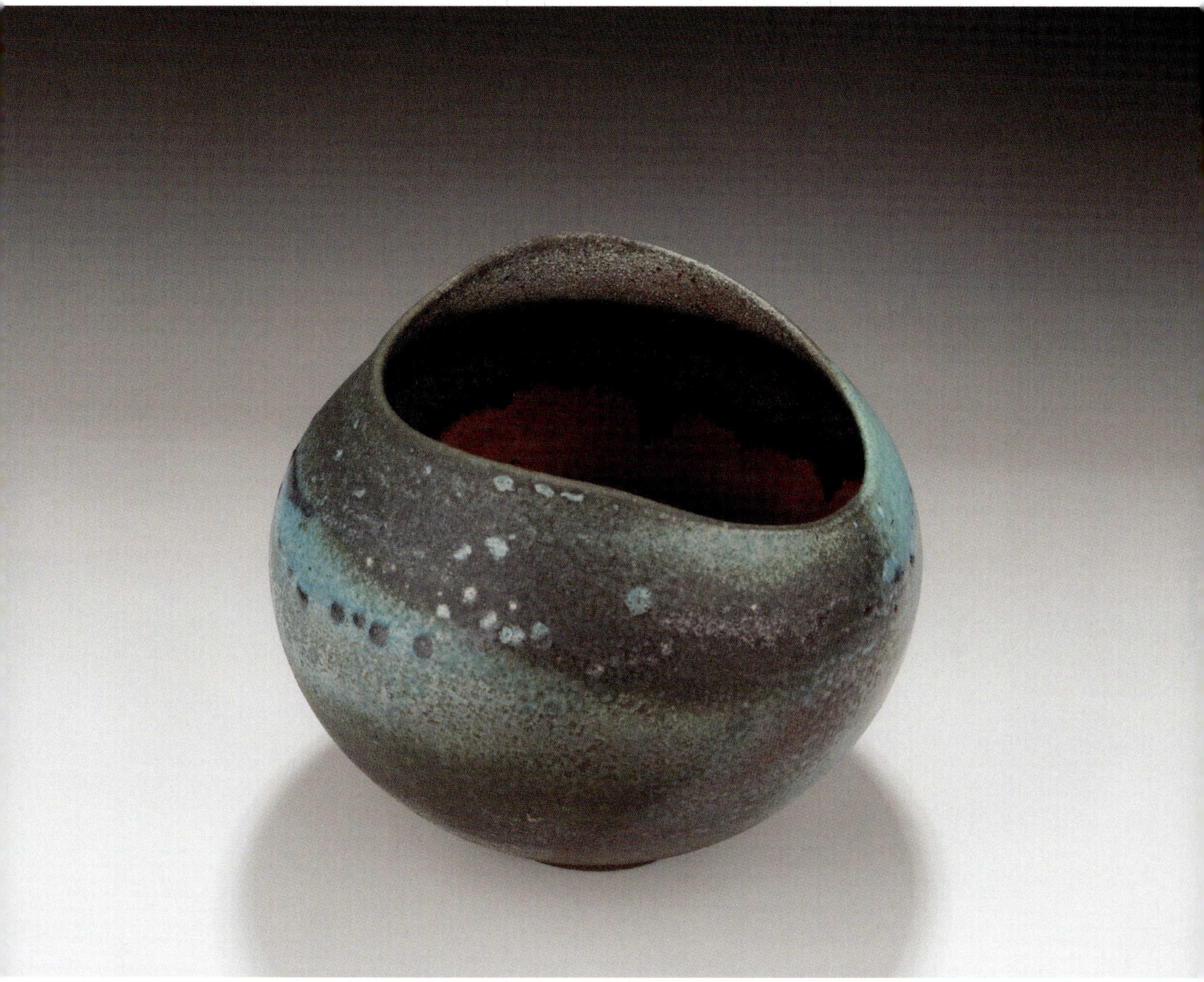

The effects from the flame varied on different areas of the vessel. Where the reduction was heavier, the effect reminded me of raku. Naturally, I wanted to learn more by trying this again, but as I had several other ideas percolating, I needed to put this exploration on hold. One idea kept tugging at me, though, so I let myself do one more experiment before moving on. Off I went in search of another sacrificial pot.

Altered Vessel, multiple layers of glaze and firings both in oxidation and reduction, final firing saggar, 22 cm W × 20 cm T.

Oh, the number of pots that have been offered up in my quest for learning! I can almost hear you saying, "There's nothing wrong with that piece—leave it alone!" And, indeed, there was nothing wrong with it. I chose it because it was in the first saggar firing I did after getting the Blaauw and I had forgotten a crucial step—applying a base layer of white terra sigillata. That base layer makes a huge difference, as it enhances and brightens the colours. Every time I looked at this piece, I remembered my mistake, so I was willing to sacrifice it—and take a chance on turning it into something even cooler!

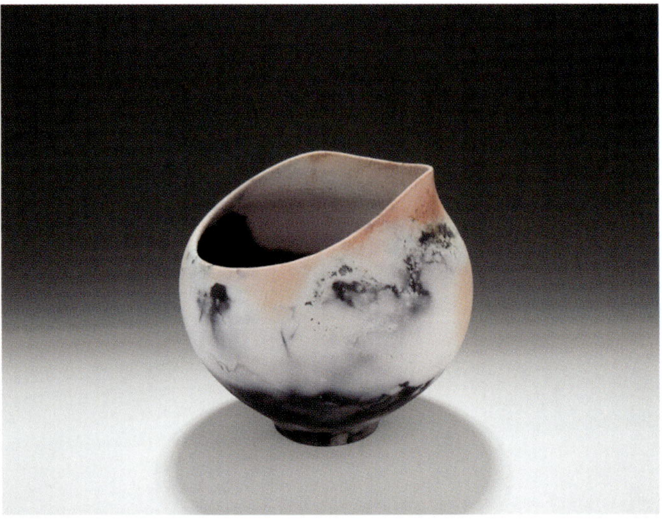

I added a sprinkling of borax to the surface to give it a bit of a sheen, then added combustibles. Most of the combustibles were in the interior of the pot, with only a small amount around the outside.

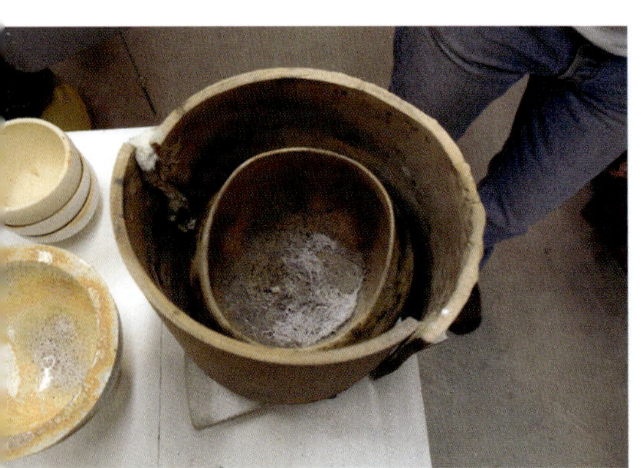

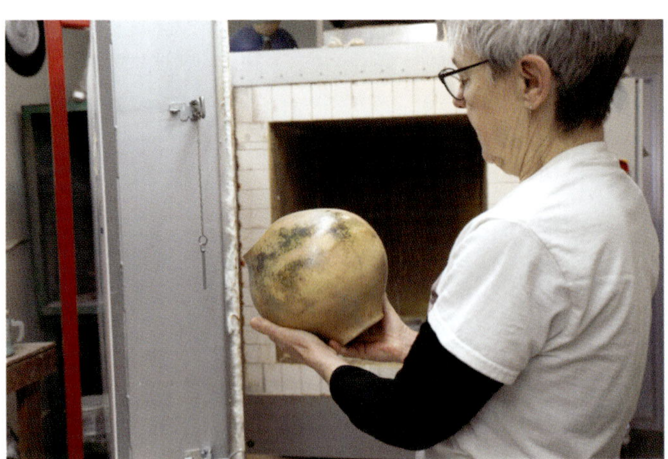

Considering results. The saggar had opened up a fair bit during the firing, and I pinned the lacklustre results on the small amount of combustibles around the outside of the vessel.

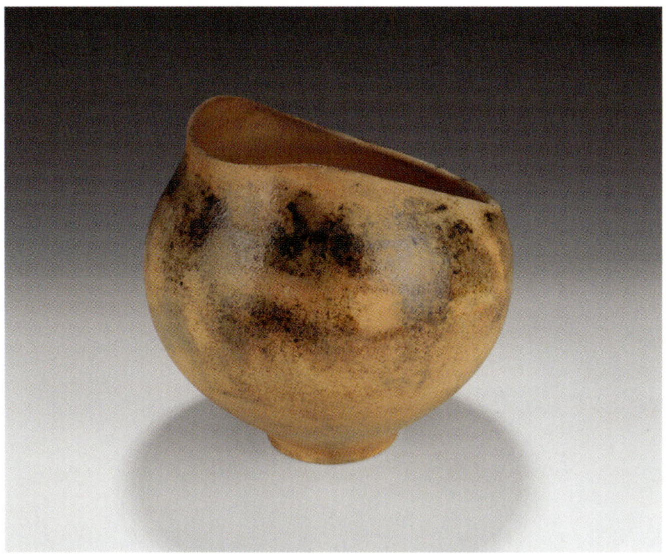

When I took it out of the kiln, I found the results underwhelming. I'm sure the thought occurred to me that I should have left well enough alone. *Oh well—what to do next?*

I decided to go back to oxidation and sprayed on a light dusting of orange terra sigillata before popping it into the next bisque firing. This time, when I lifted it out of the kiln, I was pleasantly surprised. It immediately began to inspire new ideas, but I put those on the back burner for another day.

Altered Vessel, multifired in reduction and then oxidation, 22 cm W × 23 cm T.

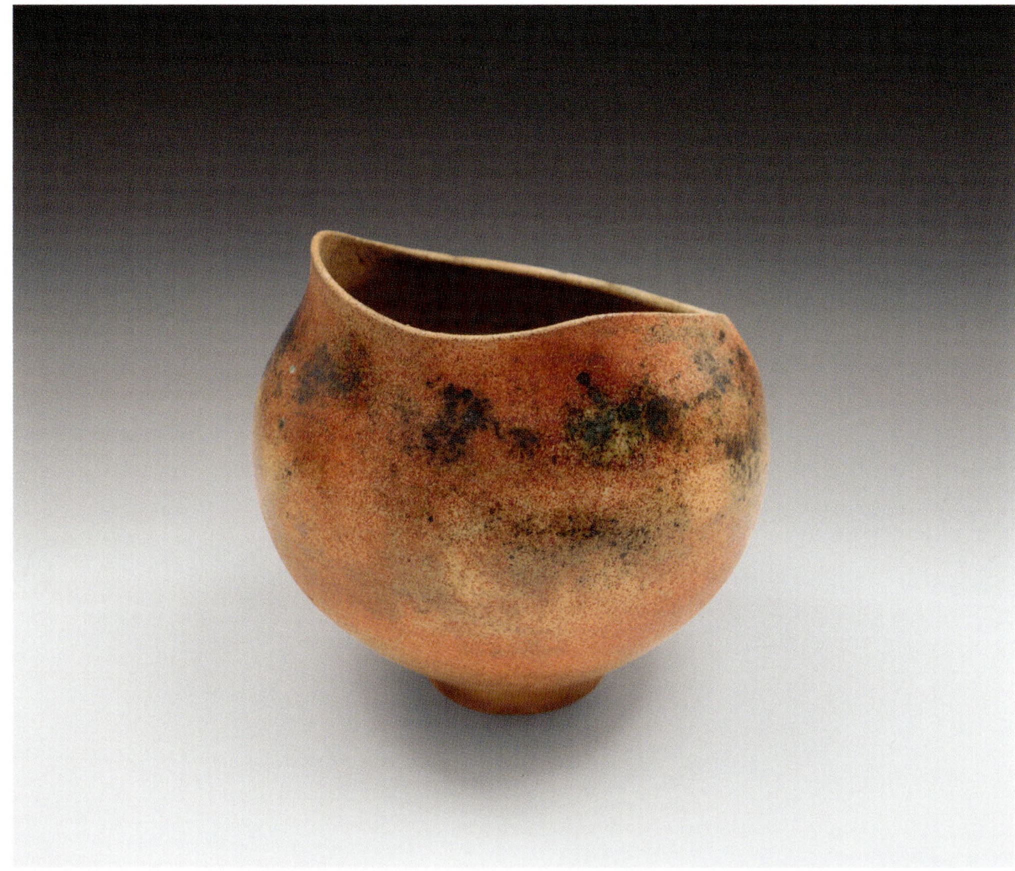

Then, months later, another day came. I was dusting pots, a never-ending job around here, and as I lifted up this vessel, I thought of one more thing I would like to try. Down to the creation room I went with my "sacrificial pot" and started to play. Here are the steps I took that day. Once more, I was glad that I took the risk.

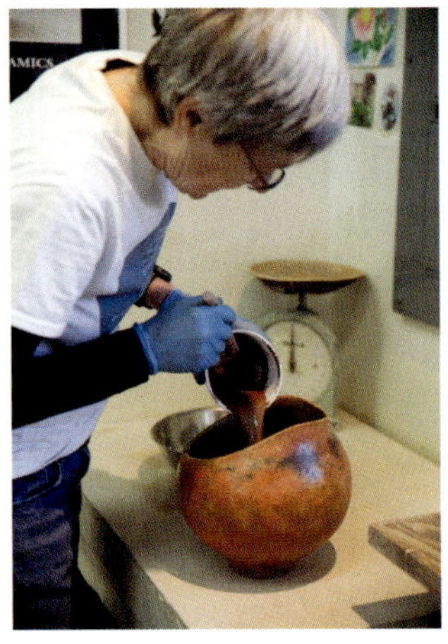

1 I start by giving the interior a thin coat of orange terra sigillata. And while it is still wet, I start to sprinkle borax on the interior.

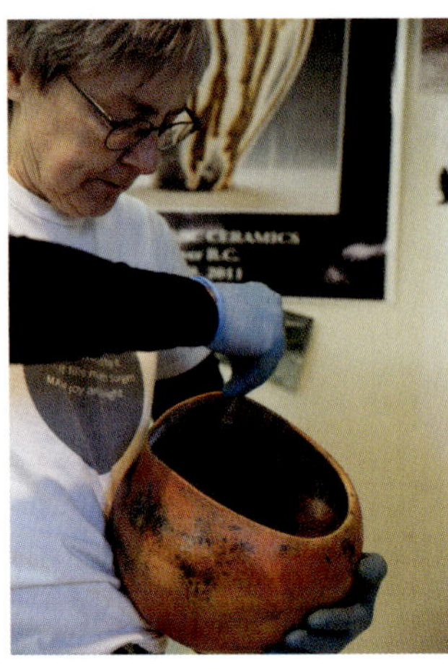

2 Turning the pot as I go, sprinkling away.

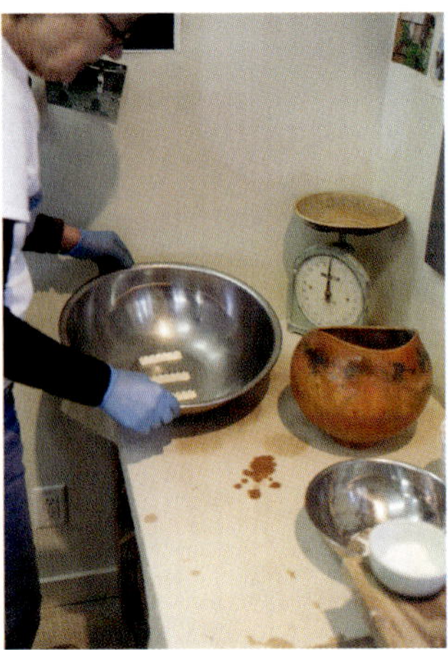

3 I put some kiln stilts in the bowl to balance the vessel when it's time to sprinkle borax on the exterior.

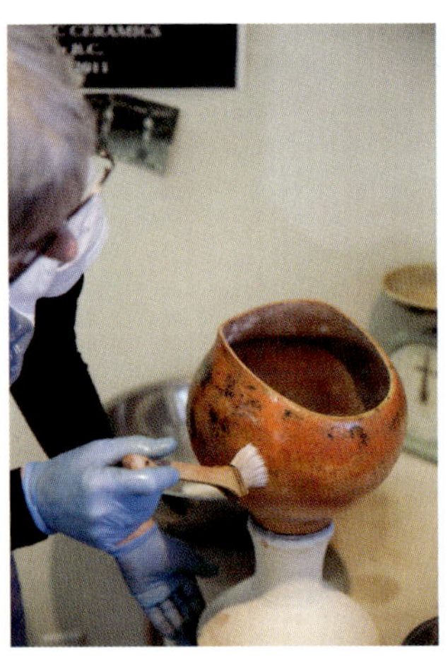

4 Brushing on a layer of gum.

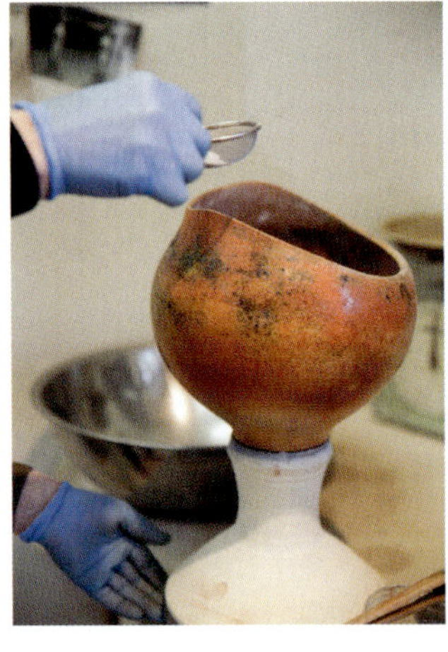

5 Sprinkling borax and some copper-lithium blend.

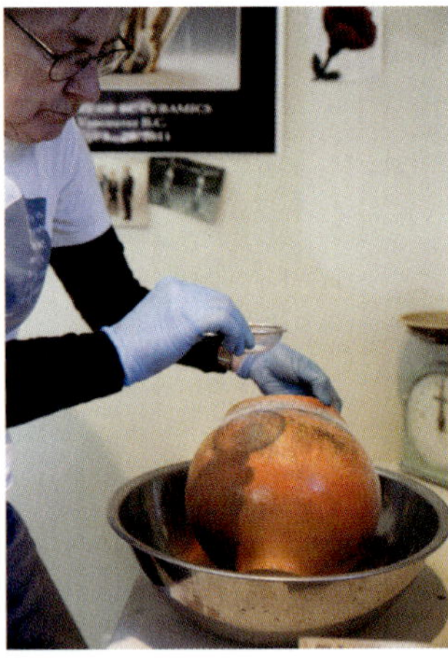

6 I balance it on the kiln stilts and sprinkle anywhere I haven't coated yet.

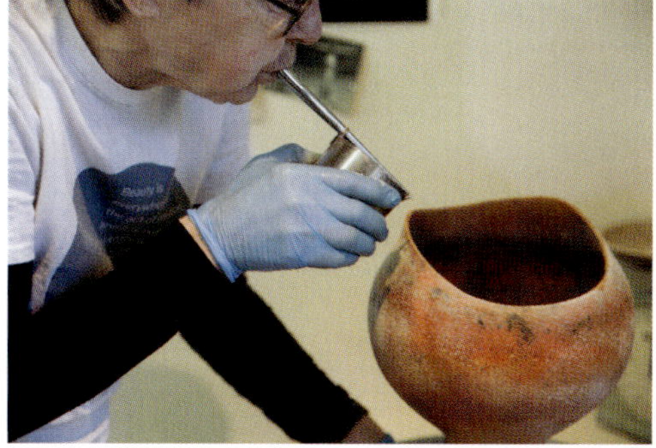

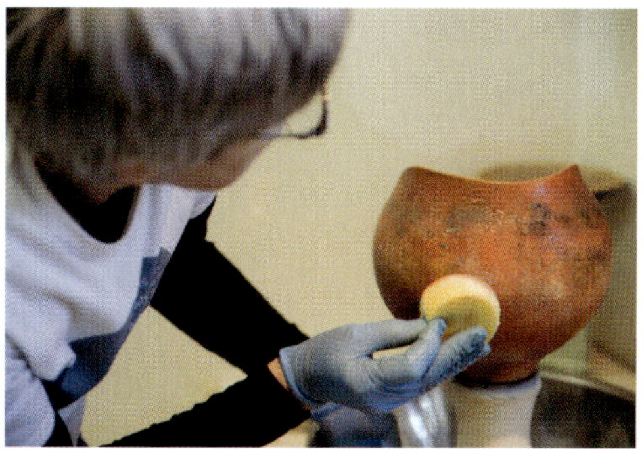

7 Spraying some more sigillata over what has been applied up till now.

8 I take a look and am not happy with the sigillata drips, I quickly grab a sponge and dab away till you can't see the drips anymore.

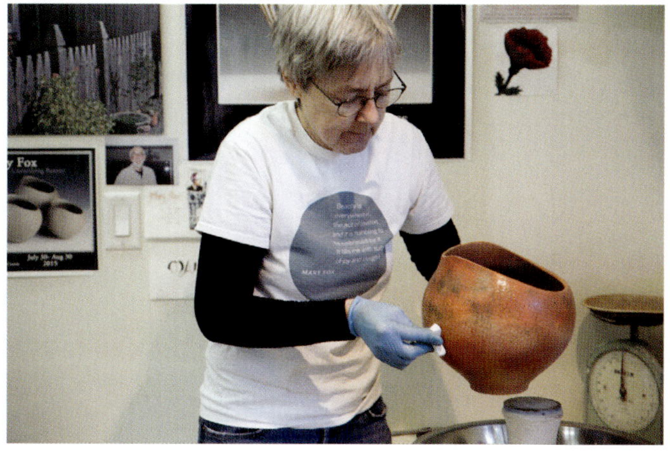

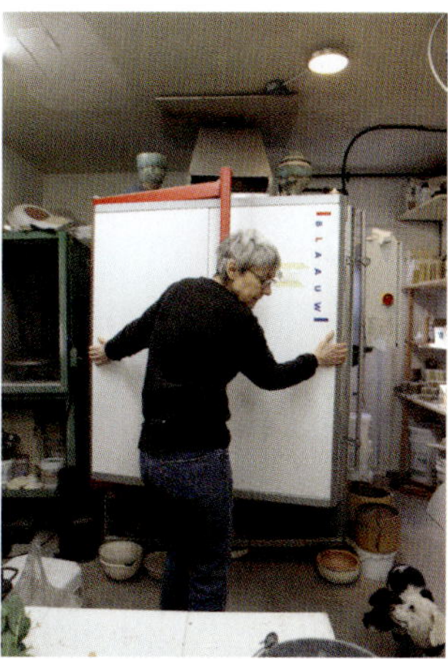

9 Carefully picking it up with the aid of kiln stilts, then off to the kiln it goes.

10 The girls are happy to see that I am closing the kiln, as they think it's quitting time.

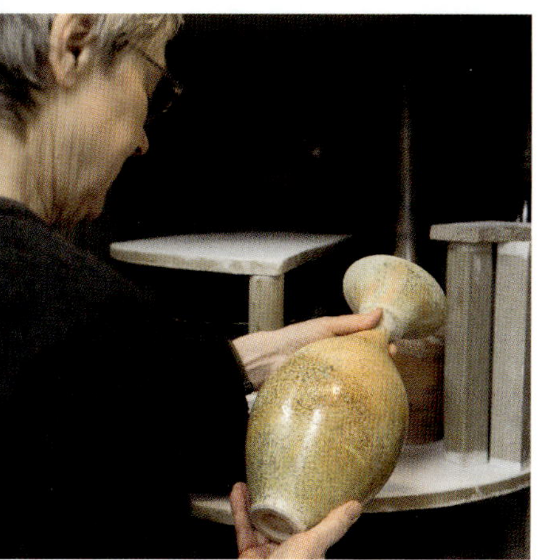

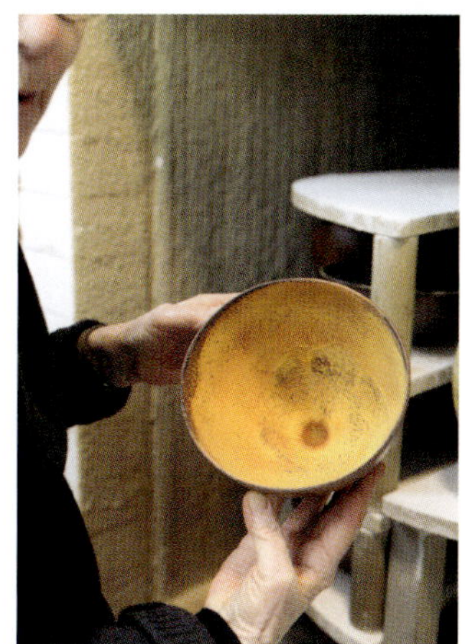

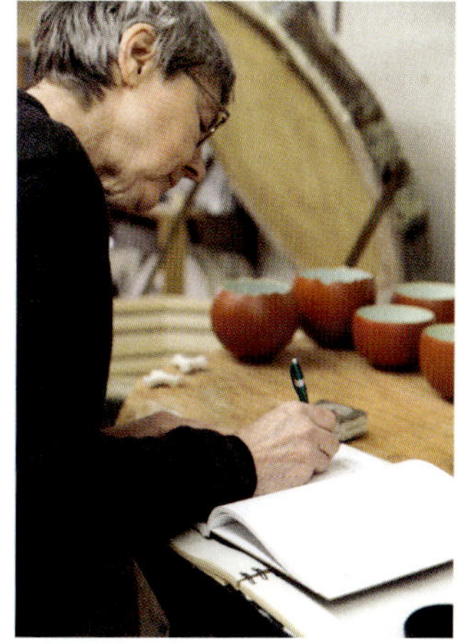

I unload the firing the next morning, making notes as I go.

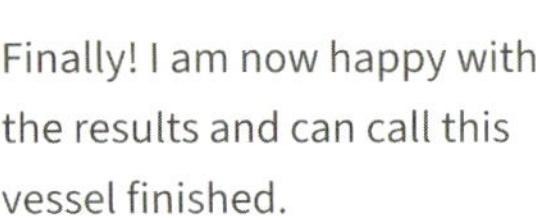

Finally! I am now happy with the results and can call this vessel finished.

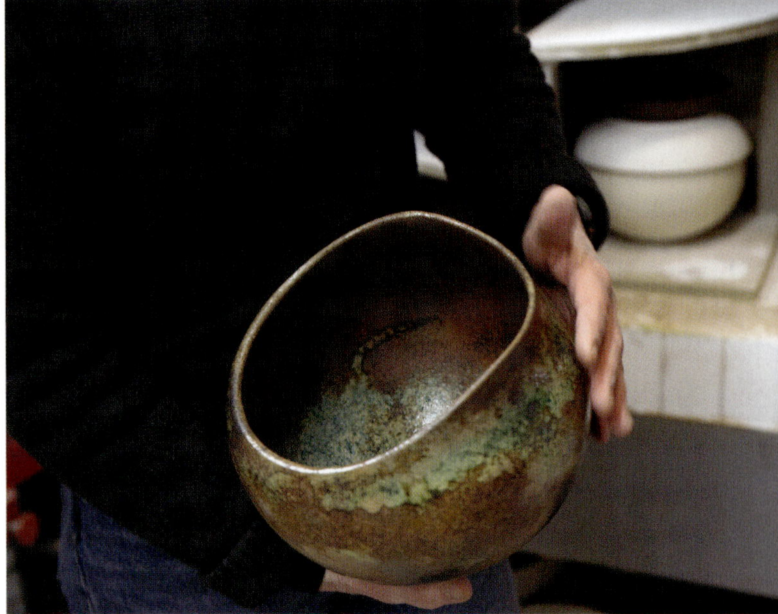

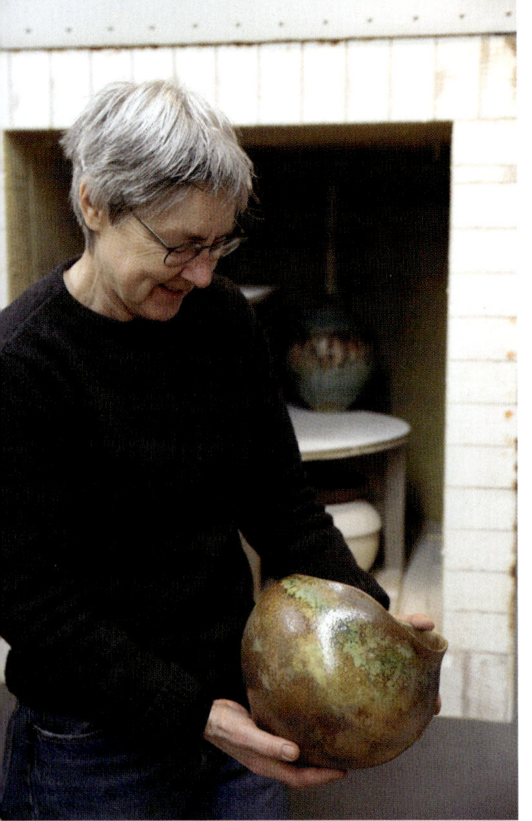

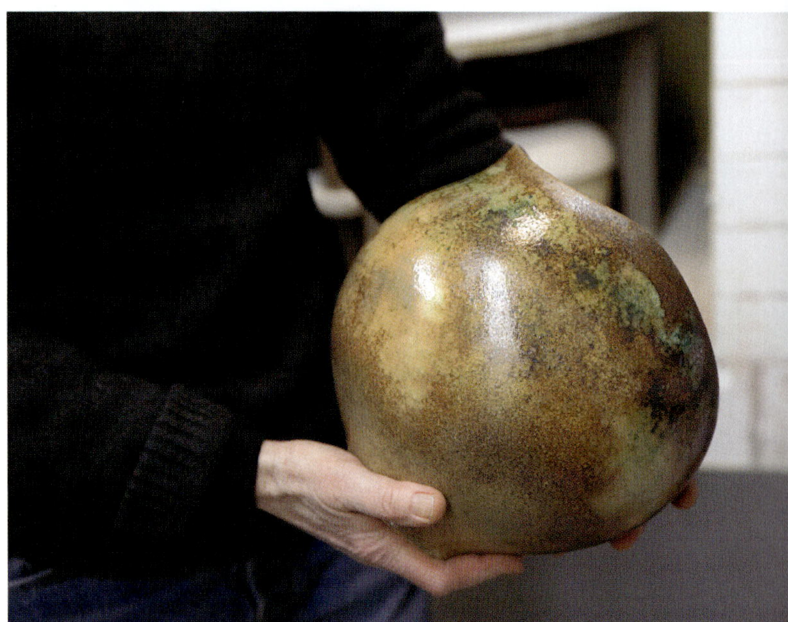

Now that I've shown you how you can play with saggars as reduction environments inside the kiln, think back to the piece that turned out looking a little like raku. In the next chapter, I describe how that outcome spurred me on to experiment further and develop techniques to produce raku-like results that I call "Faux Raku."

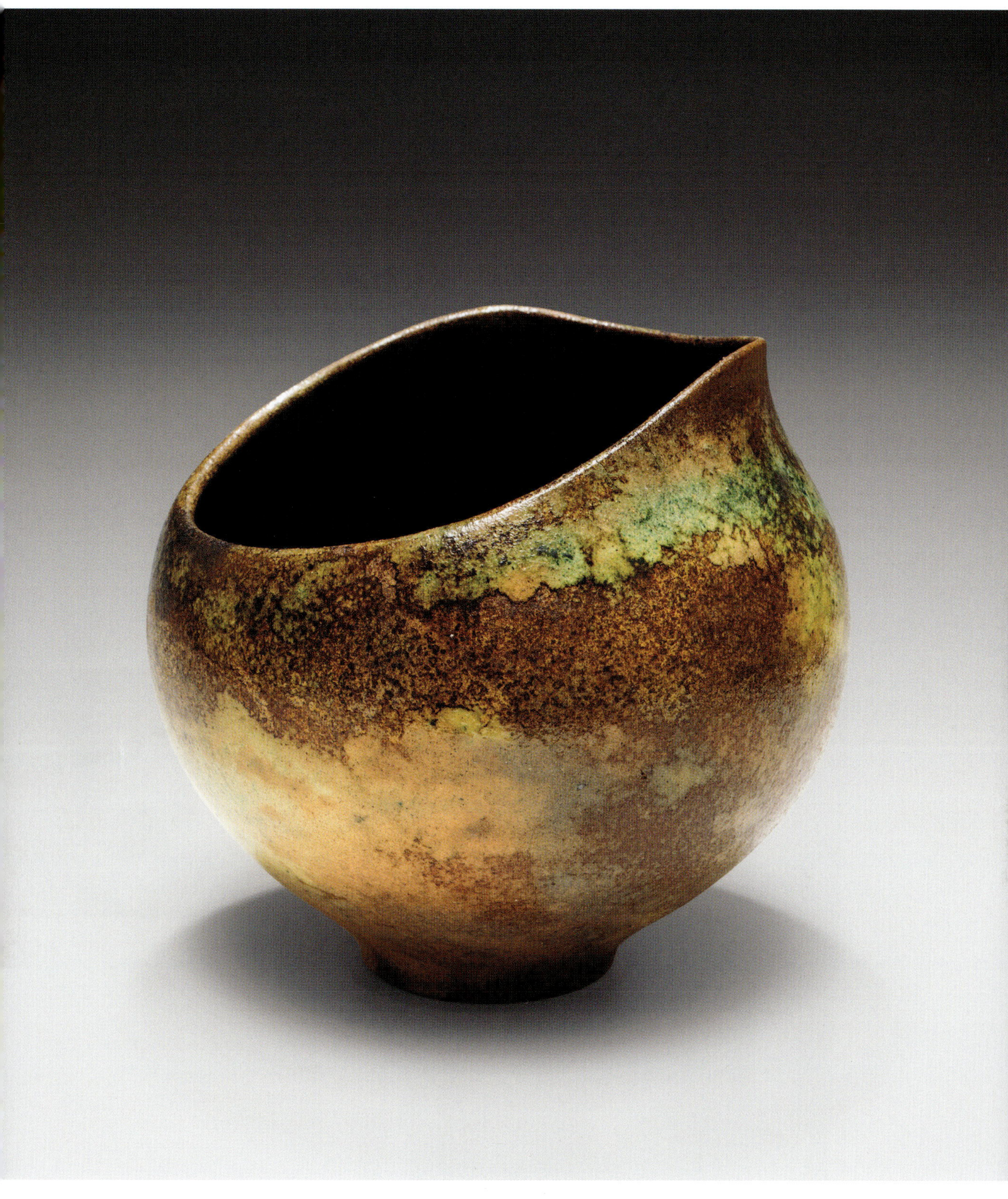

Altered Vessel, multifired in reduction and oxidation, 22 cm W × 23 cm T.

Stacking saggars—a game-changer

For years, I've made saggars either by throwing them on the wheel or constructing them from slab. Both types will start to crack after a few firings, but you can still use them many more times if you reinforce them by wrapping them with wire. These days, I throw the saggars as large cylinders and use broken kiln shelves for the bottom.

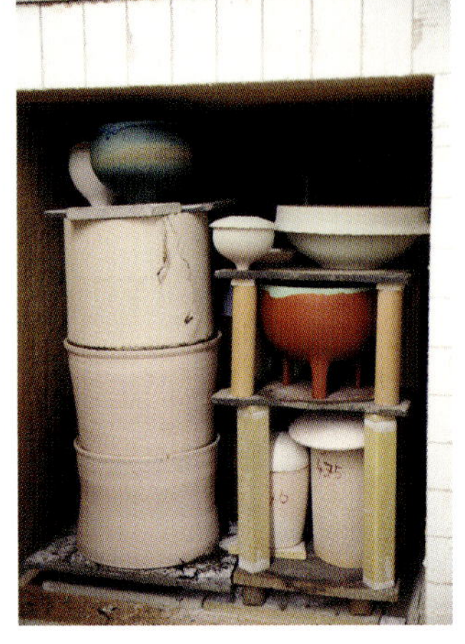

1 Packed and ready to fire.

My first stacking saggar was designed to fit my tall bottle vases and the largest slip-cast chalices that I make. As is often the case when trying something new, I encountered problems as I embarked on saggar firing these pieces, and I knew I would need to figure out some adaptations. The first issue I noticed when I started to pack the saggar for a chalice was the amount of combustibles needed to fill the void around the long, thin stem. The next challenge was how to pack the bottom section, as there was no room for my hands to get in there with the combustibles. I soon realized I needed a saggar redesign. In the meantime, I placed a narrow saggar inside the bottom saggar section and packed the stem into that. There was a lot of fiddling, but eventually I got it all packed and into the kiln.

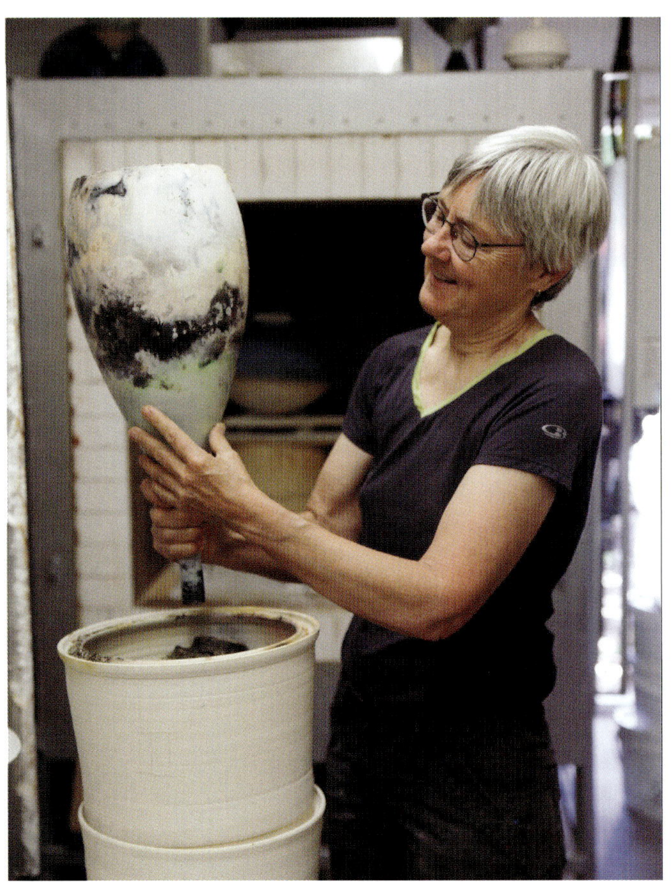

2 The reveal.

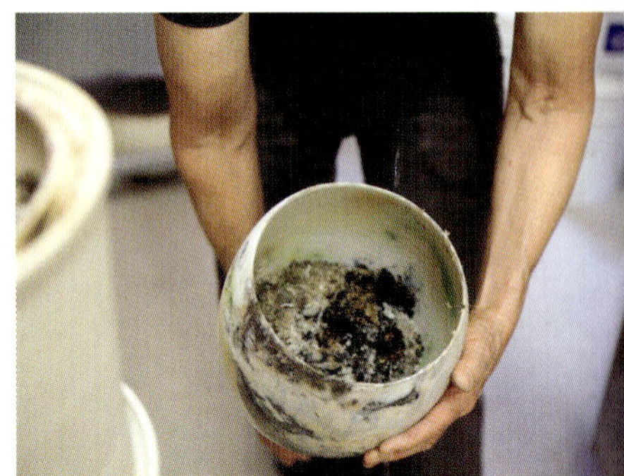

3 The remnants—the saggar and chalice were crammed full of combustibles, and this shows you how much they burn down. To promote the beautiful pink flashing achieved in saggar firing, you need air gaps to develop during the firing. I pack the combustibles with this in mind, placing larger sticks or pieces of wood where I want to promote air gaps. As the filling burns down, the larger pieces will block some of the sawdust from falling down, creating the conditions for flashing.

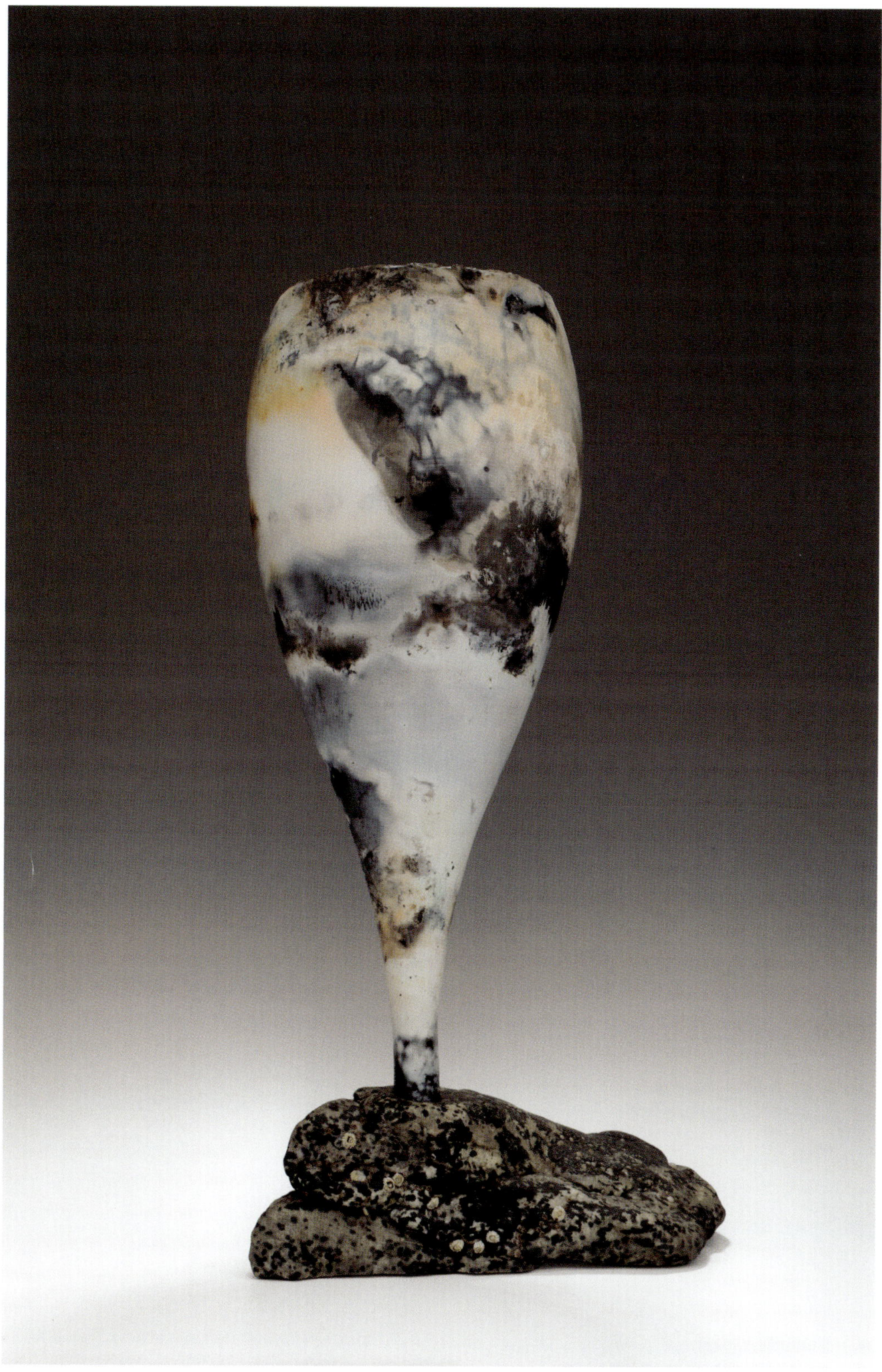

After the experience of firing the large chalice using two saggars, I realized that I would have more options packing the saggars if I had a stackable assortment of different sizes. Apprentice Sarah Wilson was charged with the job of creating them. When we were ready to do another reduction firing, I chose a previously fired piece to experiment on.

Fire Storm, clay, sawdust, seaweed, wood, copper carbonate, saggar fired, mounted in rock; chalice: 20 cm W × 53 cm T; rock base: 20 cm W × 11 cm T × 27 cm L.

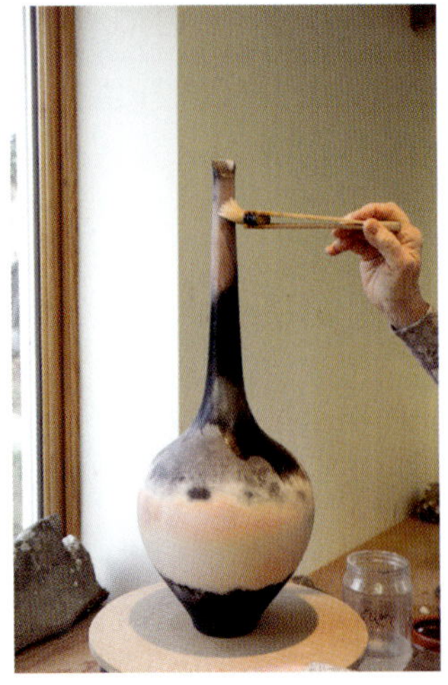

1 Brushing on gum.

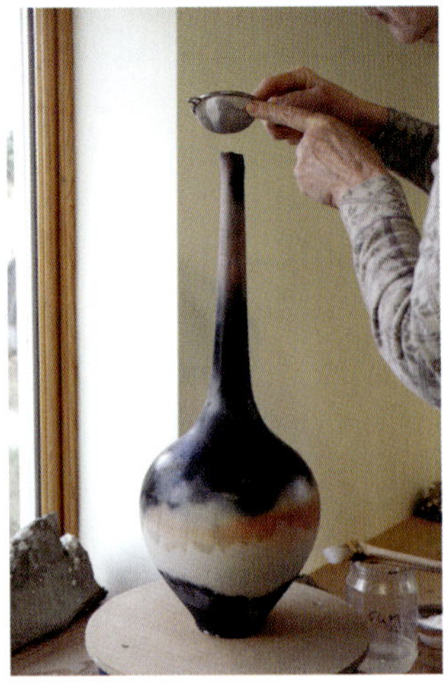

2 Sprinkling borax from above, so that it settles on the shoulder of the bottle.

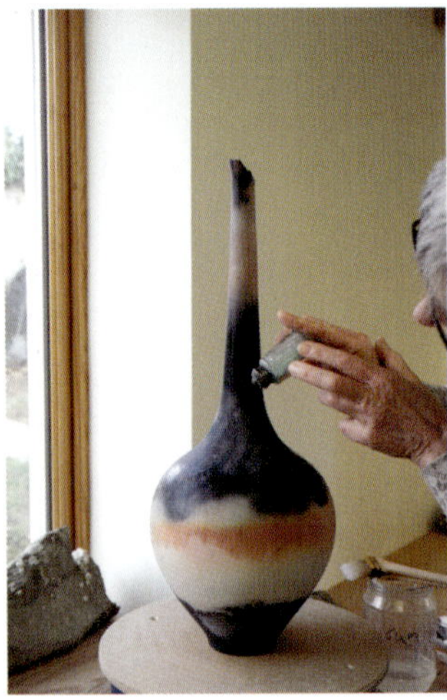

3 Adding copper carbonate.

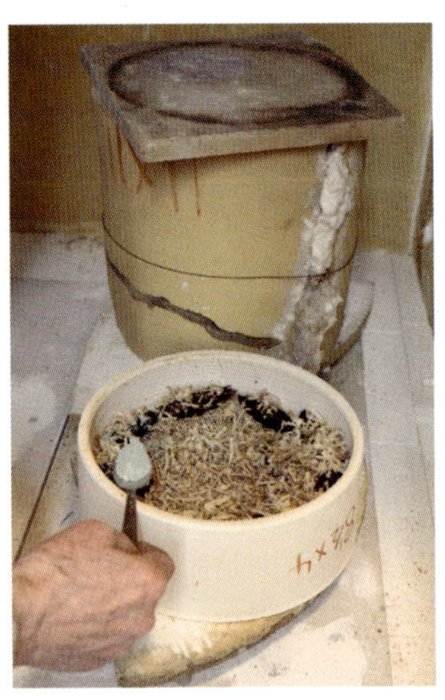

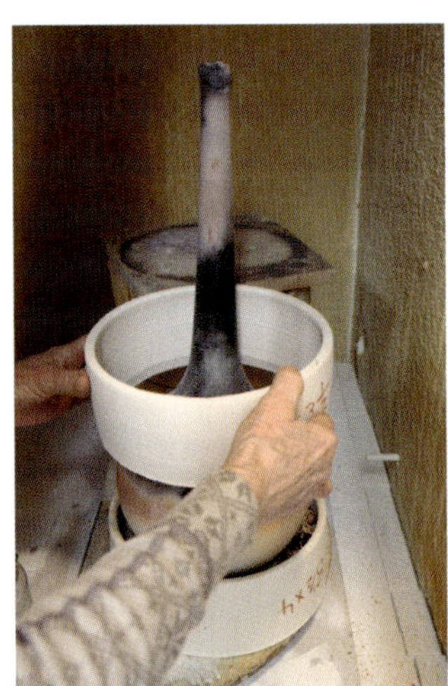

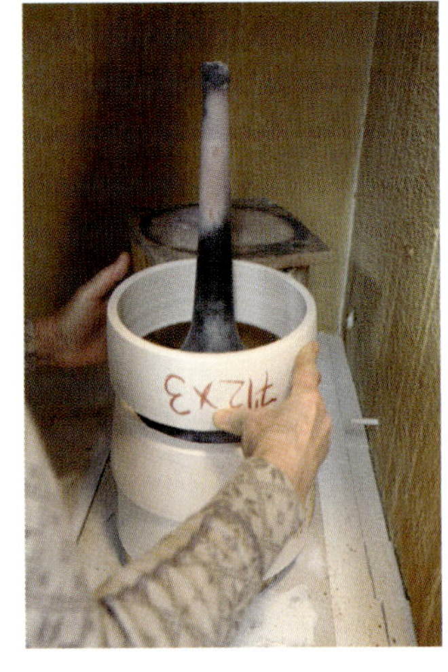

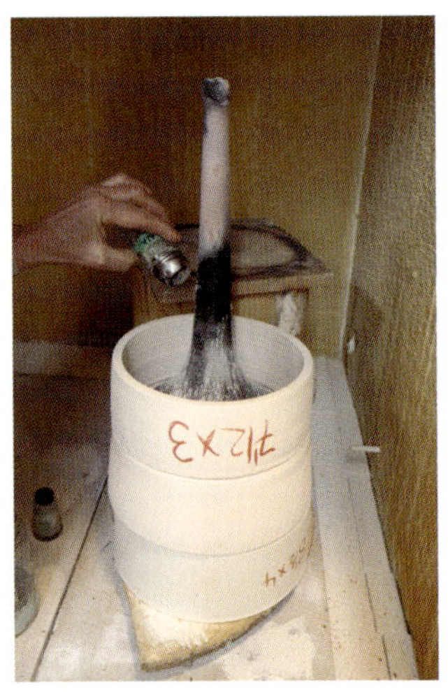

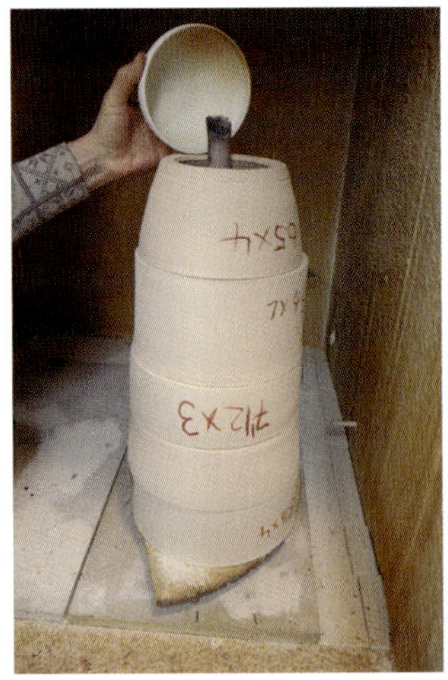

9 The stacked saggar loaded in the kiln.

4–8 Adding copper carbonate to the bottom saggar ring, then stacking saggars and adding combustibles, plus a bit more copper carbonate, until I get to the top where I add the cap.

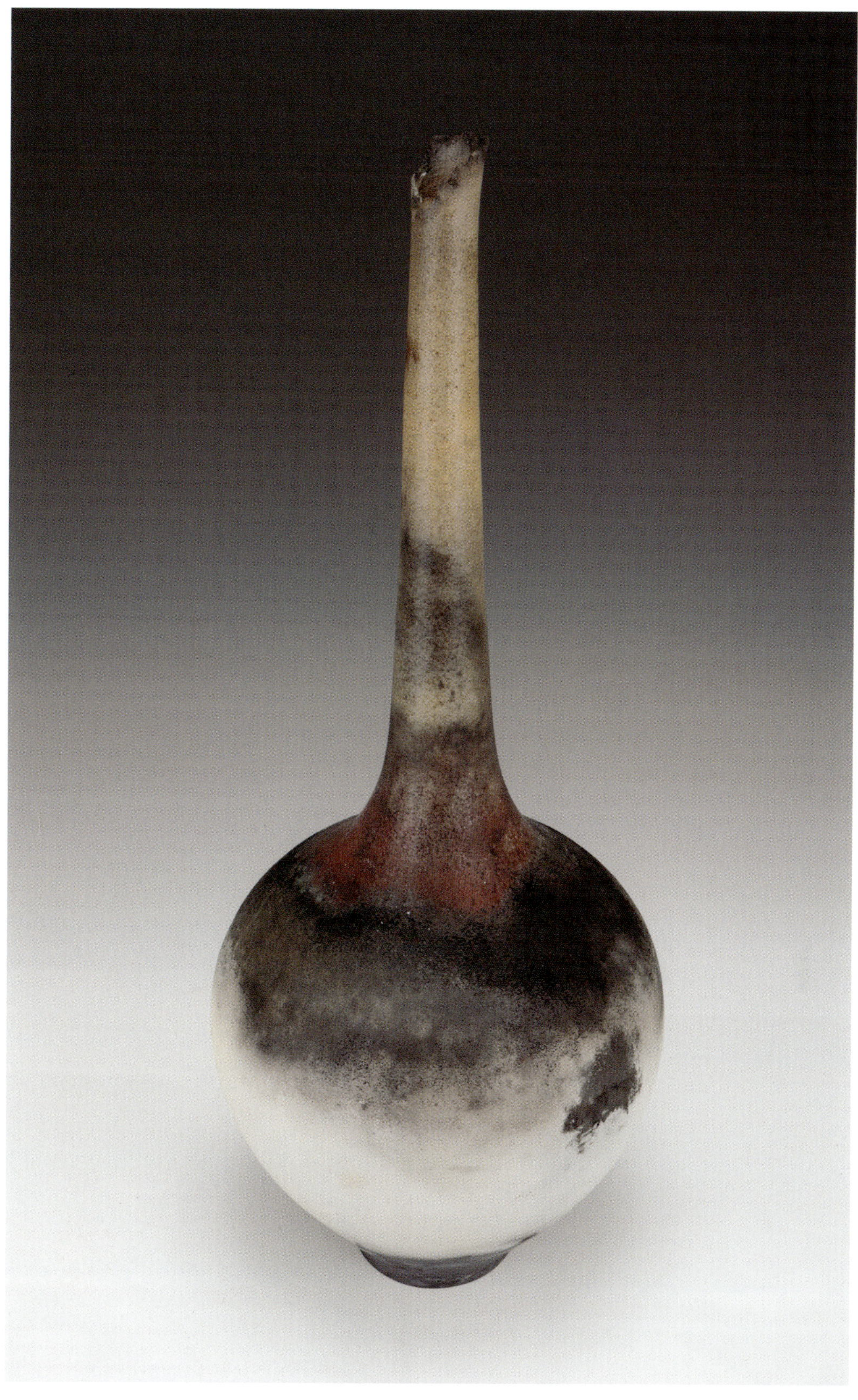

Bottle Vase, borax, copper carbonate, combustibles, cone 05, saggar fired twice, 20 cm W × 55 cm T.

I really was quite happy with how the bottle vase had turned out and didn't think I was going to go back to it. However, I change my mind at the drop of a hat. As I was loading what would be the last firing for this book, I decided to spray orange terra sigillata over the bottle and add it to the reduction firing. One is always learning—one of my favourite aspects of being a potter.

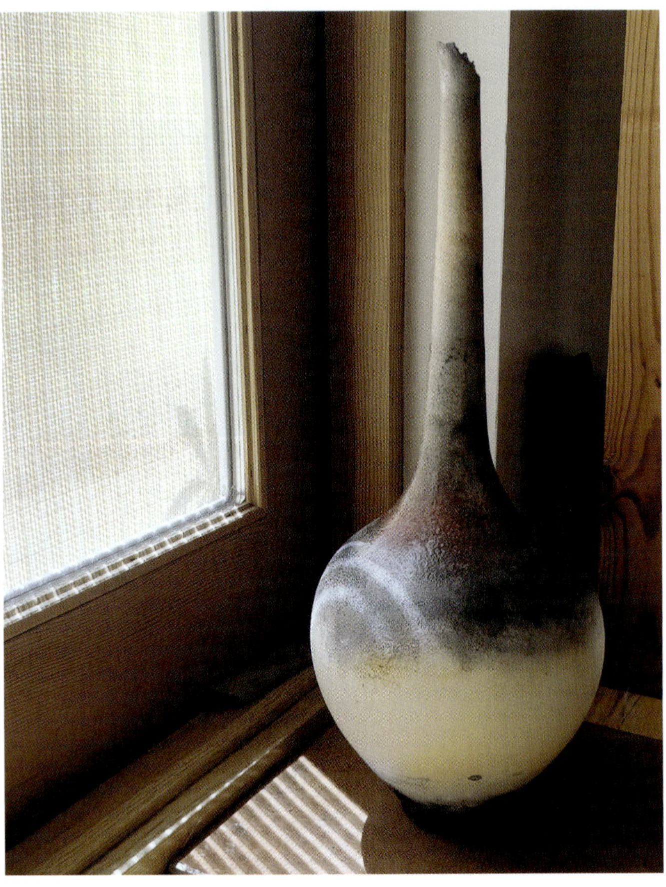

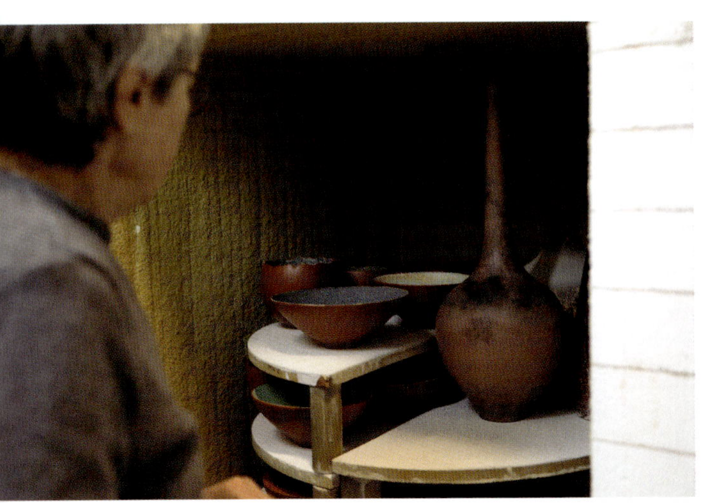

A very light dusting of orange terra sigillata; let's see what that does!

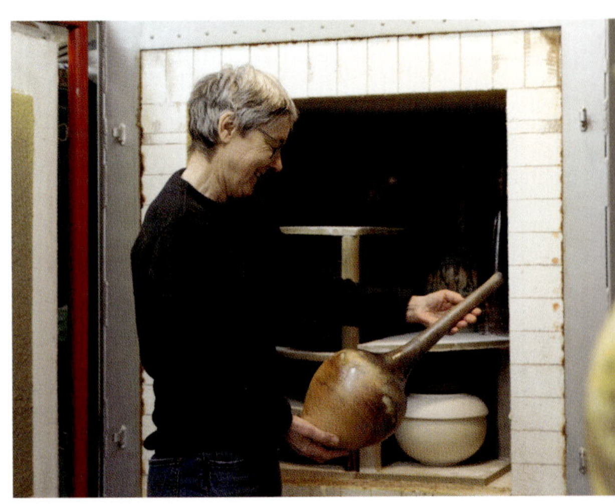

Some risks are worth taking.

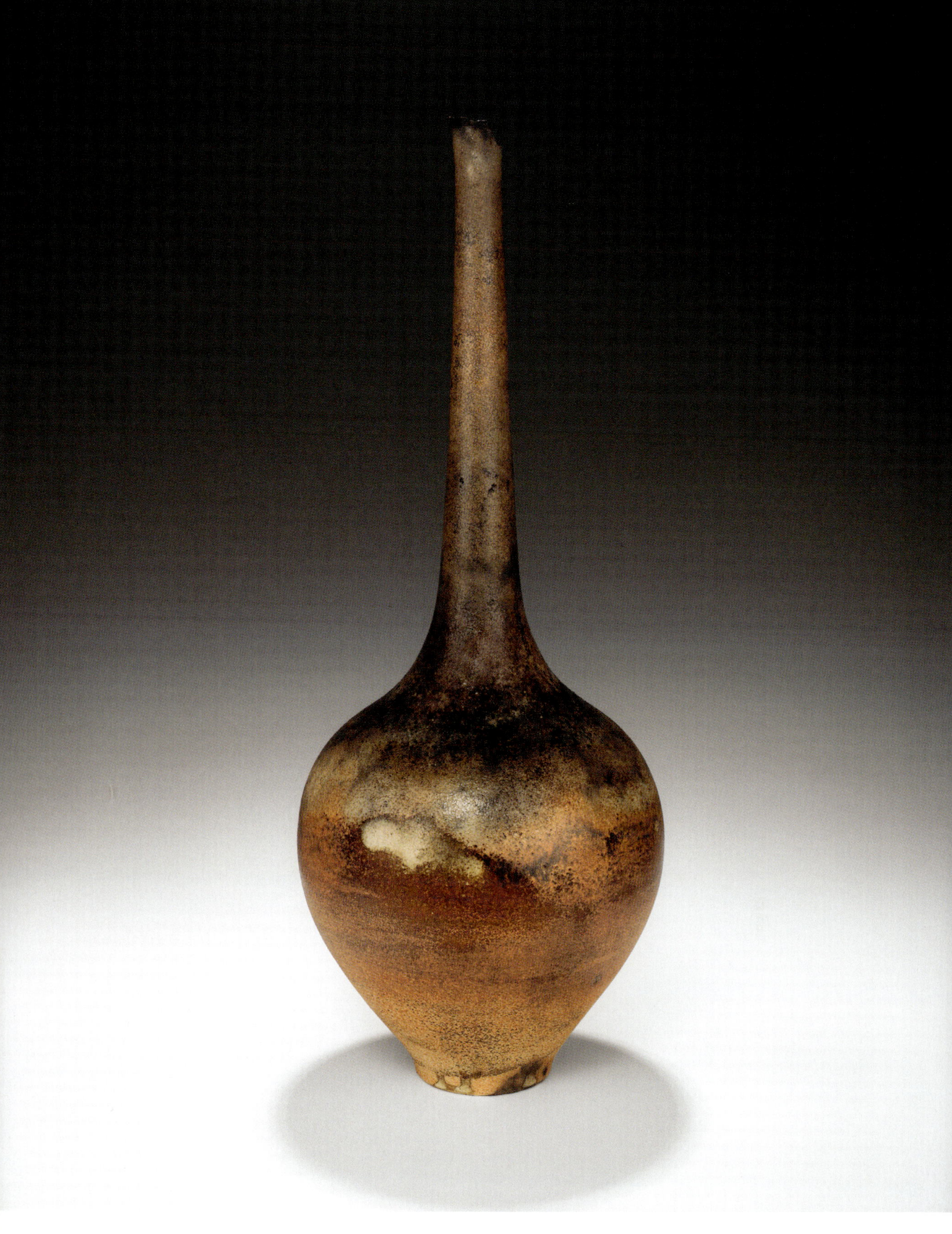

Bottle Vase, multiple saggar firings, copper carbonate; final firing, coat of orange terra sigillata sprayed overall, reduction fired, 04, 20 cm W × 55 cm T.

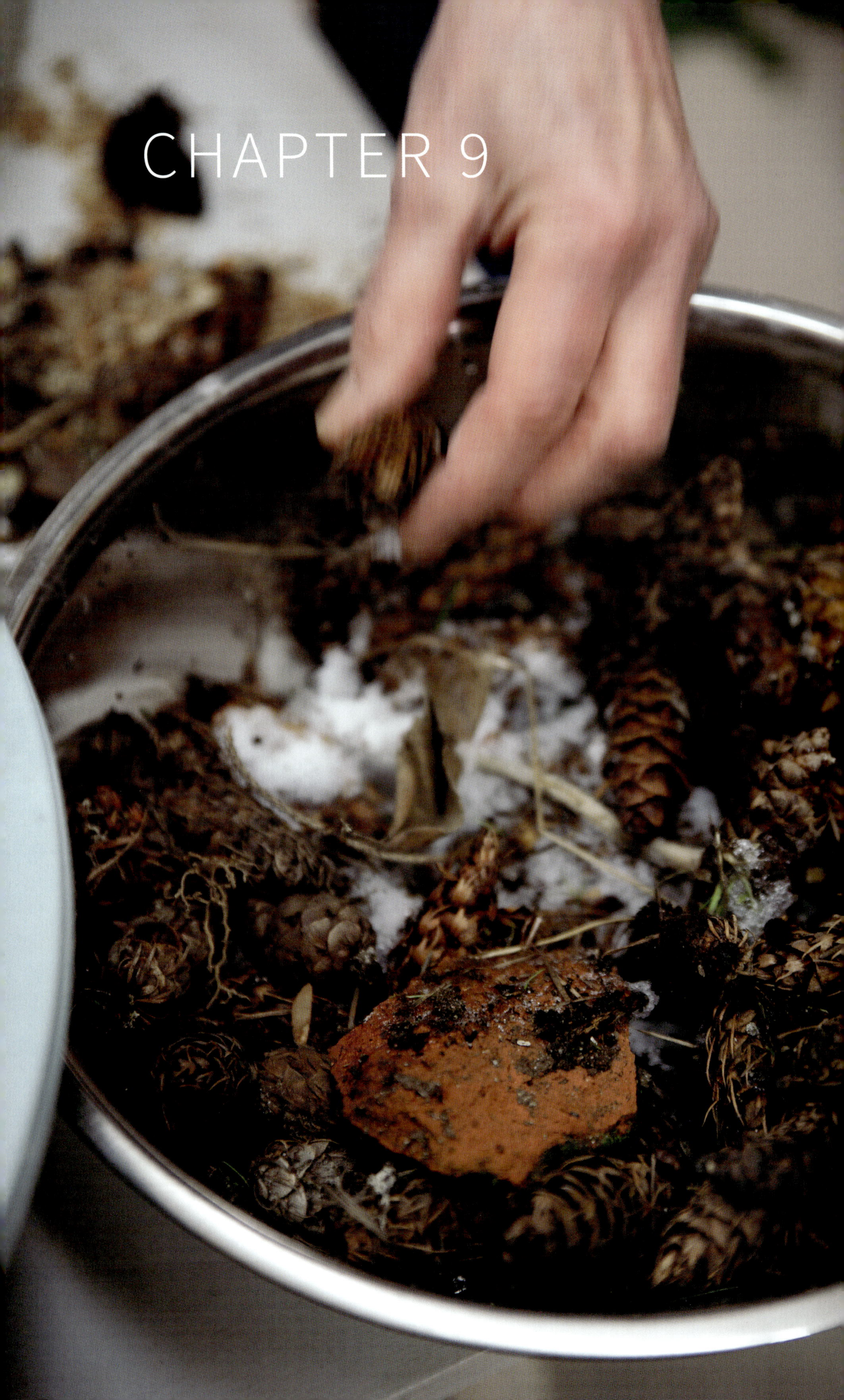

CHAPTER 9

EMULATING RAKU

Raku finishes can be eye-catching, and the traditional raku process is fast, relatively easy and has elements of the mysterious and unknown, so no wonder potters gravitate to it. As I mention in the previous chapter, however, having a Blaauw kiln gave me a glimpse of how low-fire reduction could create effects that were similar to raku. In this chapter, I share my exploration of this discovery.

For my first experiments, I placed the pots in the body of the kiln, sometimes firing them first in oxidation and then in reduction to compare results. Here is one of my early tests.

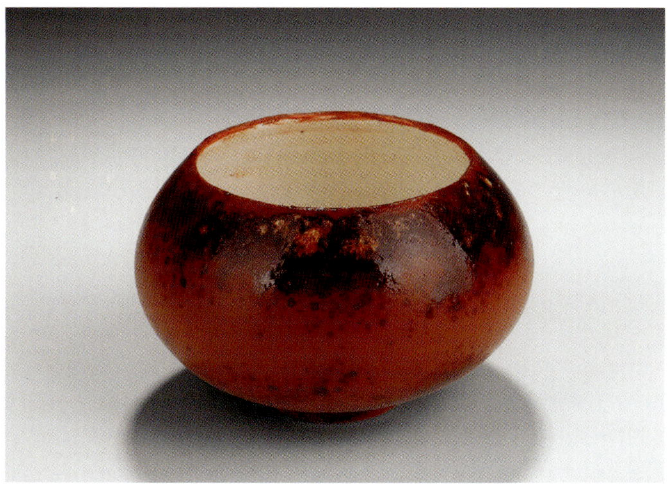

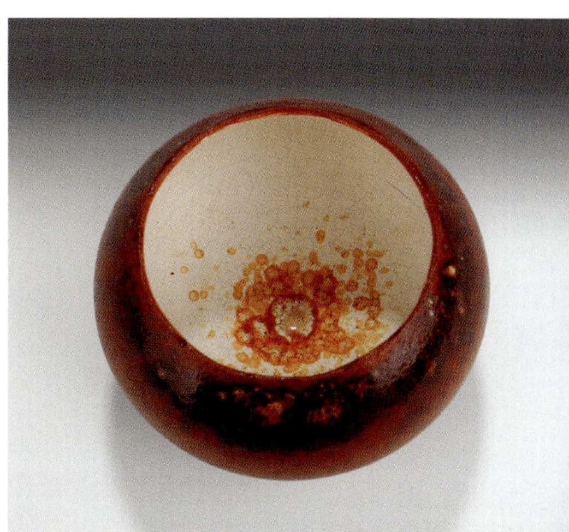

Orange and white terra sigillata, borax sprinkles, cone 05, oxidation.

Before I placed the vessel in the gas kiln to see how it would react to the reduction atmosphere, I added a light sprinkle of lithium compound to the exterior lip and interior bottom. When I lifted it out of the kiln the next day, I was pleased to find that it looked convincingly like it had been raku fired.

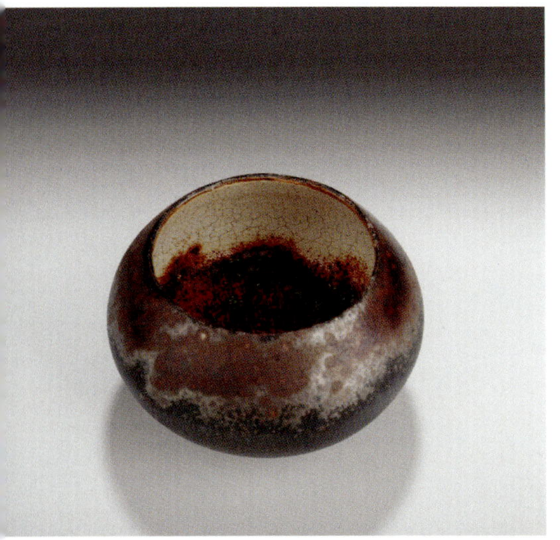

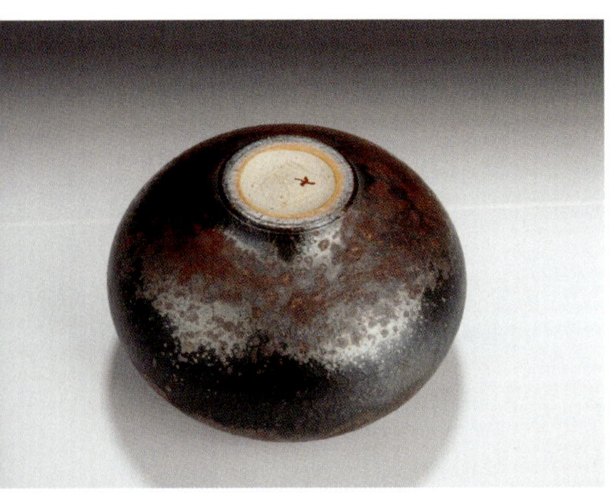

Orange terra sigillata, borax sprinkles, lithium compound, cone 05, reduction, 14 cm W × 10 cm T.

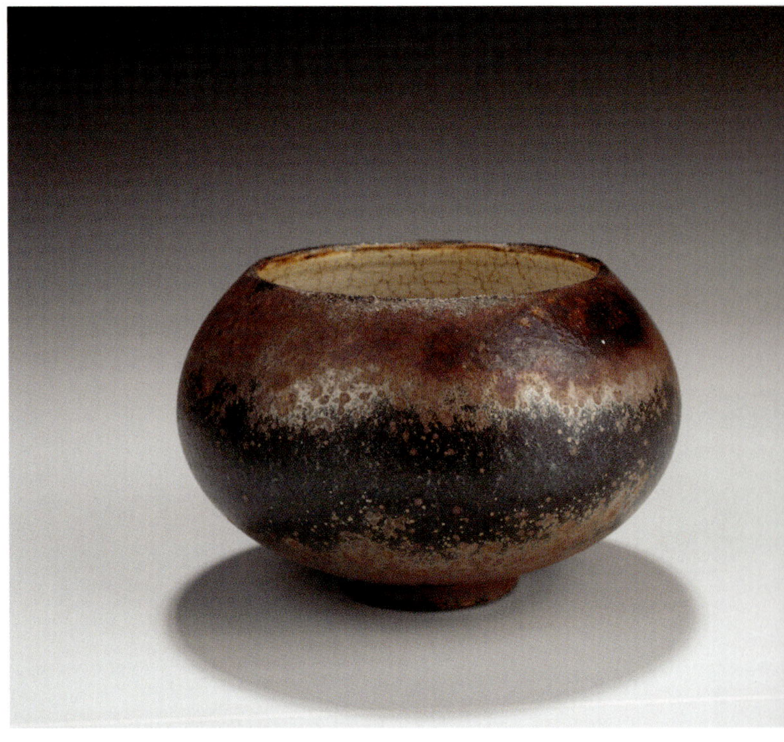

However, for the most part, my experiments with firing glazed pots in reduction weren't getting the results I had hoped for. Except for the pieces that had orange terra sigillata on them, I wasn't seeing the kind of reduction effects I had pictured. The glazes definitely looked different from when they were fired in oxidation, but the difference wasn't as dramatic as I had anticipated. It was time to try another approach.

In the '80s, when I was raku firing a fair amount, one of my favourite glazes was Copper Sand. I liked it because if you played with the amount of reduction/oxidation you could get beautiful variations that weren't like the popular oil slick look obtained by heavy reduction. The glaze had a nice dry, slightly sandy texture that varied depending on the thickness of application. Because I was somewhat familiar with the glaze, even though it had been decades since I last used it, it seemed like a good one to start with for my experiments.

I sprayed Copper Sand thickly on the upper section of a tall vessel, then gradually thinner as I worked my way down. It came out a bit underfired on the bottom half, and though I hadn't planned that result, I thought it looked pretty cool. Still, it didn't bear any resemblance to the raku-fired pots I had done years ago with this glaze. As I compared my method to the traditional raku process, I kept coming back to the fact that maybe what was missing was an enclosed environment with combustibles. *How could I achieve this and not end up with the ash from the combustibles sticking to the glaze itself?*

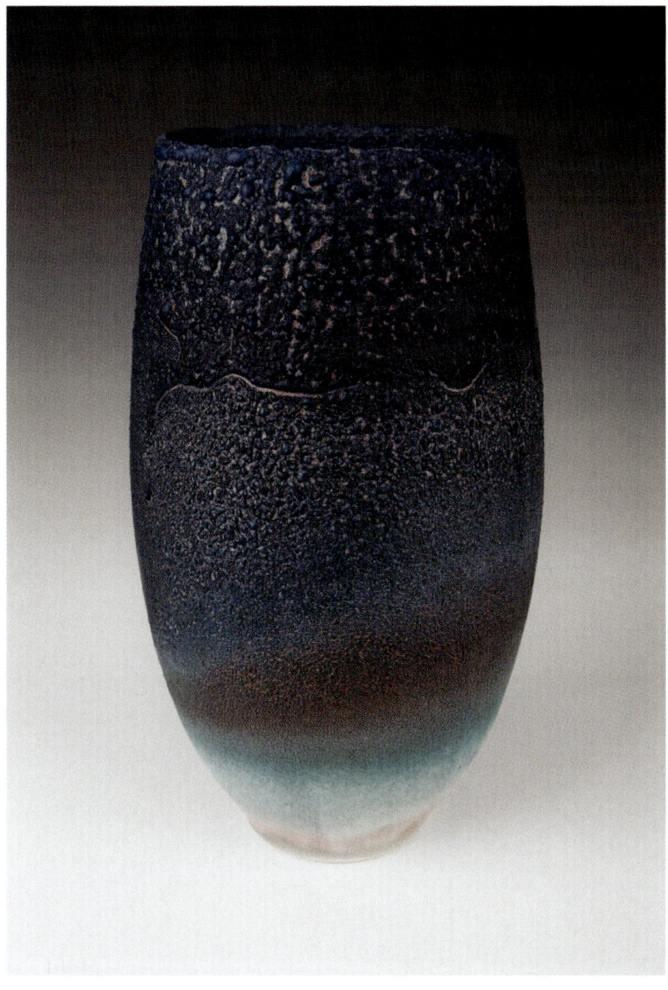

Vessel, Copper Sand glaze, reduction fired in kiln, cone 04, 10 cm W × 23 cm T.

This is what I came up with: I placed combustibles in the bottom of a saggar, put kiln posts in to keep the vessel raised above the carbon source and then put in the pot. I've tried this with the vessel upright and with it turned upside down, depending on the reduction results I am aiming for.

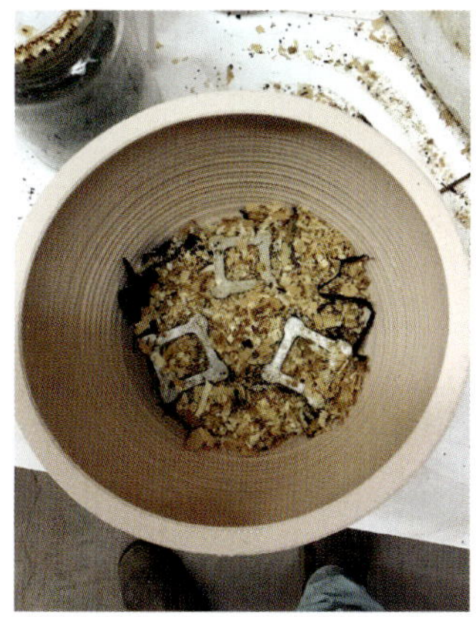

Sawdust placed in the bottom of the saggar with posts to place the pot on.

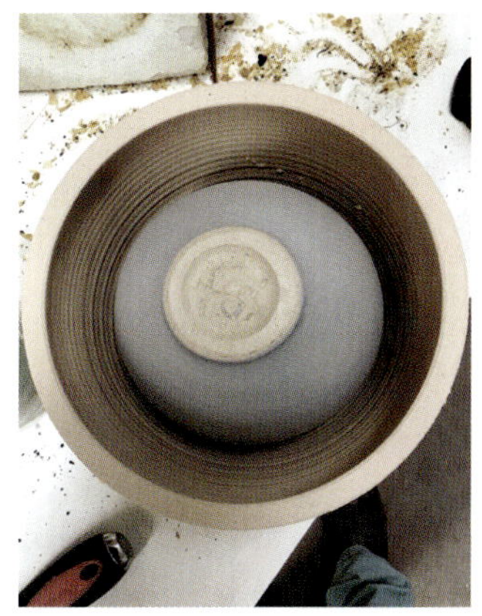

The pot placed upside down in the saggar to create heavier reduction on the inside than on the outside.

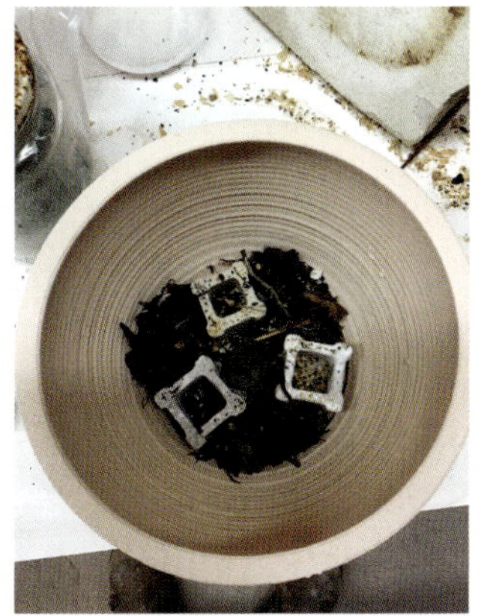

The remains of the sawdust after taking my piece out of the saggar.

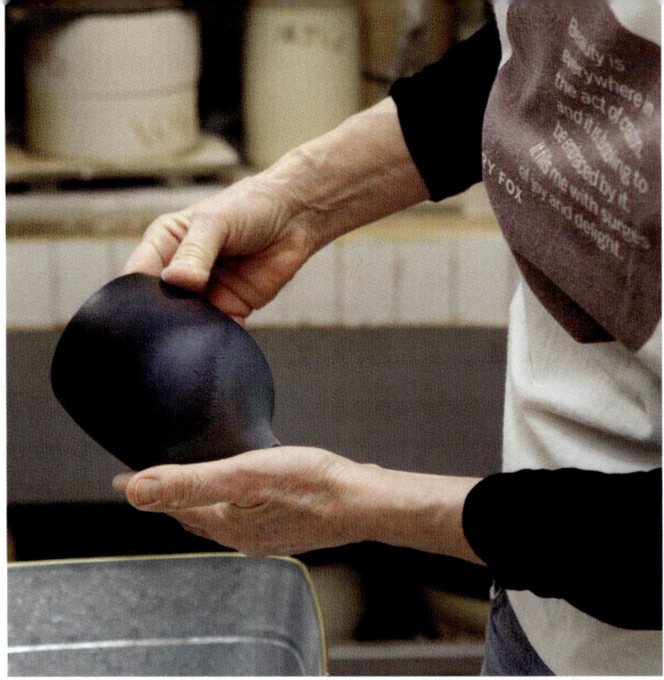

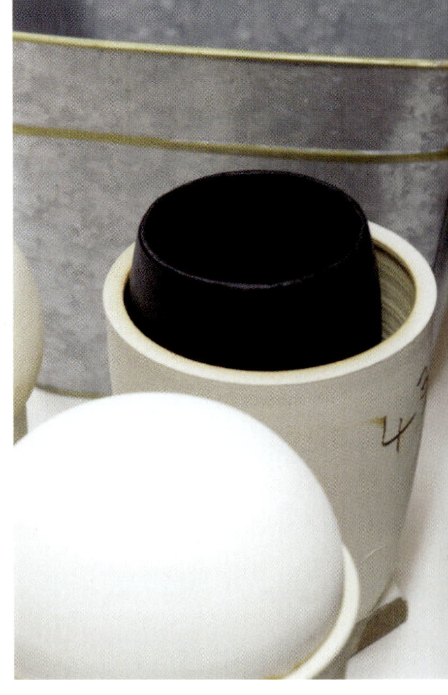

Fired using the same technique; however, this piece was fired upright in the saggar. Copper Sand was applied thinly to this vessel.

Interestingly, the dark area at the top of the vessel, that was close to the saggar wall, has influenced the colour of the glaze.

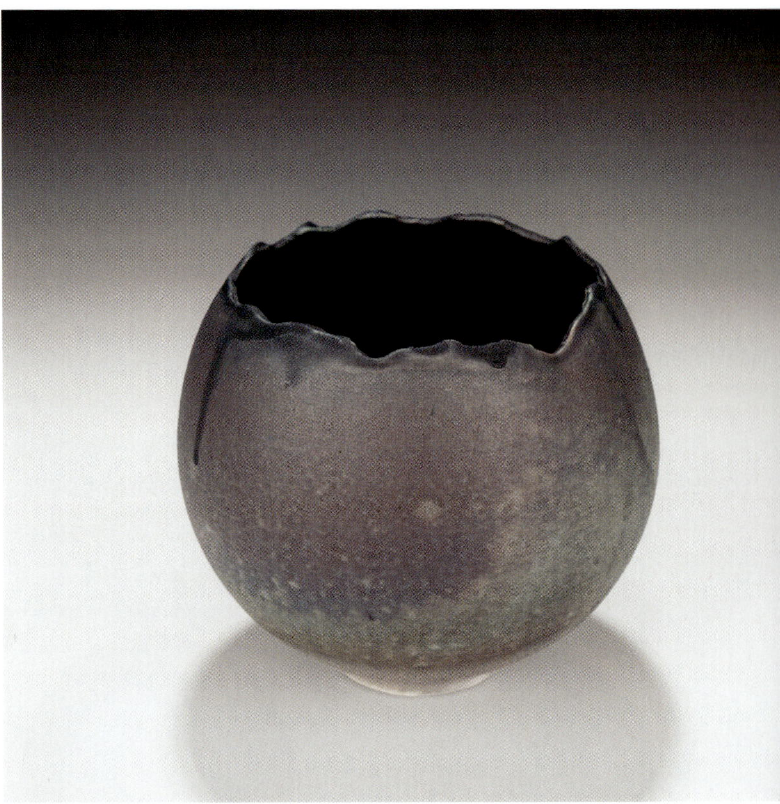

Vessel, Copper Sand glaze, cone 04, reduction/saggar, 15 cm W × 13 cm T.

I am still trying to figure out the right quantity of combustibles needed inside the saggar for this type of firing. This piece was heavily reduced, a bit too heavy in my opinion, so I made a note to use fewer combustibles next time.

Another way to approach this type of firing is to lay some sawdust on a kiln shelf with an added dish of sawdust in the centre. Use kiln posts to raise the vessel a little and place your piece upside down over the combustibles. Then put the saggar overtop. The sawdust in the dish will be contained during the firing, promoting more reduction on the interior of the vessel.

The results from placing a glazed pot in a saggar were leading me on to a new and fascinating trail. The pieces that I had raised up over the combustibles in the saggar gave me a fresh idea. I took a small chalice, glazed the top section of it in Soldner's clear raku glaze, 80/20, fired it so the glaze was well melted, then put it in a saggar and packed combustibles and copper carbonate around the lower section.

When it came out of the next firing, I was over the moon! Finally, I was seeing hints of what I had originally been wanting to achieve. The top section looked like it could have been raku fired with its black carbon trapping and crackle lines, while it also married well with the saggar effects on the lower section. I had achieved the carbon trapping I wanted, but it required an enclosed environment. So, not the same as raku, but inspired by raku.

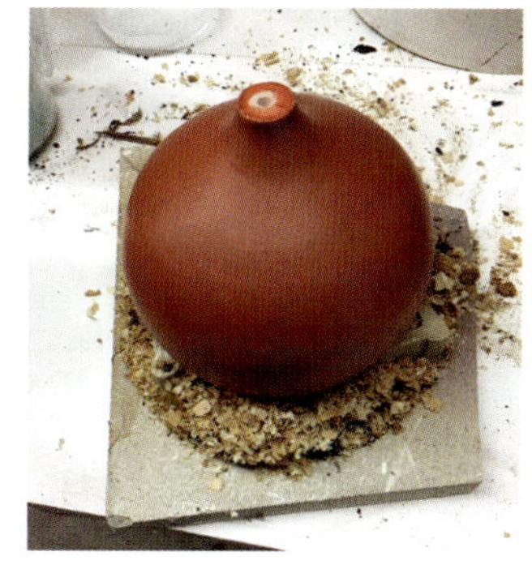

ABOVE
A small chalice ready to have the saggar placed over it.

BELOW
Chalice Mounted in Rock, clear glaze on top section, cone 05, saggar fired, 15 cm W × 17 cm T × 20 cm L (base).

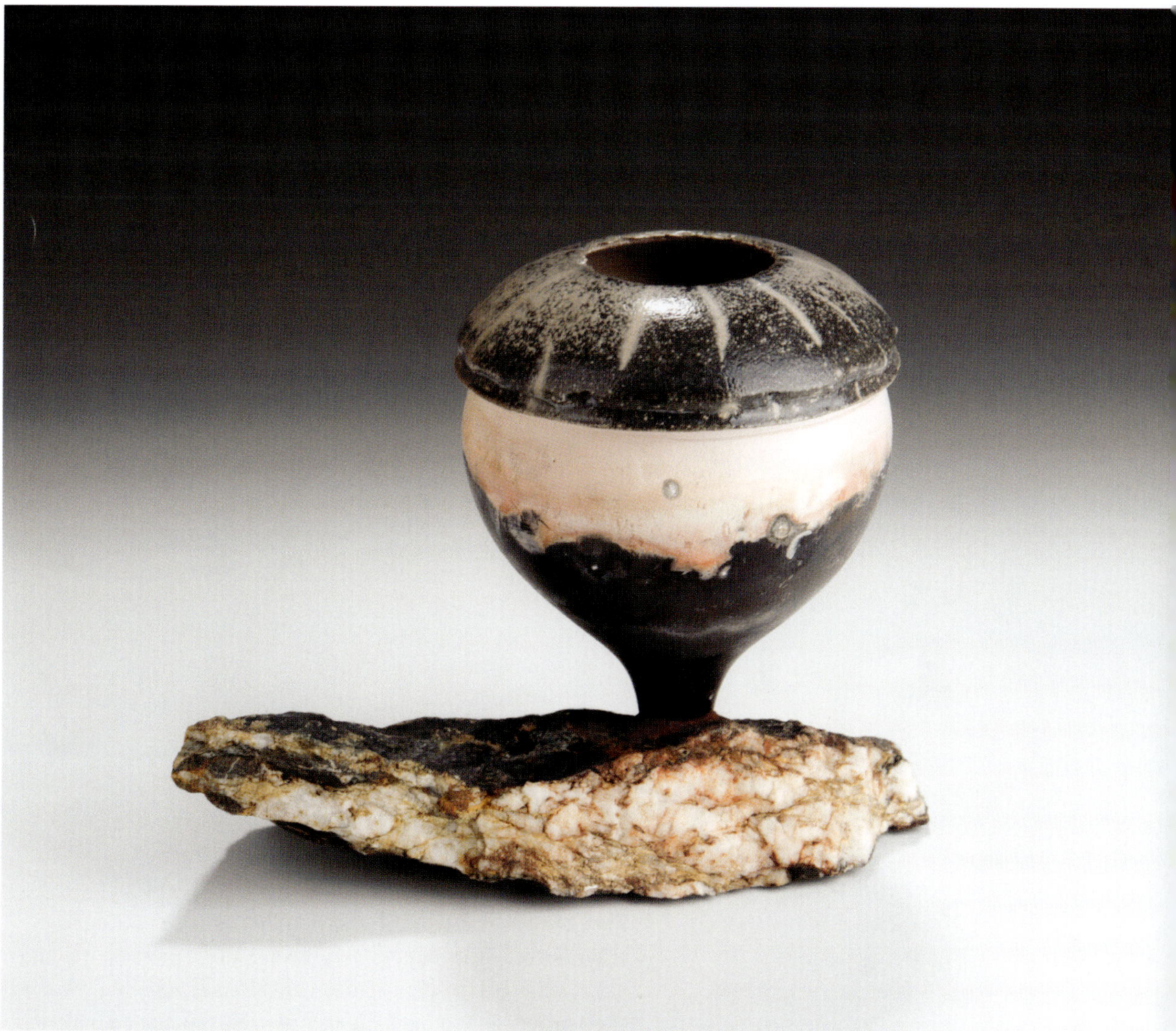

LEFT
Dish of combustibles.

RIGHT
Dish placed between tripod legs.

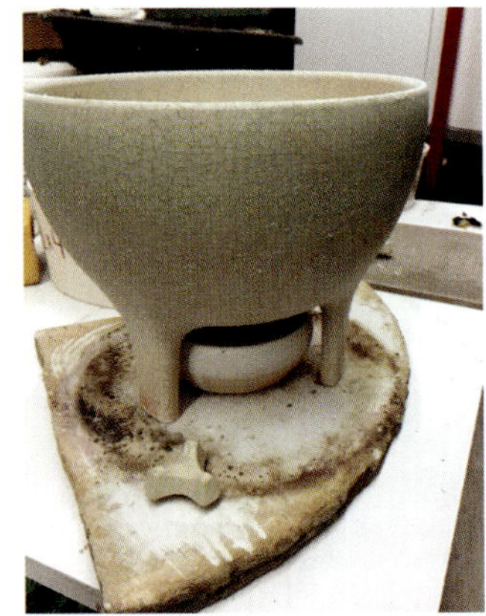

BELOW
Interior detail.

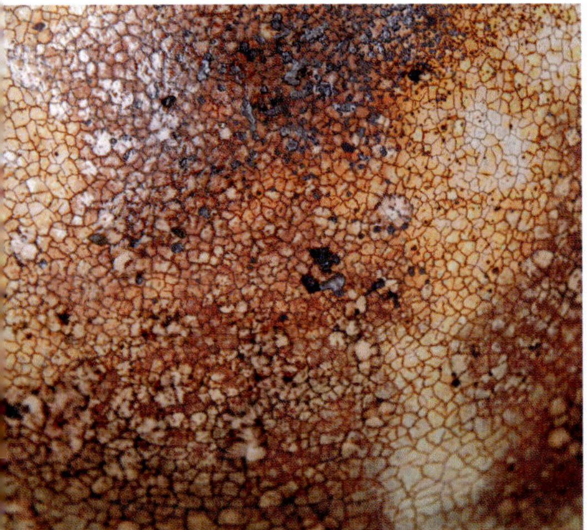

The idea of using the little dish of combustibles first came to me when I was trying to figure out how to fire one of my tripod chalices without immersing the legs in sawdust. The chalice had a base layer of white terra sigillata. After bisque firing, I applied a copper wash as well as a sprinkling of borax. I covered the bottom of the kiln shelf with about an inch or so of fine sawdust and a few chunks of wood, then placed a bowl full of sawdust underneath the chalice, between the legs. I placed the saggar overtop, and into the kiln it went. The three little black bits you see on top of the sawdust are pieces of coal that I found on the beach here in Ladysmith, remnants from when Ladysmith was a coal-mining town.

The results were stunning.

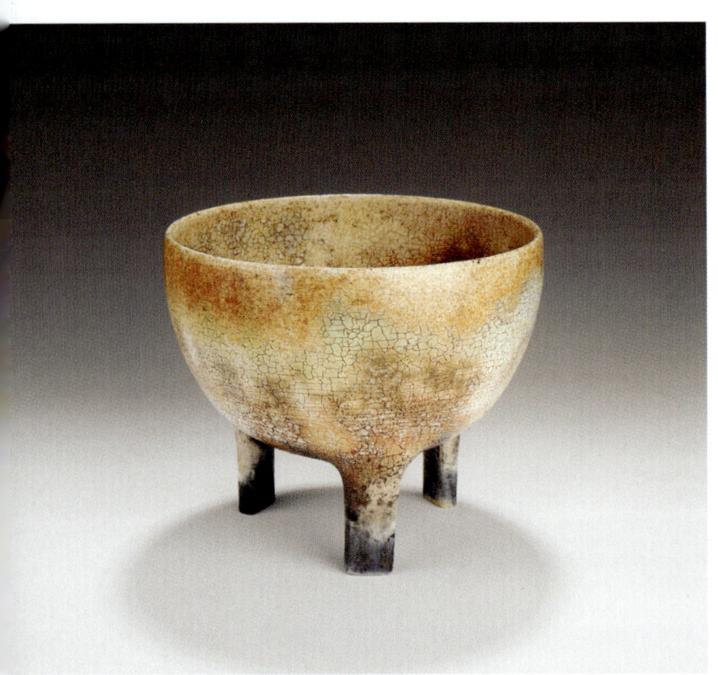

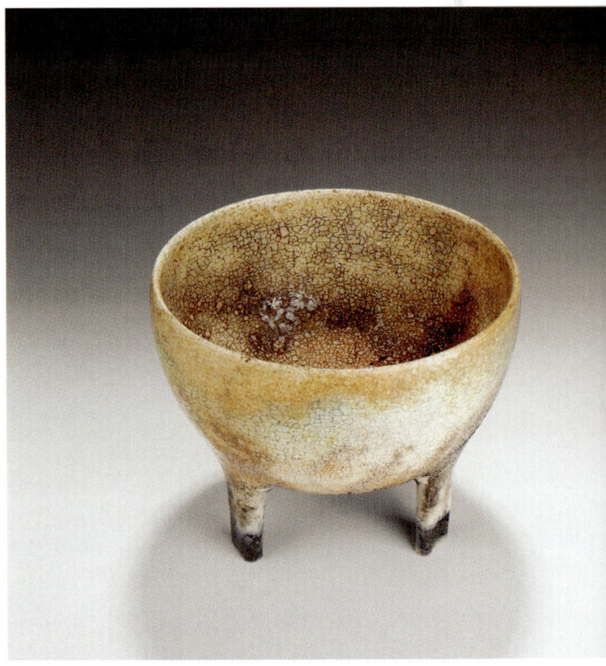

Tripod Chalice, terra sigillata, copper carbonate wash, borax, cone 05, saggar fired, 21 cm W × 18 cm T.

This, of course, led to yet another idea. I placed the next tripod in a deeper container, placed a small bowl containing sawdust and a couple of small coal bits between the legs and then proceeded to pack the saggar with sawdust, pinecones and twigs. I placed a clay saggar ring on top of the base container and then covered the open top with a piece of shelf. The result was much more carbonization than on the previous chalice and a heavier reduction because of the extra combustibles that were enclosed around the base.

The unveiling:

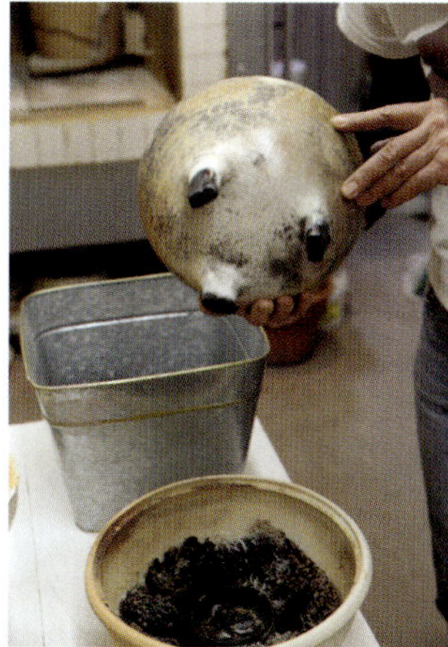

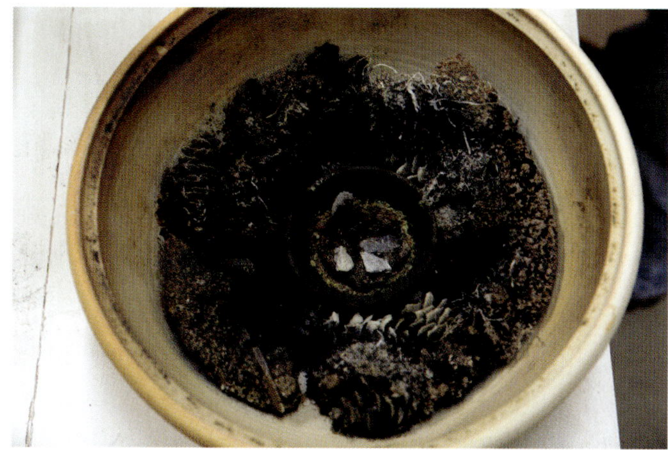

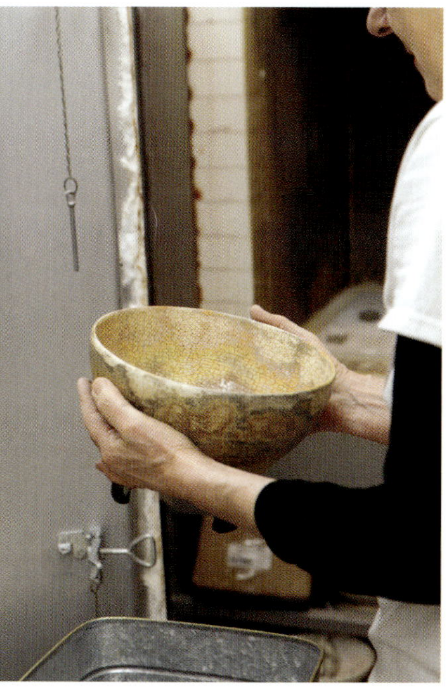

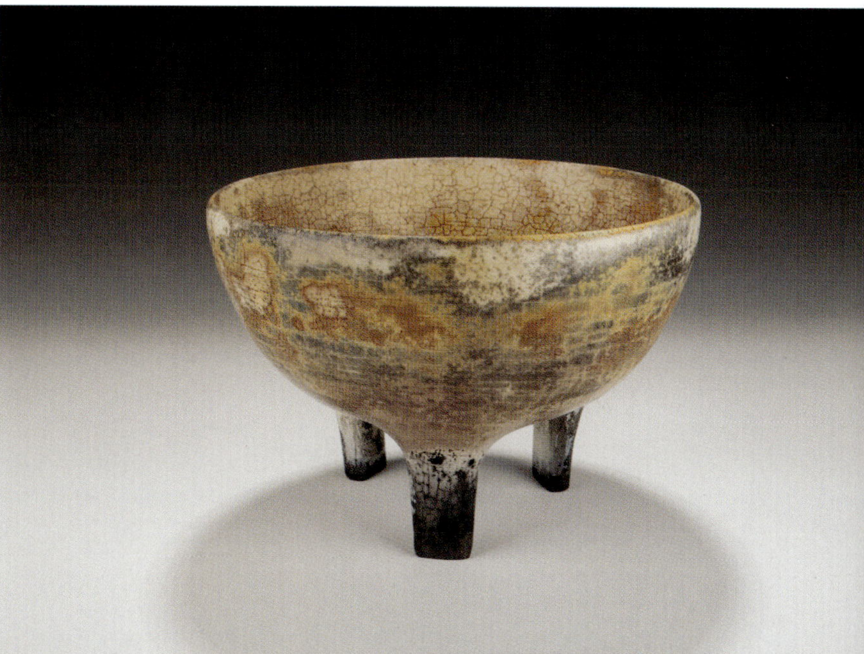

Tripod Chalice, terra sigillata, iron and copper wash, borax, cone 05, saggar fired, 23 cm W × 16 cm T.

Onward…I decided to try a wide bowl, but, once again, added some variation to my approach. I began with a base layer of white terra sigillata, then sprayed a thin layer of clear glaze on the interior and gave the interior edge a light dusting of copper carbonate with the atomizer. I left the exterior alone. I didn't prefire the bowl in oxidation after applying the glaze, as I wanted to see how the drier surface would turn out.

Because I fire these pieces quickly—3 hours to cone 05 for this firing—the glaze doesn't have much time for heat work and often comes out underfired. In subsequent test firings, I slowly increased the temperature to cone 04, but still found the clear glaze a tad underfired. I think adding a soak at the top temperature might be all that is needed for a thorough melt.

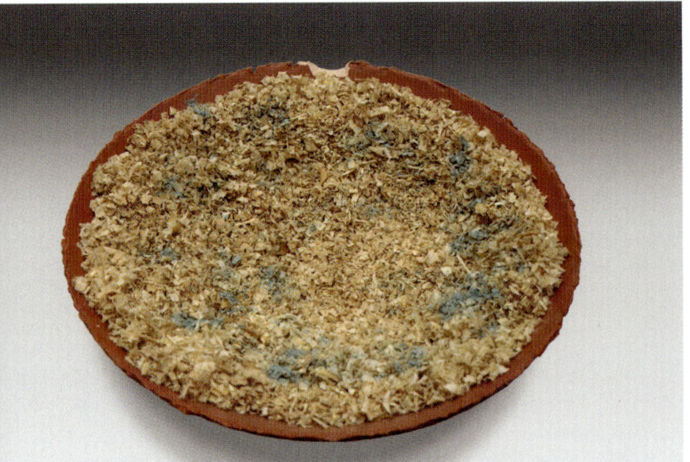

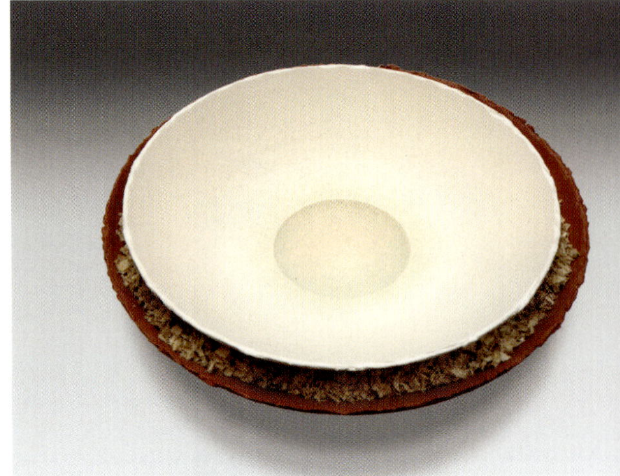

For this saggar test, I prepared the bowl as follows:

1. Filled a large container bowl (discarded due to a chip) with sawdust and then sprinkled copper carbonate on top.

2. Placed the test bowl in and then sealed the saggar by placing another slightly larger bowl overtop.

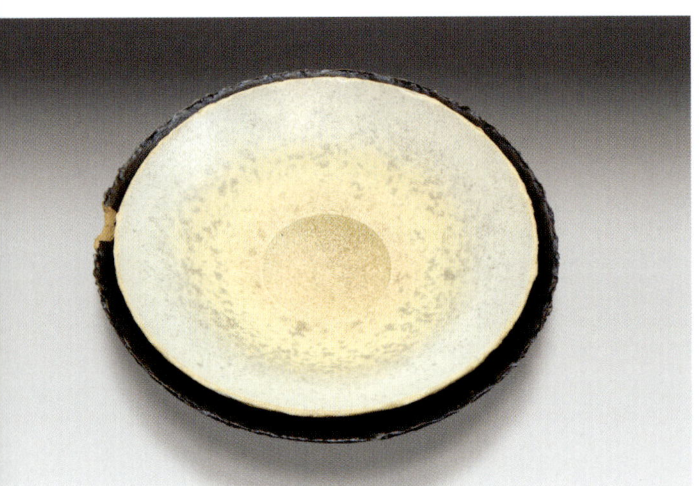

The bowl after firing, sitting in its bed of burnt sawdust.

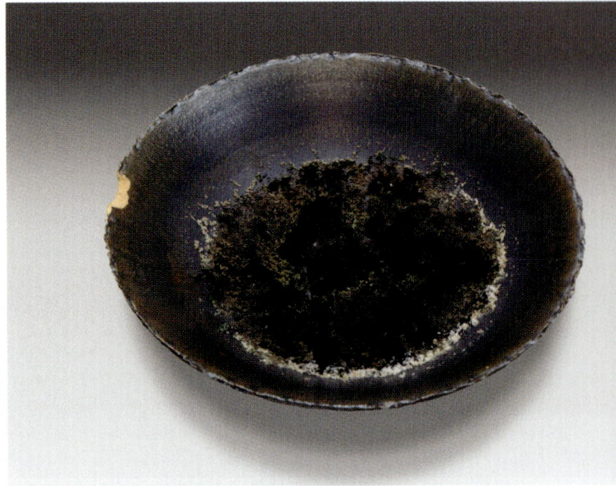

What remained of the sawdust.

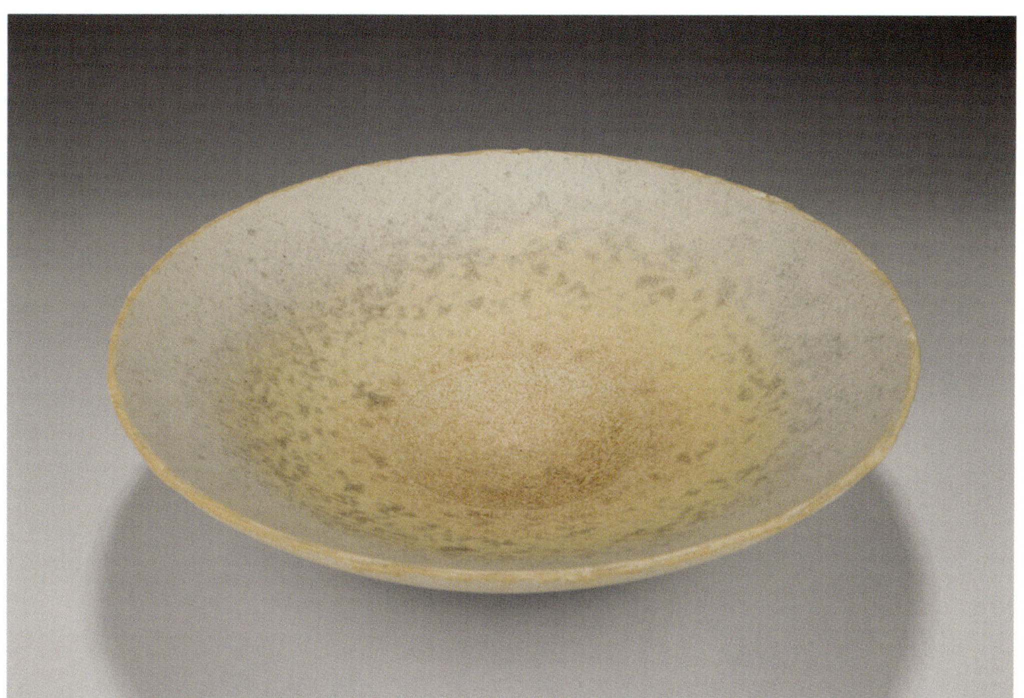

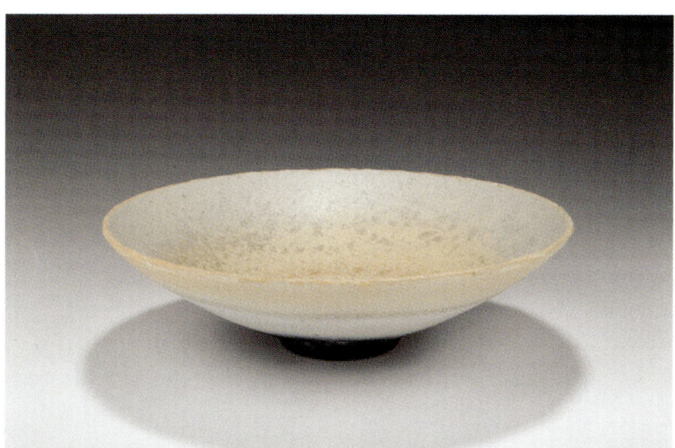

Bowl, terra sigillata, clear glaze, copper carbonate, cone 05, saggar fired, 28 cm W × 8 cm T.

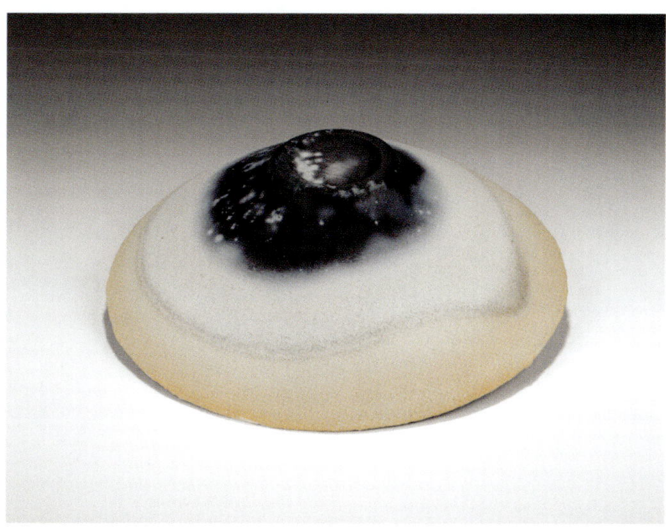

MY LATEST FAUX RAKU PIECE

We've covered a lot of ground so far, yet the possibilities are endless! I'm going to end this chapter with one of my latest pieces, so you can see where all the experiments I've described so far have led me.

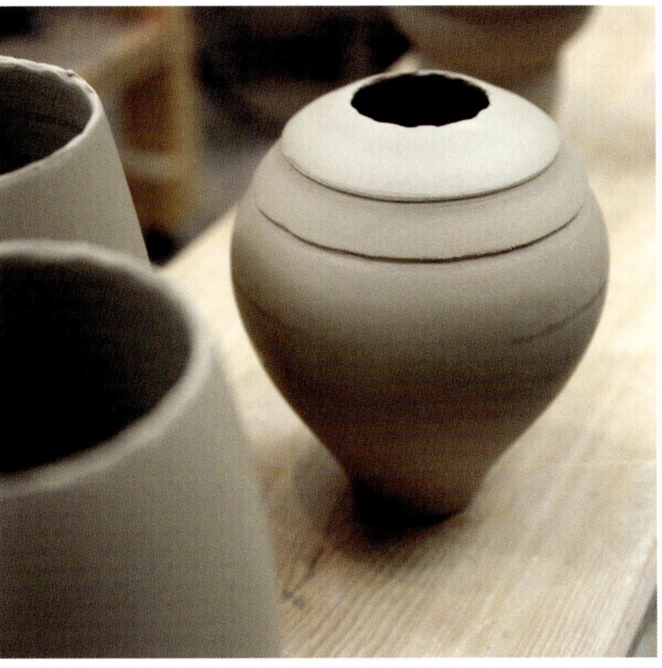

Freshly trimmed vessel, ready for testing.

Before bisque firing this vessel, I applied white terra sigillata to the top and bottom sections and a band of orange terra sigillata around the middle for contrast.

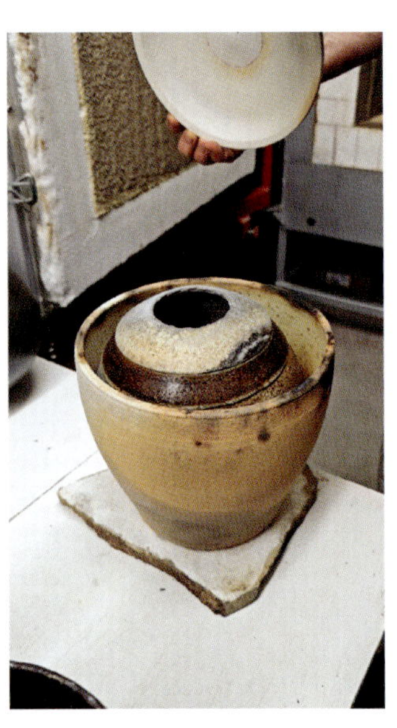

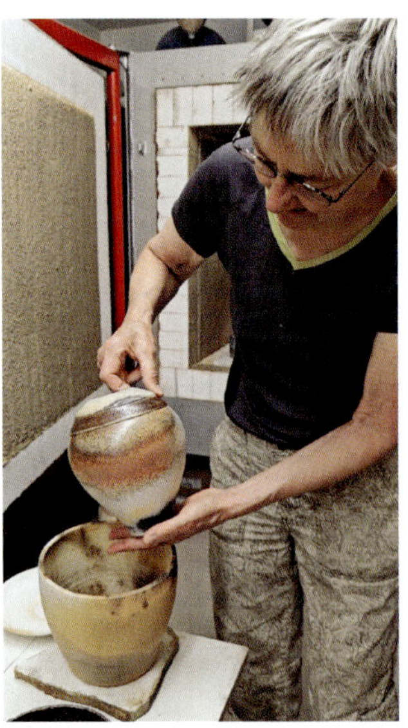

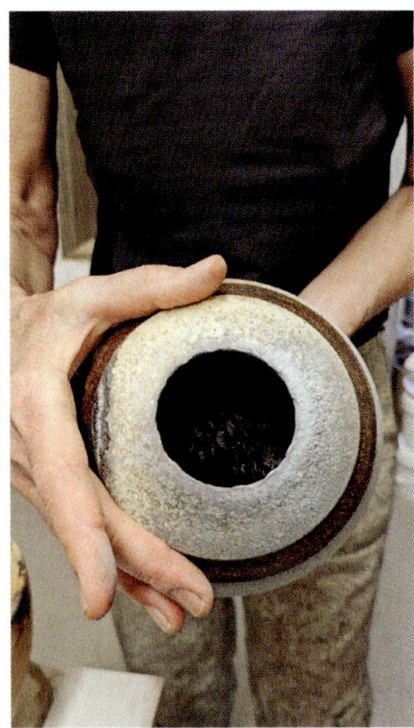

After bisque, I sprayed clear glaze primarily over the top area, following that with a light dusting of lithium compound. To prepare the saggar, I loaded it with about 3 inches of sawdust and a sprinkling of copper carbonate and filled the vessel

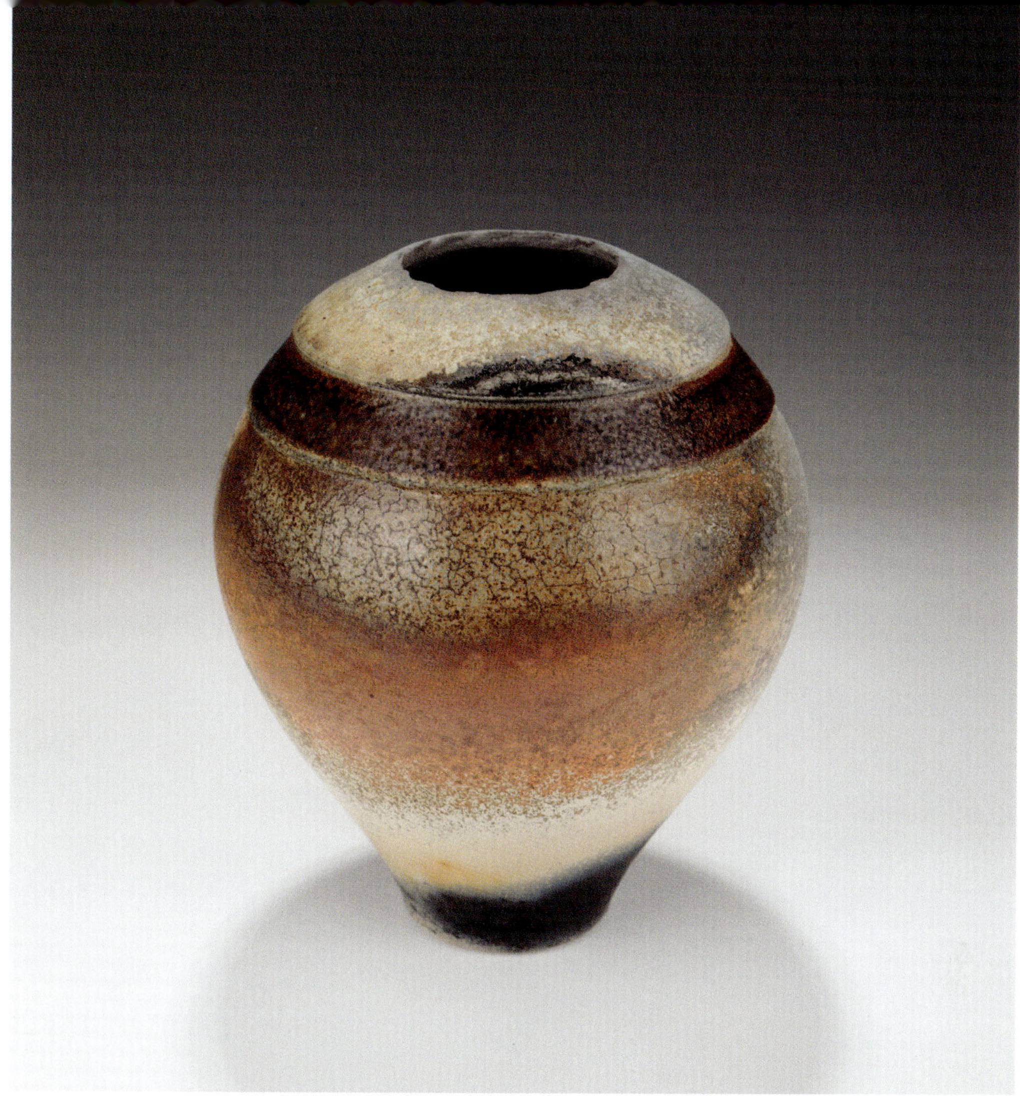

Collared Vessel, terra sigillata, glaze, cone 04, saggar fired, 17 cm W × 20 cm T.

interior with sawdust and pinecones. Finally, I cracked the saggar lid a wee bit to let in some air.

I think the beautiful flashing came about because the vessel was very close to the saggar wall. As you can see in the photo, at some point in the firing, the vessel tilted over and was leaning against the side of the saggar. I had not prefired the glaze, so it didn't completely melt, which meant that the pot, thankfully, did not fuse to the wall.

Now, I know a lot of you are probably saying, "But I don't have a gas kiln to try this stuff out in, and you can't do reduction in an electric kiln. You need a gas kiln." However, I don't see why you couldn't do the Faux Raku saggar in an electric kiln. You might not want to try it in a brand new kiln, but it's super easy to find an old kiln—with a kiln sitter, no computer—for cheap. Temperature fluctuations don't matter nearly as much in these firings. I've always had a kiln that I refer to as my "trash kiln," where I fire my spitting glazes and any other decorative pieces that I want to fire in oxidation. It's very freeing when you aren't concerned about what all these fumes are doing to a kiln that you would be firing your tableware in.

Now, let's move on to some other innovative techniques.

CHAPTER 10

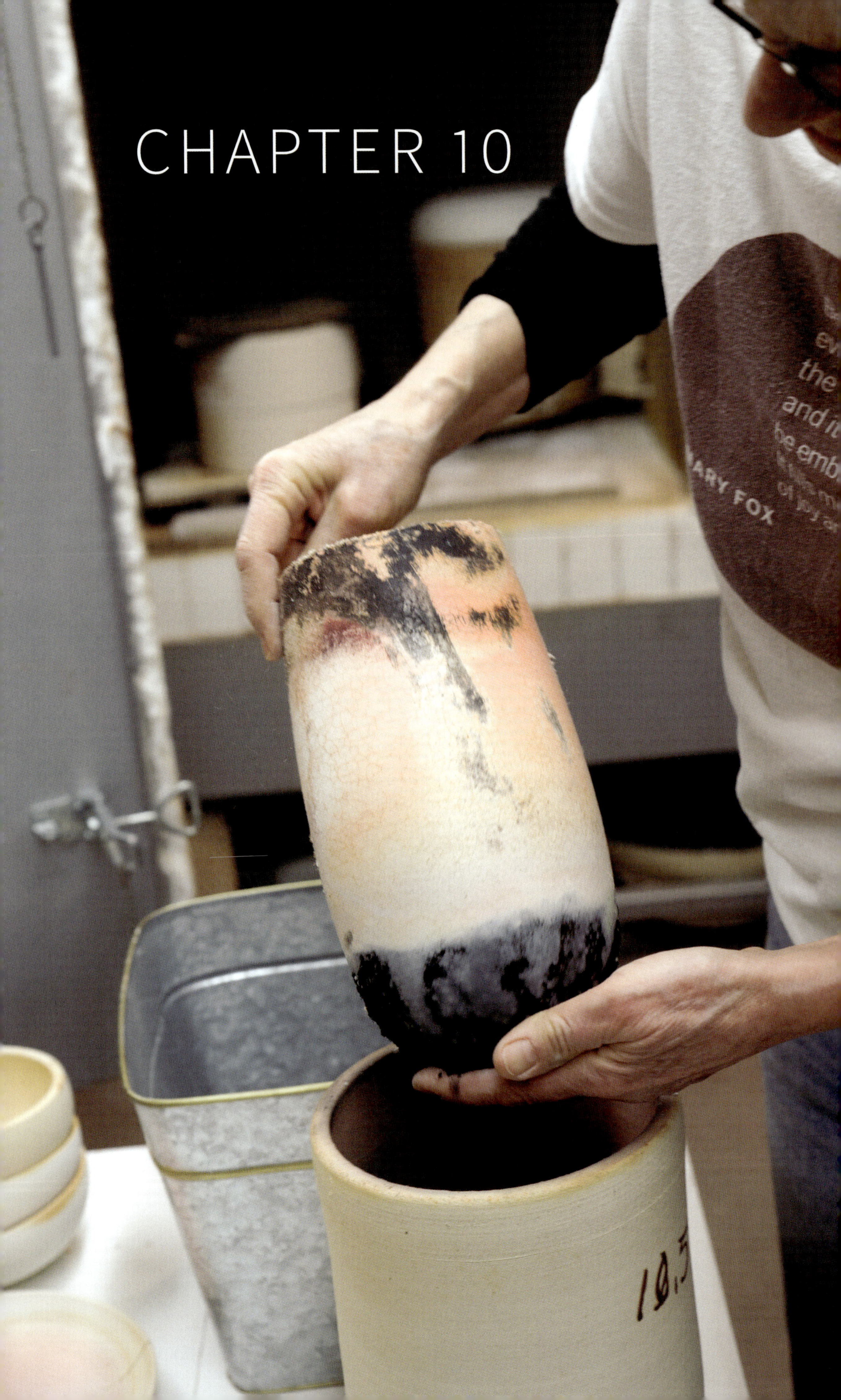

REFIRING TO REVEAL HIDDEN SURFACES

With all this experimenting, you are bound to get pieces that you aren't very happy with. I know, hard to believe, but it does happen! There are a variety of ways you can refire such pieces to learn more and often improve your results. If the piece has been saggar fired, you can saggar fire it again. I haven't had any issues with repeated saggar firings, so you can probably do this many times. Another way is to try putting a glaze over the saggar-fired vessel and firing it again in oxidation or reduction. This is always fun and can lead to unexpected results that may take you down yet another avenue of discovery.

A third strategy is to do what I used to do with my raku-fired pots. I discovered many years ago that I could put a raku-fired piece in my electric kiln and heat it up to burn off some of the surface carbon. It was a bit tricky with raku-fired pieces, as I needed to open the lid a crack and peek at the piece to see what was happening as the carbon burned off. I can't tell you what temperature I would go up to, as this was before we had computers on our kilns, but I don't think it was very high, probably under 600°F. I no longer raku fire, so I can't illustrate this for you with a raku pot, but I show you the process below with a previously saggar-fired vessel.

Discovering this technique is probably what led me to put my glazed but unfired raku pots in a bisque first to see what they would look like before the raku process. On the next page, you'll see a good example of what I am talking about. I glazed this chalice with the popular Copper Sand raku glaze and then included it in a bisque to see the results. Sometimes you strike gold, but even if you don't, you will have learned more about the glaze you are using.

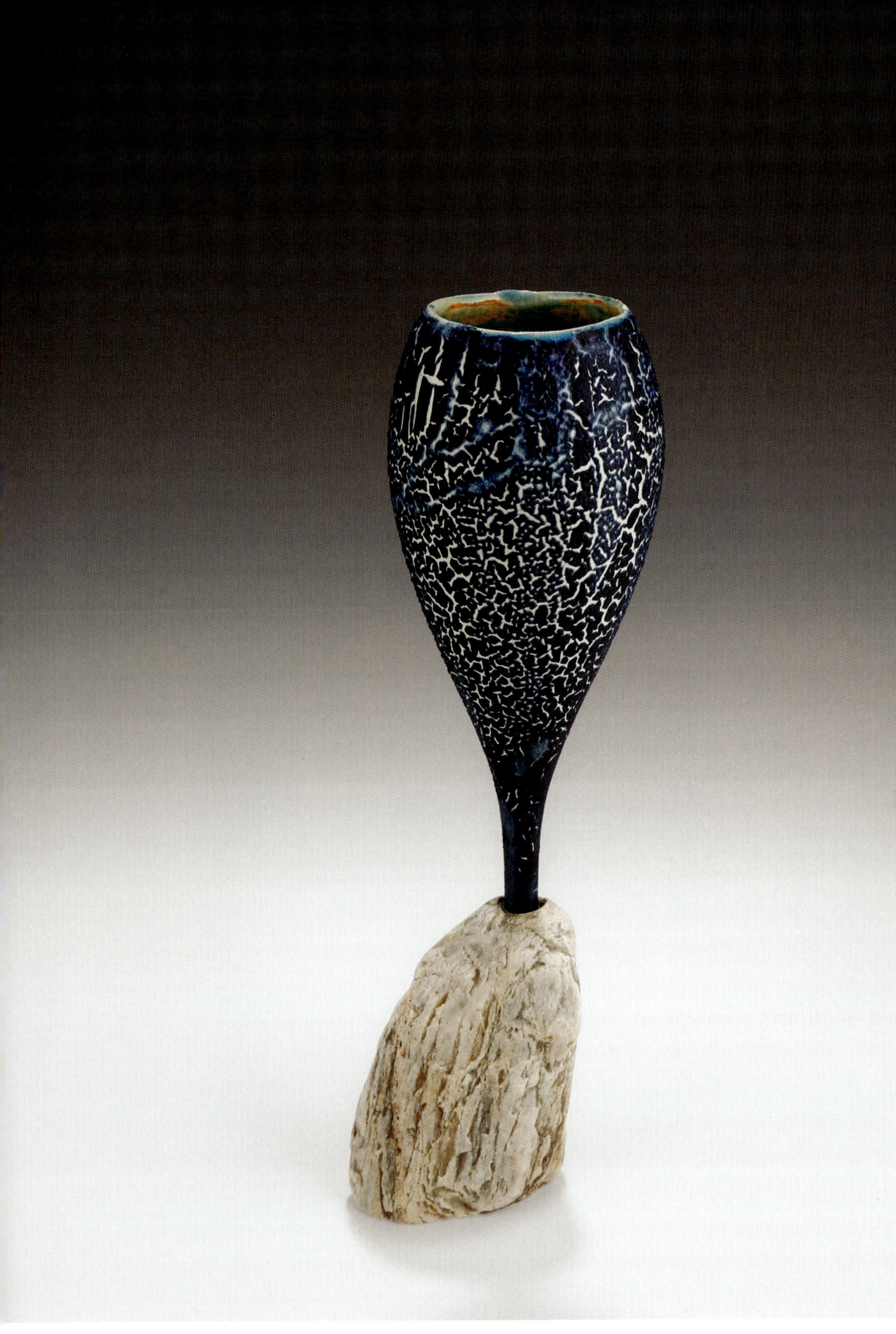

Chalice, Copper Sand raku glaze, mounted in rock, 05 oxidation, 16 cm W × 37 cm T.

This is what I like most about firing low—if at first you don't succeed, you can try another approach. I don't usually fire a piece more than six or seven times, but that is only because I am usually happy with the results by then. If I weren't, I would carry on. Raku clay bodies are well suited to this approach and hold up well through multiple firings.

Here is a piece I played with to give you an idea of what refiring can do.

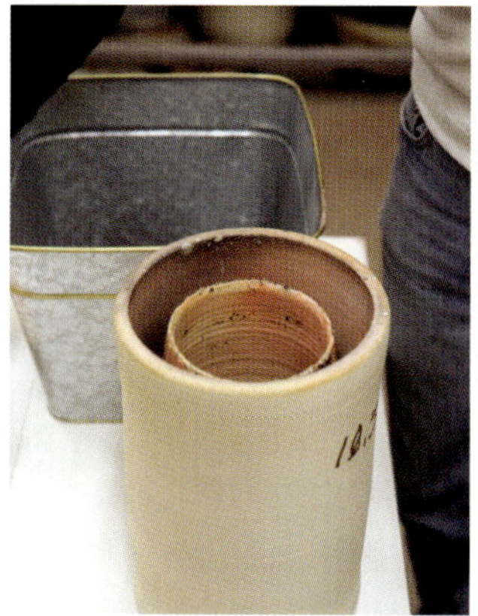

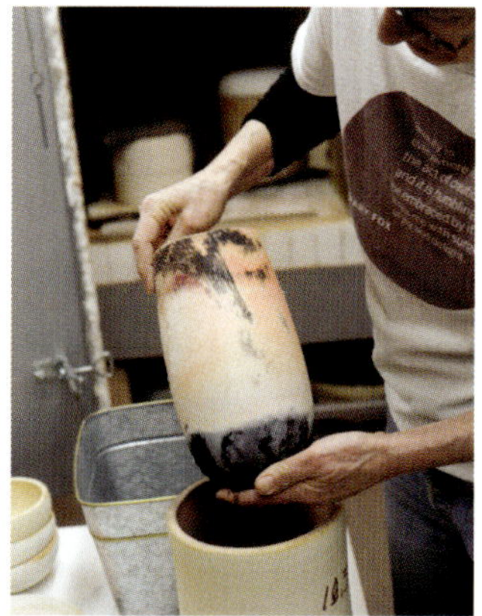

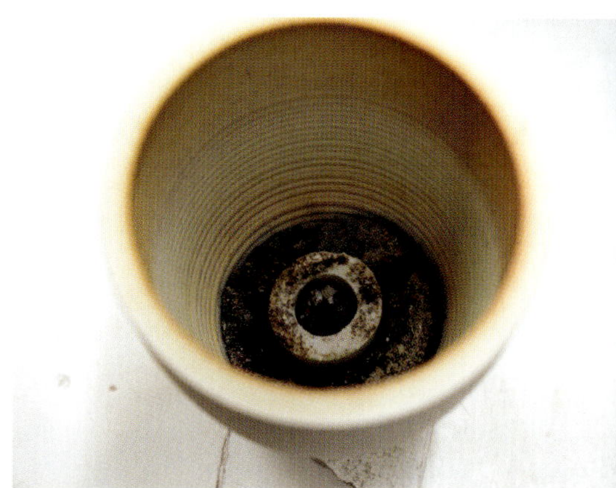

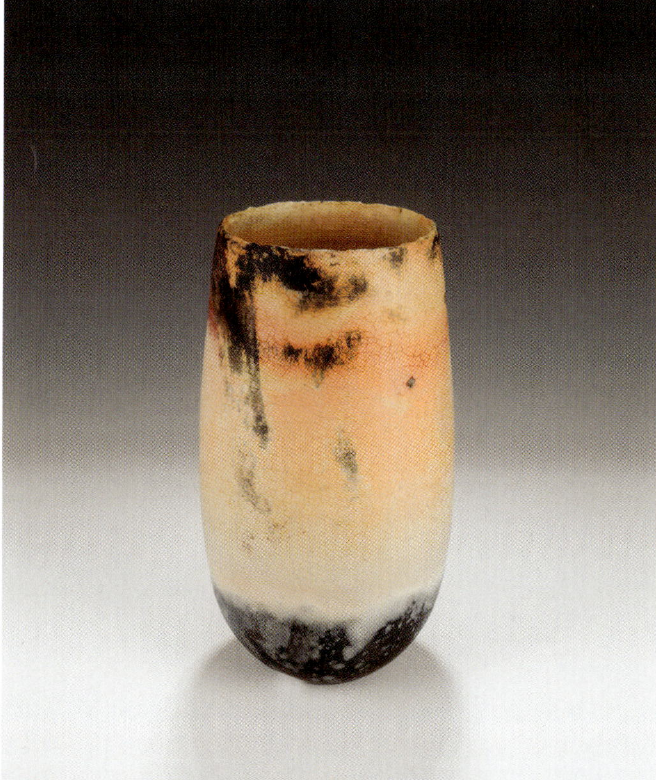

This is the vessel after its first firing in a saggar. Now, let's fill it with combustibles, put it back in the saggar and instead of packing more combustibles around the exterior of the piece like we usually do, let's leave that space empty and see what happens.

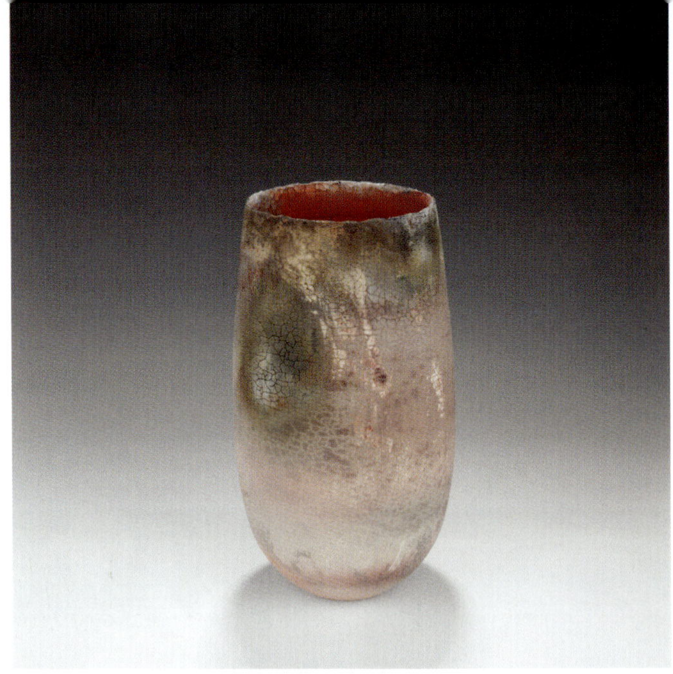

Very interesting. That dark oval area you see was brought about by the vessel being very close to the side of the saggar, which caused some flashing, one of those unforeseen outcomes of firing. *I wonder what would happen if I applied a thin layer of borax and fired it in oxidation?*

After applying some gum and sprinkling on borax, I decided to put a small piece of coal inside the vessel, along with some sticks. I then covered the upper rim and top with kiln fibre and fired the piece in oxidation. I didn't take a photo before it went into the kiln, but took one afterward with the fibre on top, so you could see what I did.

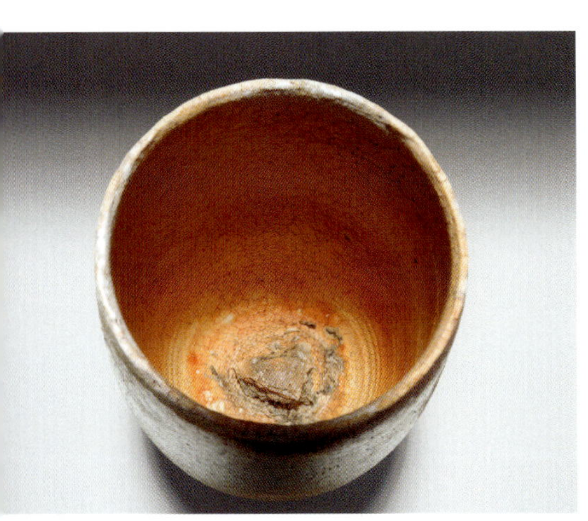

ABOVE
The interior after the oxidation firing.

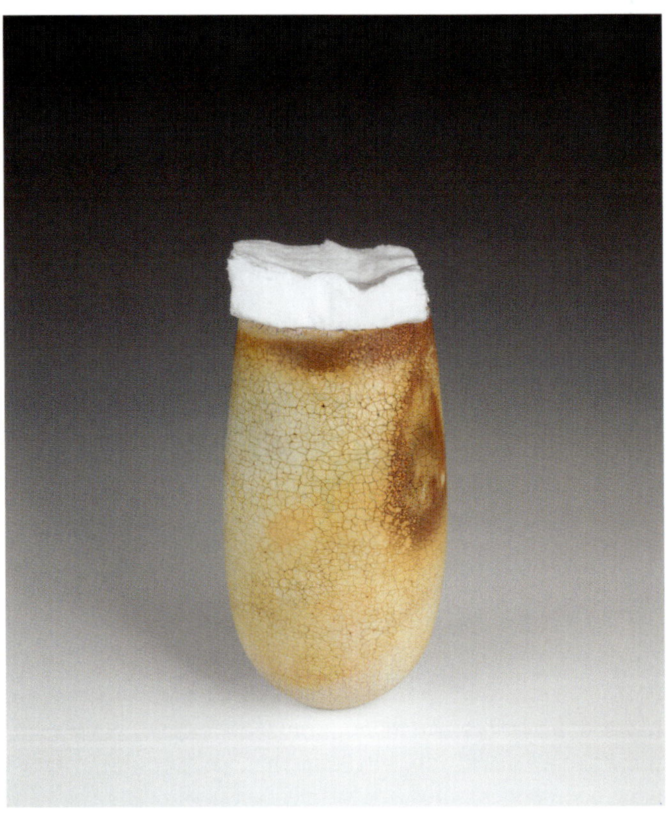

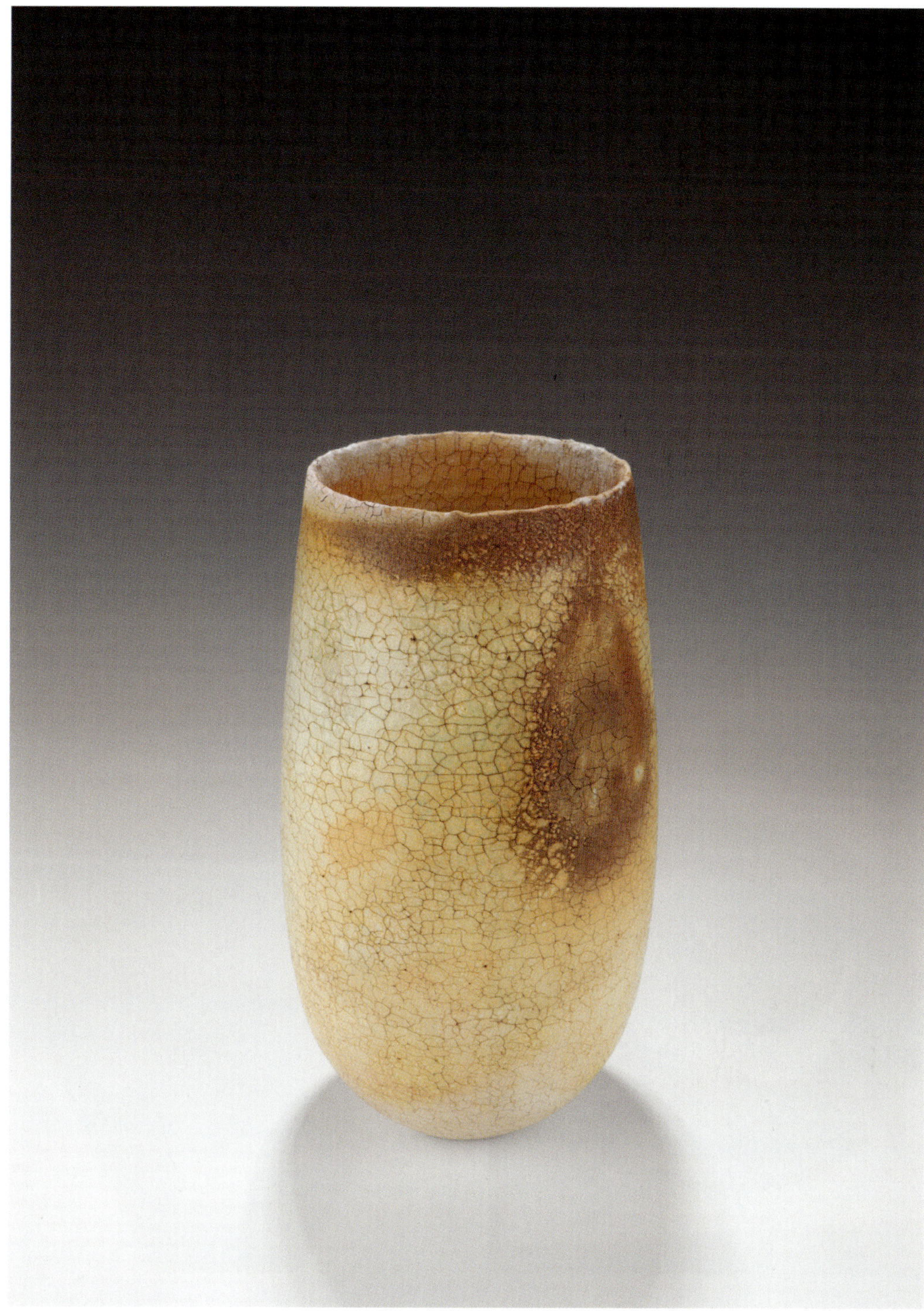

Vessel, borax, copper carbonate, cone 05, multifired in reduction and oxidation, 12 cm W × 25 cm T.

Another example of the happy surprises that come from refiring experiments is my chalice *From the Embers* (see pages 110 and 113). I had saggar fired the vessel, which resulted in flashes of pink on the top section. I was curious to see how the piece would respond to being saggar fired again, but this time with a layer of borax applied.

I coated the chalice with gum, sprinkled a heavy layer of borax on the top section and went gradually lighter with the borax as I moved downward to the thin stem.

Then I started second-guessing myself: *Had I applied enough borax to the top?* I went back and forth on whether to add more. I was nervous to try this because I knew the ashes from the combustibles would stick to the melting borax during the firing, but I forged on, dribbled some gum over the borax and sprinkled on more—the thickest layer I've applied to date. Even if it makes you nervous, this is how you learn. You can't know what is possible without going out on a limb and trying things.

I left the top few inches of the chalice poking out of the combustibles to see what would happen above the ash line. I packed the bottom section of the saggar with a lot of sawdust interspersed with layers of seaweed and sprinkles of copper carbonate, then packed the interior of the vessel primarily with sawdust, then arbutus tree twigs and pinecones to help promote some air gaps. Finally, I topped it off with seaweed, sawdust and sprinkles of copper carbonate. I crossed my fingers as I put the lid on the saggar and loaded it into the kiln.

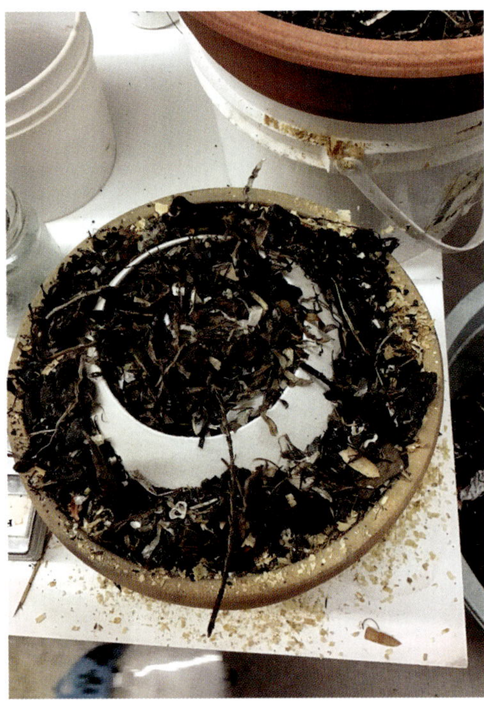

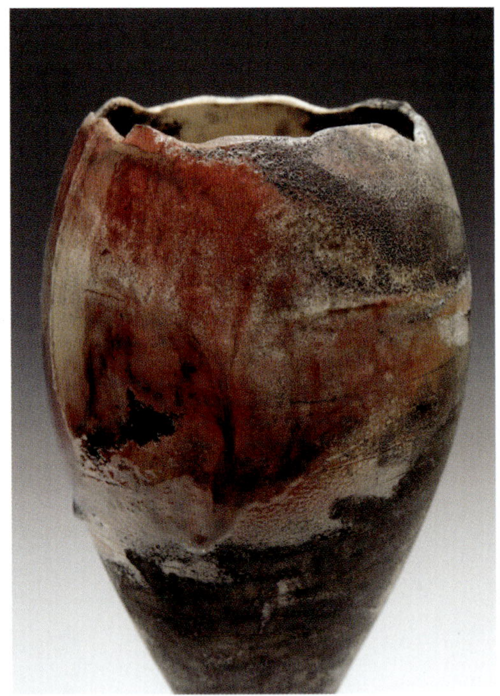

Oh my, was I in for a nice surprise! The borax was now glossy with streaks of red—gorgeous! The lower section that wasn't above the ash line was black and encased in a thick layer of burnt sawdust. I took it to the sink and started vigorously scrubbing away the ash. It took quite a while, but eventually I managed to reveal the surface underneath. The contrast between the glossy areas and the carbonized surface was stunning. I immediately knew that I had the perfect rock to mount it in. When I was last on Quadra Island with my sister and her family for our annual vacation, I had found a beautiful curvy grey rock. I remember the day well. We had headed to

Open Bay for a picnic, an area we had not visited before. As we hiked down the long steep trail to the beach, my relatives teased me mercilessly, already announcing that there was no way they were going to be hauling rocks back up that trail for me. I replied that, as the bay supposedly had a sandy beach, it wasn't likely there would be many rocks, so they were safe. As we reached the bottom of the trail, a stunningly beautiful vista opened up before us. And, sure enough, the beach was fine sand, unlike most of Quadra Island's rocky beaches.

The tide was out, and the kids kicked off their shoes and ran for the water, squealing with excitement while I sat on a log to take in the expansive view of the bay. After a while, I noticed a rocky area in the distance, where the bay began to widen out to the ocean. I started walking. As I got closer, I spotted a few nice rocks poking out of the sand, but at this point I was telling myself, *No rocks*, and I continued on my way. However, more and more enticing rocks appeared, including some unusual, intriguing ones I knew I'd find hard to leave behind. My resolve weakened, and I began to gather a small pile of my selections out on the sand, where I would be sure to see them on my way back. As I neared the area I had spied from the log, I saw that most of the rocks there were too large for my purposes, so I turned and headed back.

By this time, my niece Maia had spotted my rock pile and was heading out to help me carry them back to our picnic spot. This required a few trips! On our final trip, I saw the top of a light grey rock curving up out of the sand, and as I bent down to examine it more closely, Maia exclaimed, "NO, Aunty Mary, no MORE!"

"But, Maia," I said, "look at it; it's so beautiful! Look at these smooth curving lines, and there is a cool grey line running through it, too. We have to take it!"

My pile of rocks on the beach had grown quite large, and as I hadn't planned on rock hunting, I didn't have any strong carrying bags with me. I looked around for what we could use to haul the rocks, and my eyes fell on our picnic lunch satchels. They would soon be empty, and there were also the backpacks that had held our beach blankets and other gear. *Problem solved*, I thought, and proceeded to laze about.

When it was time to go, I surveyed the load to go up the trail, and somehow most of the bags looked full again. I lamented my dilemma, and the ribbing began. After tormenting me with threats of leaving the rocks behind, the whole family pitched in. Bags were emptied, and towels and extra clothes wrapped around people's shoulders or waists. We loaded the knapsacks with rocks, and everyone except the littlest carried one rock in their arms, along with a bag on their back, up the steep trail.

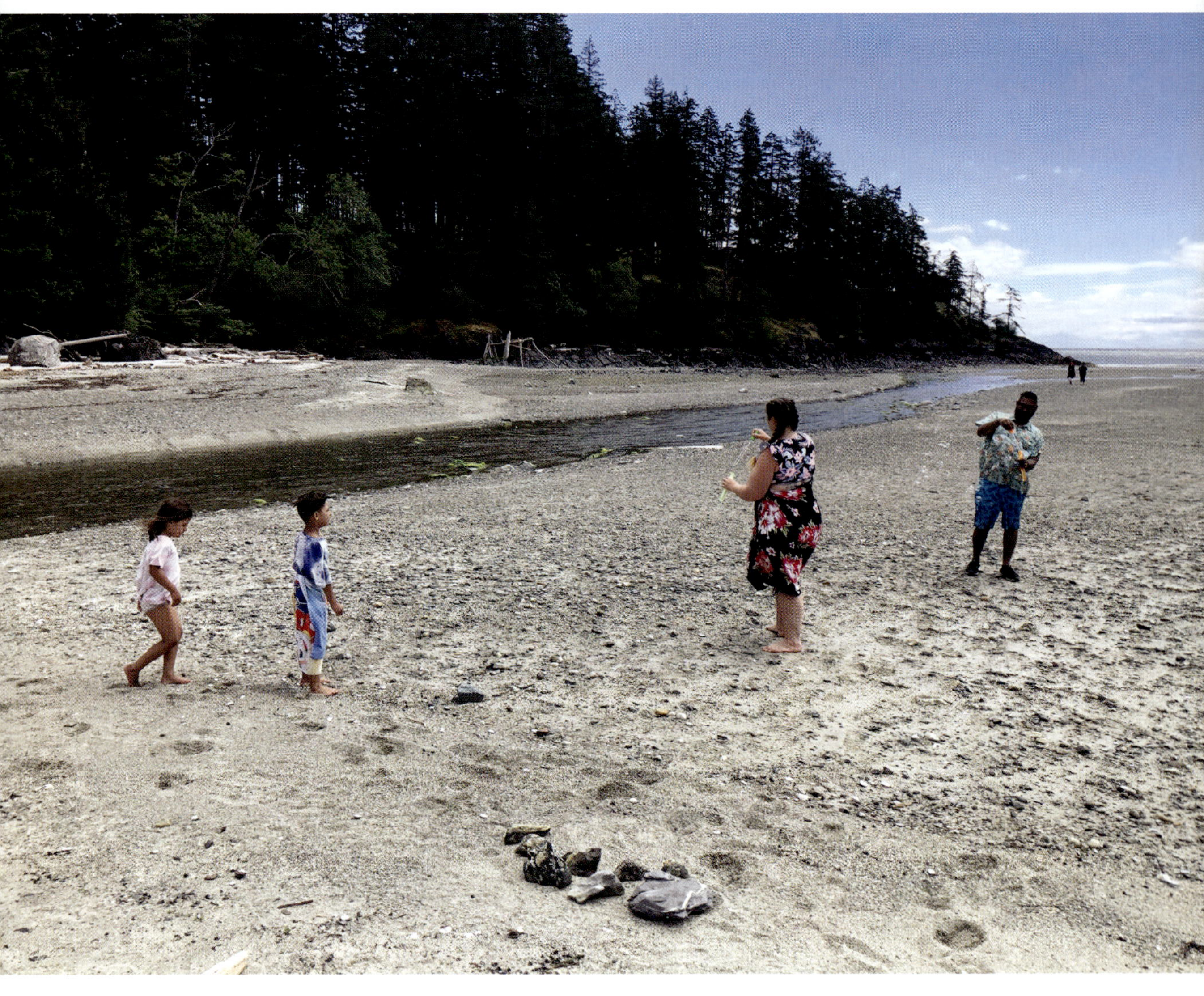

ABOVE

Here's my niece Coral and her family having fun making soap bubbles while my pile of rocks grows. If you look closely you can see, second from the right, the rock that was to become the base for my chalice.

OPPOSITE

From the Embers, chalice, white terra sigillata, copper carbonate, borax, sawdust, seaweed with coal fragments attached, cone 05, saggar fired, mounted in rock, 27 cm W × 42 cm T × 22 cm L (rock base).

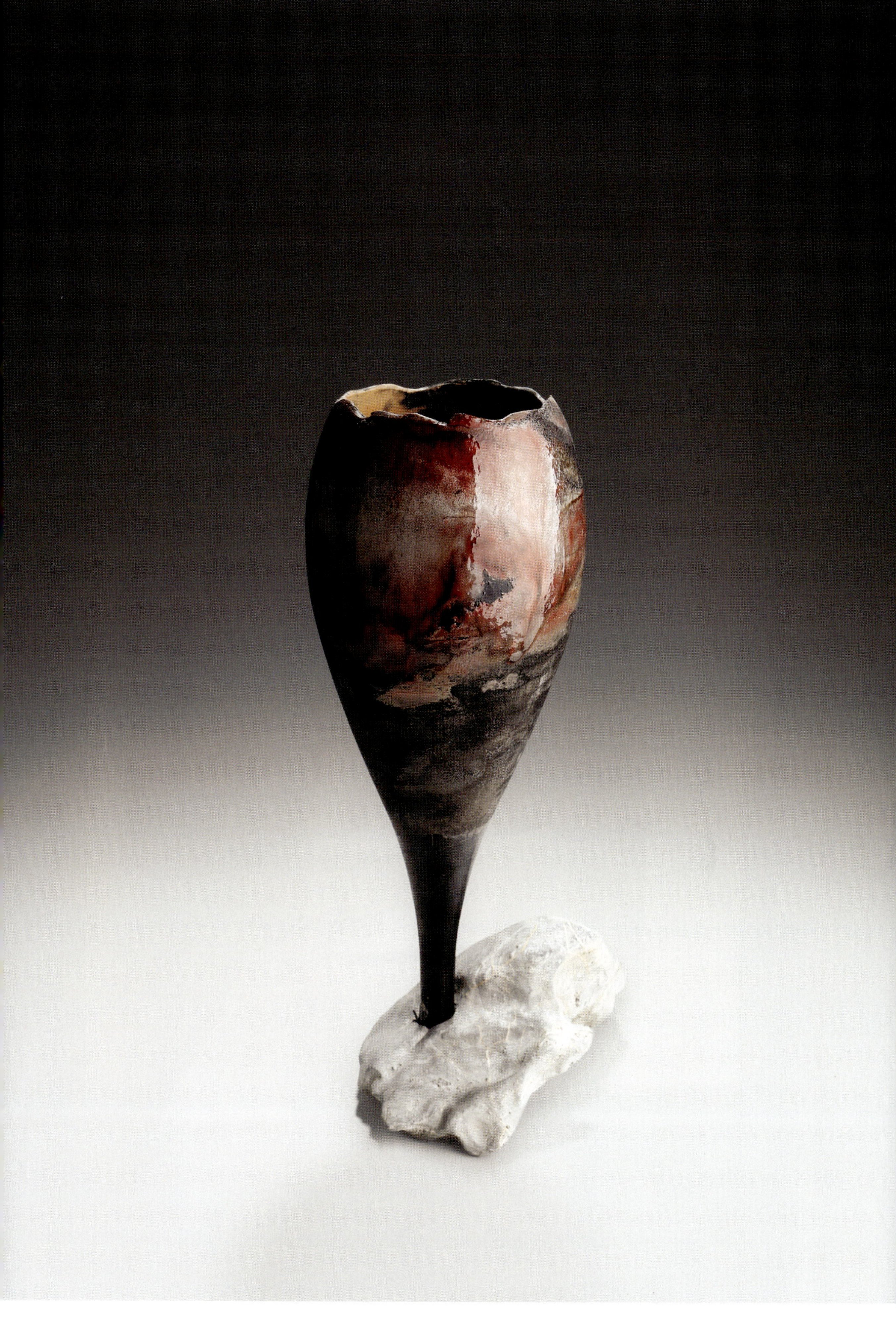

CHAPTER 11

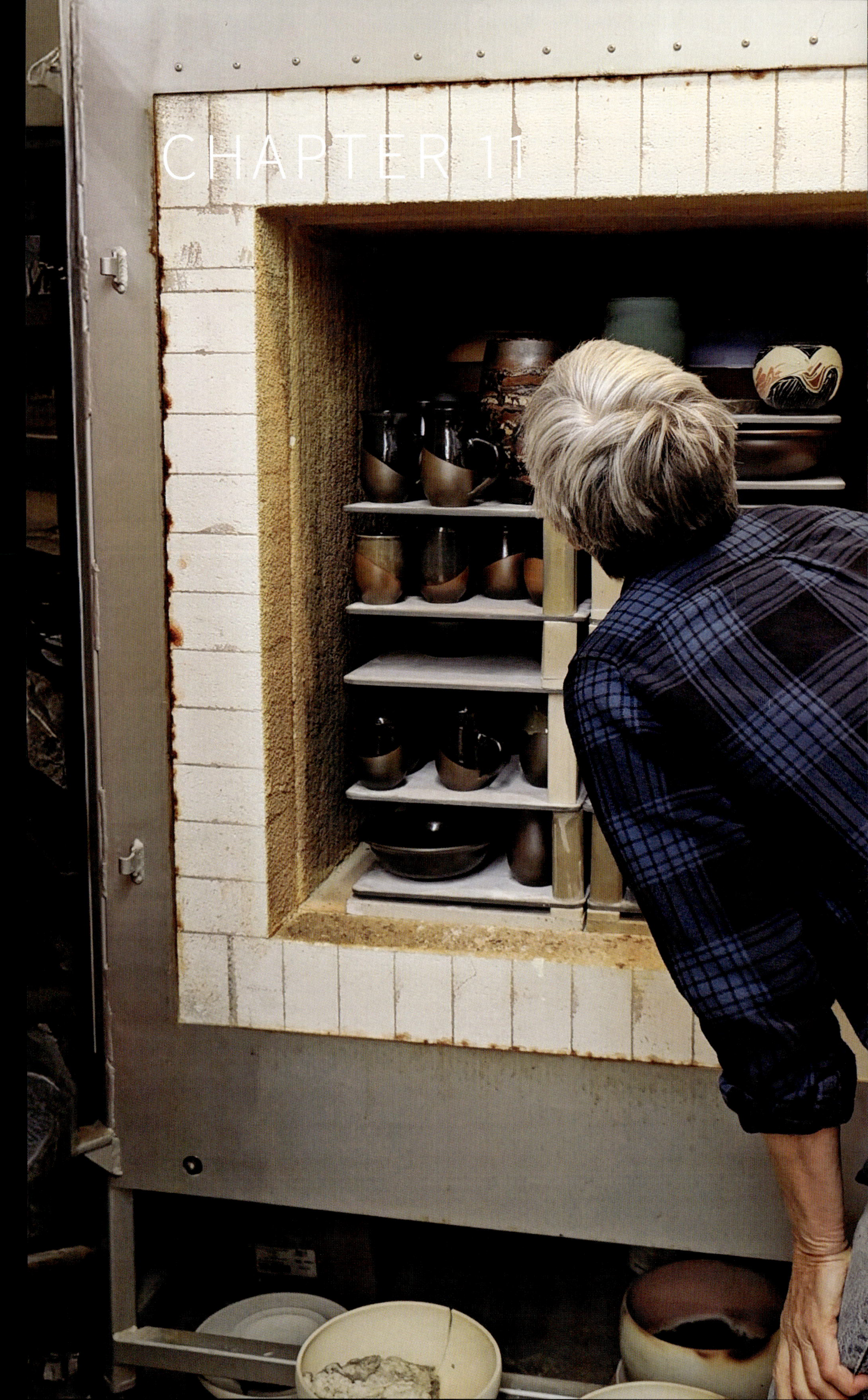

EARTHENWARE IN OXIDATION AND REDUCTION

If I were starting out as a potter today, earthenware would be among my top choices of clay to work with for a number of reasons. Because earthenware is low fire, you can fire everything—bisque, glazed tableware and decorative pieces—all in the same load. No more waiting for your next decorative firing to find out how a piece is going to turn out: you can pop in that decorative piece along with all your other pots. However, I do recommend that you keep your decorative work on a separate shelf in the kiln to avoid flashing or glazes spitting and landing on your tableware.

Firing low will also drastically increase kiln life, is much easier on your elements and will keep your shelves from warping. Finally, the obvious: climate change is forcing our hand, leading the way toward new approaches to energy use. When we fire low, we are consuming considerably fewer resources.

Until I acquired the Blaauw, I hadn't created dishes in earthenware other than my Peasant Ware line (covered in my first book). But with the new kiln, I wanted to explore cone 04 reduction-fired tableware, and that meant developing low-temperature glazes. I thought this would take me quite a while, but I was pleasantly surprised. The first tests blew me away. They were beautiful and looked great in both reduction and oxidation.

I used both white and red clay bodies for my explorations of earthenware glazes. There aren't many 04 white clay bodies readily available, but after testing the ones I could get, I found that Laguna EM 342 worked nicely. For the red clay, I used the same clay body that I make my Peasant Ware with: Tacoma Clay Art Darcy's Redart.

In order to test what the glazes looked like on both white and red clays, my apprentice Sabrina Sachiko Campbell created bowls in both clay bodies. We left the rim and outside of each bowl unglazed, but applied a coat of orange terra sigillata to those areas, so that we would get a beautiful black (in reduction) or orange (in oxidation) to contrast with the interior glaze. Honestly, I'm still amazed by the results. The bowls turned out to be absolutely gorgeous. Aside from creating a stunning contrast with the glaze colours, the terra sigillata's smooth surface greatly enhances how the bowls feel in the hand.

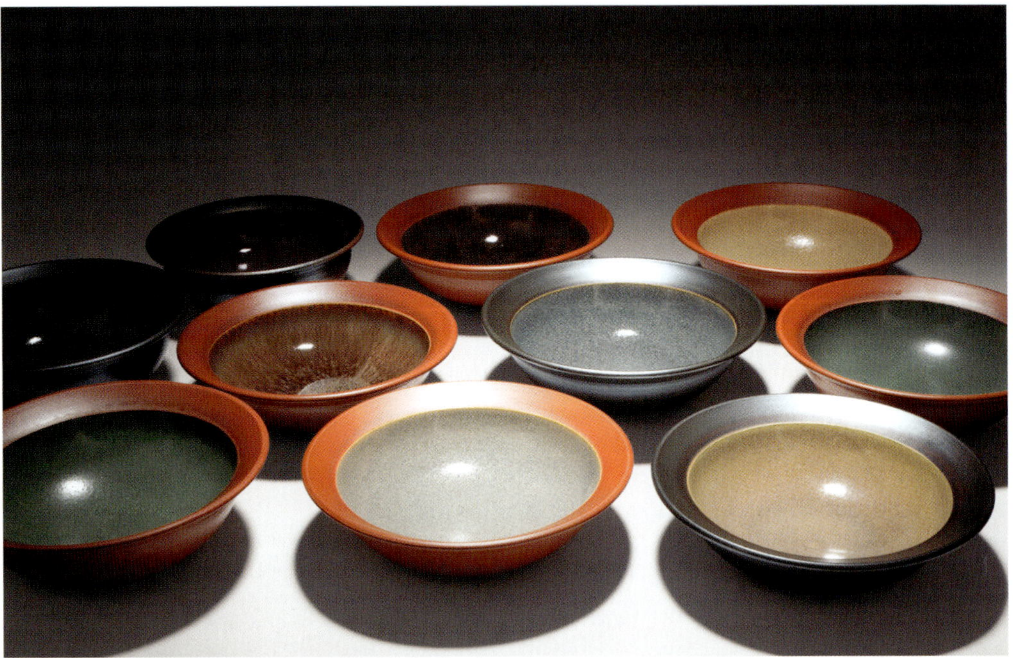

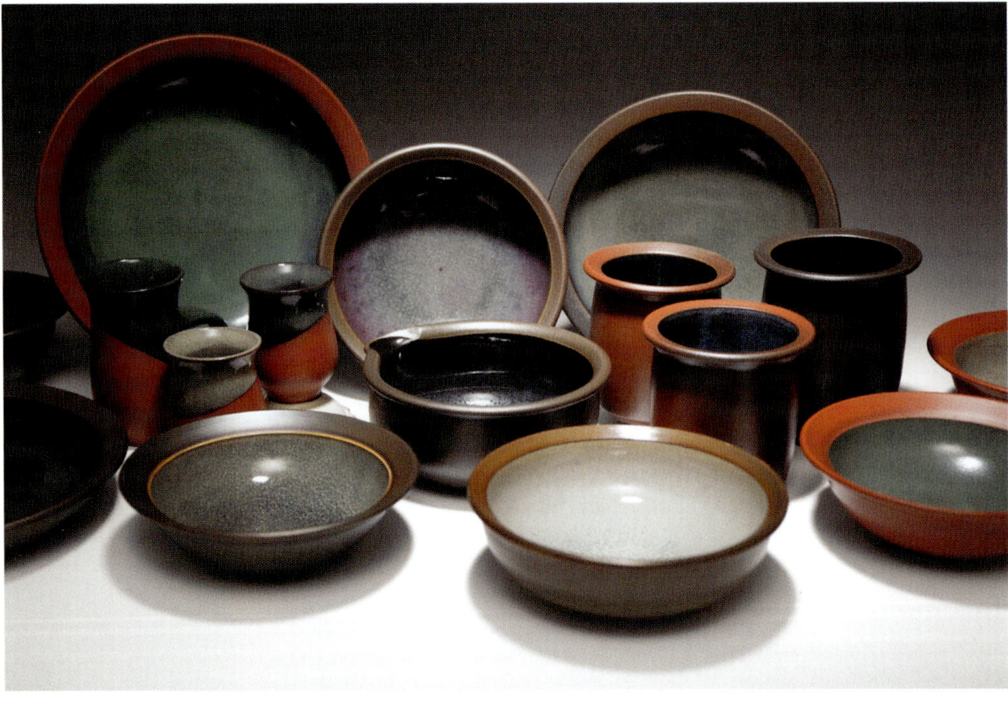

I am excited by the possibilities of this new work. I love to put these bowls into customers' hands to see how they react. And react they do, commenting on the wonderful glazes as well as how the bowls feel. Visiting potters are surprised to learn that the bowls are low-fire earthenware and even more amazed that some have been reduction fired.

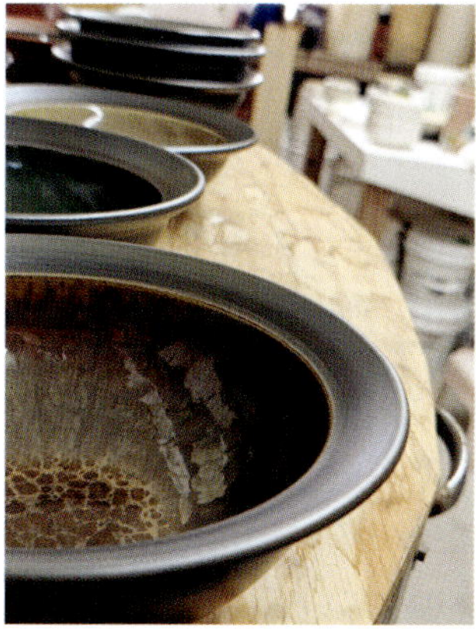

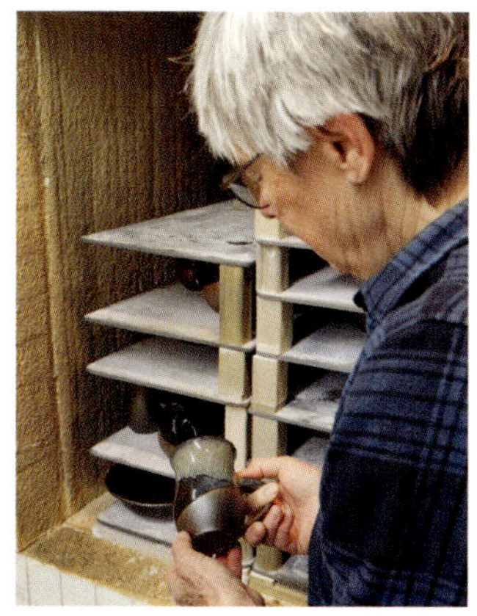

However, the joy of discovering these new earthenware possibilities has been tempered with sadness, as I reluctantly decided last year to let go of creating functional ware. It had become clear that my body wasn't able to produce like it used to, and I was pushed to capacity with my decorative work, the Mary Fox Legacy Project, the apprenticeship program and book writing. Something had to go.

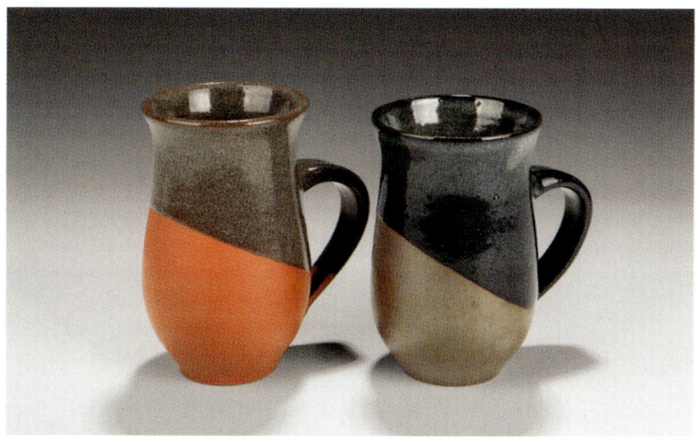

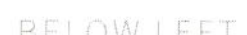

BELOW LEFT

The mug on the left was fired in oxidation, the other in reduction. I have been using one of these mugs daily and have seen no issues. This is another way for potters to save on energy, as glazing using this method requires only one firing.

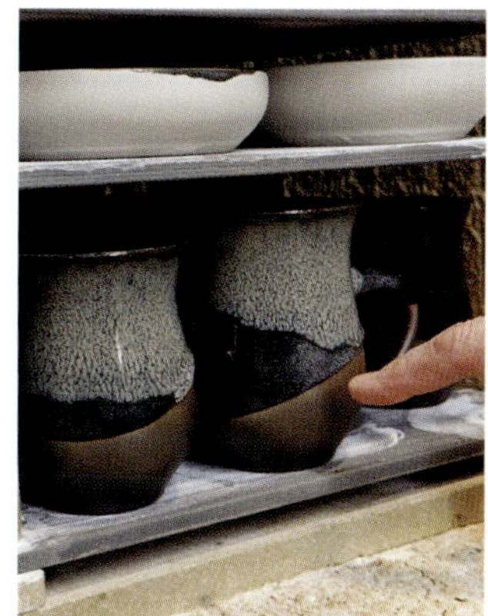

ABOVE RIGHT

Glazing greenware is something I've thought of doing, but have always been hesitant to try. As a test, I glazed both of these mugs at the greenware stage. I used a thinner glaze and shortened the dip time to account for rapid absorption.

I was surprised by how upsetting it was for me to give this up. I've been making mugs and other functional pieces since I was 15. When I was young, all I wanted to do was focus on decorative work, but that has changed over the years. Creating tableware has its own special joys—it is both gratifying and touching to witness the pleasure people get from using these pieces and how attached they become to their favourites.

However, all is not lost. I have apprentices these days who are learning what it takes to be a studio potter and I continue to learn about earthenware glazes through the functional work they are producing for me.

I might be blowing my own horn here, but I truly believe that in a few years you will be seeing more and more earthenware fired in reduction and oxidation. It is beautiful, cheaper to produce, better for our environment and holds up very well with everyday use.

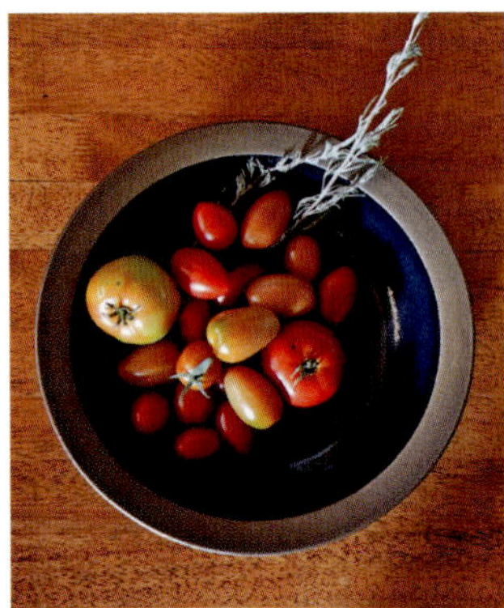

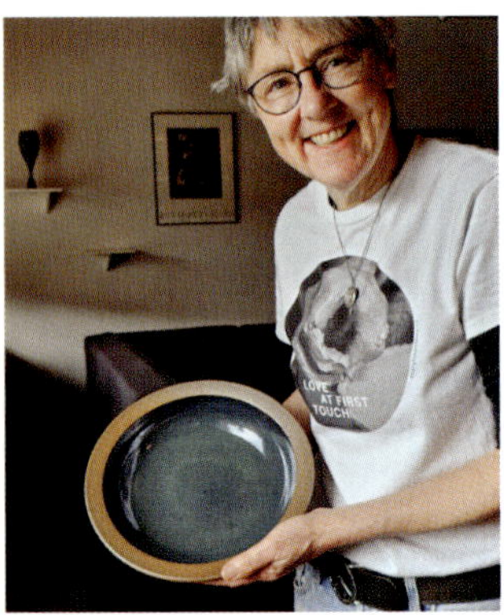

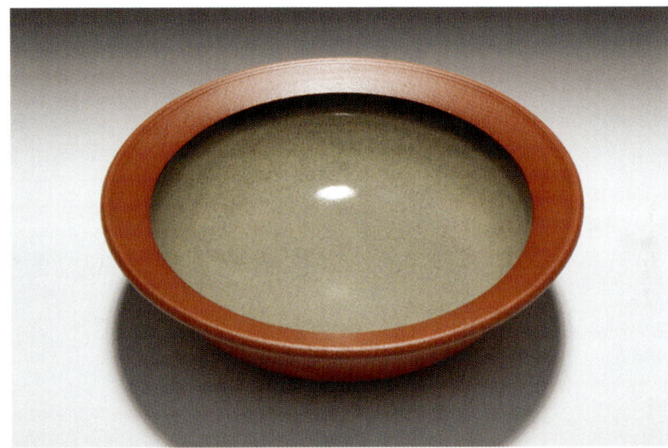

Bowl 1's Earthenware Base glaze (no colourants), fired in oxidation.

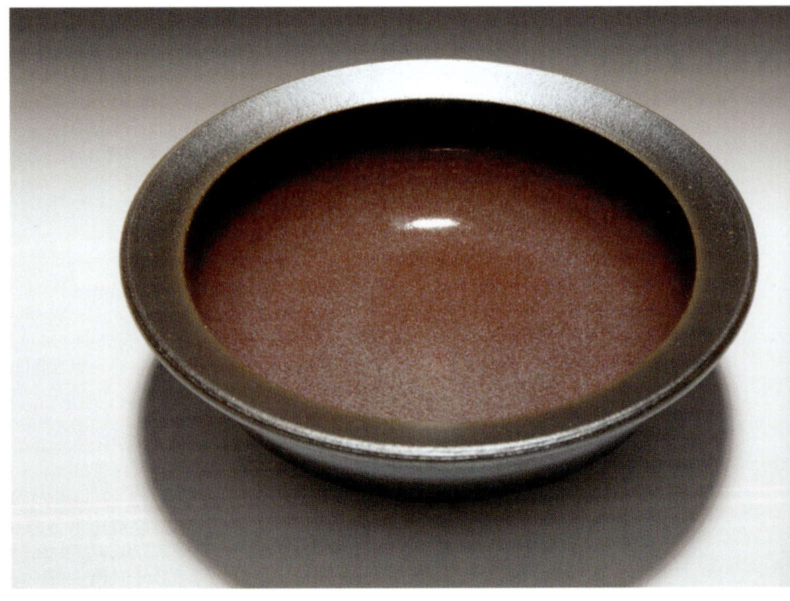

Bowl 2's Earthenware Base glaze (no colourants), fired in reduction.

When I took bowl number two out of the kiln, I couldn't believe that it was the same base glaze without colourants that I had used on bowl number one. I was convinced that there had been a mistake. There was no terra sigillata applied to the interior of either bowl; it was only applied to the rims and exteriors. That meant that the colour difference had come about because of how the glaze and clay body reacted in reduction. The base glaze on the interior of bowl number two was slightly thinner than on bowl number one, which allowed the glaze to react more with the red earthenware clay body underneath, producing that beautiful pinky-red colour.

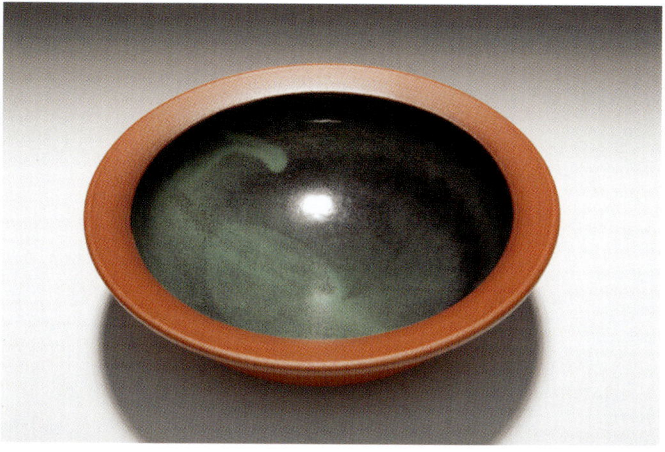

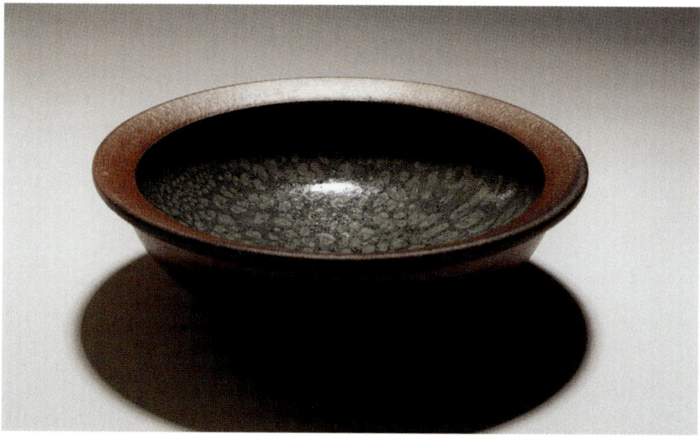

TOP
Bowl with Fox's Earthenware Galaxy Green, fired cone 04, oxidation.

MIDDLE
Bowl with Fox's Earthenware Galaxy Green, fired cone 04, reduction.

BOTTOM
This was one of my first test bowls. I didn't have any red earthenware clay on hand, so threw a few bowls with my raku clay to use for testing. I wish I could say that I've gotten this result since, but I haven't. It was glazed using coarse ilmenite instead of fine, which is what brought about that beautiful pattern. It was a very old batch of ilmenite, and I haven't achieved the same results with the coarse ilmenite that I bought recently. The rest of the tests were done using fine ilmenite, which is easier to work with, as the coarse ilmenite settles to the bottom of the glaze mixture very quickly.

The story of a mug

Mugs! How many thousands have these hands created? My approach to making mugs has changed over the years. Young Mary would produce the same form over and over again, making it easy for people who wanted sets. But as time went on, I found I wasn't going to the wheel with the same level of enthusiasm for making mugs, so I started to introduce a variety of shapes and sizes. I soon noticed people's delight as they looked at the shelves loaded with a wide range of forms and glazes and began the hunt for their new favourite mug. *What purpose would the new mug serve? Would it be for their morning coffee, cappuccino, espresso or for tea or soup? What size should it be?*

I confess that I have developed a habit of hiding away my favourite pots. As I unload them from the kiln, there are invariably some that I love more than others. With the mugs, I usually tuck them on the windowsill at the base of the stairs leading to the upper floor of the house. Every day I walk by the little collection, sometimes stopping to pick one up and look at it again. Occasionally, one or two of them make their way upstairs to my living area. The other place I tend to keep them is on my desk in the gallery. Then, if someone makes just the right comment, off the pot will go with its new owner.

Which brings me to one particular mug. I had been learning about shino glazes and the amazing variety of surface effects they can produce. In a previous firing, I had created a batch of shino mugs that I had glazed quite thin on the inside and thicker on the outside. When I unloaded the kiln, I was delighted with the results. The insides of the mugs turned out a lovely orange, and the exteriors were a creamy tan with dark speckles produced by the iron in the clay. Naturally, I kept my favourite, and over to the staircase windowsill it went, soon to make its way upstairs and into the house. It wasn't to be my morning bathtub coffee mug, as that job was taken, but it did become my cup for after my morning walk with the dogs. As I used the mug, I found myself musing that if I were to glaze the outside surface just a tad thicker with the shino, it would be a creamier colour and contrast beautifully with the orange interior. I tried this out on some mugs for my next firing, and as I came upon them while unloading the kiln, I let out a little yelp. They were gorgeous!

There was one in particular that I kept coming back to. I took it upstairs, away from hungry mug eyes, with the thought that I would swap it with the mug from the earlier firing. But, alas, I couldn't do it! I had fallen in love with the first mug and had to keep it. Now, as you can imagine, I have no shortage of mugs in my home and didn't feel I should also keep my latest

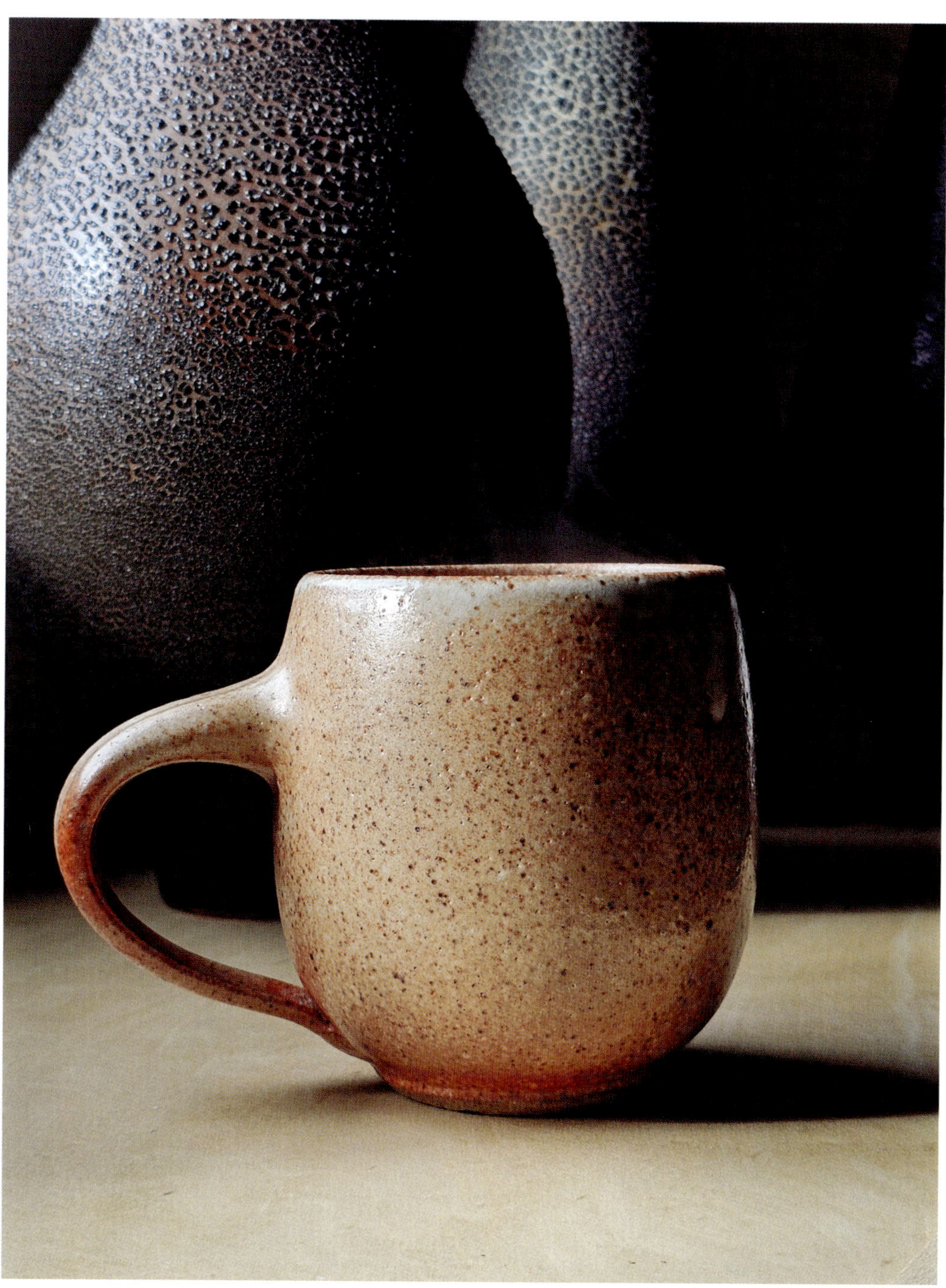

love, so back down it went to a spot on my desk in the gallery. Every day I would pick it up and spend a moment admiring it. People noticed it and would ask if it was for sale, but I wasn't ready to part with it, so I would tell them it was spoken for.

Then one day, as I picked it up, the perfect recipient flashed through my mind, and I knew where the mug belonged. Later that day, I packaged it up and popped it in the mail as a surprise gift.

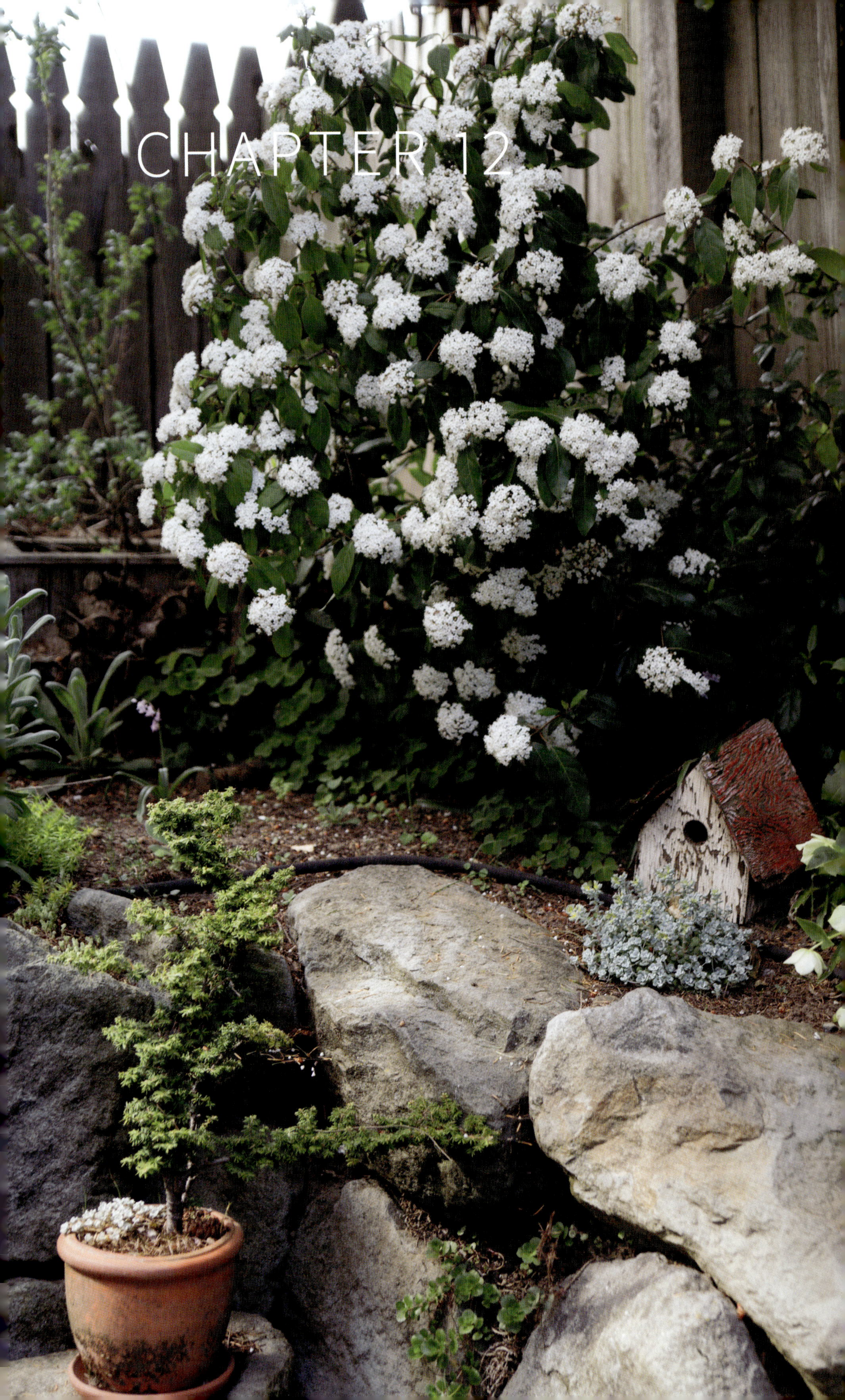

CHAPTER 12

THE INSPIRATIONAL BEAUTY OF GARDENS

My favourite book as a child was *The Secret Garden*, by Frances Hodgson Burnett. My Grade 5 teacher would read a chapter every day to the class, and we would always beg her for more. I'm not sure how many times I've read that book since, but each time it pulls me in and carries me back to my childhood fantasies of gardens and other magical places. I have always loved to create calming, hidden sanctuaries that can whisk us away from the stressors of the modern world and into a more contemplative, healing space.

Over the years, I have created five gardens here at the pottery. The first garden visitors see on arriving is on the boulevard, where raised beds overflow with an ever-changing mixture of flowers and vegetables. As folks approach the gallery, some will also notice the garden at the side of the house and pause to take it in. Next, they are greeted by the front courtyard garden, its planters bursting with seasonal mixes of flowers, vines and small shrubs. Visitors have described this welcoming entrance as "an eruption of flowers preparing them for the explosion of pots inside."

At the back of the house, hidden from the street, is my secret garden, a restful sanctuary. One of my favourite moments is when I catch a visitor's gasp as they walk into the creation room and look upon my secret garden for the first time. The fifth garden is on the upstairs balcony and only visible to those who are curious enough to walk up the back stairs to take a peek, or those who have been invited up to the middle floor of the house—my main living area.

Over time, my secret garden has become the place where damaged pots find their final resting spot. Each spring, the garden grows up around them, eventually obscuring them as the plants mature. Then as the season changes to fall and winter and the plants die back, the clay remnants reappear.

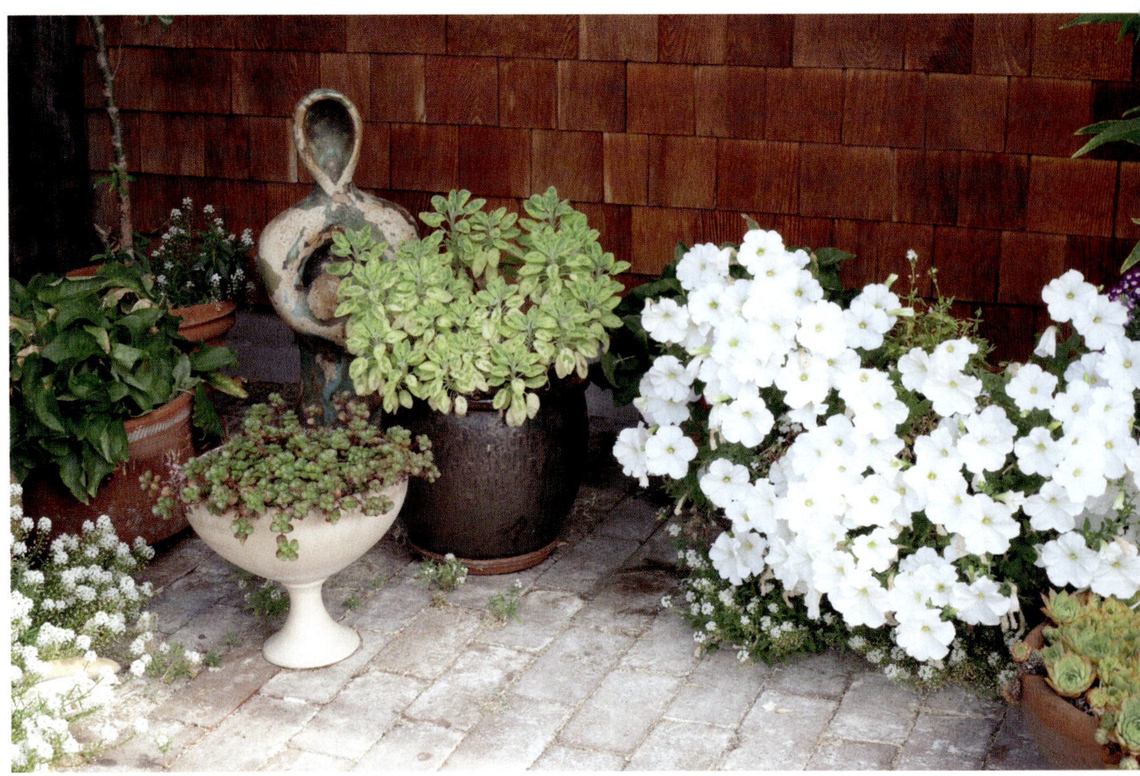

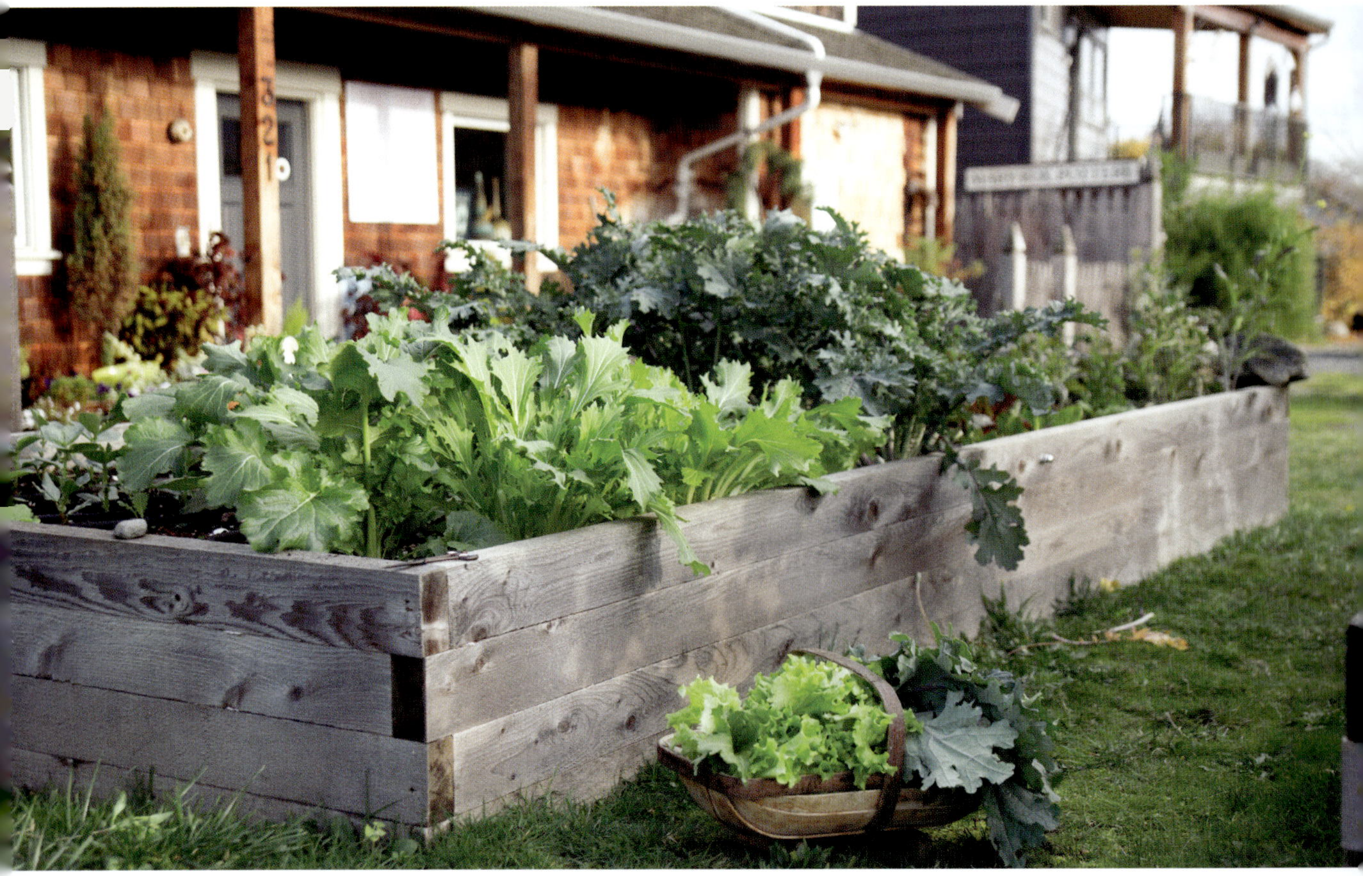

Many years ago, when I opened my front door in the morning to get my newspaper, I was greeted by this fox looking up at me from the doormat. Then, quite a few years later, as I picked up my morning paper, I found this little black mouse peering up at me. The two have been looking out for visitors ever since, though somewhere along the way, the mouse lost its tail.

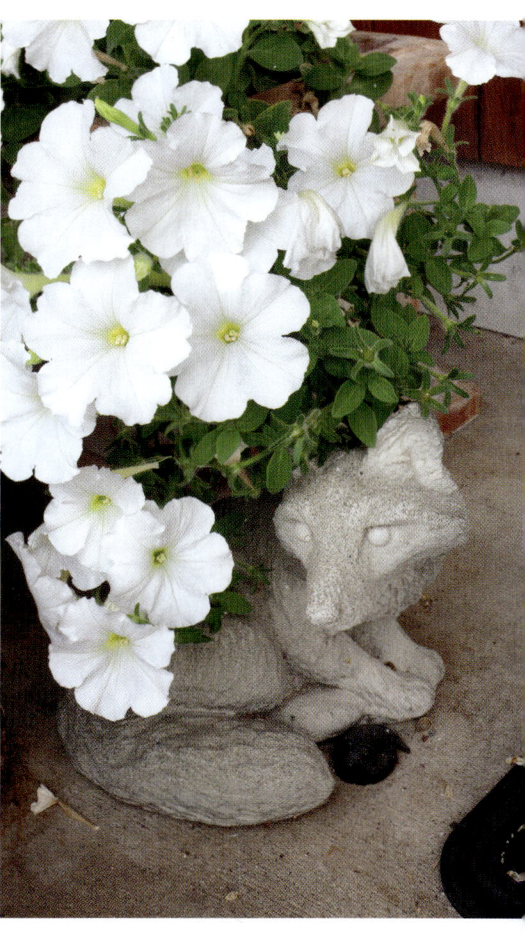

When I first started working again after my five-year illness, I made all sorts of different pieces, and this piece (below) was one of them. Decades ago I had taken pressings from some of the statues at the Ross Bay Cemetery in Victoria, and this is where the ladies' faces on these planters originated. I quite liked them, so I made a few extra and gave my dad one. Never did I think he would nickname it "The Pregnant Lady." The Pregnant Lady never made a very good planter, as the soil dried out very quickly. When I realized this, I planted sedums in mine, as they are very forgiving. My dad, however, kept replanting fresh plants each time the previous occupant died. I would see all sorts of different plants in it whenever I visited. I remember him saying he had the best luck with pansies planted in the wet spring weather. One hot summer day when I arrived, I saw, to my horror, that The Pregnant Lady had sprouted plastic flowers. He defended his actions by reminding me that everything he planted in the summer months died and so...

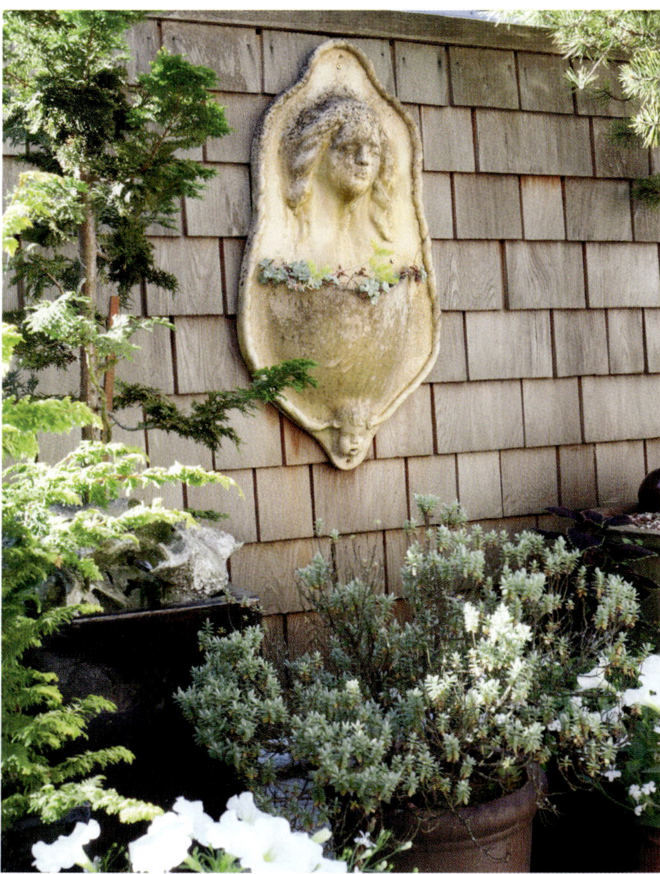

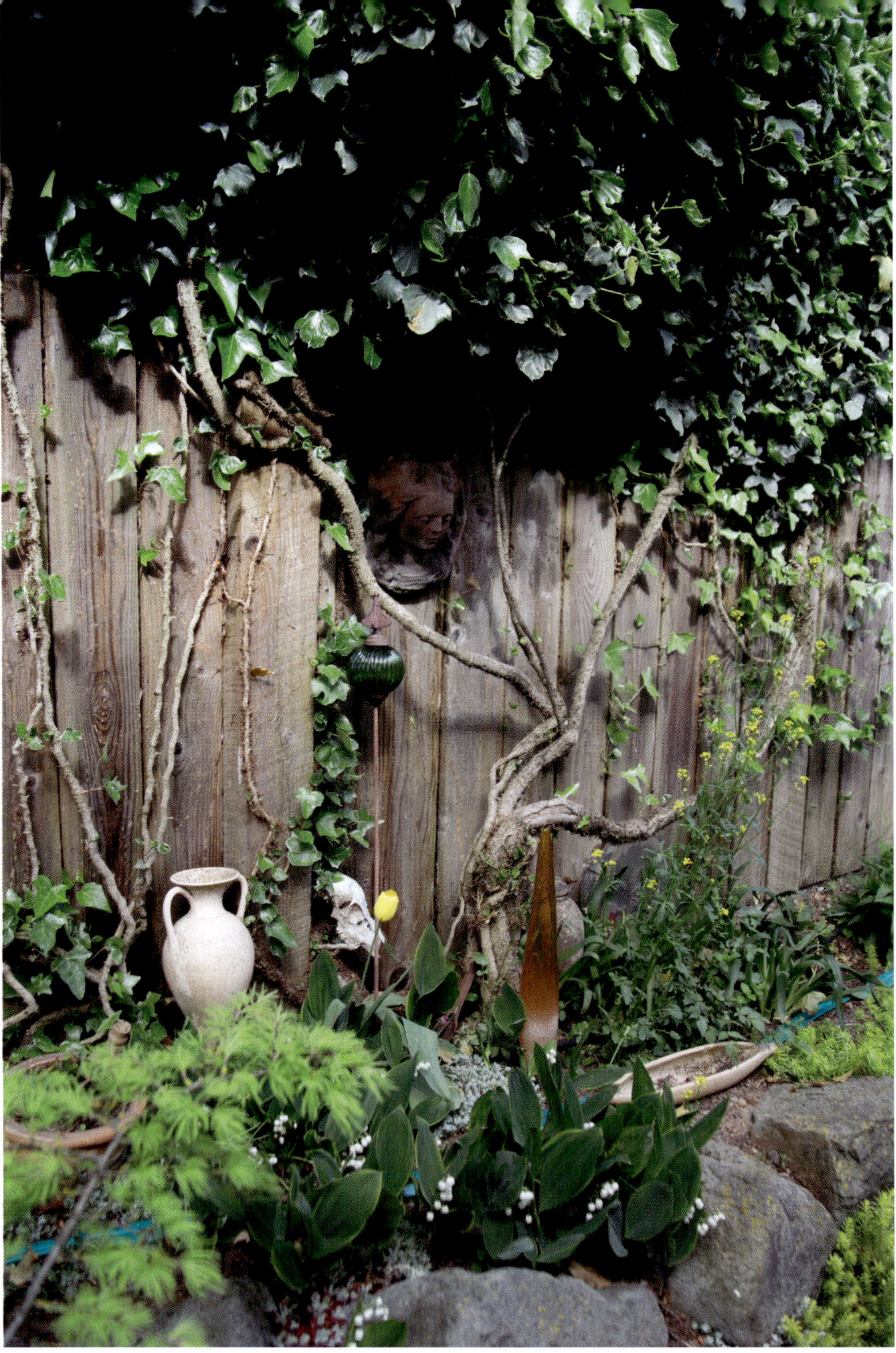

Pots made in sections can be quite challenging. Many things can go wrong, and you usually don't know you have a problem till the piece comes out of the kiln. When I unloaded this amphora from the firing, I noticed a hairline crack where I had added the bottom section. I gave the stem a little tug to see how bad it was, and the bottom section came off in my hand. Generally, whenever something like this happens, a bad mood descends on the studio as I lament the loss of the piece. But eventually I brighten and take the broken piece out to the garden, giving it a new home. This amphora may have been the impetus for me to figure out a better method for adding a bottom section on these tall pieces.

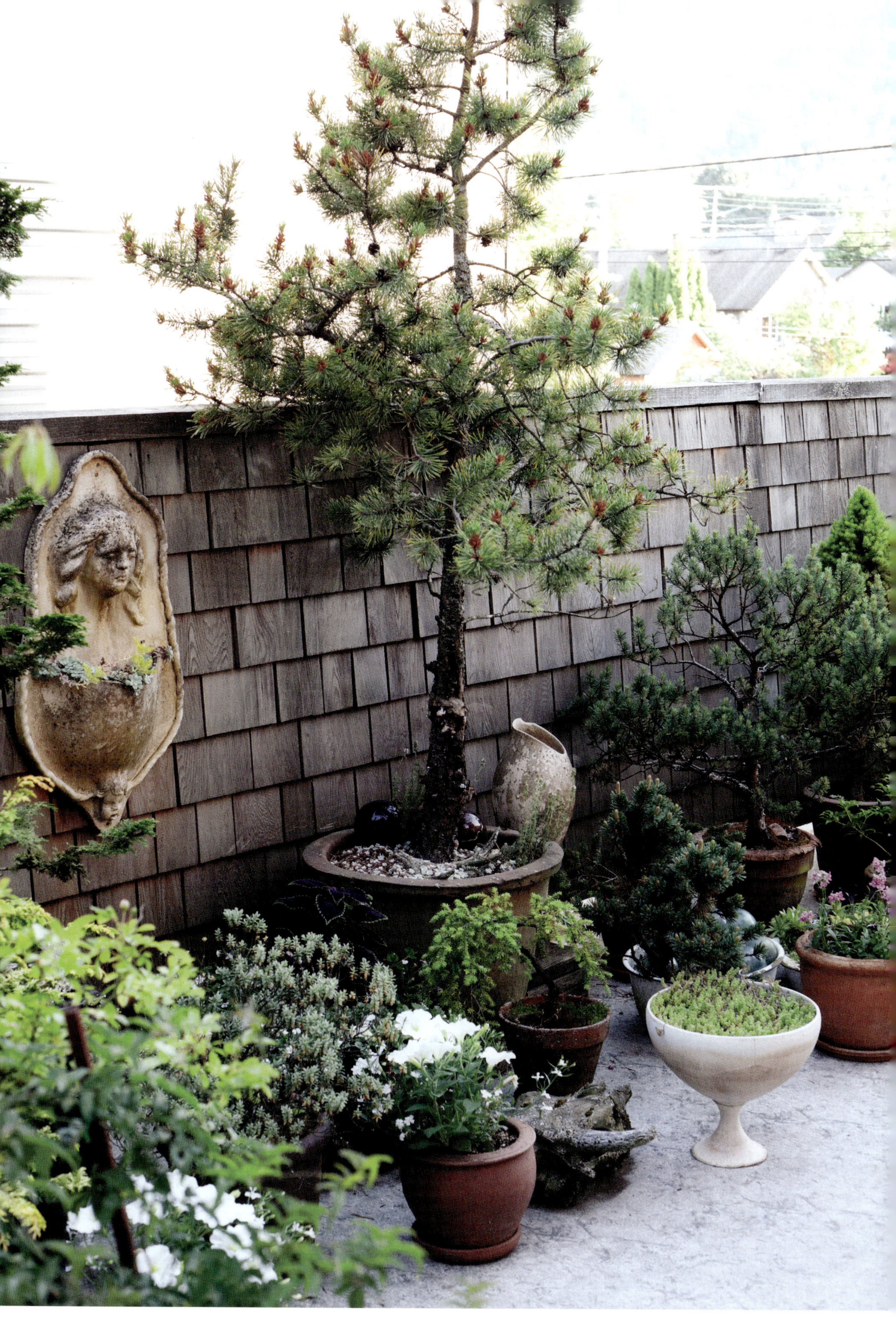

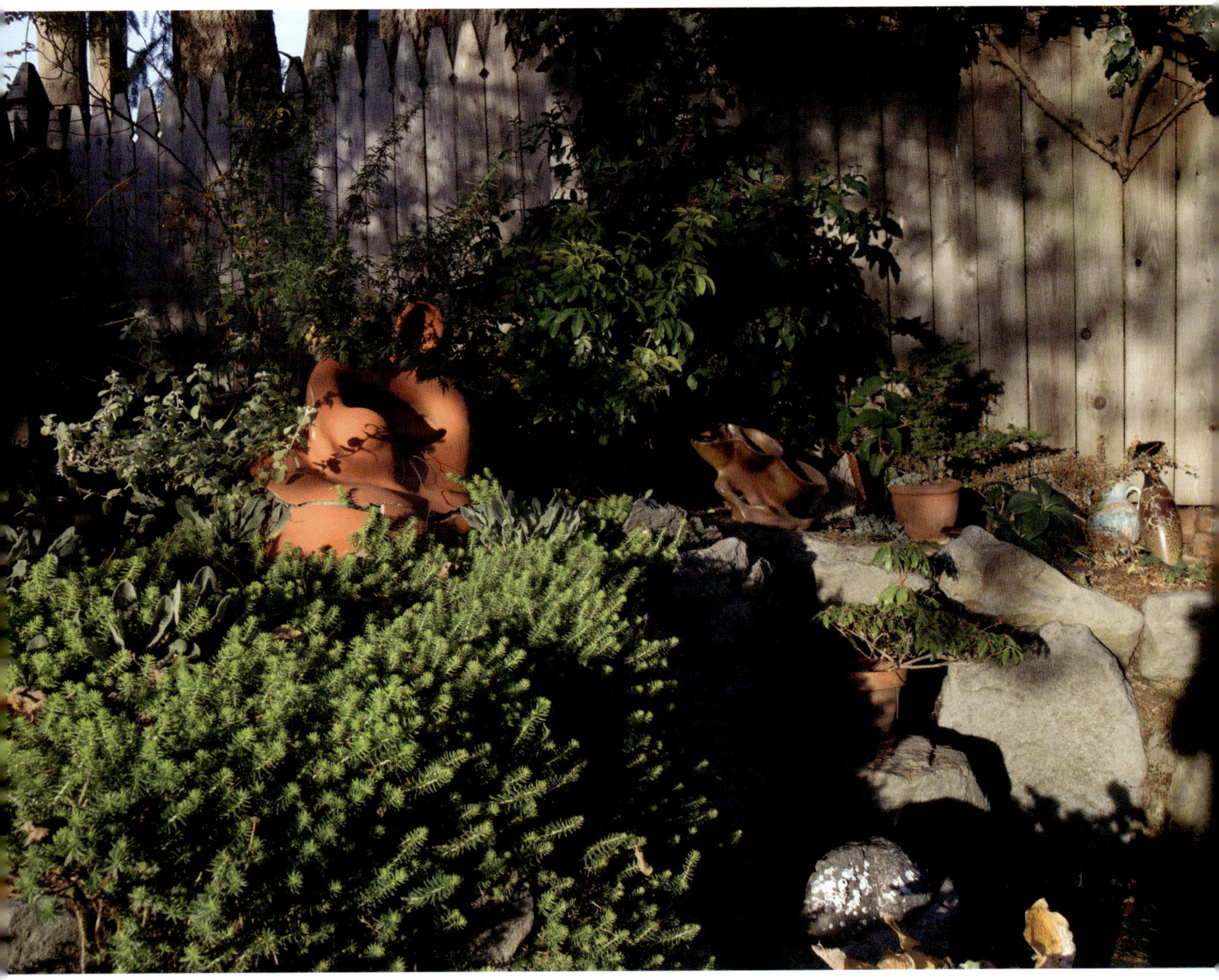

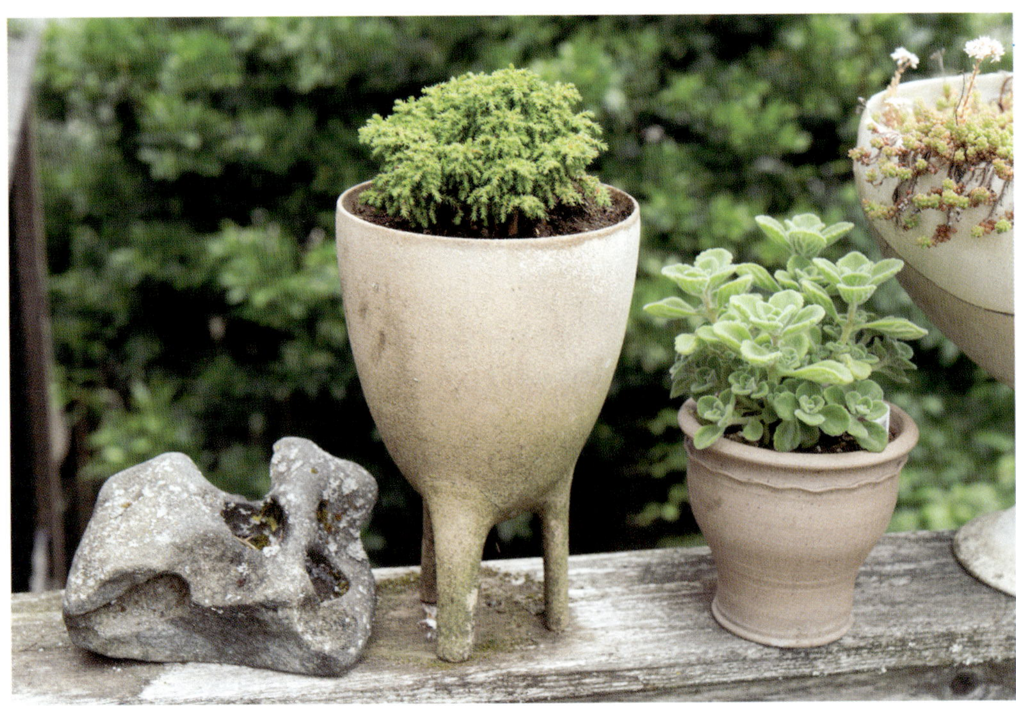

Many years ago, one of my sculptured canoe forms lost a leg, which broke my heart at the time. I wasn't to know that there would be a silver lining to this mishap when I placed the canoe to rest outside in the secret garden. Gradually, the freeze and thaw of winter broke off more bits of the canoe, and I had moments of thinking that maybe it was time to dispose of it. Yet, each time I carried it out to the garbage bin, I couldn't leave it there, and back into the garden it came.

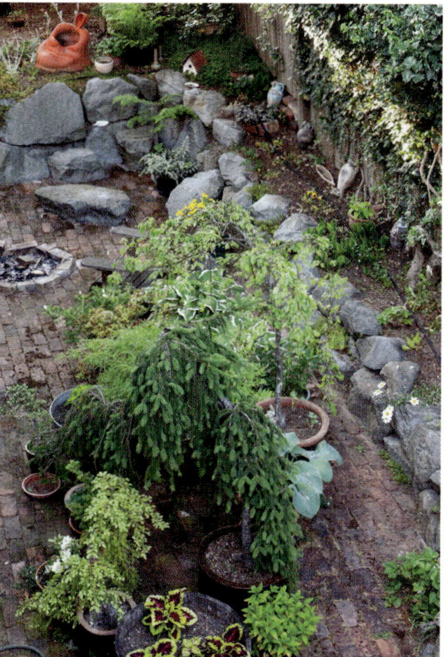

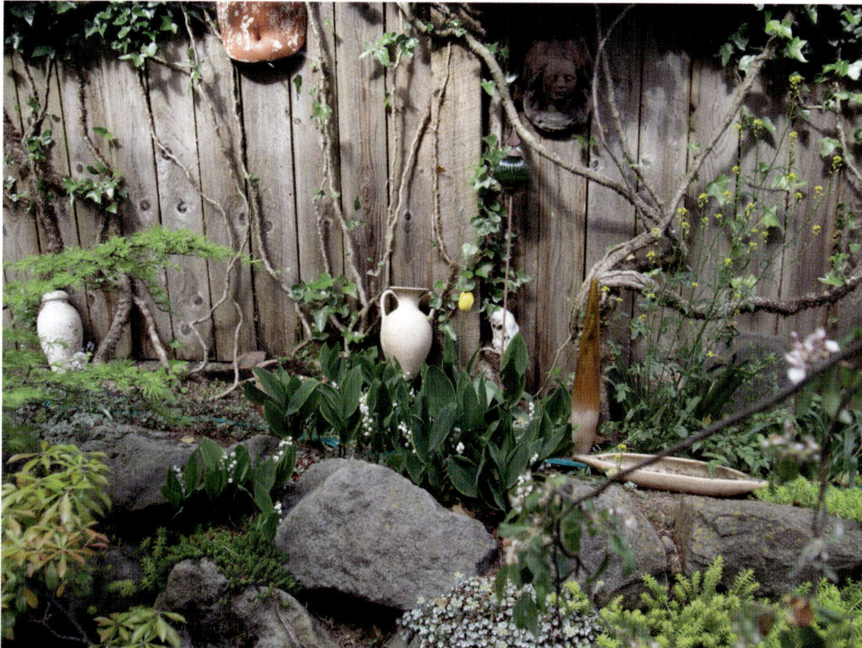

Jump forward to a decade later, when I was on a Gulf Island for my yearly vacation with my sister Angelika, niece Chelsea and her wife Amy. When we were exploring the beaches, Angelika discovered an amazing rock, which I knew I had to bring home. I was so taken with its raw beauty that I thought I would forgo using it as a base for one of my pieces and instead place it in my balcony garden, where I could admire it every day.

When I returned home, I left the rock on the front courtyard table for a while, along with the other rocks found on that trip. Then, one day, like a bolt of lightning, an idea flashed through my mind. I had often contemplated creating hand-built sculptural forms and mounting them on rusty metal or other found objects that had been weathered by nature. This rock had a deeply curved hollow running across its centre, and I suddenly envisioned a weathered beached canoe resting there. I scurried out to the garden to find my old canoe. Though the weather had chipped away more fragments, the basic form was still intact, and when I lifted it, I knew it would fit in the rock's hollow. I carried the canoe to the rock in the front courtyard to see if I was right, and—voila—it was a perfect fit!

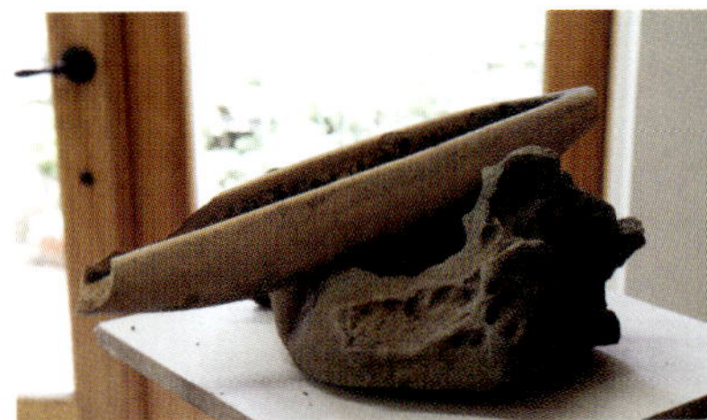

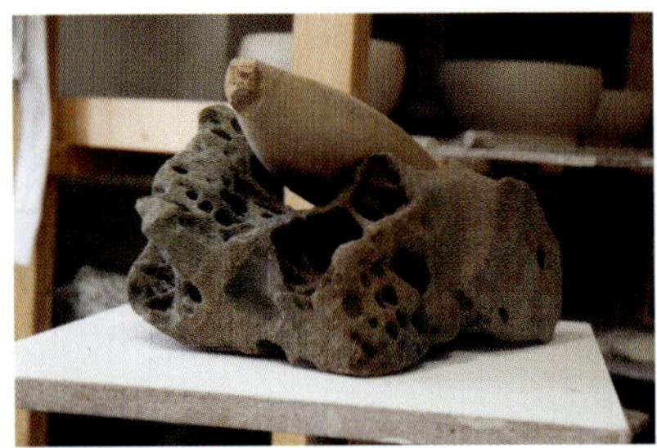

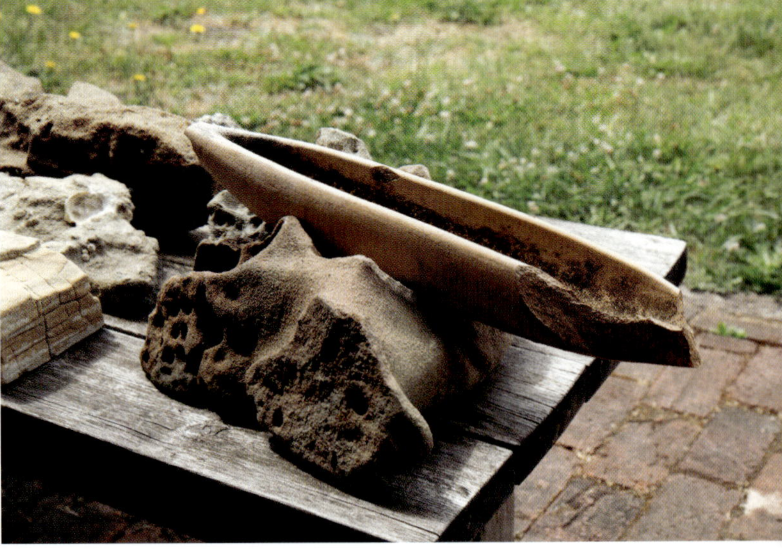

BELOW
Beached, terra sigillata, borax, iron wash, multifired in oxidation, final firing reduction 1900°F, 30 cm W × 20 cm T × 58 cm L.

I brought the rock into the creation room and, using the garden canoe measurements as a guide, sculpted a new canoe. Sometimes, while walking our shorelines, I come across old boats that have been beached for decades, the weather having given them a patina that only time and the elements can create. This is what I had in mind as I started the process of creating the finish for the canoe in *Beached*.

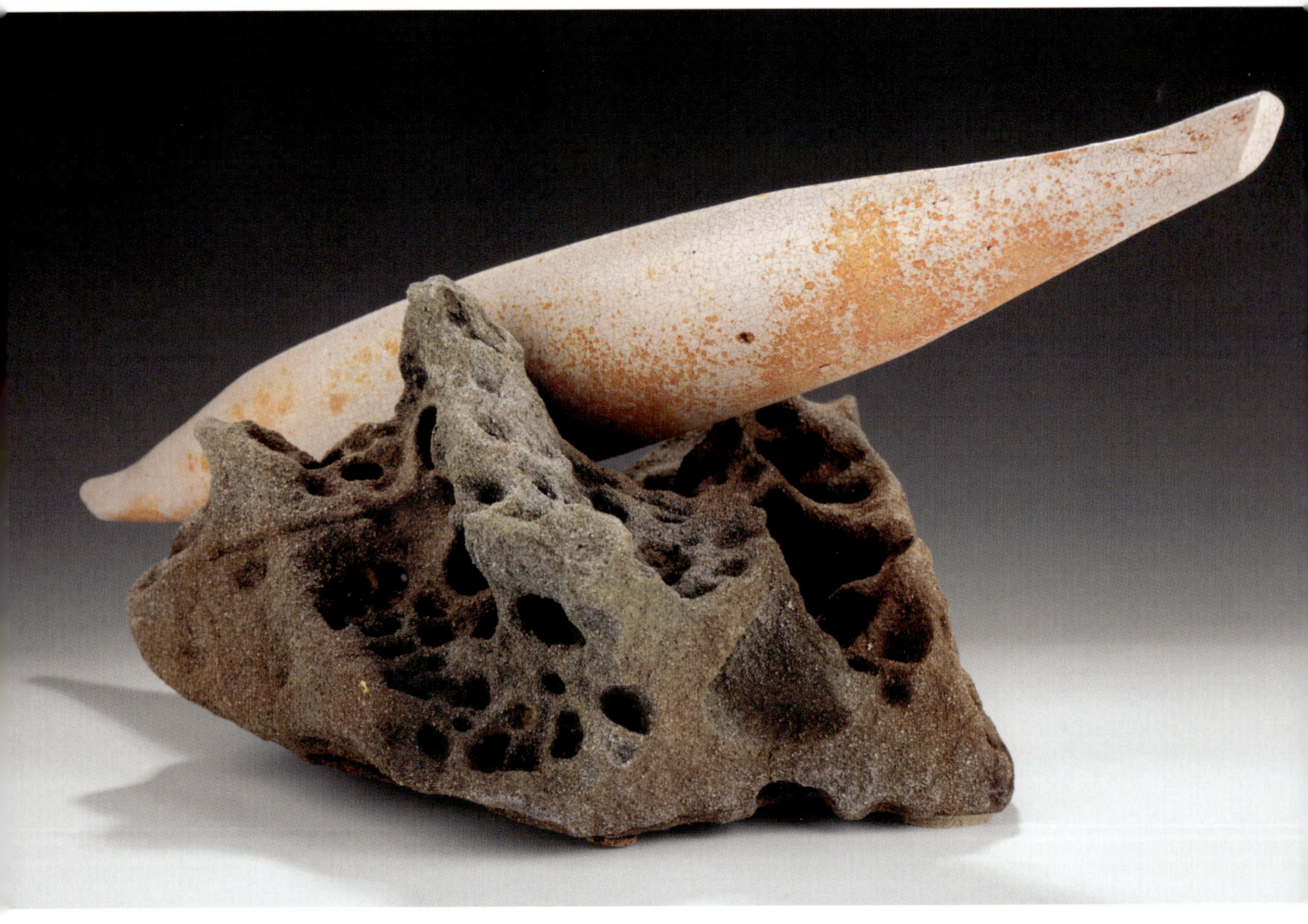

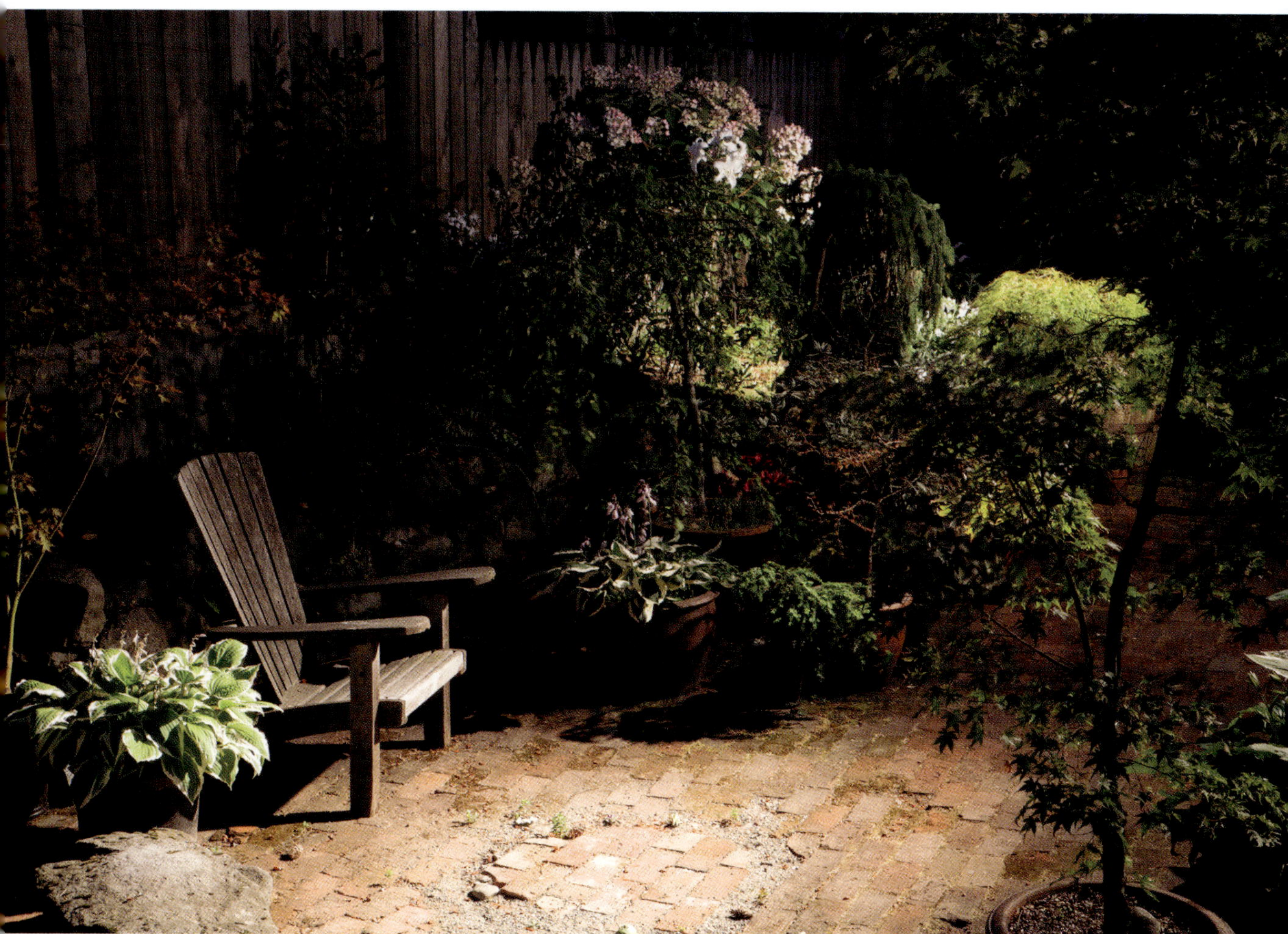

The secret garden at night.

One evening, when I was outside with Amy and Sasha for their bedtime wee, my eyes fell upon this magical scene. I felt as if I could step into the circle of light and disappear into the fantasy world of my childhood. As I stood there taking in the beauty, I contemplated getting my camera and capturing the moment, but it had been a long day and I was tired, so the girls and I went to bed.

The following evening, I went out just before dusk, set the camera up and waited for darkness to fall over the garden again, so I could capture the sublime beauty of the moment.

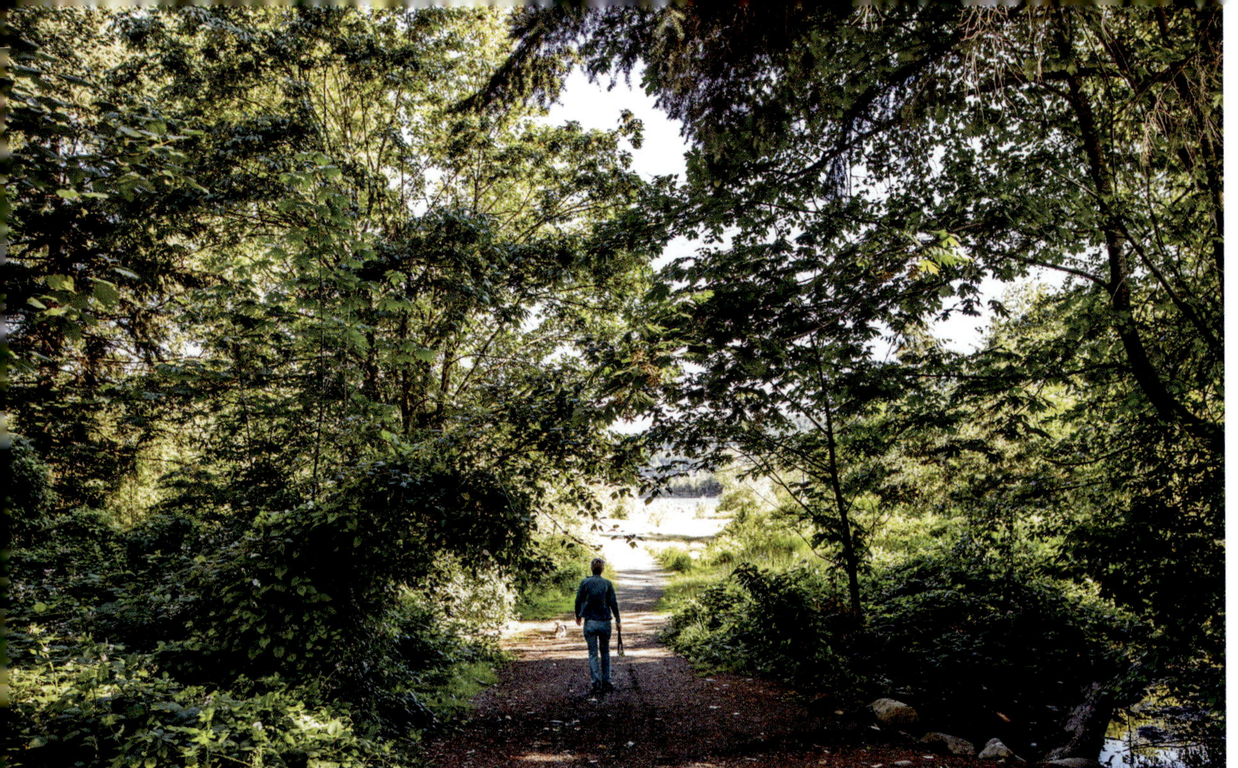

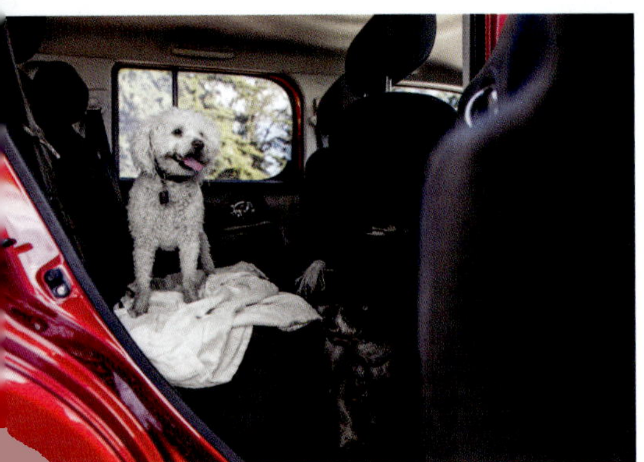

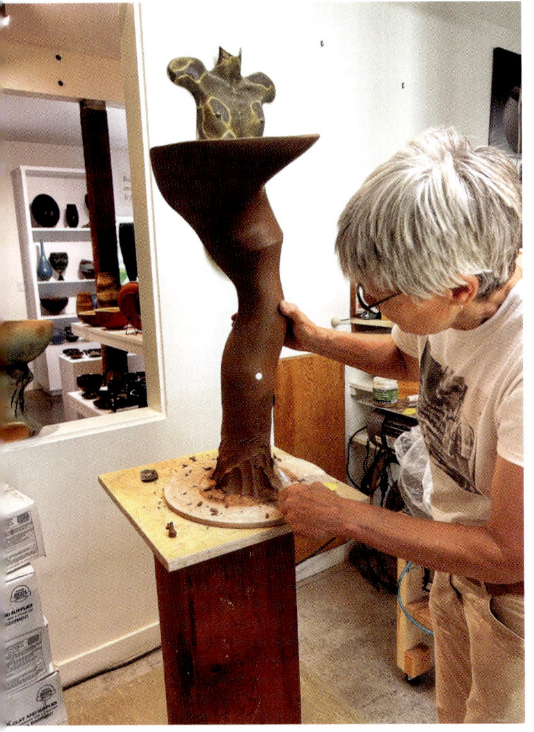

Treasures from yesteryear

On Sunday, I like to take the girls for a special walk to somewhere we don't go every day, and one of their favourite spots is Slack Point here in Ladysmith. The point came into being early in the 20th century, as coal slack and debris slowly accumulated to create a large peninsula. As the seasons go by, more of it erodes into the ocean, unearthing relics from the town's coal mining past. My eye is always on the lookout for new finds that I might use in my art, and on one of our many walks around the point I spotted a piece of our town's history that had recently emerged—a rusted iron disc poking out of the pebbly shore. As I inspected it more closely, I could see that it was attached to a long rod with more rusted parts—likely an axle attached to a wheel disc. I tried to lift it and immediately realized I would need help, so I beetled off to my neighbour Stu's house to see if he could give me a hand. We loaded a wheelbarrow into his car and headed off to the beach to retrieve my find.

With the wheel back home, Stu tried drilling the hole in its centre to enlarge it for use as a mount hole, but iron is very dense and hard, and he soon realized a machinist would be needed to do the job. As he took care of finding someone to do that, a sculpture design began to form in my mind.

LEFT MIDDLE
In the car, Amy is always eager to see where we are going for our Sunday walk, and Sasha just curls up until we get there.

TOP
Walking down to Slack Point.

LEFT
Working on the sculpture.

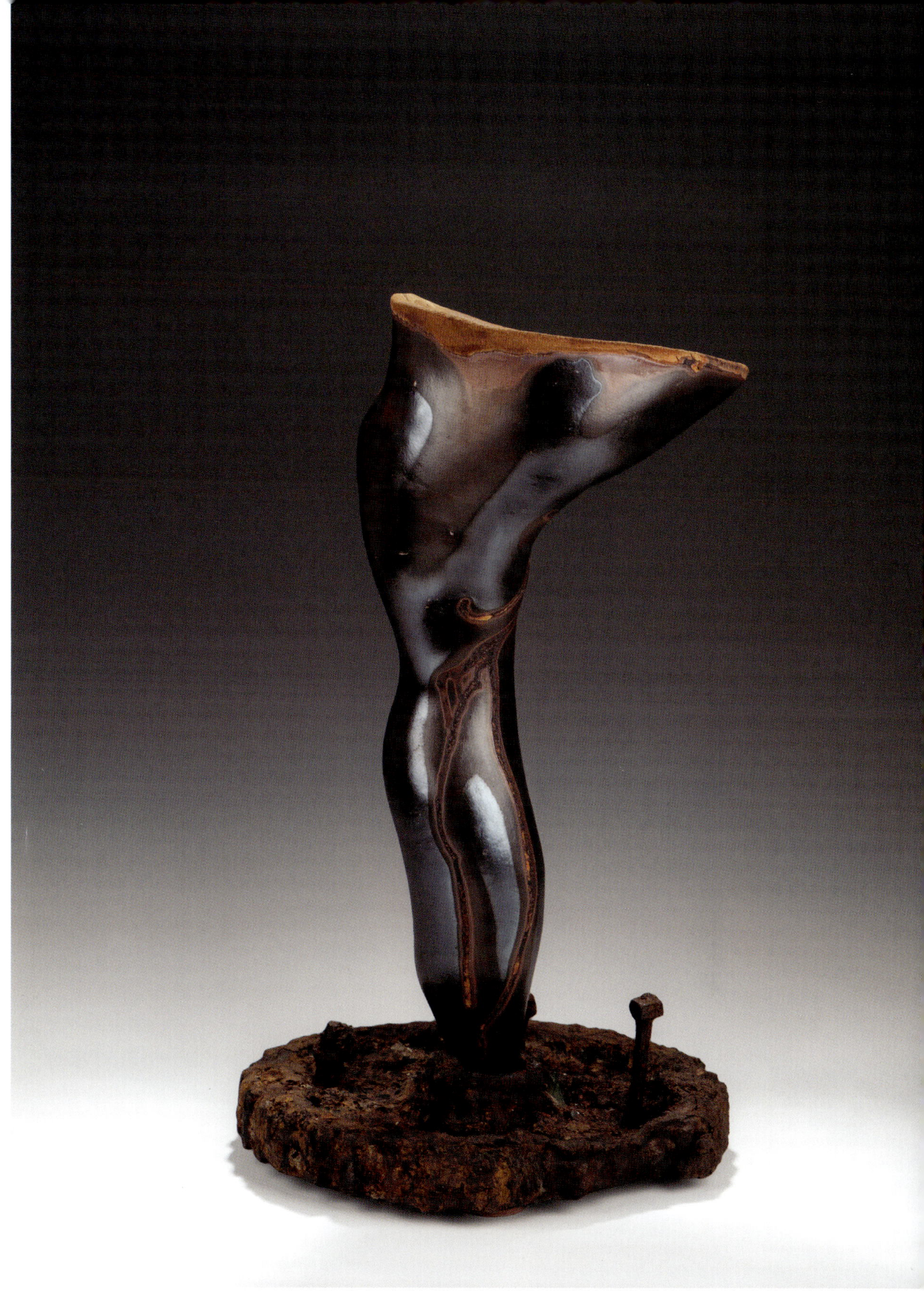

Long after we are gone, the remnants from our life here on Earth remain, persevering in even the most hostile of environments. Whoever dumped what was likely part of an old coal cart would never have imagined that a century later an artist out for a walk would come upon it and retrieve it to use in a sculpture.

From the Wreckage, terra sigillata, Lana Wilson's chartreuse, reduction fired 1900°F; base: 30 cm W, sculpture: 64 cm T.

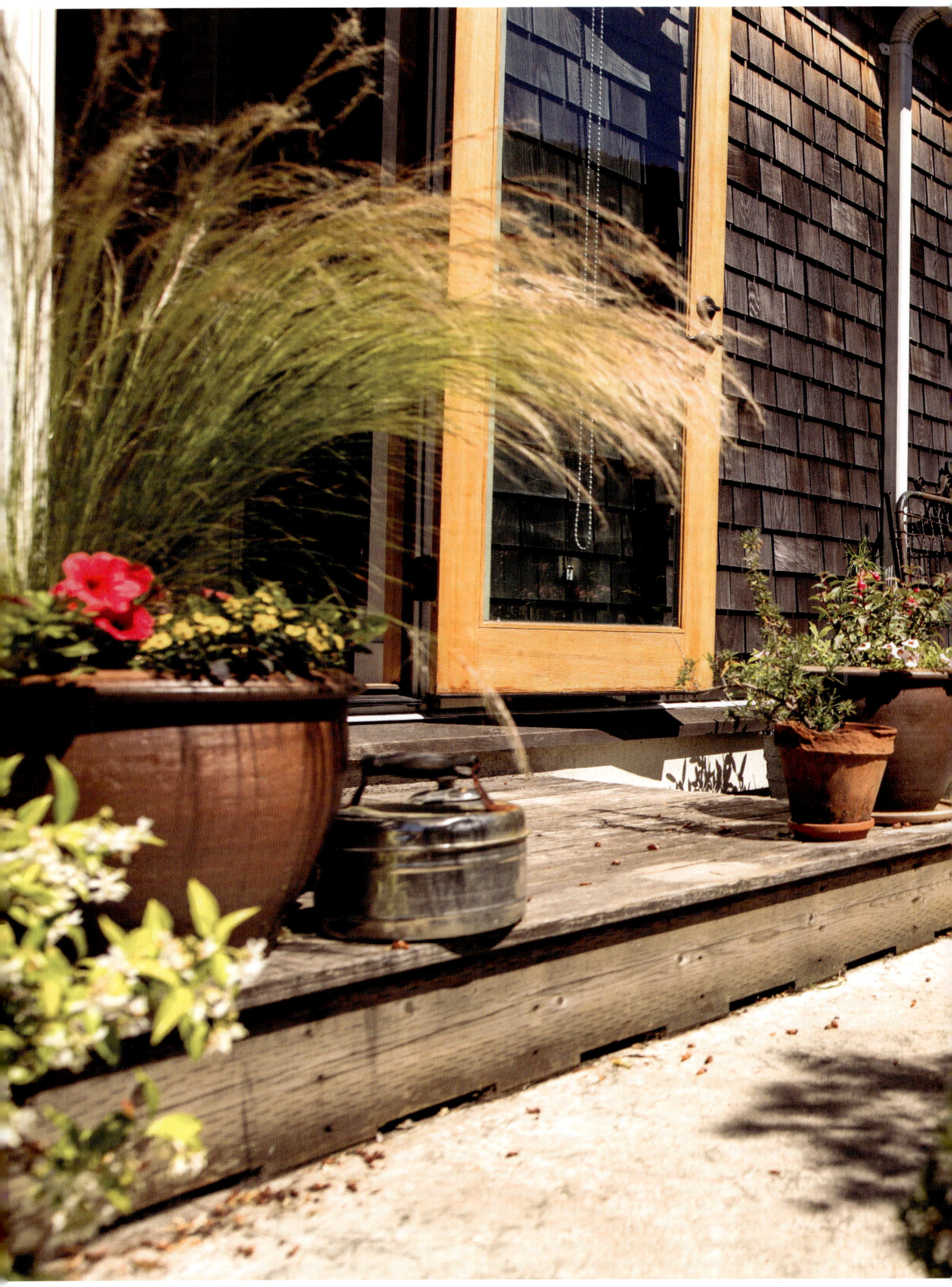

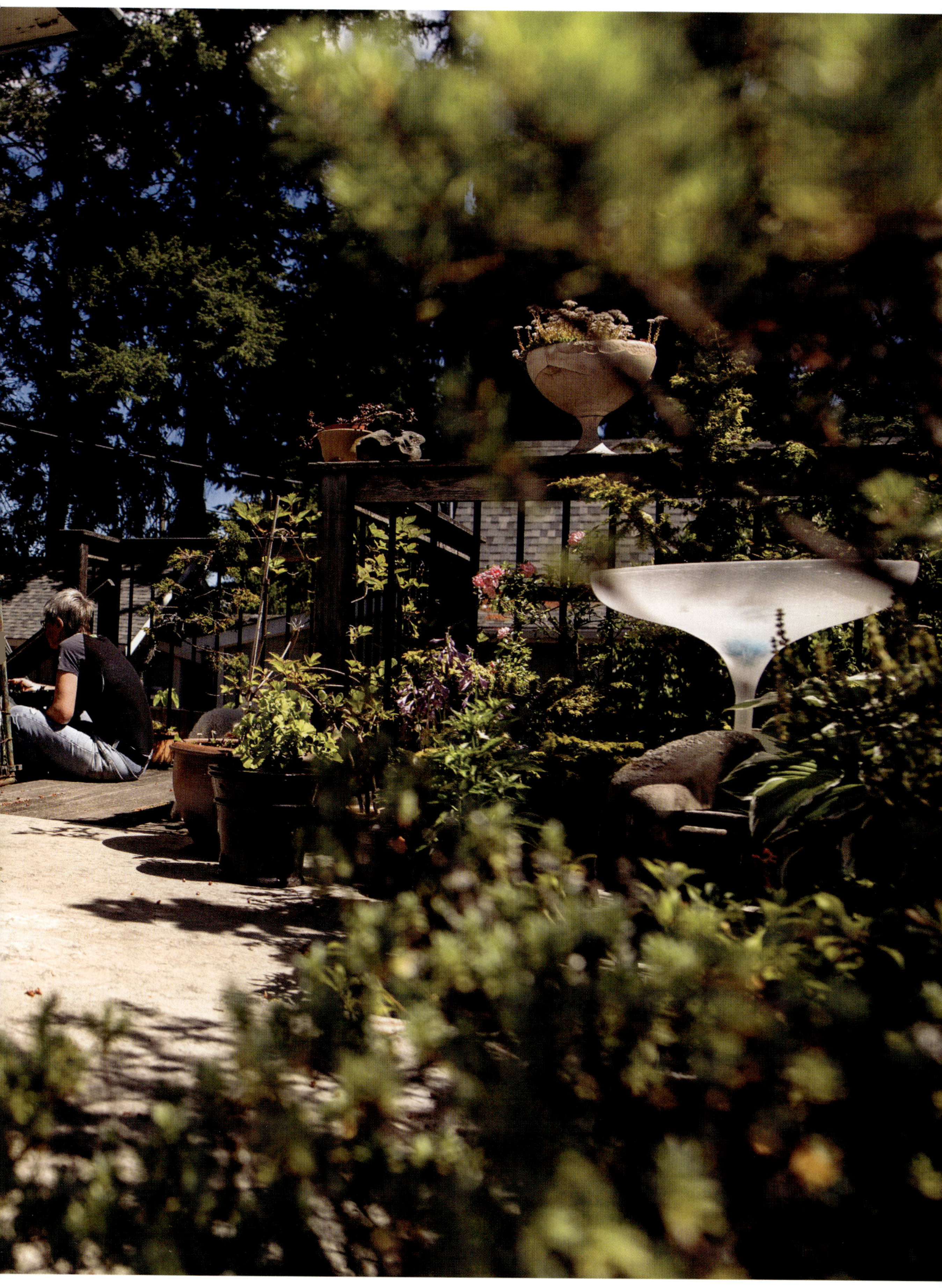

CHAPTER 13

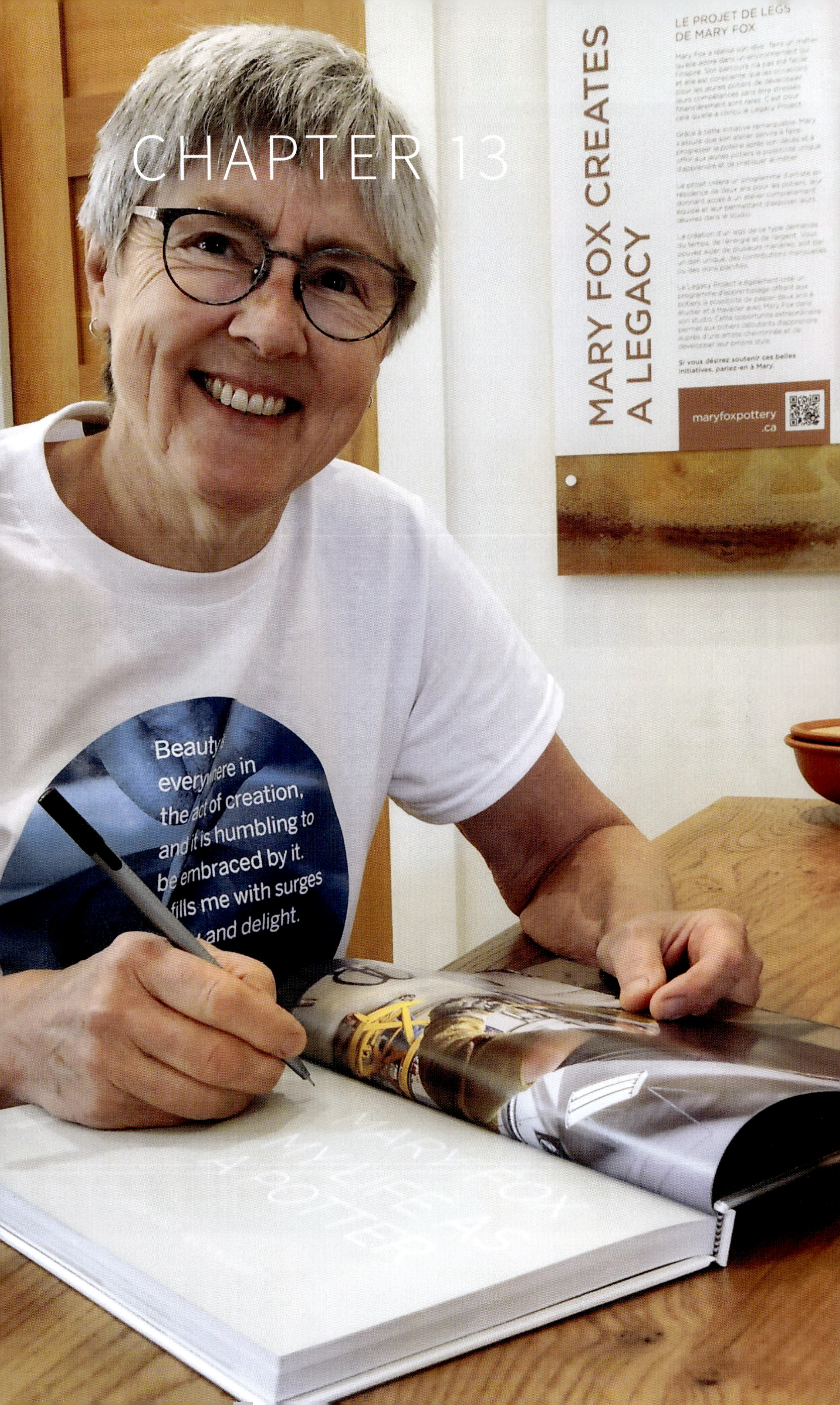
MARY FOX CREATES A LEGACY
LE PROJET DE LEGS DE MARY FOX
Si vous désirez soutenir ces belles initiatives, parlez-en à Mary.
maryfoxpottery.ca
the act of creation,
and it is humbling to
be embraced by it.
fills me with surges
and delight.
MARY FOX
MY LIFE AS
A POTTER

THE MARY FOX LEGACY PROJECT GROWS

Things are constantly shifting in life. No sooner do you start down one road than an unforeseen fork in the road appears. You choose a new path and start to wander that way when, bam, you meet another fork! That's how the Mary Fox Legacy Project feels to me as it unfolds.

When I first began work on the project in 2011, my goal was to expand my studio and gallery space and establish an endowment fund to support an artist residency program at my studio after I'm gone. Knowing how hard it is for potters just starting out to find the resources and time they need to explore their craft and establish themselves, I wanted to create an opportunity for them to do so at my fully equipped studio and gallery. However, I was completely overwhelmed by all that needed to be accomplished to make it a reality rather than just an idea I dreamed about. I felt anxious about the challenges involved, but reminded myself that every project feels that way at first. The trick is to make yourself start and trust that you will get there.

Since then, the project has grown beyond what I could have imagined. In 2014, the Mary Fox Legacy Project became a society, and under the auspices of the Vancouver Foundation and the Craft Council of British Columbia, an endowment fund was established to give donors the opportunity to support the project over the long term.

Then, in 2020, I created the two-year apprenticeship program, for which the legacy project has set up a separate donation fund. The program is modelled on traditional apprenticeships where the trainee learns to re-create the head potter's tableware and take care of the many jobs that keep a

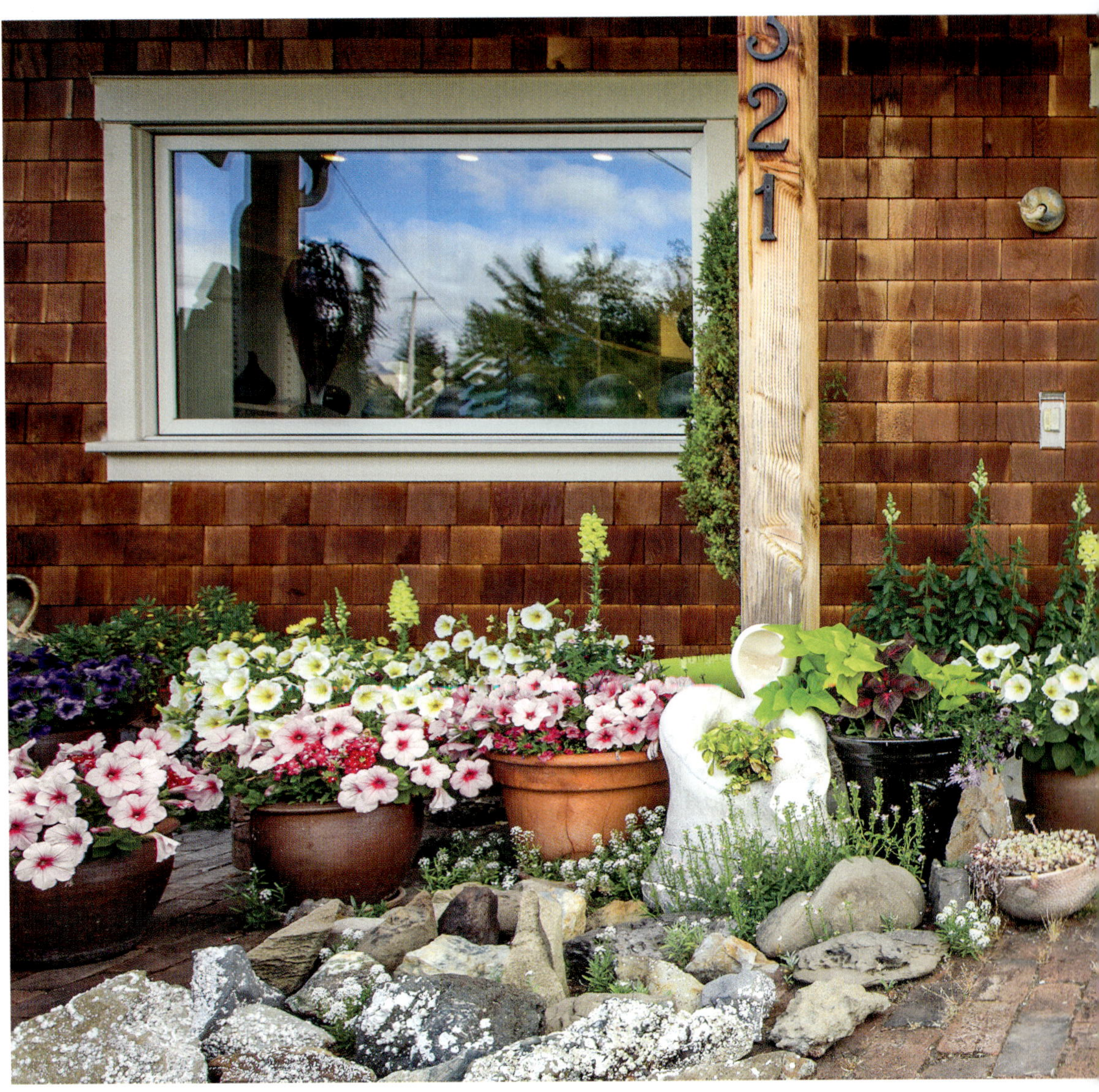

working pottery going. In the second year, the apprentice has one week a month to begin developing their own line of functional wares.

Meanwhile, my first book, *My Life as a Potter*, came out in 2020 and has produced a steady stream of royalties that are being deposited to the apprenticeship fund with the long-term goal of purchasing artist housing for both the apprenticeship program and the artist residency program in the future. The apprenticeship program has no government support and is fully funded by me at this point. I prefer to pay the apprentice's monthly wage and all other costs associated with running the pottery, so that the donation fund can continue to grow for future housing. I have my eyes on a new condo building in town that is a five-minute walk from the pottery, but we are still a long way from our goal.

To further the legacy project's objective of sharing knowledge, I have been creating a series of videos with the help of local

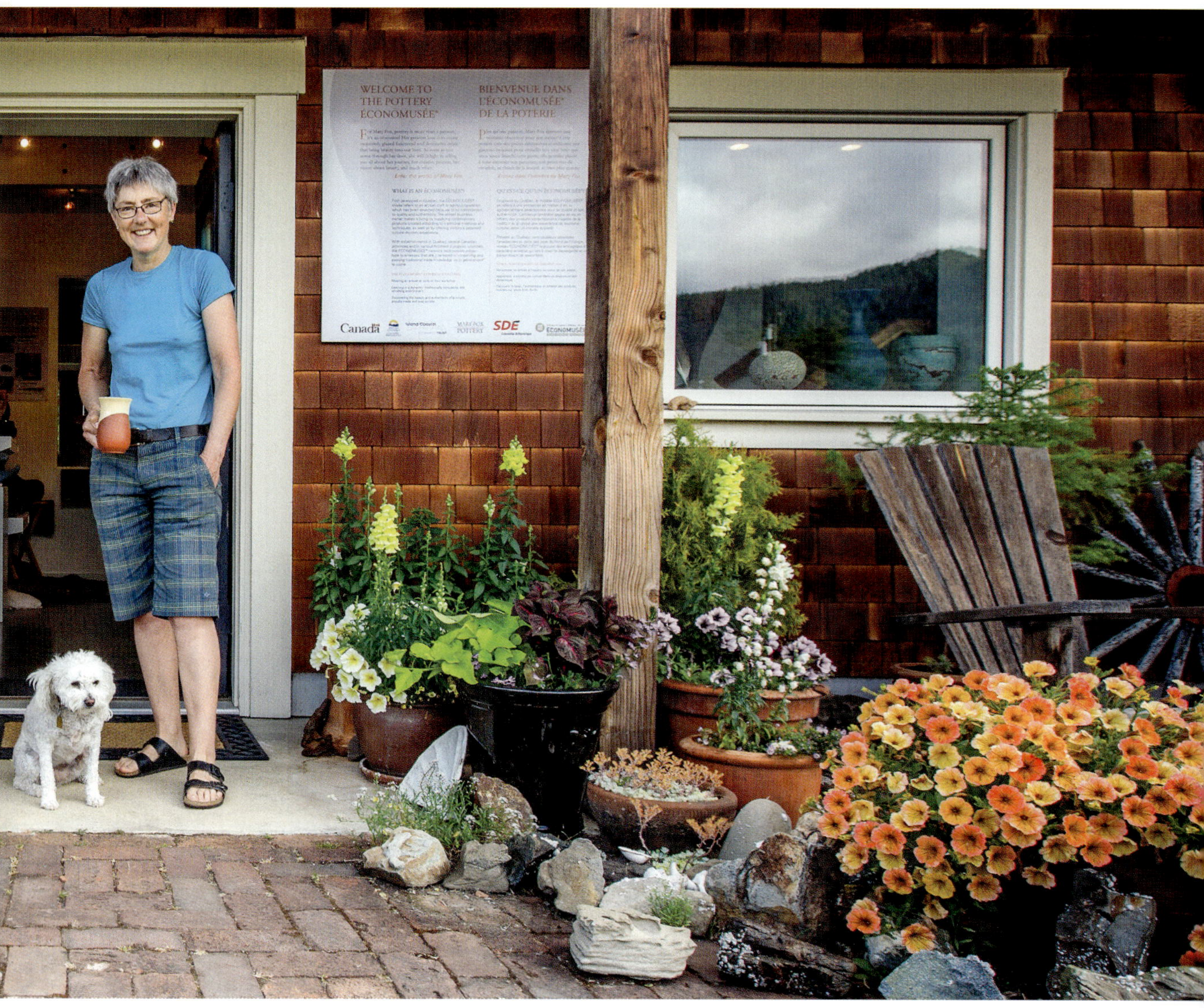

videographers Logan Steele and John Fulton. These videos assist the apprentices and are also posted online on the Creation Room page of my website, allowing other potters to access them from anywhere in the world.

In 2023, Sarah Wilson became the first graduate from the apprenticeship program, going on to set up her own pottery studio in Ladysmith. In early 2024, Sabrina Sachiko Campbell began as the next apprentice, just as I started work on this book. Alongside *My Life as a Potter*, this book is also a fundraiser—all royalties will be donated to the Mary Fox Legacy Project.

Now, here we are all caught up on most of the goings-on here at the pottery since the publication of my first book.

However, as I've said, life always presents new forks in the road. And, recently, an opportunity arose that was too good to pass up. A storefront located on the main street of my hometown became available to rent and, even though I had promised myself no more big projects, I jumped on it. I immediately messaged Sarah Wilson, whose studio was right around the corner from mine, and told her, "Opportunity is knocking! Come on over." She was in my living room five minutes later, and the plan for her very own gallery/studio started to take shape. After months and months of renovations, a working pottery studio was created in the back, and the gallery in the front now showcases Sarah's work, along with other artists she chooses to represent. When I started the legacy project, I never imagined that one of the offshoots would be a retail gallery, but Wilson & Co. is now adding to the vibrancy of downtown Ladysmith.

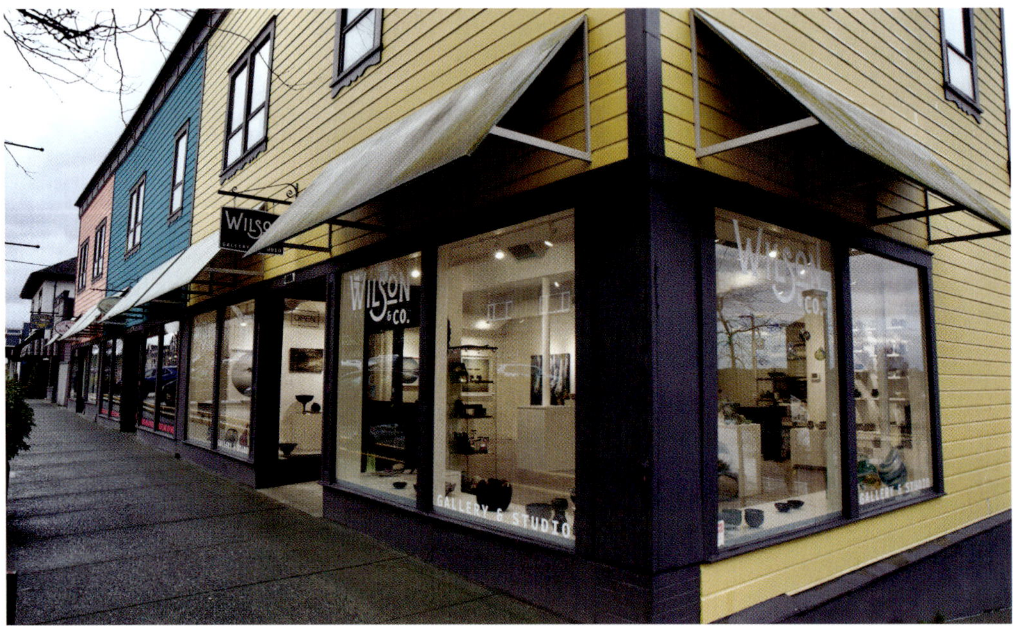

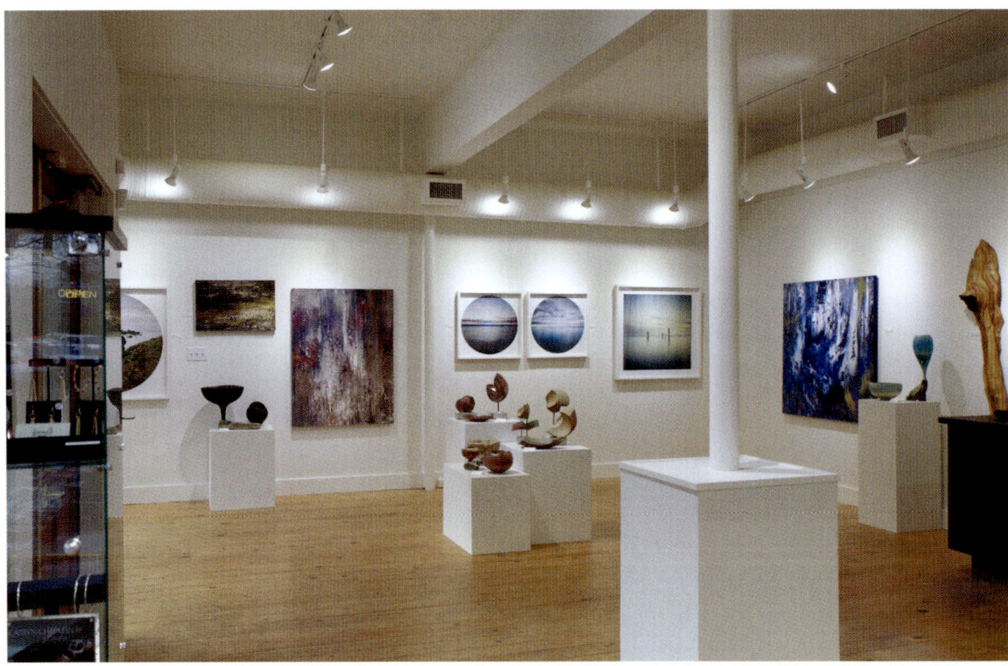

Go to my web page, maryfoxpottery.ca/legacy, for more information about the Mary Fox Legacy Project. On the page are donation buttons for both the apprenticeship program and the Mary Fox Legacy Project Endowment Fund for the artist residency program.

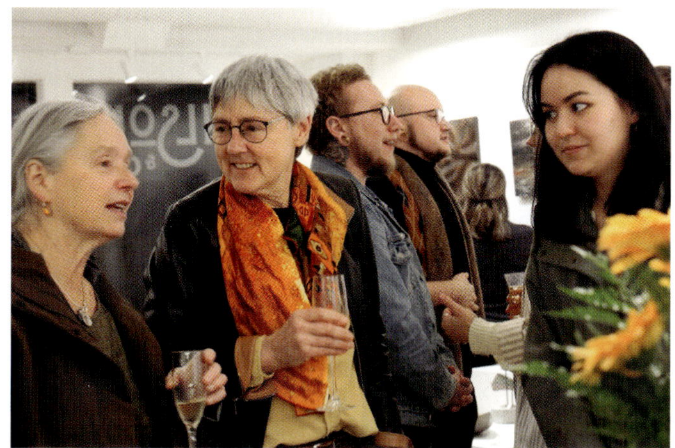

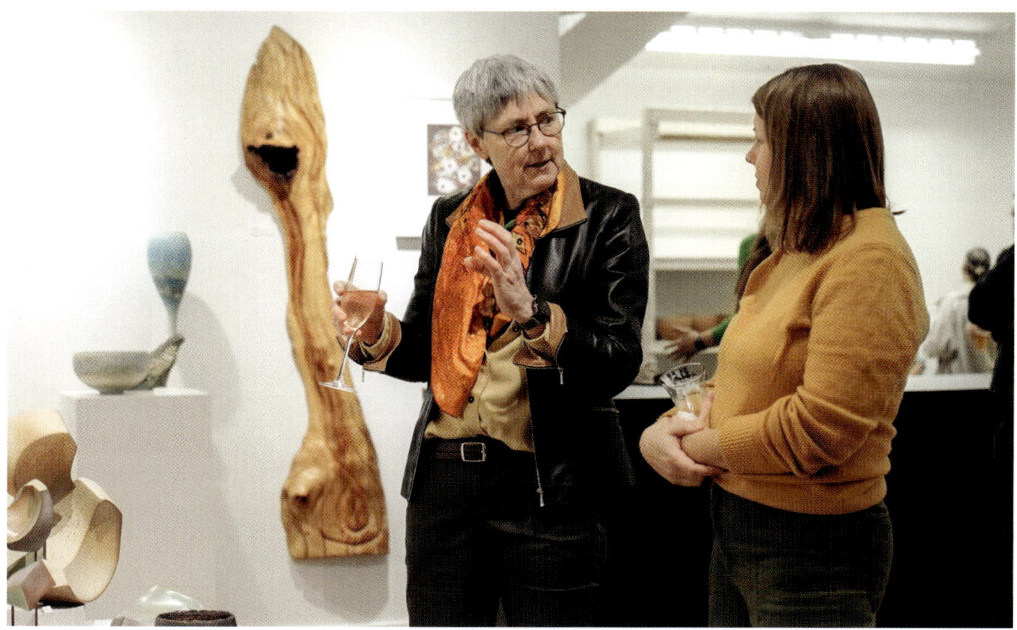

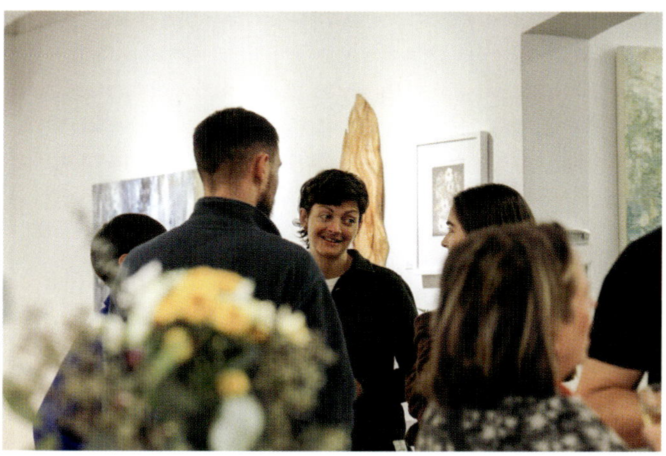

Lessons that keep on giving

BY SARAH WILSON

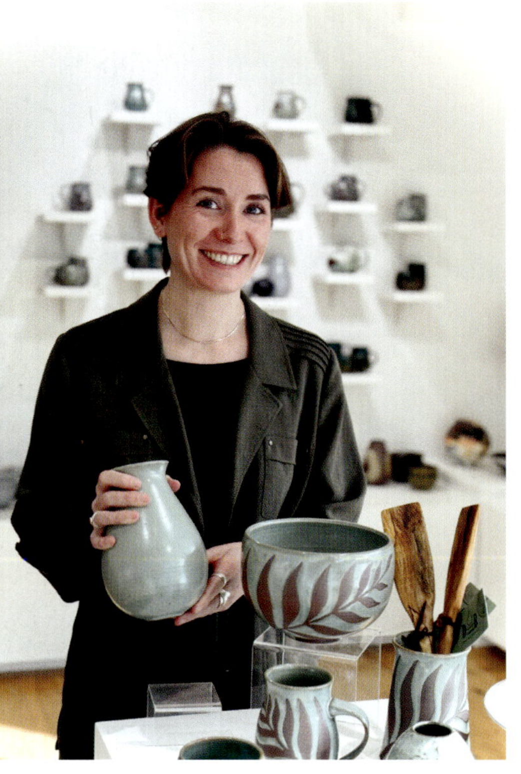

When I reflect on my journey through the apprenticeship at Mary Fox Pottery, I am struck by the stark contrast between the nervous, unsure young potter who first stepped through the door and the excited, budding entrepreneur who emerged two years later, eager to start her own pottery business. The apprenticeship program provided me with many benefits—not just the skill to produce work I was proud of, but also the confidence and road map I would need to make a living in the arts.

During my time at the pottery, I encountered obstacles and learned lessons that have served me beyond the apprenticeship. Many are the same lessons Mary herself learned in her younger years as a potter, described in her memoir, *My Life as a Potter*. Despite the fact that I had read the book before beginning my apprenticeship and despite Mary reminding me of the lessons often, there's nothing quite like learning a lesson through personal experience to make you take heed and remember it! One of the most important is that being a potter is a really physical job—a reality I underestimated at first, but quickly became aware of. It is essential to take breaks and not overwork yourself.

There were many highs and lows throughout the experience. For example, I would be incredibly hard on myself when I didn't get a form just right, or even worse, I would have it right one week and then feel like I had lost all that progress when I messed it up a few weeks later. Nothing really felt better than Mary taking a pot I made out of the kiln and being so impressed with it that she wanted to keep it herself. A hard-won compliment, as Mary is very choosy about the tableware she keeps in her kitchen!

Overall, I feel immense gratitude for my experience as an apprentice. With studio space and time being so difficult and expensive to come by, I would have faced more challenges and made slower progress improving my skills had I not been afforded the opportunity. And I gained much more than skills in the craft. Mary continues to be an incredible support, providing invaluable advice on building a successful career as a potter. Sometimes I ponder what my life would have been like had I not undertaken such an adventure...but that quickly falls by the wayside. There's too much living in the now and planning for the future to do!

The unexpected breakthroughs of applied learning

BY SABRINA SACHIKO CAMPBELL

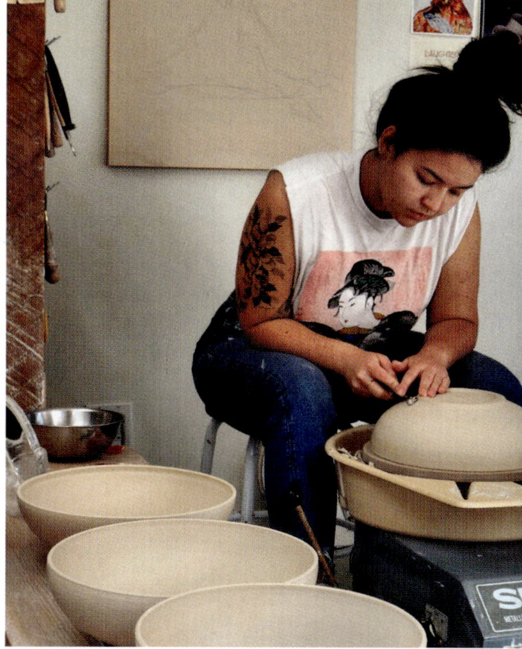

It's easy to get comfortable with what we know, and pottery is no exception. I've had my fair share of starts with pottery, from taking courses at the art gallery to diving back in at school, and more recently joining and teaching classes at a local studio. Despite the wealth of knowledge I've gained from these experiences, after just a few days of my apprenticeship with Mary Fox, it was clear I had only scratched the surface.

When I started the apprenticeship program, I was already intrigued by the world of glazes, but prior to working with Mary, I had little exposure to the process of creating them. I knew there was much to learn. What surprised me was how much simply weighing up different ingredients for glazes expanded my capacity to understand a subject I never thought I'd grasp.

After completing my first week, during which I weighed up various glaze tests for Mary, I took the ferry back to Vancouver with my partner, buzzing with excitement and questions. We spent the trip engrossed in discussing the chemical composition of minerals and their effects on glazes. With his background in science and my new exposure to glazes, I was surprised to find myself grasping chemistry in ways that I never had in school. After just one short week of hands-on learning and a ferry ride, I was beginning to understand a field that had been daunting to me only a few days earlier.

Time flies when you're immersed in a program like this. Though it feels like I started just yesterday, the progress I've made over the last several months speaks volumes to the value of the hands-on experiences I've been fortunate enough to take part in. The chance not only to learn from Mary, but also to see how a lifelong potter continues to experiment and ask questions gives me hope that I, too, will never stop learning.

Mary's thrill over unexpected outcomes and new creations makes me eager for the journey that lies ahead. I'm excited to embrace the new discoveries and many challenges I'll encounter as I continue to explore the vast world known as pottery.

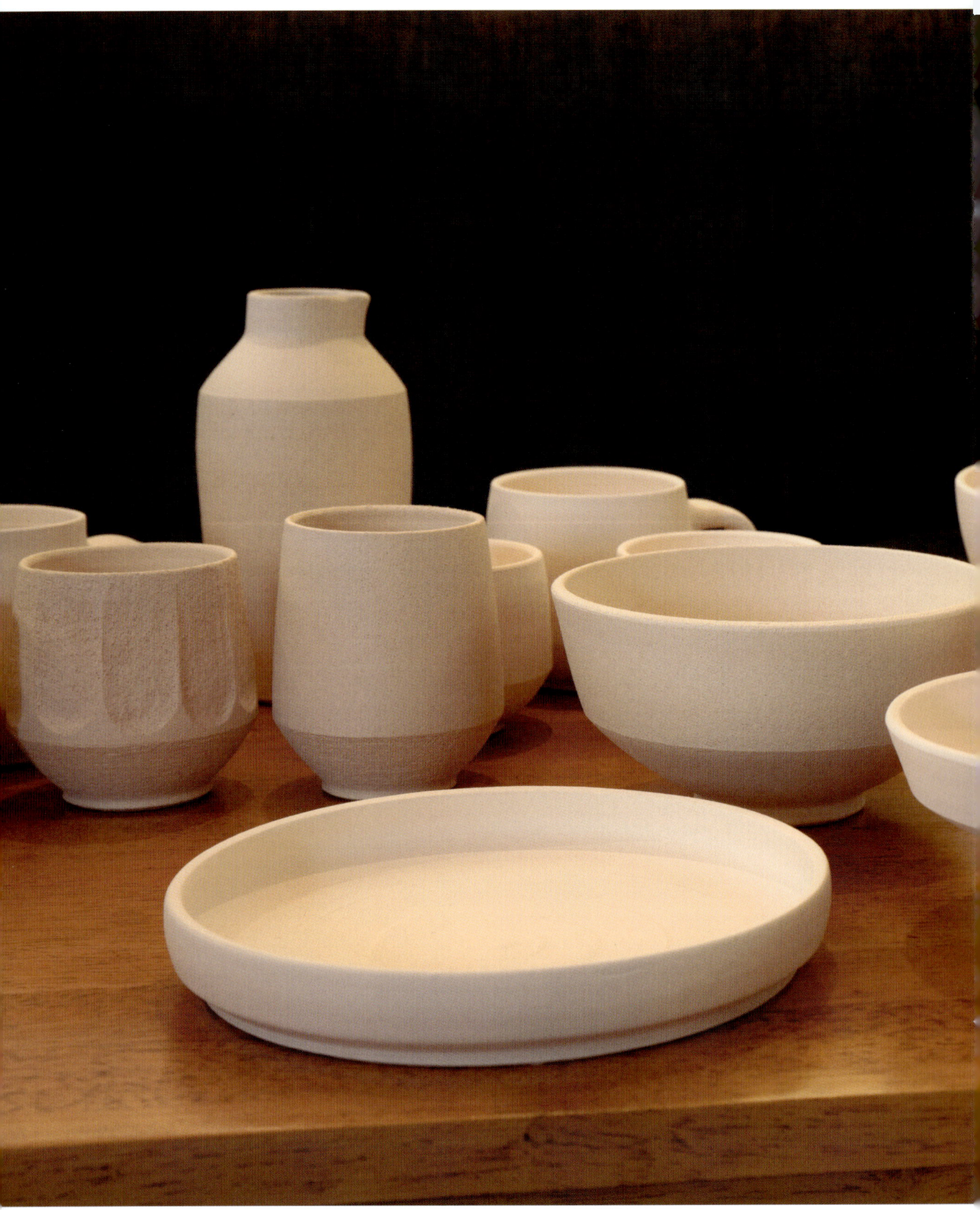

Sabrina's first bisque pieces from what will become her line of tableware laid out on my living room table for discussion.

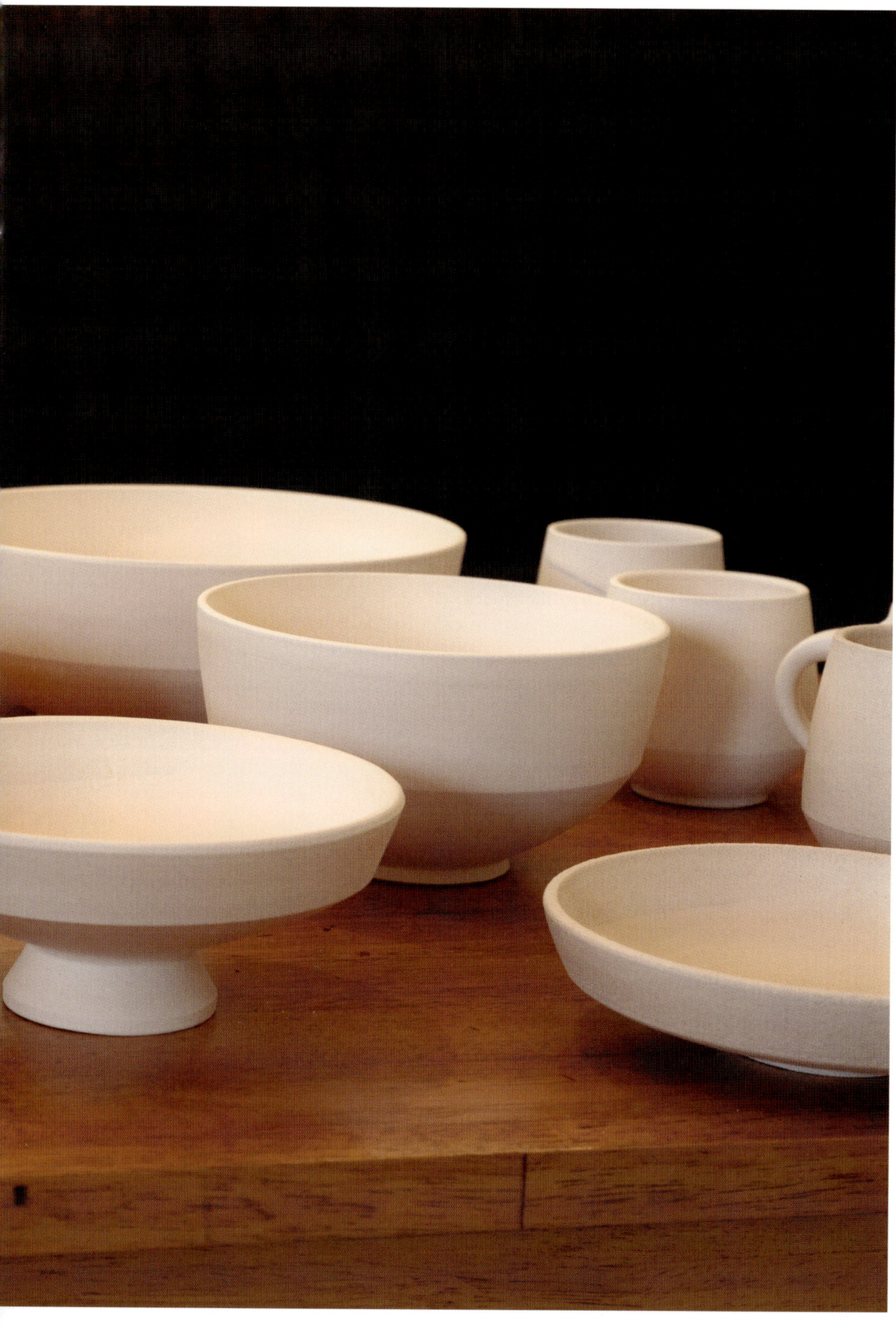

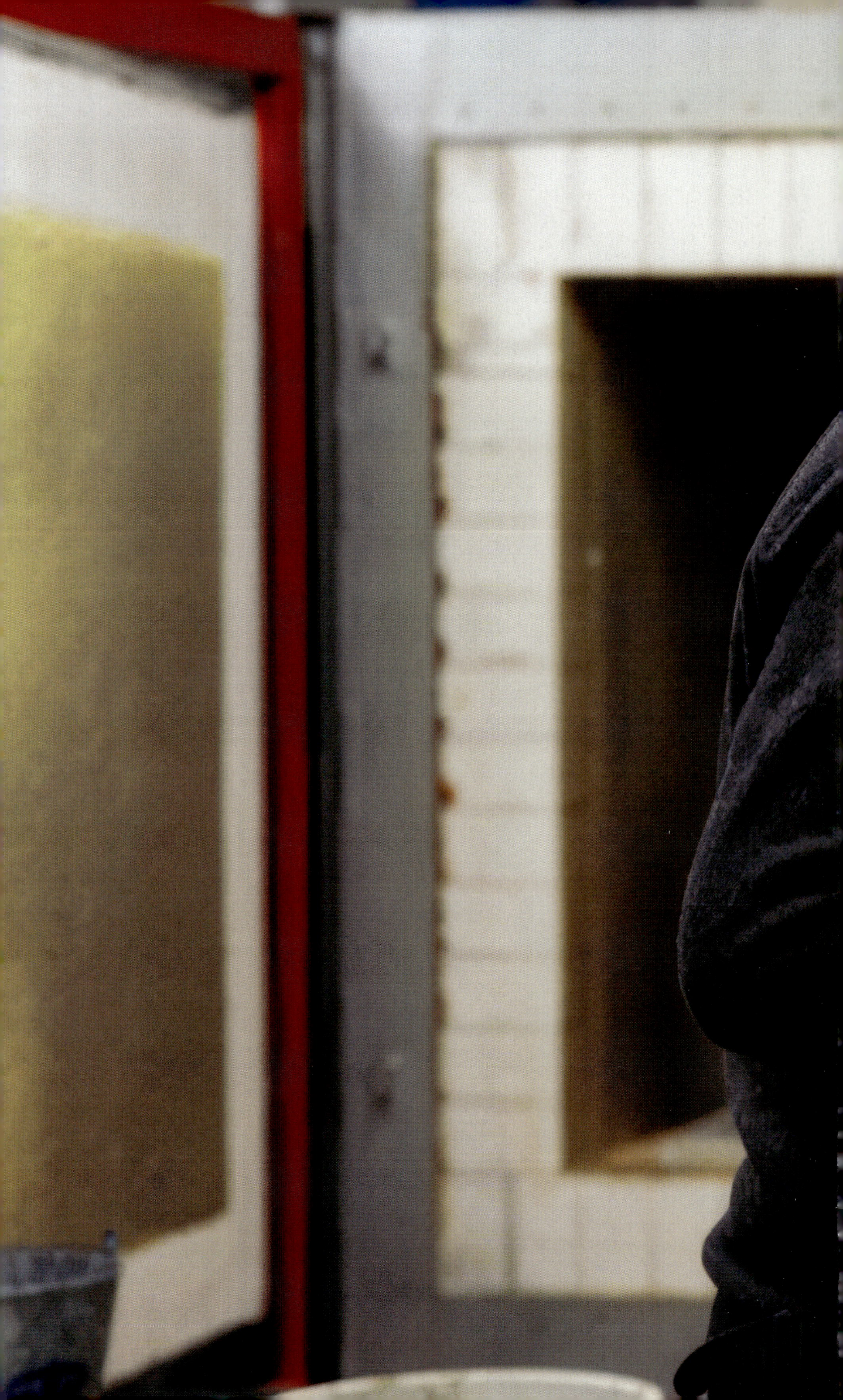

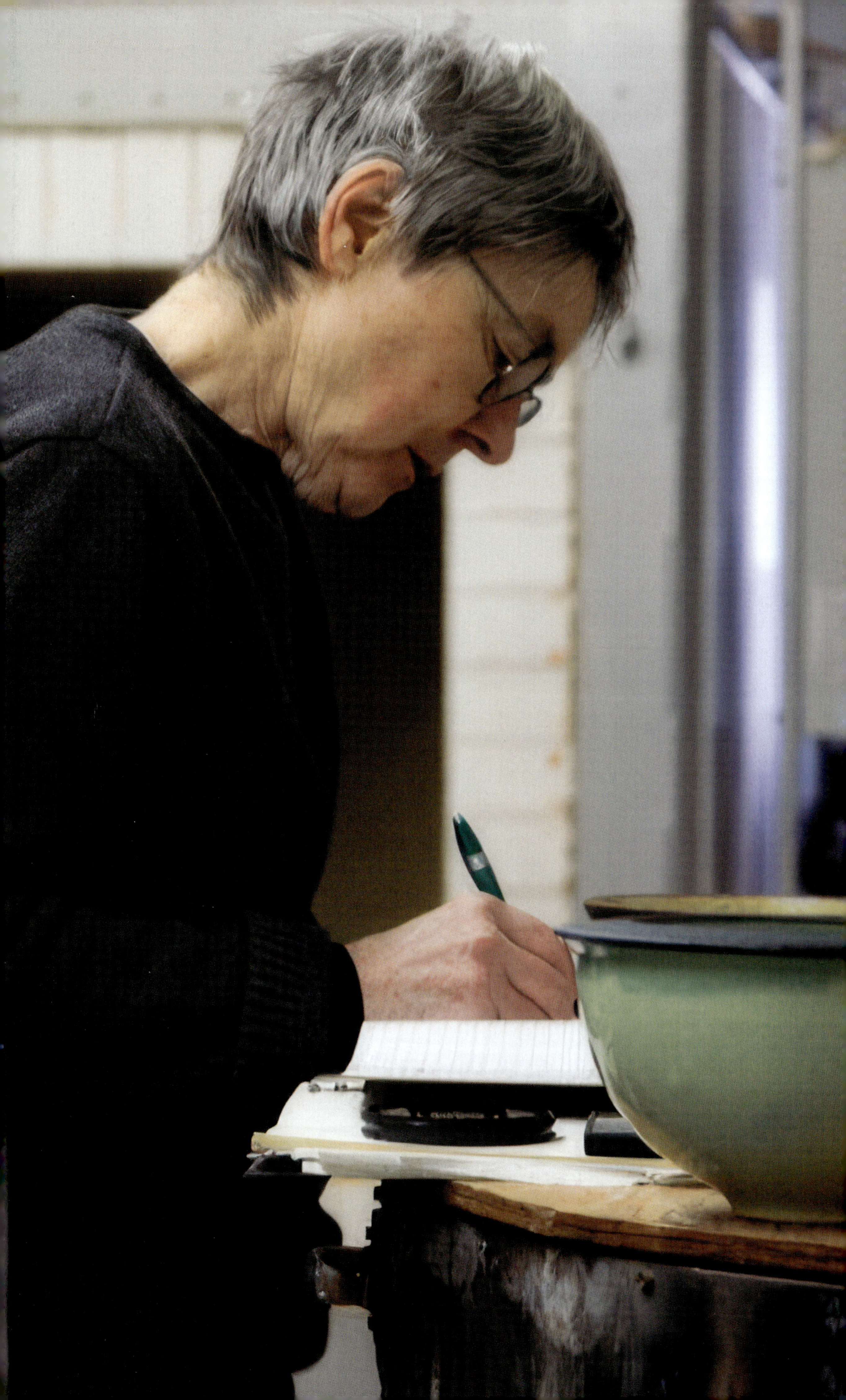

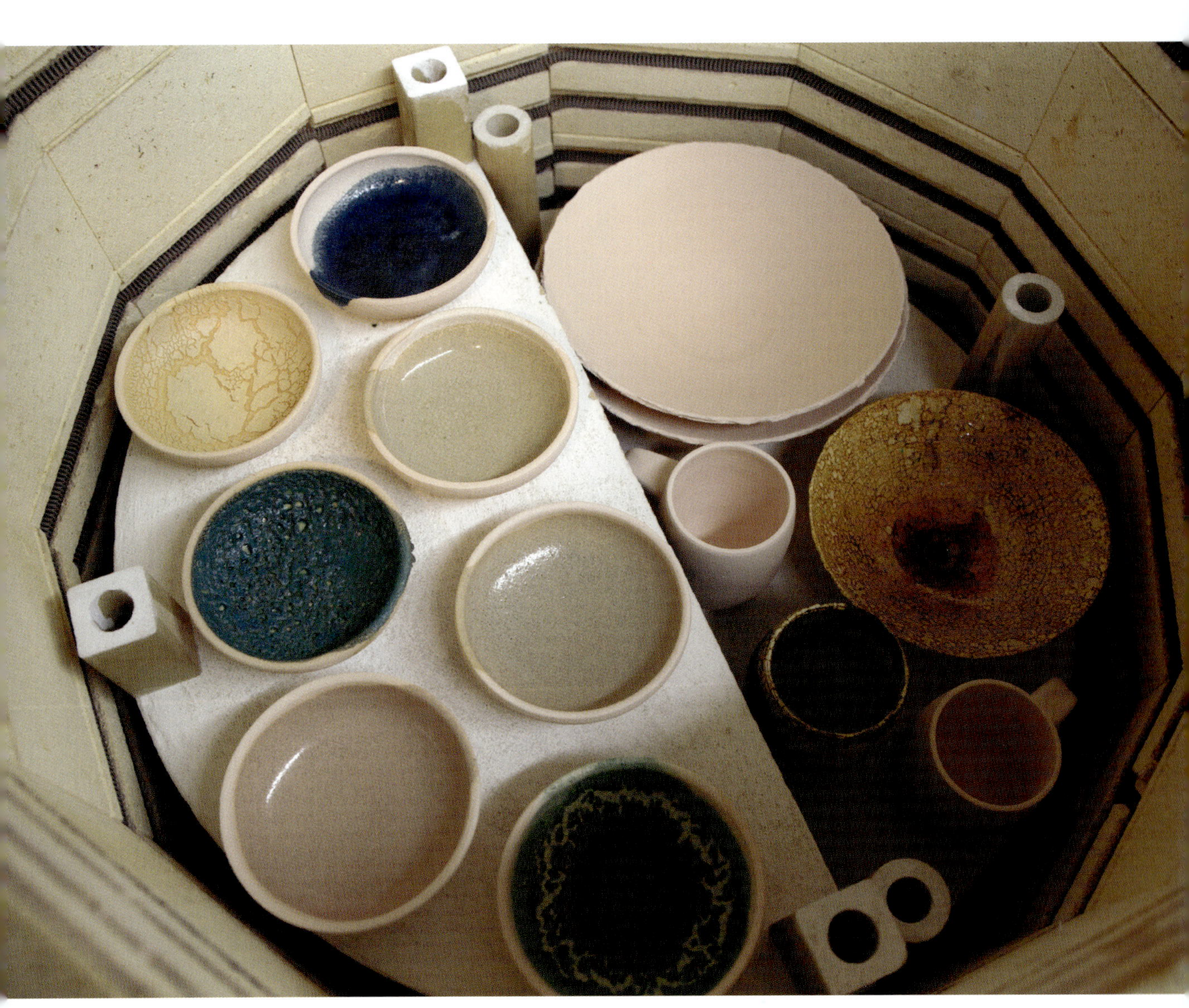

ALKALINE BLUE, CONE 04

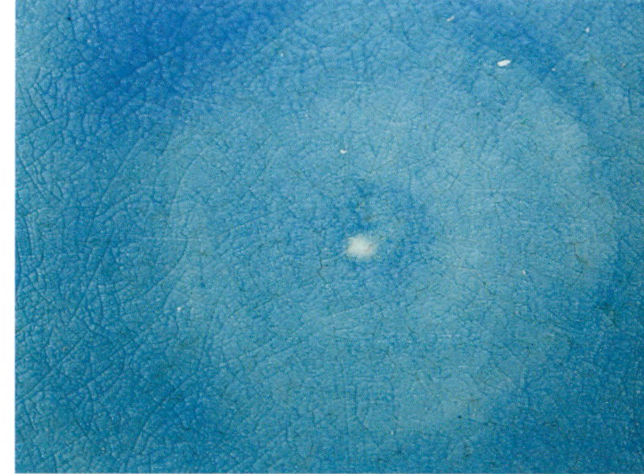

Frit 3110	70%
Soda Ash	10%
Kaolin	10%
Silica	10%
+ Copper Carbonate	2%

This is one of the glazes I have played with the most. It is forgiving when it comes to temperature. I've used it as low as 06 in both wet form and dry sprinkled form.

BARIUM MATTE BLUE, CONE 04

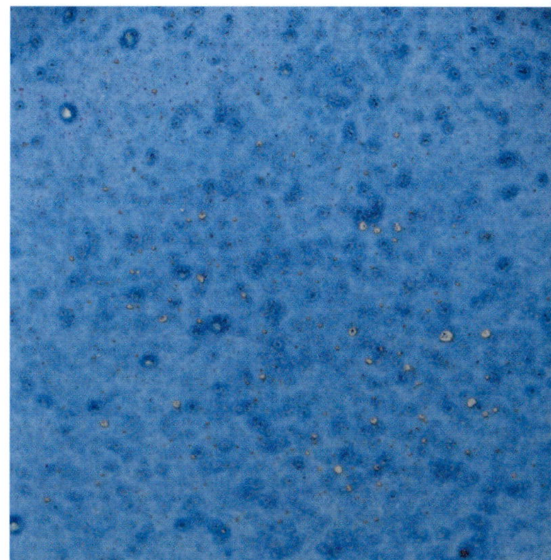

Nepheline Syenite	55%
Barium Carbonate	26%
Silica	7%
Kaolin	6%
Lithium Carbonate	2%
Copper Carbonate	4%

I haven't used this glaze very much yet, so I still have much to learn about it. Fired by itself, it has a dry matte surface. I have played with applying it over more fluxed glazes as well as using it in the dry sprinkled form. It can pair well with the dark blue terra sigillata, as the colours complement each other.

CHARTREUSE MOONELIS—FOX'S ADAPTATION, CONE 06–04

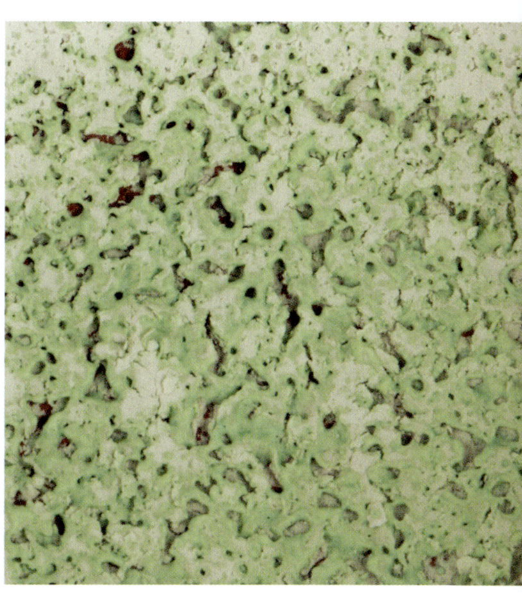

Nepheline Syenite	55%
Dolomite	15%
Borax	15%
Talc	10%
Feldspar (soda spar)	5%
* Frit 279	5%
+ Chrome Oxide	1%
Bentonite	1%

* I found the above recipe to be too dry, so I added 5% Frit 279, and that helped make it more stable. I doubt that the form of feldspar used will matter much with this glaze. For my tests, I used soda spar.

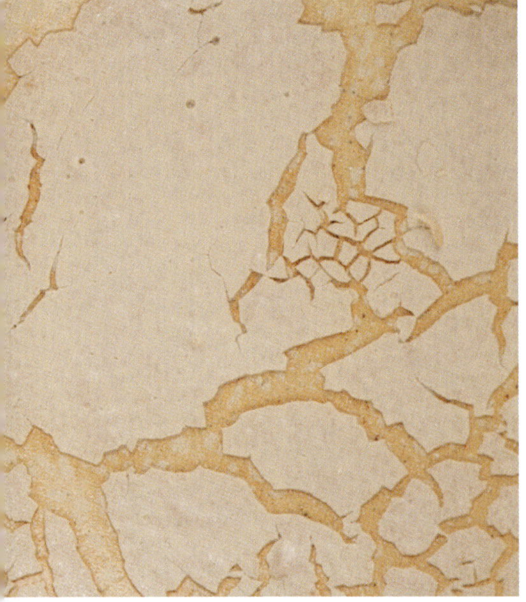

CRUSTY GLAZE BASE, CONE 04

Gillespie Borate	40%

(A blended borate material designed to replace Gerstley Borate in glazes.)

Kaolin	10%
Cryolite	20%
Titanium Dioxide	30%

Note: When no colourants are added to the base, it produces creamy gold tones, and I refer to it as "Crusty Desert."

For a browner version I call "Crusty Mudflat," add 3% rutile + 3% red iron oxide.

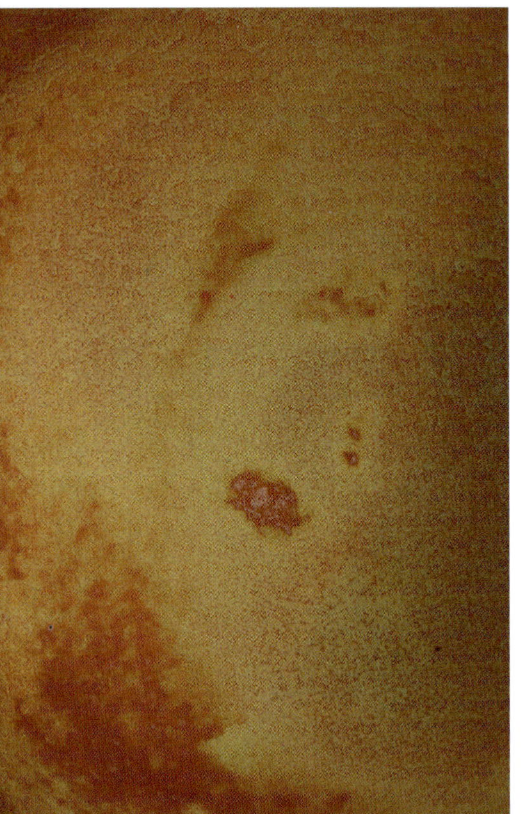

LANA'S CHARTREUSE MOSS, CONE 06–04

Lithium Carbonate	80%
Silica	15%
Gillespie Borate	5%
+ Bentonite	2%
Chrome	3%
Tin	7%

This is a pricey glaze to make, but I am including it here because I've used it on pieces in this book.

Great in oxidation or reduction, it's a glaze that requires a bit of experimenting to learn how best to apply it. As it has a lot of lithium in it, you will find that it settles very quickly, and frequent stirring is necessary. Lithium comes in various grit sizes, and the results you get will be affected by this.

I often use it over an orange terra sigillata, and the thickness really affects how it turns out. If applied on the thicker side, you can get the beautiful chartreuse colour, but the drawback is that the glaze can be more unstable when thick.

Another problem you may have if it's applied on a slip is shivering. I have found that pouring a thin first layer followed by a thicker layer overtop solves this. When pouring the second layer, try not to come to the edges of the first layer.

LANA'S CHUN, CONE 06–04

Frit 3195	50%
Frit 3124	40%
Kaolin	10%
+ Copper Carbonate	0.5%
Titanium	5%

This is a great glaze to play with, beautiful by itself and stunning with terra sigillata overlays. In this book, it's used on my decorative work, but it can also be used on functional ware.

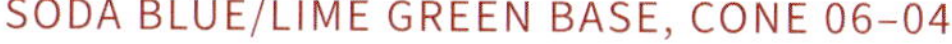

SODA BLUE/LIME GREEN BASE, CONE 06–04

Frit 3110	76%
Gillespie Borate	6%
Silica	10%
Kaolin	7%
Bentonite	1%

SODA BLUE

+ Copper Carbonate	3%

This is a blue-turquoise colour and crazes nicely.

EMERALD GREEN

+ Copper Carbonate	1%
Chrome Oxide	0.62%

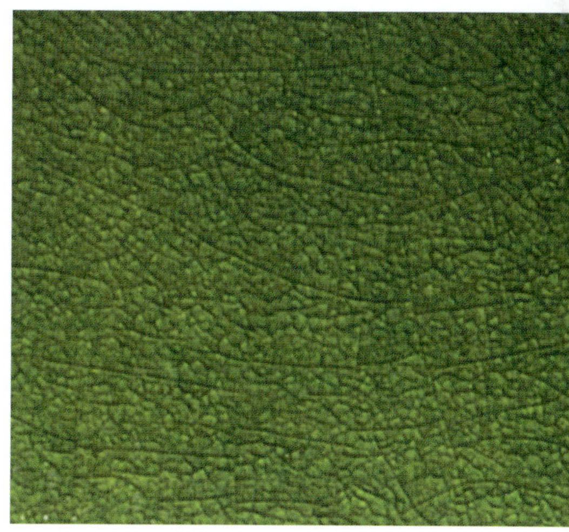

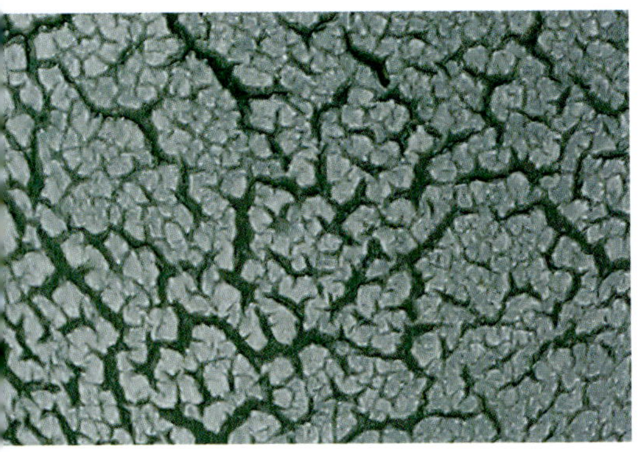

White crawl over soda lime green.

WHITE CRAWL GLAZE, CONE 06–04

Gerstley Borate	46.51%
Magnesium Carbonate	31.01%
EPK	18.6%
Borax	3.88%
+ Zircopax	5.43%

LITHIUM COMPOUND, CONE 08–05

Lithium	95%
Copper Carbonate	5%

For more information on crawl glazes and the lithium compound, please refer to the first book, *My Life as a Potter*, where they are covered extensively.

WHITE & ORANGE TERRA SIGILLATA

1 L (.26 gal) water
400 g ball clay
2 g sodium silicate
2 g soda ash

or

1 L (.26 gal) water
400 g ball clay
11 g Darvan 7

* For orange terra sigillata substitute ball clay for Cedar Heights Redart clay.

Let sit for at least 24 hours to allow the heavier particles to settle. Then siphon off the finer particles above, discarding the heavier sludge below.

DARK BLUE TERRA SIGILLATA

2 cups white terra sigillata
12 g copper oxide
20 g cobalt oxide
10 g manganese dioxide

For a darker blue-black terra sigillata, use 1 cup of white terra sigillata instead of 2 cups.

FOX'S EARTHENWARE GLAZE, CONE 04 (FUNCTIONAL WARE)

Photographed in oxidation.

EARTHENWARE BASE

Frit 3134	44%
Cedar Heights Redart clay	44%
Whiting	6%
Custer Feldspar	6%

By itself, the base is a beautiful tan colour. It will be influenced by the colour of the clay body used.

STONY GREY

Ilmenite	9%

I have been making this glaze with both the coarse and the fine grade of ilmenite. Both are good, with subtle differences between the two. The fine grade is easier to work with, but you might also want to try the coarse, just to see the variation between them.

GALAXY GREEN

Black Copper Oxide	1.5%
+ Chrome Oxide	.5%

A stunning glaze with lots of variation, depending on thickness. It has hints of blue as well as the green tones.

FAUX RAKU AND SAGGAR FIRING

#	Temp	Time	Rate	Mode	Oxid %	Time Elapsed
1	250°F	0:24	455°F/h	Firing	0%	0:24
2	500°F	0:23	652°F/h	Firing	0%	0:47
3	1112°F	1:53	325°F/h	Firing	0%	2:40
4	1562°F	0:23	1174°F/h	Main On	85%	3:03
5	1900°F	1:22	247°F/h	Main On	87%	4:25
6	1116°F	1:14	-636°F/h	Cooling	0%	5:39
7	930°F	1:01	-183°F/h	Cooling	0%	6:40
8	570°F	1:00	-360°F/h	Cooling	0%	7:40
9	120°F	2:30	-180°F/h	Cooling	0%	10:10
10	120°F	3:00	0°F/h	Cooling	0%	13:10

TABLEWARE 04 REDUCTION

#	Temp	Time	Rate	Mode	Oxid %	Time Elapsed
1	250°F	0:35	312°F/h	Firing	0%	0:35
2	500°F	0:50	300°F/h	Firing	0%	1:25
3	1022°F	1:10	447°F/h	Firing	0%	2:35
4	1200°F	0:50	214°F/h	Firing	0%	3:25
5	1350°F	0:20	450°F/h	Firing	0%	3:45
6	1650°F	0:35	514°F/h	Main On	80%	4:20
7	1940°F	0:30	580°F/h	Main On	85%	4:50
8	1940°F	0:30	0°F/h	Main On	90%	5:20
9	1562°F	0:50	-454°F/h	Cooling	0%	6:10
10	1112°F	0:42	-643°F/h	Cooling	0%	6:52
11	932°F	1:00	-180°F/h	Cooling	0%	7:52
12	572°F	1:00	-360°F/h	Cooling	0%	8:52
13	120°F	2:30	-181°F/h	Cooling	0%	11:22
14	120°F	5:00	0°F/h	Cooling	0%	16:22

In the tableware firing program shared here, I have set the reduction fairly high. I am still learning and experimenting with the reduction levels for tableware and suggest you treat this program as a guide. Play around, as all kilns fire differently.

ACKNOWLEDGEMENTS

This book was challenging on many levels. It required a lot of experimenting, thinking, testing and documentation. Unlike my first book, *My Life as a Potter*, which recounted the challenges and learning that led to my career as a potter, this book required a new experimentation process and couldn't be written until that was well under way.

Right when I was in the thick of it all, Sabrina Sachiko Campbell started her two-year apprenticeship. Not only did she have to adjust to life at the pottery, but she also had to navigate a head potter who was more than a little overwhelmed. And navigate it she did. Suddenly, I was tossing all sorts of new jobs her way—loads of test bowls to throw, glaze tests to mix, pots to carry upstairs to be photographed, computer work to catch up on and more. Meanwhile, she also had to learn how to throw my forms, glaze to my specifications, keep the studio clean, take care of customers and lastly—the most important job of the day—make our 3 p.m. cappuccinos. It would be an understatement to say I could not have done this book without all her help in the studio.

As with my first book, Roberto Dosil was my chosen designer, but unfortunately he had to stop working on the book partway through the process. I wasn't sure we could continue, but the team at Harbour Publishing jumped in with both feet, encouraged me to carry on and brought designer Libris Simas Ferraz on board to deftly take over.

As it turns out, Sabrina is an ace at getting things organized and, putting aside her studio work, she got down to business helping me reassemble the manuscript and images. Using Roberto's design draft as a guide, we worked our way through the book, tweaking and adding photos and captions, where needed. We were finally set free when the revised manuscript was on Harbour's desk and the photos had been sent off to Fidelis Art Prints for prepress work. Of course, after a short break, we were back at it going through the new layout with Libris.

To say I am grateful for the help we received on short notice would be an understatement. A technical book such as this is challenging for everyone involved. The editors had to familiarize themselves with a lot of information that was new to them, while catching mistakes or areas needing clarification. Libris worked to Roberto's design, adding the changes required and bringing the book to life.

As always, my editor, Pat Feindel, was a beacon in the wilderness every step of the way. Pat has been my editor for more than a decade, and it's safe to say I wouldn't be the writer I am today without her guidance. She has a keen eye, and I have never been more grateful for her expertise and patience than while working on this challenging book. I suspect another editor might have headed for the hills.

My heart is filled with gratitude to everyone involved and to you, my readers, who make it all worthwhile.

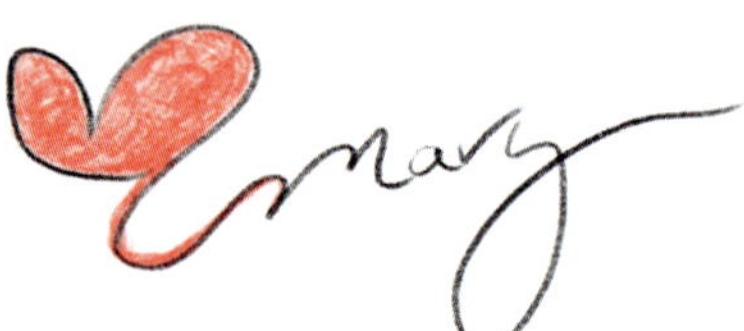

IMAGE CREDITS

All photos courtesy of Mary Fox unless otherwise credited.

FRONT COVER
Sabrina Sachiko Campbell

TITLE PAGE (P. XII–XIII)
Sabrina Sachiko Campbell

DEDICATION PAGE (P. XIV)
Sabrina Sachiko Campbell

CONTENTS PAGE (P. XVI)
Sabrina Sachiko Campbell

CHAPTER 1
Sabrina Sachiko Campbell: p. 4, p. 8 (top left)

CHAPTER 2
Sabrina Sachiko Campbell: p. 14, p. 16, p. 17, p. 18 (bottom), p. 19, p. 20, p. 26

CHAPTER 3
Sabrina Sachiko Campbell: p. 28, p. 29, p. 32 (bottom right)

CHAPTER 4
Sabrina Sachiko Campbell: p. 34, p. 36, p. 37

CHAPTER 5
Sabrina Sachiko Campbell: p. 44, p. 46 (top), p. 47 (bottom), p. 48 (top and bottom left), p. 49 (top), p. 50 (bottom)

CHAPTER 6
Sabrina Sachiko Campbell: p. 55 (top), p. 59, p. 60 (top)
Sarah Wilson: p. 54

CHAPTER 7
Sabrina Sachiko Campbell: p. 64

CHAPTER 8
Sabrina Sachiko Campbell: p. 78, p. 80 (bottom left and right), p. 82, p. 83, p. 84, p. 88, p. 90
Sarah Wilson: p. 86 (bottom left and right)

CHAPTER 9
Sabrina Sachiko Campbell: p. 92, p. 96 (top left and right), p. 98 (top left and right), p. 99 (top left and right, bottom left), p. 102

CHAPTER 10
Sabrina Sachiko Campbell: p. 104, p. 107 (top left, right and centre)
Angelika McLenan: p. 112

CHAPTER 11
Sabrina Sachiko Campbell: p. 114, p. 117 (top left, top right, bottom right), p. 118 (top left and right), p. 121

CHAPTER 12
Ashley Marston: p. 132 (top and centre), p. 134, p. 135.
Sarah Wilson: p. 132 (bottom)

CHAPTER 13
Sabrina Sachiko Campbell: p. 136, p. 140, p. 143, p. 144–145
Linda Mitsui: p. 141
Sean Sherstone: p. 138–139
Jane Zatylny: p. 142

GLAZE RECIPES
Sabrina Sachiko Campbell: p. 149, p. 150 (top), p. 151 (top), p. 153

ADDITIONAL IMAGES
Sabrina Sachiko Campbell: p. 146–147 (two-page spread), p. 148 (page before glaze recipes)
End sheets: Sabrina Sachiko Campbell
Sean Sherstone: first page (signing pot before the page spreads start)

Mary Fox is a self-taught exploratory potter who has been working with clay since she was thirteen years old and as a professional potter for over forty years. Her innovative and inspired creations have garnered national and international acclaim. Fox creates contemporary pieces based on classic lines that express the beauty and strength of pure form. With inspired original glazes and shapes that seem to spring up from the earth, each of Fox's pieces tells its own story, evoking a sense of wonder and intensity that is both delicate and powerful. Fox is also the author of a memoir, *My Life as a Potter* (2020). She lives and works in Ladysmith on Vancouver Island, BC.

1 2 3 4 5 — 29 28 27 26 25

Harbour Publishing Co. Ltd.
P.O. Box 219, Madeira Park, BC, V0N 2H0
www.harbourpublishing.com

Edited by Pat Feindel
Cover and text design by Roberto Dosil and Libris Simas Ferraz
Printed and bound in South Korea

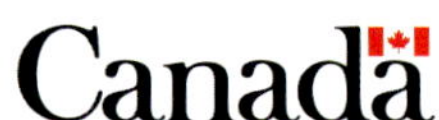

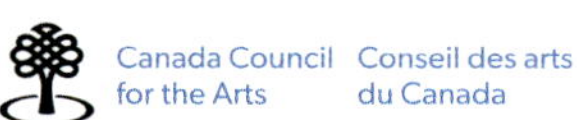

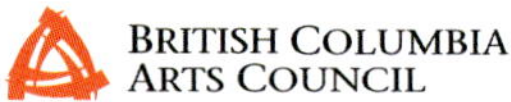

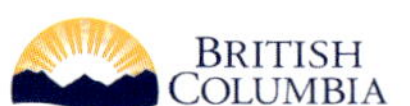

Harbour Publishing acknowledges the support of the Canada Council for the Arts, the Government of Canada, and the Province of British Columbia through the BC Arts Council.

Library and Archives Canada Cataloguing in Publication
Title: Developing glazes : low-fire reduction and oxidation / Mary Fox.
Names: Fox, Mary, 1959- author.
Identifiers: Canadiana 20250158434 | ISBN 9781998526253 (hardcover)
Subjects: LCSH: Glazes. | LCSH: Glazing (Ceramics) | LCSH: Pottery craft—Technique.
Classification: LCC TT922 .F69 2025 | DDC 738.1/27—dc23